ECONOMIC AND SOCIAL COMMISSION FOR ASIA AND THE PACIFIC

ECONOMIC AND SOCIAL SURVEY OF ASIA AND THE PACIFIC 2002

UNITED  NATIONS

New York
2002

UNITED NATIONS
ECONOMIC AND SOCIAL SURVEY OF ASIA AND THE PACIFIC
2002

ST/ESCAP/2144

UNITED NATIONS PUBLICATION
Sales No. E.02.II.F.25
Copyright © United Nations 2002
ISBN: 92-1-120085-7   ISSN: 0252-5704

FOREWORD

The strong economic recovery that had been under way in parts of Asia in 1999-2000 came to a halt this past year. Many economies were hit hard by the global economic downturn, which itself was amplified by the terrorist attacks of 11 September 2001 and their ripple effects. Although several countries managed to continue on a high-growth path, and inflation, by and large, remained muted, social distress was on the rise, not only because of the economic setback but also because Governments pursuing a course of economic and financial prudence necessarily had fewer resources available for public spending. Still, despite these new and re-emerging constraints, the process of reform and restructuring must be sustained for, over the long term, this remains the surest path to durable and equitable economic growth.

This edition of the *Economic and Social Survey of Asia and the Pacific* reviews the efforts in the region to cope with the slowdown and the dislocations it has generated. It provides a preliminary assessment of activities aimed at reaching the millennium development goals set out in the Declaration adopted at the Millennium Summit in September 2000. It examines official development assistance, long of critical importance to this most populous region of the world, with a particular focus on economic and technical cooperation among developing countries in Asia and the Pacific.

One of the main messages that emerges is that the contents of growth are as important as its pace. The need to protect the environment, preserve and foster social cohesion and eradicate hunger and poverty will have to feature prominently in national policies as well as in international cooperation for development. I hope this *Survey* will contribute to our collective efforts, in the ESCAP region and beyond, to translate this message into action that brings real, positive change to the daily lives of the peoples the United Nations exists to serve.

Kofi A. Annan
Secretary-General

March 2002

ACKNOWLEDGEMENTS

The *Economic and Social Survey of Asia and the Pacific 2002* was prepared under the direction of Raj Kumar and coordinated by N.V. Lam of the Development Research and Policy Analysis Division of ESCAP.

Experts from within and outside the ESCAP secretariat contributed to various stages in the preparation of the *Survey 2002*. The team of staff members of the Development Research and Policy Analysis Division who prepared the *Survey 2002* comprised: Shahid Ahmed, Lene Andersen, Eugene Gherman, Fareeda Maroof Hla, Nobuko Kajiura, Muhammad Hussain Malik, Hiren Sarkar, Hirohito Toda, Seok-Dong Wang and Marin Yari. Staff analysis was based on data and information available up to the end of February 2002. Research assistance was provided by Somchai Congtavinsutti, Kiatkanid Pongpanich and Amornrut Supornsinchai. All graphics work and the cover design were done by Somchai Congtavinsutti. The logistics of processing and production, and the organization of the meetings referred to below, were handled by Dusdeemala Kanittanon and Woranut Sompitayanurak.

Inputs for the *Survey 2002* also came from the International Trade and Industry Division and the Environment and Natural Resources Development Division. Andrew Flatt, Chief of the Statistics Division, provided useful comments and suggestions on data presentation in all draft chapters of the *Survey 2002*.

Major reports for the *Survey 2002* were received from the following external consultants: Mushtaq Ahmad, Tarun Das, Yuba Raj Khatiwada, Mohammad Kordbache, Theodore Levantis, George Manzano, Aun Porn Moniroth, Muhammad Abul Quasem, Djisman Simanjuntak, Hadi Soesastro, Vo Tri Thanh and Wang Tong.

Chapter I was the anchor paper for discussion at the Meeting of Eminent Persons on Current and Prospective Economic Performance in the ESCAP region held at ESCAP, Bangkok, on 18 and 19 October 2001. The eminent persons, who attended the meeting in their personal capacity, were: Peter G. Warr (Australia), Rehman Sobhan (Bangladesh), Lu Aiguo (China), Suman K. Bery (India), Djisman Simanjuntak (Indonesia), Shinichi Ichimura (Japan), Jomo K. Sundaram (Malaysia), Tilak Bahadur Rawal (Nepal), Bernardo M. Villegas (Philippines), Suk Bum Yoon (Republic of Korea), Victor Y. Rosin (Russian Federation), Linda Low (Singapore), Amarakoon Bandara (Sri Lanka), Thirachai Phuvanat-Naranubala (Thailand) and Pisit Leeahtam (Thailand). J.K. Robert England (UNDP, Bangkok), Ejaz Ghani (World Bank, Bangkok), Lorenzo Giorgianni (IMF, Bangkok) and C. Houser (ADB, Manila) also participated in the Meeitng.

Chapters III and IV were discussed at the Expert Group Meeting on Development Issues and Policies, held on 3 and 4 December 2001. The experts, who participated in the Meeting in their personal capacity, were: Pingyao Lai (China), Lorraine Seeto (Fiji), Mohammed Saqib (India), Ofelia Templo (Philippines), Woosik Moon (Republic of Korea), Dushni Weerakoon (Sri Lanka), Amara Pongsapich (Thailand), Mingsarn Kaosa-ard (Thailand) and Vo Tri Thanh (Viet Nam).

CONTENTS

CONTENTS *(continued)*

BOXES

TABLES

TABLES *(continued)*

TABLES *(continued)*

FIGURES

FIGURES *(continued)*

EXPLANATORY NOTES

The term "ESCAP region" is used in the present issue of the *Survey* to include Afghanistan; American Samoa; Armenia; Australia; Azerbaijan; Bangladesh; Bhutan; Brunei Darussalam; Cambodia; China; Cook Islands; Democratic People's Republic of Korea; Fiji; French Polynesia; Georgia; Guam; Hong Kong, China; India; Indonesia; Iran (Islamic Republic of); Japan; Kazakhstan; Kiribati; Kyrgyzstan; Lao People's Democratic Republic; Macao, China; Malaysia; Maldives; Marshall Islands; Micronesia (Federated States of); Mongolia; Myanmar; Nauru; Nepal; New Caledonia; New Zealand; Niue; Northern Mariana Islands; Pakistan; Palau; Papua New Guinea; Philippines; Republic of Korea; Russian Federation; Samoa; Singapore; Solomon Islands; Sri Lanka; Tajikistan; Thailand; Tonga; Turkey; Turkmenistan; Tuvalu; Uzbekistan; Vanuatu; and Viet Nam. The term "developing ESCAP region" excludes Australia, Japan and New Zealand.

The term "Central Asian republics" in this issue of the *Survey* refers to Armenia, Azerbaijan, Georgia, Kazakhstan, Kyrgyzstan, Tajikistan, Turkmenistan and Uzbekistan.

The designations employed and the presentation of the material in this publication do not imply the expression of any opinion whatsoever on the part of the Secretariat of the United Nations concerning the legal status of any country, territory, city or area, or of its authorities, or concerning the delimitation of its frontiers or boundaries.

Mention of firm names and commercial products does not imply the endorsement of the United Nations.

The abbreviated title *Survey* in footnotes refers to *Economic and Social Survey of Asia and the Pacific* for the year indicated.

Many figures used in the *Survey* are on a fiscal year basis and are assigned to the calendar year which covers the major part or second half of the fiscal year.

Reference to "tons" indicates metric tons.

Values are in United States dollars unless specified otherwise.

The term "billion" signifies a thousand million. The term "trillion" signifies a million million.

In the tables, two dots (..) indicate that data are not available or are not separately reported, a dash (–) indicates that the amount is nil or negligible, and a blank indicates that the item is not applicable.

In dates, a hyphen (-) is used to signify the full period involved, including the beginning and end years, and a stroke (/) indicates a crop year, a fiscal year or plan year. The fiscal years, currencies and 2001 exchange rates of the economies in the ESCAP region are listed in the following table:

Country or area	Fiscal year	Currency and abbreviation	Rate of exchange for $1 as at November 2001
Afghanistan	21 March to 20 March	afghani (Af)	3 000.00
American Samoa	..	United States dollar ($)	1.00
Armenia	1 January to 31 December	dram	566.51
Australia	1 July to 30 June	Australian dollar ($A)	1.92
Azerbaijan	1 January to 31 December	Azeri manat (AZM)	4 677.00[a]
Bangladesh	1 July to 30 June	taka (Tk)	54.00[b]
Bhutan	1 July to 30 June	ngultrum (Nu)	47.99
Brunei Darussalam	1 January to 31 December	Brunei dollar (B$)	1.83
Cambodia	1 January to 31 December	riel (CR)	3 925.00
China	1 January to 31 December	yuan renminbi (Y)	8.28
Cook Islands	1 April to 31 March	New Zealand dollar ($NZ)	2.42
Democratic People's Republic of Korea	..	won (W)	2.20
Fiji	1 January to 31 December	Fiji dollar (F$)	2.29
French Polynesia	..	French Pacific Community franc (FCFP)	133.75[c]

Country or area	Fiscal year	Currency and abbreviation	Rate of exchange for $1 as at November 2001
Georgia	1 January to 31 December	lari (L)	2.08[b]
Guam	1 October to 30 September	United States dollar ($)	1.00
Hong Kong, China	1 April to 31 March	Hong Kong dollar (HK$)	7.80
India	1 April to 31 March	Indian rupee (Rs)	47.99
Indonesia	1 April to 31 March	Indonesian rupiah (Rp)	10 430.00
Iran (Islamic Republic of)	21 March to 20 March	Iranian rial (Rls)	1 747.86
Japan	1 April to 31 March	yen (¥)	123.95
Kazakhstan	1 January to 31 December	tenge (T)	148.55
Kiribati	1 January to 31 December	Australian dollar ($A)	1.92
Kyrgyzstan	1 January to 31 December	som (som)	47.90
Lao People's Democratic Republic ...	1 October to 30 September	new kip (NK)	9 540.00[d]
Macao, China	1 July to 30 June	pataca (P)	8.03
Malaysia	1 January to 31 December	ringgit (M$)	3.80
Maldives	1 January to 31 December	rufiyaa (Rf)	12.80
Marshall Islands	1 October to 30 September	United States dollar ($)	1.00
Micronesia (Federated States of)	1 October to 30 September	United States dollar ($)	1.00
Mongolia	1 January to 31 December	tugrik (Tug)	1 100.00[b]
Myanmar	1 April to 31 March	kyat (K)	6.81
Nauru	1 July to 30 June	Australian dollar ($A)	1.97
Nepal	16 July to 15 July	Nepalese rupee (NRs)	76.48
New Caledonia	..	French Pacific Community franc (FCFP)	133.75[c]
New Zealand	1 April to 31 March	New Zealand dollar ($NZ)	2.42
Niue	1 April to 31 March	New Zealand dollar ($NZ)	2.42
Northern Mariana Islands	1 October to 30 September	United States dollar ($)	1.00
Pakistan	1 July to 30 June	Pakistan rupee (PRs)	60.86
Palau	1 October to 30 September	United States dollar($)	1.00
Papua New Guinea	1 January to 31 December	kina (K)	3.80
Philippines	1 January to 31 December	Philippine peso (P)	52.02
Republic of Korea	1 January to 31 December	won (W)	1 273.00
Russian Federation	1 January to 31 December	rouble (R)	29.90
Samoa	1 July to 30 June	tala (WS$)	3.52
Singapore	1 April to 31 March	Singapore dollar (S$)	1.83
Solomon Islands	1 January to 31 December	Solomon Islands dollar (SI$)	5.43[b]
Sri Lanka	1 January to 31 December	Sri Lanka rupee (SL Rs)	93.15
Tajikistan	1 January to 31 December	somoni	2.58
Thailand	1 October to 30 September	baht (B)	43.99
Tonga	1 July to 30 June	pa'anga (T$)	2.20
Turkey	1 January to 31 December	Turkish lira (LT)	1 552 330.00[d]
Turkmenistan	1 January to 31 December	Turkmen manat (M)	5 200.00
Tuvalu	1 January to 31 December	Australian dollar ($A)	1.97
Uzbekistan	1 January to 31 December	som (som)	686.00
Vanuatu	1 January to 31 December	vatu (VT)	146.88[b]
Viet Nam	1 January to 31 December	dong (D)	15 068.00

Sources: United Nations, *Monthly Bulletin of Statistics*, available at <http://esa.un.org/unsd/mbs/mbssearch.asp> (13 February 2002); IMF, *International Financial Statistics* (CD-ROM), January 2002; and Economist Intelligence Unit, *Country Reports*, available at <http://db.eiu.com/countries.asp> (13 February 2002).

[a]   August 2001.
[b]   October 2001.
[c]   7 December 2001.
[d]   September 2001.

ABBREVIATIONS

ADB	Asian Development Bank
AFTA	ASEAN Free Trade Area
ASEAN	Association of Southeast Asian Nations
c.i.f.	cost, insurance, freight
CD-ROM	compact disk read-only memory
CEPT	Common Effective Preferential Tariff
CIS	Commonwealth of Independent States
CPI	consumer price index
DAC	Development Assistance Committee
ECDC	economic cooperation among developing countries
f.o.b.	free on board
FAO	Food and Agriculture Organization of the United Nations
FDI	foreign direct investment
GDP	gross domestic product
GNP	gross national product
HIV/AIDS	human immunodeficiency virus/acquired immunodeficiency syndrome
ICT	information and communications technology
IMF	International Monetary Fund
IT	information technology
M2	broad money supply
NPLs	non-performing loans
ODA	official development assistance
OECD	Organisation for Economic Cooperation and Development
OPEC	Organization of the Petroleum Exporting Countries
SEACEN	South East Asian Central Banks
SMEs	small and medium-sized enterprises
TCDC	technical cooperation among developing countries
TRIPs	trade-related intellectual property rights
UNCTAD	United Nations Conference on Trade and Development

UNDP	United Nations Development Programme
UNEP	United Nations Environment Programme
UNESCO	United Nations Educational, Scientific and Cultural Organization
UNFPA	United Nations Population Fund
UNICEF	United Nations Children's Fund
UNIDO	United Nations Industrial Development Organization
VAT	value added tax
WHO	World Health Organization
WTO	World Trade Organization

GLOBAL AND REGIONAL ECONOMIC DEVELOPMENTS: IMPLICATIONS AND PROSPECTS FOR THE ESCAP REGION[1]

OVERVIEW

The global economy slowed dramatically in 2001, recording its slowest rate of growth since 1992 as well as being associated with a sharp reduction in the growth of world trade. Those adverse developments were led by an abrupt deceleration in the economy of the United States of America, an interrupted recovery of the Japanese economy and weaker growth in the European Union. The global down-turn was then intensified by the terrorist attacks in the United States on 11 September 2001. This and related events in its aftermath caused a major loss of business and consumer confidence, among several other constraints on economic activity, in the United States and elsewhere.

Global slowdown was intensified by terrorist attacks of September 2001. Significant recovery in 2002 is however possible

The situation appears to have essentially stabilized and indeed some visible signs of recovery have emerged on the horizon, such as improved consumer confidence in the United States, in the early part of 2002. It is thus possible that world output in 2002 could grow significantly faster than in 2001.

In the ESCAP region, the main impact of the global slowdown has been felt in East and South-East Asia, especially in economies with high trade-to-GDP ratios. China and India have been relatively unaffected thus far. However, the slowdown carries major implications of concern to the ESCAP region, some of which are highlighted below.

Setback in poverty alleviation likely

Most ESCAP economies had made impressive progress in raising employment and reducing poverty up to the 1997 crisis in East and South-East Asia. Those gains were partially eroded in 1998, but the rapid recovery in 1999 and 2000 enabled most regional economies to address

---

[1] This is a revised and updated version of "Global and regional economic developments: patterns, implications and prospects for the ESCAP region", in *Bulletin on Asia-Pacific Perspectives 2001/02* (United Nations publication, Sales No. E.02.II.F.2).

the issues of social welfare, protection and safety nets. The current economic slowdown in several parts of the region, if prolonged by the inauspicious external environment, could seriously interrupt progress in those critical areas in social development.

Interruption in the
reform process

In the months ahead, the present setback could serve to delay the ongoing policy reforms, including those in governance and the restructuring of the financial and corporate sectors, especially in dealing with the non-performing-loan (NPL) problem. Indeed, there is some evidence that the economic recovery in 1999 and 2000 had dampened to some degree the enthusiasm for reform and a prolonged slowdown could reduce it further. It is therefore essential that Governments in the region remain committed to addressing the post-1997 reform challenges as well as to maintaining their commitment to the realization of the United Nations millennium development goals, especially with regard to poverty alleviation and human development.

Finding alternatives
to export-led growth

It is clear that economies which have grown successfully over two decades via an export-led strategy would need to consider and develop a more balanced approach in order to sustain growth in the near term. The policy options include counter-cyclical stimuli of a fiscal or monetary nature. There are, however, clear limits on either or, indeed, both such options, especially in view of the possible risks impinging upon the strong macroeconomic fundamentals that the majority of the developing economies of the ESCAP region have built up over the years, and thus adversely affecting market confidence and longer-term growth prospects in the region.

The costs and
benefits of
globalization

From an international perspective, the downturn brings into sharper focus the debate on the costs and benefits of globalization. Both the 1997 crisis and the 2001 slowdown were significantly intensified by the ripple effects and contagion from trade and financial market linkages, global and regional ties which have become closely integrated since the mid-1990s. While most developing economies of the ESCAP region are less susceptible to the conditions that led to the 1997 crisis, certain downside risks, such as financial market instability and setbacks to export gains, may still be unavoidable.

A coordinated
international
response to counter
the slowdown

In the immediate aftermath of the September events the developed countries took coordinated measures, in the form of interest rate cuts and provision of liquidity to the financial markets, to counter the threat of a prolonged global slowdown. At a time of weakened consumer confidence, and weak commodity prices similarly robust and coordinated measures may be needed should recovery in 2002 falter for any reason.

Greater regional cooperation appears to offer a viable and effective supplement to more coordinated effort at the international level. Such cooperation can and does have several layers, for example, among the developed countries, between the developed and developing countries, and among the developing countries. The objectives are not purely economic, that is, to boost trade, investment and other financial interaction. Joint efforts are increasingly needed in the provision of public goods in areas ranging from the prevention of money-laundering and trafficking in drugs and human beings, to terrorism. Combating terrorism entails higher expenditure on national security, which can have significant budgetary implications in the short term. The effects of this are clearly regional and thus joint efforts might be more appropriate.

Close international and regional cooperation required to counter money-laundering, terrorism and trafficking in drugs and human beings

The announcement from the fourth WTO Ministerial Conference, held at Doha, Qatar, in November 2001, of a new round of multilateral trade negotiations under WTO auspices was an important and welcome development in the above context. It signified a newly formed consensus between developed and developing economies towards achieving a balanced trade agenda, reflective of the needs of all developing countries but pushing forward the process of liberalization of trade in both goods and services. In particular, the developed countries could give a valuable additional impetus to that process by accelerating the implementation of commitments already made to improve market access for developing countries.

New round of multilateral trade negotiations at WTO a welcome development

Humanitarian assistance for reconstruction and development to countries such as Afghanistan rightly takes precedence in the current circumstances. But this should represent an additional effort on the part of the international community and not be at the expense of ODA for the purposes of promoting longer-term capacity-building, poverty alleviation and human development, especially among the least developed countries and other economies with special needs. In this connection, it is vital to address the longer-term challenges of financing for development raised by the International Conference on Financing for Development, scheduled to be held at Monterrey, Mexico, in March 2002.

Need to sustain and preserve ODA flows for long-term development

RECENT GLOBAL MACROECONOMIC TRENDS

Estimates of GDP for 2001 and forecasts for 2002, which are primarily based upon United Nations sources plus other pertinent information, are summarized in table I.1 and figure I.1. Following the terrorist attacks in the United States in September 2001, the world's principal central banking authorities reduced interest rates in unison and provided substantial additional liquidity to their respective financial markets to counter the loss of business and consumer confidence.

The terrorist attacks have undermined business confidence and intensified the global slowdown

Table I.1. Selected indicators of global economic conditions, 1998-2002

		1998	*1999*	*2000*	*2001[a]*	*2002[b]*
Economic growth (percentage change in GDP)						
World		2.3	2.9	4.0	1.3	1.5
Developed economies		2.5	2.7	3.5	0.9	0.8
Japan		−1.1	0.7	2.4	−0.5	−1.2
United States		4.6	4.0	4.1	1.2	0.7
European Union		2.6	2.3	3.5	1.6	1.5
Developing economies		1.6	3.5	5.8	2.3	3.5
Economies in transition		−0.7	3.0	6.0	4.3	3.8
Growth in volume of trade (percentage)						
World[c]		4.2	5.4	12.4	1.0	2.1
Developed economies	Export	3.9	5.2	11.6	−0.3	0.5
	Import	5.9	7.7	11.5	−0.3	1.4
Developing economies	Export	4.9	4.7	15.0	3.4	4.5
	Import	−1.4	1.7	16.1	5.0	6.5
Commodity prices **(annual percentage change; US dollar terms)**						
Non-fuel primary commodities		−14.7	−7.0	1.8	−5.5	1.7
Oil		−32.1	37.5	56.9	−14.0	−23.7
Inflation rate (percentage)[d]						
CPI in the developed economies		1.5	1.4	2.3	2.3	1.3
CPI in the developing economies		10.5	6.8	5.9	6.0	5.3
Interest rates						
United States		5.1	5.9	6.3	1.8	..
Japan		0.5	0.2	0.5	0.02	..
Euro area		3.4	3.5	4.9	3.4	..
Exchange rates (nominal units per US dollar)[e]						
Yen per US dollar		130.9	113.9	107.8	121.5	129.0
Euro per US dollar			0.939	1.085	1.118	1.087

Sources: United Nations, *World Economic Situation and Prospects 2002* (January 2002); IMF, *World Economic Outlook* (Washington, December 2001) and *International Financial Statistics*, vol. LV, No. 2 (February 2002); *The Economist*, various issues; and national sources.

[a] Preliminary estimate.

[b] Forecast.

[c] Exports and imports (goods and services).

[d] Developed and developing economies ratios weighted at purchasing power parity.

[e] Period average.

Other supplementary stimuli were applied or are being implemented in various countries. Major uncertainties remain, however, as regards the nature of the post-11 September economic situation itself, that is, whether the world economy is now facing a shock-related downturn over and above the cyclical slowdown that had become evident prior to September 2001 or whether it is primarily facing longer-term structural problems.

Between October and December 2001, IMF, for its part, revised its forecast for global economic growth from 2.7 to 2.4 per cent for 2001, with a similar prognosis for 2002. Among other reasons for this reduction were the widespread spillovers from the 11 September events in the form of higher transaction costs, especially in insurance and transport, and lower receipts from tourism and foreign remittances. Many developing countries are also likely to be constrained in their access to foreign capital, and external demand for goods and services is likely to weaken. These adverse factors, together with the sharp downturn in world trade that became evident in late 2000, have resulted in slower growth in much of the developing world. Largely as a result, the World Bank estimated that, as a consequence of the 11 September events, some 10 million more people could be condemned to live in poverty in 2002 in the world as a

Figure I.1. Rates of GDP growth of major developed economies, 1998-2002

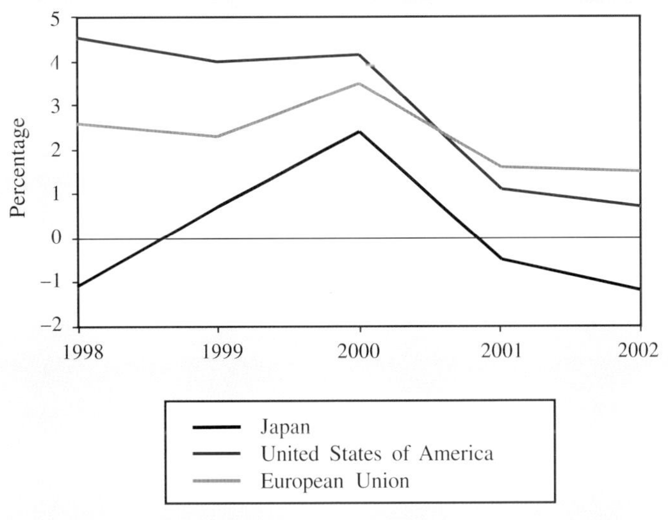

Sources: United Nations, *World Economic Situation and Prospects 2002* (January 2002); IMF, *International Financial Statistics,* vol. LV, No. 1 (January 2002); *The Economist,* various issues; and national sources.

Note: Figures for 2001 are estimates and those for 2002 are forecasts.

whole.[2]   Whatever the precise extent of the slowdown to be experienced in 2002, developing countries of the ESCAP region will almost certainly be faced with a major challenge in the medium term, namely, to preserve the post-1997 momentum of gains in income and employment. The many factors impinging on the possible patterns of development in 2002 and their implications for various ESCAP subregions are discussed more fully in chapter II of this *Survey*.

United States growth decelerated sharply

As reported in the *Survey 2001*, global economic growth accelerated sharply in the first half of 2000 after a relatively gentle recovery in 1999. This trend rested primarily on the sustained, dynamic performance of the United States economy, which had expanded at an unprecedented, annualized rate of 5 per cent by the second quarter of 2000. The subsequent, drastic correction in the high-tech sector caused stock markets to tumble and contributed to an abrupt economic downturn in the United States, to an annual rate of 1.5 per cent in the second half of the year and further to 0.6 per cent by the third quarter and 1.4 per cent in the fourth quarter of 2001 on a year-on-year basis; there was, in fact, an actual contraction of 1.1 per cent in the third quarter itself. Those setbacks spread with remarkable speed to other countries and regions, not only via trading links but also through a dramatic weakening of stock markets and their adverse knock-on effects on new capital issues and business confidence. That was particularly evident in the Asian economies with large ICT sectors depending heavily on exports of such equipment and services to the United States.

Japan slid into recession – again ...

The slowdown in the United States was accompanied by a significant reversal of growth in Japan, where GDP had grown, until the second quarter of 2000, at a more modest annual pace of 2.4 per cent. Such expansion was driven by the fast pace of growth in the United States, by the still-buoyant Asian economies and by a surge in ICT capital expenditure on the part of Japanese corporations. As the external stimuli faded, however, new domestic corporate investment expenditure came to a halt, while the long-standing structural problems of the Japanese economy again came back into sharp relief, further weakening business and consumer confidence. Largely as a result, the Japanese economy had slid into recession by the third quarter of 2001, registering negative growth of 0.5 per cent on a year-on-year basis, including a massive contraction of 2.2 per cent in the third quarter alone. Japanese stock prices also fell to their lowest level since 1984 in the latter part of 2001, with further deleterious effects on market sentiment and confidence in the economy.

---

[2] The World Bank has estimated that the terrorist attacks could shave 0.50 to 0.75 percentage points off the GDP growth of developing countries in 2002 (World Bank press release, 1 October 2001).

The European Union did not provide an offsetting expansion in 2001, as might have been expected from the apparent insulation of the euro area from developments in the rest of the world. While the European Union trades primarily within itself, falling demand for its exports in non-European Union markets weakened its growth perceptibly in 2001. Initially, GDP expansion declined and the European Union also slowed marginally from 3.5 per cent in the first half of 2000 to 3.0 per cent by the end of 2000 in 11 economies of the European Union, and to a similar extent also in the United Kingdom of Great Britain and Northern Ireland. Thereafter, the policy stance of the European Central Bank was tightened somewhat in response to the weak euro combined with the lagged effect of high oil prices which raised headline inflation above the target range of 0-2 per cent. The adjustment, however, served to slow investment expenditure, particularly in Germany, the largest economy in the European Union. By the third quarter of 2001, overall growth in the euro area had declined to 1.3 per cent on a year-on-year basis and in the United Kingdom, to 2.2 per cent. Recession had thus far been only narrowly avoided in the European Union as a whole. However, Germany registered negative GDP growth of 0.6 per cent in the third quarter of 2001.

... and the European Union also slowed down

There was one particular event worthy of note in the European Union. It related to the smooth introduction on 1 January 2002 of euro notes and coins as legal tender in 12 member States of the European Union, and the simultaneous withdrawal of the national currencies of those countries.[3]

RECENT DEVELOPMENTS AND PROSPECTS

Developed economies

The United States commands a large weight in the global economy (some 30 per cent of world GDP); it has also played a critical role as an engine of growth for much of the rest of the world in the last 4-5 years. Japan, the United States and the European Union together account for 54 per cent of the exports of the ESCAP developing region and are also the preponderant sources of external resources and capital. In addition, Australia and New Zealand play a major role in the Pacific island subregion in various ways.

Sustained GDP growth and sudden economic reversal

The most recent phase of American economic expansion, which ended in 2001, began in the second quarter of 1991 and was the longest on record. Indeed, there has been concern in recent years that the United

---

[3] For an initial assessment of the economic implications of the euro, see *Survey 1999*, box I.1.

States economy was growing unsustainably fast, and the strength of domestic demand relative to output growth has been reflected in a sharp widening of the current account deficit. The United States deficit has its counterpart in current account surpluses in Japan, a smaller one in the euro zone and significant surpluses in much of Asia. Clearly, such global imbalances have been the driving force of international capital flows between markets in recent years. They have also been instrumental in the development of new instruments and new risk-minimization techniques in the financial markets. However, the orders of magnitude involved have at times intensified volatility across countries and regions.

Signs of a slowdown in the United States first emerged in the third quarter of 2000. First, persisting high oil prices in 2000 had triggered a slight rise in inflation in the first half of the year; this induced the Federal Reserve to raise interest rates modestly in May 2000. Second, productivity growth slowed in the United States in the second half of 2000. The combined effect of these setbacks contributed to a sharp drop in the last quarter of 2000 in corporate capital investment, which has shown few indications of recovery thus far.

The contribution of productivity to growth in the United States since the mid-1990s

It is most notable that above-trend GDP growth in the United States economy since the mid-1990s has been associated with benign inflationary pressure, in strong contrast to previous phases of expansion. This phenomenon has been attributed to a marked acceleration in the rate of labour productivity growth. As a result, the uplift in wages and salaries has remained modest, thus reducing the need for any significant policy tightening over the last few years. Against this, the timing and pace of recovery in 2002 will depend to a large extent on the conditions and impulses for a resumption of productivity growth, including through an upturn in capital spending by corporations and a sustained rise in consumer spending. However, the pointers in this regard are somewhat ambiguous at this stage.

While there is a broad consensus that productivity has improved significantly in recent years, there is less agreement as to how much of this improvement is structural and how much cyclical. If the former turned out to be the primary cause, then recent patterns of very high price-earnings ratios in the stock markets would acquire a firmer basis and the extraordinary bull run in equity markets between 1998 and April 2000 would be more or less justified. However, to regain such a comparable rate of productivity growth in the medium term would require correspondingly high rates of capital spending by corporations, as recorded in the second half of the 1990s. This could be a rather doubtful proposition, given their sharply weaker financial positions at present, which embody high debt and low profitability.

If, however, productivity growth was also partly cyclical in nature, then the output and productivity growth path in the long run and, by inference, share prices have recently been overstated. Thus, any recovery in 2002 would depend more on the beginning of a new inventory cycle and relatively less on an investment rebound. Furthermore, the inventory build-up would need to be financed in the normal way, such as by internal cash flows or debt, rather than new equity. On the basis of past experience, an inventory-led recovery would be less sustained than an investment-driven rebound.

Regardless of the merits of these two views, the slowdown in the United States has once again drawn attention to some of the latent economic fragilities which have been masked by rapid growth over the last 4-5 years. These relate to the aggregate imbalance in the private sector as embodied in a decline in private savings by households, a trend aided by the marked rise in equity prices and its associated wealth effects, and the rise in corporate debt caused by debt-financed share buy-backs and other expenditures. The two phenomena are reflected in the widening of the current account deficit (noted earlier), which now exceeds 4.5 per cent of the GDP of the United States, equivalent to nearly 8 per cent of the world's gross savings.[4] Such imbalances appear unsustainable at these orders of magnitude. Their correction accordingly has important implications for the pace and depth of United States recovery, for world financial markets and for all developing countries in the near term.

This structural overhang would be likely to test the strength of the United States as an engine of global growth. Meanwhile, how long could the present recessionary phase last? It is not entirely clear at this stage whether the present slowdown is primarily cyclical or structural in nature. The available evidence indicates that positive growth impulses are likely to remain weak in the United States economy for some time, despite the unprecedented 11 cuts in interest rates in 2001, the spending boost from the tax rebates in fiscal 2001/02 and the extra expenditure approved by Congress in the wake of the terrorist attacks. Unwinding the excess inventories and overinvestment in ICT by corporations cannot be achieved overnight, but the decline in corporate profitability and increase in unemployment are likely to dampen further output growth and consumer confidence in the months ahead. Against this backdrop, the prospects for the United States economy in 2002 are rather uncertain at this time (March 2002). Consumer spending remains tentative, owing in part to rising unemployment, and the performance of key sectors of the economy does not suggest a major upturn in the near future.

Prospects for the resumption of productivity growth in the United States

United States recovery remains uncertain in 2002

---

[4] Bank for International Settlements, *71st Annual Report: 1 April 2000-31 March 2001* (Basel, June 2001).

Japan: still grappling with the post-bubble economy

Japan's pattern of economic growth is not unlike that of the United States in 2000 and 2001. Following an expansion of 0.8 per cent in 1999, economic activity was driven by an upturn in industrial production, so that GDP was 2.4 per cent higher in the first quarter of 2000. However, economic growth went down to a mere 0.1 per cent in the second quarter, and overall GDP expansion reached 2.4 per cent in 2000. Growth was barely discernible in the first and second quarters of 2001, so that unemployment began to climb upwards over the psychologically significant level of 5 per cent; the unemployment rate stood at 5.6 per cent in December 2001, the highest since 1953, when official records were kept in their current form. Japanese consumers have become far more inclined to save than to spend, having suffered massive losses in personal wealth in recent years and being faced with increasing threats to both earnings and employment. In fact, deflation has been both a cause and an effect of such consumer behaviour since 1999.[5]

The corporate sector in Japan is thus faced with a harsh and unenviable environment. Although manufacturing productivity remains high in the larger corporations, the corporate balance sheets have weakened considerably as a result of stagnant demand and the persisting problem of overcapacity in the sector as a whole; this applies particularly to the many small-scale subcontracting companies. In this context, the Japanese economy is still grappling with the multidimensional consequences of the bubble economy of the 1980s, in the shape of low profits, falling or depreciated asset values and chronic problems in the financial sector arising from impaired assets and undercapitalization. In particular, the financial system remains in a precarious condition, with grave systemic consequences. Popular perceptions have become mired in chronic pessimism regarding the future, despite the considerable and costly efforts made by the authorities thus far.

For their part, the Japanese authorities have adopted the standard macroeconomic remedies to revive growth and rehabilitate insolvent banks, including the implementation of a long series of stimulus and rescue packages. In the process, gross public debt currently stands at an extraordinary 130 per cent of GDP compared, for example, with the European Union benchmark of 60 per cent of GDP for participation in the euro. Meanwhile, continuing slow growth has greatly weakened the financial system. The Japanese Financial Services Agency disclosed in April 2001 that banks and other financial institutions were sitting on a massive 150 trillion yen (about $1.2 trillion) of potentially problematic loans, an amount equivalent to about 25 per cent of Japanese GDP.[6]

---

[5] IMF, *Japan: 2001 Article IV Consultation,* Country Report No. 01/144 (Washington, August 2001).

[6] *Bangkok Post,* 20 July 2001.

Short-term prospects for the Japanese economy are therefore bleak, especially in view of these extraordinarily severe financial constraints and the seeming inability of both fiscal and monetary measures to revive growth. Consumer confidence remains stubbornly weak, while a renewed bout of stock market declines in recent months has raised fears that Japan could re-enter a long-term phase of slow or negligible growth, a rising number of bankruptcies and intensified fragility in the banking system. Private consumption is thus unlikely to show any significant upswing, while both private and public capital spending will either be flat or, more likely, decline in the months ahead. With the current global slowdown the stimulus to growth from net exports will also be dissipated, notwithstanding the weaker yen early in 2002. GDP is estimated to have declined by around 0.5 per cent in 2001 and there is the likelihood of economic stagnation or worse a further contraction in 2002.

Low consumer confidence and a fragile financial sector

The economy of the European Union enjoyed relatively brisk growth in the first half of 2000, although the pace was significantly slower than in the United States, among other things a reflection of the slower uptake of ICT in the European Union, as was also the case in Japan. A competitive exchange rate and favourable global conditions in 2000 stimulated higher net exports in the first half of 2001, which not only served to underpin growth but also stimulated investment spending, some of which was in ICT. In addition, lower unemployment levels boosted private consumption. In common with developments in Japan and the United States, however, the members of the European Union also experienced some cooling-off during the first half of 2001.

European Union slowdown: less severe than in the United States and Japan

The slowdown, which persisted into 2001, has been comparatively less pronounced than that of the United States so far, although it has differed widely across the member countries. Moreover, the four largest economies, France, Germany, Italy and the United Kingdom, are in general less involved with ICT. Consequently, with the exception of telecommunication equipment, the European Union was exposed to a much smaller risk of downward adjustments in capital stock and associated corporate balance-sheet deterioration than the United States in 2001. However, Finland, Ireland and Sweden are three of the smaller economies considered to be at the forefront of ICT in the European Union. Their sharper decline in economic activities was led by a major reversal of corporate investment in ICT. In turn, this has produced significant adverse spillover effects on the high-tech sectors in the rest of the European Union.

As indicated previously, the beginning of 2002 saw the successful launch of euro notes and coins in 12 member States of the European Union and, after a brief period, the withdrawal of the national currencies as legal tender in those countries. This event is without parallel in world history, and presages further integration of the world's largest economic union. While its long-term impact can only be assessed after a period of time, the successful changeover in January 2002 should benefit consumer confidence in the euro zone in the months ahead.

Developing economies

All developing regions affected by the global slowdown

The rate of economic growth in the developing countries fell from 5.8 to 2.3 per cent in 2000-2001, a setback attributable to a sharp deterioration in the external environment; domestic factors played only a minor role in the majority of those countries. All developing regions were affected by the global slowdown in one way or another. Countries heavily dependent on ICT-related exports suffered acutely from the slowdown in the industry; those exporting commodities saw low prices falling to even lower levels; and those relying on foreign finance experienced reduced inflows and higher costs of capital.

ICT downturn constrained growth in East and South-East Asia dramatically, except in China

Economic growth in East and South-East Asia slowed dramatically in 2001. Singapore and Taiwan Province of China have a major concentration in the ICT sector and a large exposure to the United States market; they fell into recession, and Malaysia was expected to be in the same situation by the end of 2001. The Republic of Korea recorded a sharp reduction in GDP growth of around 6 percentage points along with the contraction of exports to the United States and Japan. This was particularly noticeable in the year-on-year decline in industrial output. Indonesia was cushioned from a further economic setback owing to stable oil revenues and the low rupiah exchange rate. Meanwhile, domestic demand buffered the export decline and provided some support to economic growth in other countries, such as the Philippines and Thailand. Private investment declined faster than consumption across most of the subregion, while increases in public spending in several economies were insufficient to offset the negative external shock. Weakening exports and domestic demand led to a slowdown in virtually all sectors, except for agriculture. The negative repercussions on aviation and tourism of the terrorist attacks affected Malaysia, Singapore and Thailand especially. China, however, provided a sharp contrast, with its GDP growing by an impressive 7.3 per cent in 2001. Strong domestic demand, particularly public investment, more than offset a negative contribution to GDP from net exports; capital spending on technological innovations, infrastructure and housing were the leading subcomponents.

Divergent growth trends in South and South-West Asia

Economic activity in South Asia increased slightly to 4.6 per cent in 2001 from 4.5 per cent in 2000. The deteriorating external environment acted as a main drag on growth during the year; other constraints included such domestic factors as political uncertainties, a somewhat increased oil bill, the fiscal debt burden, infrastructure bottlenecks and other structural problems. In addition, poor weather hurt a number of countries, depressing agricultural output and constraining consumption early in the year. South Asia in general, and India and Pakistan in particular, were affected by the conflict in Afghanistan in terms of war risk premiums on shipping in the Arabian Sea, which hampered exports in the last quarter of 2001 and reduced tourist arrivals in the subregion (see box II.2 of this *Survey*). Turkey plunged into a serious financial and currency crisis that resulted in a deep economic recession.

Western Asia was confronted with uncertainty in the energy markets in 2001. There were restraints on oil production in the oil-exporting countries in an attempt to shore up prices. However, sluggish global consumption softened both oil demand and earnings. Largely as a result, growth in the region decelerated from 6.3 per cent in 2000 to just under 1 per cent in 2001.

GDP growth in Latin America fell to 0.5 per cent in 2001 as a result of a sharp deceleration in the region's major economies and the deepening recession in Argentina. Among other causal factors of this poor performance were the impact of weaker external demand, a poorer external financial environment (including more costly finance and reduced capital inflows), and worsened terms of trade, as commodity prices fell. In particular, GDP growth decelerated sharply in the Dominican Republic, Mexico and other economies in Central America and the Caribbean, which have a large exposure to the United States economy. Chile and Colombia were hard hit by the lower prices of copper and coffee respectively. In addition, tight macroeconomic policies in some key economies of the region and a severe energy crisis in Brazil constrained domestic demand. However, economic activities in Ecuador and Venezuela were sustained or expanded in 2001 owing to buoyant internal demand and relatively strong oil revenues. The terrorist attacks affected many Latin America's economies adversely by accentuating the negative trends already present in the external environment and by further reducing opportunities for growth in the near term, such as through the sharp decline in tourism.

Latin America suffered a sharp downturn

In Africa, growth remained almost unchanged at 3.3 per cent for both 2000 and 2001. Economic activities in that region were supported by the recovery of agricultural production in several countries, although some others suffered from adverse weather conditions and lower agricultural output. In oil-exporting countries, relatively stable oil revenues underpinned domestic demand. Meanwhile, the deepening global economic slowdown, reinforced by the September terrorist attacks, weakened external demand, depressed foreign investor sentiment, reduced tourist arrivals and lowered the export prices of many commodities of importance to Africa. Political instability and violence, although reduced, continued to curtail economic activities in several parts of the region.

Africa remained largely unaffected

Developing countries to recover gradually in 2002

Overall growth in the developing economies is expected to recover gradually to 3.5 per cent in 2002 from 2.3 per cent in 2001, still well below the rate achieved in 2000 and the mid-1990s. Such an enhanced performance would owe much to improved domestic conditions, particularly in countries where agriculture generates a large share of GDP; it could also be expected in those economies having greater leeway for policy stimulus. The external environment is unlikely to provide any powerful impetus because of the probable slowness of the recovery process among the developed countries.

Trade and capital market trends

World trade fell sharply in 2001

In 2000, world trade expanded by 12.4 per cent, more than twice its growth rate in the previous year. Trade as a proportion of global GDP also rose, continuing a trend that has been one of the hallmarks of the globalization process, especially in the 1990s. Over the last few years, this rising trend has induced and embodied rapid changes in the organization and arrangements of production, a transformation driven partly by intensified global competition and partly by attempts of individual companies to exploit to the fullest the benefits of returns to scale. Growth in world trade declined sharply, to 1.0 per cent in 2001, thus posing a major challenge for the world economy and, in particular, for the developing economies in the near to medium terms. On present evidence, there is likely to be only a marginal recovery in 2002, with much of it concentrated in the second half of the year.

Commodity and manufactured goods prices softened in 2001

The acceleration in foreign trade in the 1990s was accompanied by a softening in international trade prices, including those of many (but not all) commodities, energy products and manufactured goods, for most of the decade. The trend continued apace in 2000 and 2001, with the notable exception of oil prices. Coffee prices, for instance, have fallen by half in two years, and cotton by two thirds since 1995. Weak prices are the result of excess capacity or supply overhang in both commodity production and manufacturing (in such sectors as steel, motor cars, computers and microprocessors). In turn, excess supplies have severely constrained producer efforts to improve rates of return or carry out urgent balance-sheet restructuring. As regards energy products, in 2000 production restraints and low inventory levels in the United States contributed to a sharp rise in oil prices, which, apart from occasional bouts of weakness, have remained at a relatively stable level (in the range of $20-$22 per barrel as of February 2002), compared with those of the 1990s. These trends are expected to continue into 2002, although oil prices in the spot market remain very sensitive to political developments involving West Asia as well as to domestic factors, including the severity of the winter in the northern hemisphere, among other transient phenomena. Above all, gains in production and prices of commodities, energy products and manufactures are likely to be driven by a strong recovery in global demand, at least in the short term, and not via investment because of current excess capacity. The performance of the United States economy would have a major bearing in this regard.

Notwithstanding the continuing stagnation of private capital flows (figure I.2), the global economic slowdown gave rise to reappraisals and re-pricing of financial risks and asset prices in a wide range of financial markets during the 12 months from mid-2000 to mid-2001. In late 2001 and early 2002, the bankruptcy of Enron and Kmart served to underline the uncertainty in stock markets. In contrast to 1998, however, when the fear of a global credit crunch was pervasive, market sentiment and concerns in 2000-2001 were influenced largely by the possible impact on capital flows as a result of the fast downturn of the United States economy, the interrupted growth momentum in Japan, slower expansion among the European Union economies and a slowdown in much of the ESCAP developing region.

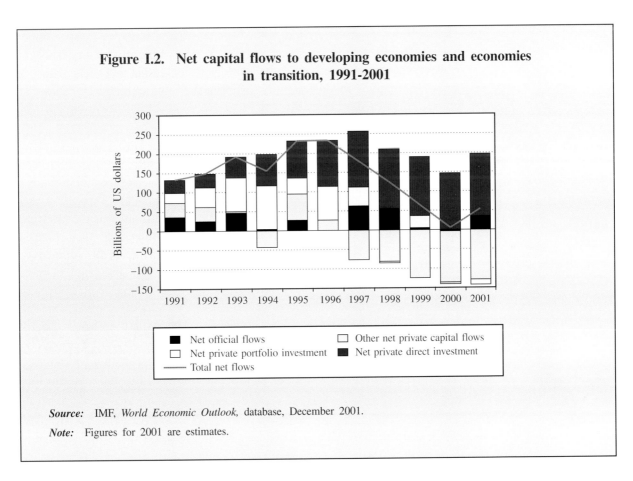

Figure I.2. Net capital flows to developing economies and economies in transition, 1991-2001

Source: IMF, *World Economic Outlook,* database, December 2001.

Note: Figures for 2001 are estimates.

Weaker capital flows and investors more risk-averse

What is likely to happen to capital flows, especially corporate and sovereign equity and bond issues and bank loans, as a result of these developments? In the post-11 September situation, uncertainty has risen to new levels, inducing investors to shift into less risky assets. From an ESCAP perspective, external capital is not required for recovery per se as several economies enjoy current account surpluses; it is needed more for the balance-sheet restructuring of corporations where the existing owners are unable or unwilling to put in new capital and reduce indebtedness. In this regard, the slowdown in global growth is bound to have a negative impact on the ability of companies both to raise capital in foreign capital markets and to attract bank loans to the region. Private capital is likely to become risk-averse, seeking more "safe haven" type outlets such as precious metals, and even cash, for the foreseeable future. In this connection, the following considerations are worthy of note.

Unstable financial markets

The initial impact of a growth slowdown is normally felt by corporations in the form of lower demand for their output, lower production and profits, and inevitably lower share prices. The financial repercussions emanating from poor corporate earnings in 2001 would therefore automatically have an adverse impact on the capital markets, as has already been observed in the United States and elsewhere. In addition, there is the likelihood of significant fluctuations in, and eventual realignment of, the exchange rates of the world's major traded currencies, since a portion of capital market activity is influenced by cross-border flows of funds. These developments imply a very uncertain environment for investors.

Constrained access for developing countries

Equity prices fell dramatically in 2001, especially those of high-tech company shares. The general deterioration in equity markets, in turn, has been compounded by economic and financial strains in Argentina and Turkey that have spilled over onto debt markets in other countries. Indeed, for some borrowers, credit spreads have widened to their highest levels since the early 1990s[7] while new issues, whether of equities or bonds, have dried up almost completely. Global equity and bond markets rebounded briefly in the early months of 2001, in response to monetary easing in the United States, but fell back as the depth of the economic slowdown there became more pronounced. The overall trend is clearly bearish, though with occasional bouts of strength. By and large, therefore, the access to capital markets by developing countries, including those in the ESCAP region is likely to remain constrained for the present (see table 1.2 and figure I.2).

---

[7] *The Economist*, 22 September 2001.

Table I.2. Net capital flows to developing Asian economies, 1991-2001

(Billions of US dollars)

	1991	1992	1993	1994	1995	1996	1997	1998	1999	2000	2001
Net private direct investment	14.2	14.3	33.1	44.7	49.9	57.3	59.8	59.9	51.9	46.8	43.7
Net private portfolio investment	2.1	12.9	25.9	20.8	20.7	31.1	8.7	−15.3	13.8	3.7	−4.7
Other net private capital flows	19.6	−1.1	−5.5	4.6	22.0	36.1	−51.6	−89.4	−74.4	−66.4	−46.0
Net official flows	12.4	11.1	11.4	3.6	5.3	−12.4	6.8	17.0	−1.2	−6.1	−2.1
Total net flows	48.3	37.2	64.9	73.7	97.9	112.1	23.7	−27.8	−9.9	−22.0	−9.1

Source: IMF, *World Economic Outlook*, database, December 2001.

Note: Figures for 2001 are estimates.

More volatile foreign exchange markets

The short-term outlook in the foreign exchange markets also remains very uncertain. Strikingly, however, the United States dollar remained generally strong on both a multilateral and a bilateral basis. Apart from minor wobbles, its trade-weighted exchange rate had appreciated by about 5 per cent in the 12 months to December 2001, while that of the yen had weakened by about 12 per cent over the same period. The euro and pound sterling had remained broadly stable against the dollar, while the Swiss franc had strengthened. ESCAP regional currencies have followed a roughly similar pattern. The Chinese yuan renminbi, Hong Kong dollar and Malaysian ringgit have fixed parity with the United States dollar, and this situation has been maintained. Other currencies, however, have tended to weaken moderately against the United States dollar as the prospects of the countries concerned have deteriorated. The weakening has, by and large, reflected their dependence on the United States economy or is an indication of long-standing political problems, as in Indonesia and the Philippines. Since January 2002, the yen has weakened significantly against the dollar; so far, the yen weakness has not had an impact on other currencies but the situation could change once a broader recovery begins.

ODA flows unlikely to rise

ODA trends are more difficult to discern in that data for 2001 are not yet available (see chapter IV of this *Survey*, relating to Regional development cooperation in Asia and the Pacific). Up to the end of 2000, however, ODA was on a declining trend vis-à-vis 1999, the largest falls being registered in the category of multilateral non-concessional loans and IMF assistance. This was largely the result of the completion of IMF-led assistance to the crisis economies in the ESCAP region. These trends are likely to have been temporarily reversed in view of the large emergency financial packages for Argentina and Turkey arranged by

IMF in 2001. On the whole, ODA is unlikely to rise except for emergencies, such as that affecting Afghanistan and its neighbours, or for natural disasters. It is worth stressing that the substantial amount of ODA pledged in support of Afghanistan in January 2002 was a development of great significance; it could herald a more sustained, positive attitude on the part of donors. If so, this would have major implications for three important groups of countries in the ESCAP region, the least developed countries, the economies in transition and the Pacific island economies.

Impact on the ESCAP region

What impact is the 2001 downturn likely to have on the developing economies of the ESCAP region? Notwithstanding the huge diversity of ESCAP economies in terms of geography, population size, level of development and approaches to development, certain similar and dissimilar features can be discerned.

The 2001 downturn to have an impact on economies with high trade-to-GDP ratios

The adverse effects are likely to be marginal in the short term for economies with a large domestic component, such as China and India, or a preponderance of traditional commodity production with low price and income elasticities in their exports. However, most of the fastest-growing economies, and especially the crisis economies of East and South-East Asia, have high trade-GDP ratios and relatively large inflows of external capital. They are likely to be affected more adversely and directly by global economic setbacks.

Malaysia, the Republic of Korea, Singapore and Taiwan Province of China have comparatively high trade-GDP ratios, larger concentrations in ICT-related exports and a greater dependence on the United States economy as an export destination. Their GDP performance in 2002 is likely to be directly affected by the strength of recovery of the United States economy.

ESCAP region less vulnerable as a whole

Many developing economies of the ESCAP region are not as vulnerable to the current slowdown as they were in 1997, thanks to their improved external current account positions, built-up foreign exchange reserves and reduced short-term indebtedness. Indeed, the Argentine crisis, while obviously affecting overall market sentiment, has had little impact on the rest of the world, including the ESCAP developing region, whether in terms of exchange rate volatility or tighter financing conditions in the international capital markets. Contagion, thus far at any rate, has been contained, with Argentina being classed as a sui generis risk (box I.1).

Box I.1. Lessons for the Asian and Pacific region from the Argentine crisis

After a decade or more of virtually no output growth and hyperinflation in the 1980s, Argentina introduced the currency board system in 1991.[a] As a result of this, the exchange rate and convertibility of the Argentine peso was fixed at par with the United States dollar. The purpose of this step was to squeeze inflation out of the economy and establish conditions in which domestic and foreign investors would be able to operate in a more stable and predictable framework of rewards and incentives. The policy anchor for achieving this objective would be provided by the fixed exchange parity of the peso to the dollar.

The initial results were very impressive. Inflation fell almost immediately from an average of over 300 per cent in the 1980s and over 80 per cent in 1991 to 17 per cent in 1992, and averaged only 4.5 per cent between 1992 and 1998. GDP growth, which had averaged –0.3 per cent in the 1980s, rose to nearly 10 per cent in 1992 and, despite one dip into recession in 1995, averaged well over 5 per cent between 1992 and 1998, Argentina's best record of sustained output growth since the Second World War. On the negative side, however, Argentina's current account deficit shot up from 0.4 to nearly 5 per cent of GDP during this period, while gross external debt increased from $63 billion in 1992 to $142 billion in 1998, or from 32 to 47 per cent of GDP, equivalent to well over five times the annual merchandise exports. The financial position of the public sector also deteriorated significantly in this period: the fiscal deficit rose from 0.1 per cent of GDP in 1992 to over 2 per cent in 1998.

In a progressively more integrated world economy with interlinked financial markets, the 1997 Asian financial and economic crisis was the first major test for Argentina's currency and exchange rate regime. The 1994 Mexican crisis was limited in impact with its effects dissipating quite quickly. The Asian crisis caused interest rate spreads for emerging markets to reach unprecedented levels, raising the cost of both external debt servicing and, via the exchange parity, domestic debt servicing for Argentina. Net interest payments on external debt increased from 9.4 per cent of GDP in 1992 to 16.5 per cent in 1998, while high and rising domestic lending rates, which jumped from 3.1 per cent in 1993 to 9.6 per cent in 1998 and to 12.4 per cent in 1999, effectively shut out large swathes of domestic borrowers from the banking system. More significantly, perhaps, Brazil, Argentina's major trading partner and competitor, experienced a substantial depreciation in the exchange rate of the real. Inevitably, as a result, Argentine unemployment began to rise, reaching 14 per cent in 1998 and, what is worse, exports declined after six years of relatively robust growth. In short, Argentina had fallen victim to a classic "scissors" crisis, in which the burden of external and internal debt service begins to rise at a time of declining economic activity.

In the period 1998-2000, asset markets in most countries experienced considerable turbulence, partly on account of the uncertainty generated in international financial markets by the fallout of the Asian crisis and partly by the "flight to quality" phenomenon that came in the wake of the Long Term Capital Management hedge fund rescue in the United States. The international portfolio, i.e. equities and bonds, and FDI flows were both depressed; spreads on developing country bonds reached very high levels, around 1,200 basis points in 1999, although these had eased down to 800 basis points by mid-2000. These developments inevitably had adverse repercussions on Argentina's domestic policies. Apart from the rise in borrowing costs, tax revenues came under pressure in response to a lower level of activity in the economy; doubts intensified about the Argentine Government's ability to finance the growing fiscal and current account deficits and ultimately whether it would be able to maintain the exchange rate peg with the dollar. By late 2000, private foreign funding had effectively dried up for Argentina in view of those doubts.

---

[a] The currency board system is an arrangement whereby the quantity of money is fixed by the quantity of external reserves and the board undertakes to exchange domestic currency for the foreign reserve currency at a specified and fixed rate. The Hong Kong, China, Monetary Authority is a notable example of a currency board system. Bosnia and Bulgaria have also adopted the currency board arrangement.

(Continued overleaf)

(Continued from preceding page)

The 2000-2001 global slowdown sealed the fate of Argentina's monetary and exchange rate arrangements. Industrial production had declined by a massive 18 per cent by December 2001 on a year-on-year basis, while GDP had contracted by nearly 5 per cent. The current account deficit had widened to nearly 7 per cent of GDP by the third quarter of 2001. Despite significant IMF assistance, the country was faced with a major crisis of confidence as bank deposits, both peso- and dollar-denominated, became subject to unrelenting attrition. Argentina's risk premium on foreign bond issues soared from 228 basis points in June 2001 to a staggering 2,090 points in September 2001. Against these inexorable trends, domestic lending contracted, as did output and employment. Bank deposits were frozen in December 2001 in a last-ditch effort to save the financial system from collapse, but by then the economy had started on a downward spiral from which there appeared to be no immediate respite. In January 2002, after three changes of government following large-scale street protests, the exchange rate peg was abandoned and the peso allowed to float freely against the dollar.

What lessons can the Asian and Pacific region draw from Argentina's crisis? Debate about the nature and efficacy of Argentina's reforms of the 1990s and the adequacy of IMF intervention will obviously go on for many years, but some tentative conclusions can be drawn now:

- First, there were major adverse international developments in the 1990s, such as dollar appreciation, Brazilian real depreciation and two global slowdowns. These events significantly undermined Argentine competitiveness, reduced exports and caused the country's current account deficit to widen.

- Second, there was slow progress in overcoming the structural fiscal imbalance. Many publicly owned enterprises were indeed privatized, but this process perversely produced a false picture of fiscal health. A bloated and rather well-paid civil service remained effectively untouched by reform.

- Third, little was done to address the problems of low labour productivity and the poor international competitiveness of the Argentine economy. In consequence, few new industries with a strong export orientation were developed. These deficiencies had existed in the economy for a long time; the discipline of a fixed exchange rate, if anything, exacerbated them.

- Fourth, an unsustainable external debt in relation to foreign earnings made the currency board arrangement untenable in the final analysis. Argentina's overall external debt as a proportion of GDP was not particularly high by international standards. However, its poor external competitiveness suggested that the debt would become increasingly difficult to service given the slow growth of exports. Rising interest rates aggravated the problem.

- Fifth, in a globalized world, a fixed exchange rate regime introduces unnecessary rigidity in the policy-making arena. Globalization exposes economies to external shocks; these can be more easily absorbed with flexible exchange rates. A focus on inflation is a worthwhile objective of policy but needs to be balanced against other objectives. There is little justification for maintaining a commitment to low inflation in the face of declining output and rising unemployment.

- Finally, any one of the above factors might have necessitated significant policy adjustments in the Argentine economy; all five together clearly posed an impossible challenge for Argentina. An internationally agreed system of debt workouts might well have given Argentina room to reorganize its debts, but would not have addressed the fundamental weaknesses that created them in the first place.

None of the countries in the Asian and Pacific region exhibits the combination of factors that led to the Argentine crisis. Nevertheless, it does drive home the message that maintaining sound economic fundamentals and international competitiveness and confidence lies at the heart of running a viable economy in a dynamic global setting. The low inflation policy goal, though necessary, is not sufficient to face the challenges of a volatile economic environment.

THE CHALLENGES AHEAD

Predicting the future remains hazardous in the extreme, given the continuing underlying uncertainties and the coexistence of a number of conflicting scenarios, all of which have some plausibility. A huge element of uncertainty for the global economy obtruded from the terrorist attacks on the United States. Moreover, the effects could be long-lasting in terms of capital expenditure by corporations. A further uncertainty lies in the patterns of consumer expenditure in the developed economies once the current slowdown begins to be reflected in significant job losses. All these possibilities are already visible in the travel and travel-related sectors of the economy in the United States, including aircraft manufacture. Largely in consequence, unemployment rose from 4.0 per cent in November 2000 to 5.7 per cent in November 2001. Until the unemployment rate stabilizes in the United States and other major world economies, it would be unrealistic to assume a sustained recovery in consumer confidence. The recovery process in the United States, and hence global recovery, could therefore take the shape of "V", "U" or even "W". Notwithstanding, such uncertainties, certain historical patterns in the process could shed light on how events might unfold in the coming months.

Uncertain growth prospects for 2002

On present evidence, the current global downturn could be the most geographically synchronized in a generation, affecting virtually all regions, with both developed and developing economies slowing at the same time. Thus a feature of concern is that there is no obvious engine of recovery immediately in view, though world economic performance will continue to depend on the speed of economic recovery in the United States.

No engine of recovery in sight

The low levels of inflation may have paradoxically put a limit on further policy easing on the monetary front, and hence on further monetary stimulus to recovery and growth. Lower interest rates by themselves are not having the desired stimulating effect on investment and consumption in Japan and the United States even bearing in mind the normal lags in monetary policy transmission through interest rate cuts. Interest rates are now very low (0.03 per cent in Japan and 1.70 per cent in the United States for three-month money market rates) and room for further cuts is small.

Limited impact of monetary stimulus

The current slowdown in the world economy, although initially triggered by an inventory correction in the United States, is in essence an investment-led downturn. Such downturns reflect previous debt-financed excesses in investment in ICT and, for the European Union in telecommunications. They therefore tend to be deeper and to last longer as excess capacity cannot be eliminated very quickly. However, recent experience with ICT suggests that the rates of ICT obsolescence can be very high, so that capital expenditure, driven by the very low interest rates, could recover quickly when the rebound starts.

Recovery could be rapid – when it comes

*Need for
counter-cyclical
policies as well as
macroeconomic
prudence*

The principal policy issue for the ESCAP region in the next 12 months is therefore to maintain the momentum and intensity of economic activities in the face of an unfavourable external environment. This means sustaining growth without the stimulus provided by net exports or capital inflows, as was the case in 1999-2000 and much of 2001. This policy approach involves the creation of stronger domestic growth stimuli, through either fiscal or monetary measures, in consonance with the parallel need to preserve market confidence and sound macroeconomic fundamentals. Counter-cyclical fiscal and monetary policies would need to be eased off gradually with the emergence of a broad-based recovery in the world economy. Meanwhile, well-targeted public spending, with emphasis on quality rather than quantity, could be initiated; the development of both economic and social infrastructure comes to mind in this regard.

*Costs and benefits
of globalization*

The speedy transmission of weaknesses in the United States economy to the rest of the world is a direct consequence of the increasingly close integration in trade and finance that has been a hallmark of the current process of globalization. There is broad agreement that developing countries have had significant new opportunities to integrate into the world trading system, to access a bigger pool of international private capital and thus to benefit from the technology, modern management practices and marketing know-how that the process facilitates. But globalization has also posed new challenges for many countries, including sharp declines in export markets and contagious effects in international capital markets, some of which have served to magnify or intensify significantly the initial fall in export demand or financial instability in the developing economies. These were witnessed in 1997/98 and once again in 2001.

An examination of the 1997 crisis and the 2001 downturn shows unmistakable evidence of the substantial costs of globalization, via externally induced macroeconomic and financial instability and contagion, for virtually all economies. Globalization has also raised the frequency and intensity of episodes of volatility in exchange rates, fluctuations in stock markets, and changes in investor sentiment that have tended to occur independently of domestic developments. All these have greatly increased the complexity of economic policy-making and management for government in many, if not all, developing economies, regardless of their levels of development, pattern of resource endowments or geographical location.

*Governments should
use opportunities
more realistically
in managing
globalization*

What are the policy options available to developing countries in general and to those in the ESCAP region in particular? At a general level, it should be emphasized that globalization is an exogenous reality over which individual countries have little or no control. It is, nevertheless, interesting to note that France and Germany have taken a new interest in the Tobin tax[8] as a means of reducing the volatility of

---

[8] The primary aim of the Tobin tax is to reduce exchange rate volatility.

international capital flows. But it is clear that any attempt at insulation by an individual country, for example, by introducing new tariffs or other restrictions on trade and capital flows, is likely to be counterproductive and increase the risk of retaliatory trade restrictions and possible exclusion from international financial markets. At the same time, in managing globalization, it is imperative for Governments to take more realistic account of both the strengths and weaknesses inherent in their own economies, in the institutional structure and in the availability and quality of human resources for policy implementation purposes.

That overdependence on a narrow range of markets and on a narrow range of exported goods and services, whether primary, manufactured or high-tech in nature, carries enormous downside risks is not in dispute. Nevertheless, a diversified pattern of exports and exports embodying higher domestic value added may not offer a complete respite, as the experiences of several countries both inside and outside the region have shown. Moreover, efforts to move up the value chain as well as to diversify the domestic economic structure and sectors are far from being a feasible option for many countries in the region and elsewhere.

Greater diversity in exports and in export markets required

The sequencing and speed of financial sector liberalization also require special attention. In the region as a whole, domestic banks have poor risk management capabilities and are, in general, undercapitalized. Regulatory and oversight functions are also not as extensive and sophisticated as could be desired. Thus, liberalization measures should not merely seek to implement an external blueprint but should also keep in view the financial, institutional and human resource capacity available in individual countries. In a period of great turmoil, the option of capital controls as a temporary measure, with a strict timetable for their removal, could be useful in calming the situation and providing some breathing space for remedial action to be in place. Orderly debt-workout mechanisms would be similarly beneficial.

Measured liberalization of the financial sector

Externally induced fluctuations in capital markets and exchange rates became a fact of life in the 1990s and apparently little can be done to avoid them entirely. Nevertheless, there may be some justification in proposing that, in the area of financial contagion and external shocks, the coordination of policies and institutions between countries can be addressed more effectively at the regional than at the international level. This also applies to other areas for regional cooperation, including through information sharing, combating money-laundering, traffic in human beings and terrorism.

More regional cooperation against money-laundering; terrorism ...

By and large, it seems inappropriate to burden global institutions such as IMF or the World Bank with yet more mandates and responsibilities, at least from a practical point of view. Interest in the regional approach, as a supplement to interregional efforts, attracted attention following the 1997 crisis. Among other things, there was a heightened perception that the advice and conditionality of IMF were not sufficiently

... in the financial markets ...

sensitive to the regional nuances of the crisis and may even have aggravated it to some extent. This perception gave rise to the proposal for an Asian monetary fund. Even though the arrangement has not materialized, the Chiang Mai Initiative of 2000[9] can be seen as a regional response on how to deal with a new bout of financial market volatility through the provision of liquidity among regional countries.

... and in matters concerning exchange rate volatility

Another regional response is embodied in tentative discussions on ensuring greater stability in exchange rates, specifically on the merits and demerits of a common currency peg system in the region along the lines of the European exchange rate mechanism. The need to choose between a fixed and floating exchange rate regime has posed a dilemma to countries, especially in relation to the policy complications and business uncertainties created by floating rates, an arrangement that has come into vogue since 1997. There is a presumption that some economies of the ESCAP region could avoid their current difficulties more successfully by establishing a common exchange rate peg and supporting it collectively with their considerable foreign exchange reserves. This approach, as reflected in the European Monetary Union and euro, is now encouraging policy harmonization in other areas as well, an additional bonus. Above all, it has created a zone of financial stability within the euro area. Some subregions within the ESCAP region certainly have the resources and institutional sophistication to make considerable progress in the area of exchange rate cooperation. In any event, there is a strong case for greater consultation among all countries on financial issues generally.

Regional approaches thus offer a viable option for many countries by combining financial cooperation with preferential trade within the region, not least to regain and sustain the momentum of growth, employment generation and poverty alleviation lost in the 1997 crisis and apparently lost again in 2001. There is, of course, no guarantee that regional arrangements are a recipe for long-term success. The regional approach nevertheless offers an important alternative for addressing the challenges of globalization and liberalization that some countries are clearly finding it difficult to face and manage effectively and sustainably on their own. It is inevitable that the Governments will need to adjust their policy parameters and institutional setting to function better in a globalized economy, one which entails an ever-greater reliance on market mechanisms. However, the adjustment process should not be construed as the exclusion of all public sector initiatives and interventions. Indeed, a predictable framework for intervention would reduce uncertainty and increase consistency, and thus allow markets to operate on a more efficient and accountable basis.

---

[9] Under the Chiang Mai Initiative, ASEAN members plus China, Japan and the Republic of Korea have agreed to set up a swap facility to provide liquidity for mutual support in times of need.

Box I.2. The WTO Doha Development Agenda: outcome and future prospects

After the breakdown of the third WTO Ministerial Conference, held at Seattle, Washington, in 1999, the need to narrow the gap between the developed and developing countries and reach a consensus on a wide range of divisive issues became increasingly imperative. Subsequently, the intensified global economic slowdown following the 11 September 2001 terrorist events, and their aftermath, rendered even more important a global commitment to push forward the momentum of trade liberalization. The major implications of the Doha Development Agenda, as agreed at the fourth WTO Ministerial Conference, held at Doha, Qatar, in November 2001, are briefly discussed below:

Results of the Doha Conference

- The main Ministerial Declaration spells out the objectives and timetables for the Uruguay Round-mandated negotiations on agriculture and services, which started in 2000, and brings both sectors within a framework for comprehensive negotiations.

- With regard to agriculture, the Declaration reaffirms the work already undertaken since 2000 and reconfirms the commitment to a fair and market-oriented trading system. It embodies a commitment to the reduction, and eventual phasing out, of all forms of export subsidies, while noting that the outcome of pertinent negotiations should also not be prejudged. Modalities for further commitments, including provisions for special and differential treatment for developing countries, are to be established by 31 March 2003 and comprehensive draft schedules submitted by the time of the fifth Ministerial Conference.

- With regard to services, the Declaration reaffirms that the Guidelines and Procedures for the Negotiations on Trade in Services, adopted at the special session of the Council for Trade in Services held in March 2001, provide the basis for continuing negotiations. The Declaration also stipulates that initial requests for specific commitments should be submitted by 30 June 2002, while the initial offers should be submitted by 31 March 2003.

- The Declaration also extends negotiations to other areas, such as industrial tariffs, anti-dumping rules, regional trade agreements, and dispute settlement procedures. Most significantly, for the first time negotiations are envisaged on the so-called "Singapore issues", namely the relationship between trade and investment, the interaction between trade and competition policy, transparency in government procurement and trade facilitation. However, these issues are subject to further study for another two years. Certain aspects of trade and environment linkages are also covered, specifically the relationship between WTO rules and multilateral environmental agreements, the "reduction or, as appropriate, elimination" of tariff and non-tariff barriers to trade in environmental goods and services, and disciplines governing subsidies that have negative environmental effects. The Declaration also makes specific reference to the fisheries sector and its importance to developing countries. Negotiations will also include, under the framework of TRIPs, a multilateral system of notification and registration of geographical indications for wine and spirits (e.g. champagne) to be completed by the fifth WTO Ministerial Conference. However, on the question of whether to extend geographical indicators to other farm products (notably cheese), the issue will continue to be addressed in the Council for TRIPs.

- The work programme on electronic commerce will continue, while issues relating to the special trade problems of small and vulnerable economies will be taken up under a new work programme under the auspices of the General Council. New working groups will be set up to examine and study issues related to trade, debt and finance as well as trade and transfer of technology. The Declaration reaffirms the decision taken at the first WTO Ministerial Conference, held in Singapore in 1996, that issues relating to core labour standards should be addressed by ILO.

(Continued overleaf)

(Continued from preceding page)

- Negotiations are to be concluded no later than 1 January 2005, the only exception being the negotiations on improving and clarifying the Dispute Settlement Understanding, which are set to conclude by the end of May 2003. Other elements of the negotiation work programme are to be concluded by the end of 2002, or by the time of the fifth Ministerial Conference.

- The Declaration on the TRIPs Agreement and public health spells out the recognition that WTO rules on intellectual property rights should not stop developing countries from gaining access to affordable medicines.

- A separate decision was adopted on outstanding implementation issues. Furthermore, the main Declaration makes specific reference to the integral role that implementation issues will play in the future work programme.

Narrowing the gap between the developed and the developing countries

- The failure to launch a new round of multilateral trade negotiations at Seattle was partly due to the developing countries' concern that the developed countries might use labour standards and environmental issues as protectionist tools. Hence, to narrow or bridge the gap between the developed and developing countries, there was a need for a restatement and reaffirmation of commitments from the European Union to re-examine its Common Agricultural Policy and from the United States to re-examine its anti-dumping rules. There was also a need to avoid any threatening positions in the area of labour and environment. The Doha Conference was a clear and concrete success in those aspects.

- The Doha Development Agenda gives developing countries better prospects for accessing the developed country markets in the areas of agriculture and textiles, on which the economies of the least developed countries especially remain highly dependent. Phasing out trade-distorting farm export subsidies and the quota-driven system that now governs the trade in textiles is squarely on the agenda. Further, issues such as food security and rural development have been re-emphasized. Developing countries might also benefit from the negotiations to clarify and improve the rules on anti-dumping.

- The current global slowdown is a major setback for the developing countries in their poverty reduction and development efforts. An element in the Doha Development Agenda that might benefit the developing world, especially least developed countries, is the commitment to provide further technical assistance for capacity-building and a guarantee of special and differential treatment. Of special interest is the political declaration that intellectual property rules should not impede developing country access to affordable medicines.

- Overall, the agreement so far is limited to setting the agenda and the time-frame for negotiations in those areas. Negotiations are to be concluded by 1 January 2005, after progress has been reviewed at the fifth Ministerial Conference, in 2003. The challenge over the next few years will be how to give the Doha Development Agenda a concrete outcome. This challenge is underlined by the fact that the Agenda comprises a list of outstanding issues awaiting implementation. Nevertheless, the Agenda shows that developing countries are now better placed than before to play a more proactive role in agenda-setting and negotiation in the forthcoming multilateral trade round.

The globalization process and regional trade agreements

- Another significant innovation in the Doha Agenda is the inclusion of the Singapore issues, thus re-emphasizing the important role of WTO in the globalization process. In the period until the fifth Ministerial Conference in 2003, a working group will look more intensively into these issues, and its work will be the basis for negotiations after the Conference.

- In recent years, regional trade arrangements have become increasingly popular in many parts of the world. In fact, prior to the Doha Conference, the Director-General of WTO had raised the issue that the current 170 regional trade agreements (with another 70 under discussion), covering around 43 per cent of world trade, could pose a systemic risk to the WTO rules-based multilateral trading system. Further, it was argued that global rules for the global firms in ICT, especially in telecommunications, financial services, data processing and electronic commerce, seemed more logical than regional protocols, thus questioning the relevance of regional agreements, for example, in e-commerce or preferential access to the Internet.

- Nevertheless, WTO is not likely to splinter into regional trading blocs. In the ESCAP region, for example, subregional trading blocs are an important supplement or a building block in the work of WTO in the area of multilateral trade liberalization. There is, indeed, an implicit acceptance of this in the Doha Development Agenda, when it states: "account should be taken, as appropriate, of existing bilateral and regional arrangements on investment". Another notable development from an ESCAP perspective was the admission of China and Taiwan Province of China into membership of WTO.

- The future patterns of globalization and the role of WTO in facilitating an equitable distribution of the substantial benefits of liberalized trade are likely to be determined, in the final analysis, by the commitments and speed of implementation of the agreements reached by the member countries themselves.

Finally, the fourth WTO Ministerial Conference, held at Doha, Qatar, in November 2001, agreed to launch a new round of negotiations (box I.2). While the portents are encouraging, it would not be out of place to stress that WTO members will still need to consider dispassionately the reasons for the debacle in Seattle and what constitutes a balanced agenda of trade reform for the next few years. While a new round of negotiations is clearly a laudable aim, it would be appropriate to give simultaneous consideration to the faster implementation of Uruguay Round agreements. In particular, there is a need to address the marginalization of the least developed countries in international trade, as well as issues related to the global integration efforts of small economies. Multilateral cooperation through trade and investment creates mutually beneficial interdependence and trust; it is therefore an essential building block for both economic well-being and world peace and security. This implies helping developing countries to participate more effectively in, and benefit more equitably from the world trading system, including by facilitating the accession of all developing countries that have applied for WTO membership, particularly the least developed countries and the economies in transition.

WTO: Qatar an encouraging portent

MACROECONOMIC PERFORMANCE, ISSUES AND POLICIES

REGIONAL OVERVIEW

The 2001 *Survey* forecast that GDP growth in developing economies in the ESCAP region would decline by around 1 percentage point to 6 per cent in 2001 and that there would be a slight rise in inflation in those economies. It was predicted that in the three developed countries as well, output expansion would be just over 2 per cent in 2001 compared with 1.8 per cent in 2000, but that inflation would be minimal. In the event, both forecasts proved to be off the mark. GDP growth declined by 3.9 percentage points in the developing economies of the region and by over 2 percentage points in the developed economies. Inflationary pressures were marginally more subdued than forecast in the *Survey* in both groups of countries (see table II.1).

Sharp falls in output along with subdued prices in many subregional economies

The poorer GDP outcome in 2001 was associated with a sharp downturn in world trade growth, from over 12 per cent in 2000 to 1 per cent in 2001. This was triggered by a decline in ICT imports by the United States, the knock-on effects of which spread rapidly to ICT component suppliers, particularly those in East and South-East Asia. Although some economies and subregions, for instance, China, India, Australia, New Zealand and the economies in transition in North and Central Asia, remained relatively immune, the slowdown was not restricted to ICT but subsequently spread to a broader range of manufacturing activities and services. Economies with high trade-to-GDP ratios were especially vulnerable to the downturn in external demand. The events of 11 September 2001, in turn, significantly intensified the downturn, while it translated into only slightly higher inflation in the developing economies. Among the developed countries of the region, Japan experienced deflation, Australia recorded lower inflation and New Zealand experienced only modest price pressures. Excess capacity and easier commodity and energy prices were major factors in the more favourable price environment that prevailed in most parts of the region in 2001.

But strong growth was sustained in China and India, among others

The dramatic suddenness of the global downturn in 2001 and its surprising severity meant that countervailing measures in the form of growth-enhancing domestic policies, such as a stimulative fiscal and easy monetary policy approach, proved to be insufficient. A number of

Table II.1. Selected economies of the ESCAP region: rates of economic growth and inflation, 2000-2004

(Percentage)

	Real GDP					Inflation[a]				
	2000	*2001[b]*	*2002[c]*	*2003[c]*	*2004[c]*	*2000*	*2001[b]*	*2002[c]*	*2003[c]*	*2004[c]*
Developing economies of the ESCAP region[d]	7.0	3.1	4.2	5.4	5.9	2.1	3.1	3.0	3.4	3.6
South and South-West Asia[e]	4.5	4.6	5.5	6.0	6.6	6.1	6.9	7.3	6.7	6.3
Bangladesh	5.9	6.0	4.3	..	..	3.4	1.6	4.0	..	..
India	4.0	5.4	6.0	6.3	7.0	3.7	4.2	5.0	5.0	4.5
Iran (Islamic Republic of)	5.9	5.5	6.5	6.5	6.1	12.6	12.0	14.0	14.0	11.5
Nepal	6.4	5.9	5.0	6.0	6.5	3.5	2.4	4.5	5.0	5.0
Pakistan	3.9	2.6	4.0	4.7	5.2	3.6	4.7	5.0	5.0	5.0
Sri Lanka	6.0	0.9	3.3	5.5	5.9	6.2	13.0	9.1	7.5	6.6
Turkey	7.1	−8.4	2.0	4.4	4.1	54.9	65.0	51.2	43.0	34.9
South-East Asia	6.5	1.8	3.2	4.4	4.6	2.3	5.0	4.3	3.9	3.9
Cambodia	5.4	5.3	4.5	6.3	6.0	−0.8	−0.6	3.0	5.0	5.0
Indonesia	4.8	3.3	3.8	4.9	4.6	3.7	11.1	9.8	6.3	5.3
Lao People's Democratic Republic	5.7	6.4	5.0	..	..	25.1	9.0	12.0	15.0	..
Malaysia	8.3	0.4	3.2	5.1	6.1	1.6	1.5	1.6	3.4	4.0
Myanmar	13.6	5.0	5.1	5.9	..	−0.1	9.6	..	..	..
Philippines	4.0	3.4	4.0	3.4	4.0	4.4	6.3	5.7	5.3	5.0
Singapore	9.9	−2.0	2.0	5.8	5.7	1.4	1.0	0.8	1.5	1.7
Thailand	4.4	1.5	2.5	2.5	3.5	1.6	1.6	1.8	2.5	3.1
Viet Nam	6.8	6.8	6.1	6.8	7.3	−1.7	−0.1	2.0	3.8	7.6
East and North-East Asia	8.0	3.2	4.3	5.7	6.2	0.8	1.1	1.2	2.1	2.7
China	8.0	7.3	7.0	7.5	7.6	0.4	0.7	1.1	2.2	2.5
Hong Kong, China	10.5	−0.2	1.0	6.0	6.3	−3.8	−1.6	−1.0	2.5	4.0
Mongolia	1.1	1.4	4.0	5.0	6.0	11.8	8.8	6.0	5.0	5.0
Republic of Korea	8.8	3.0	3.9	4.6	5.0	2.3	3.2	2.8	2.6	3.4
Taiwan Province of China	5.9	−2.2	1.7	4.0	5.4	1.3	0.0	0.0	1.0	1.5
Pacific island economies	−1.0	−1.2	2.7	2.7	2.5	7.1	7.2	8.2	7.1	5.9
Cook Islands	3.2	3.2	3.3	..	..	2.0	1.0	1.0	..	..
Fiji	−2.8	1.5	5.0	4.0	3.0	3.0	2.3	2.5	3.0	3.0
Papua New Guinea	−0.8	−3.3	1.2	1.8	2.1	10.0	10.3	12.0	10.0	8.0
Samoa	7.3	6.5	4.8	4.3	4.1	1.0	1.5	2.0	2.0	2.0
Solomon Islands	−14.5	−7.0	5.5	3.0	2.0	6.0	8.0	10.0	6.0	5.0
Tonga	6.1	3.0	2.5	2.9	3.0	7.1	8.0	3.0	3.0	3.0
Vanuatu	4.0	2.0	3.0	3.5	3.5	4.1	3.0	2.0	2.5	2.5

(Continued on next page)

Table II.1 *(continued)*

(Percentage)

	Real GDP					Inflation[a]				
	2000	*2001[b]*	*2002[c]*	*2003[c]*	*2004[c]*	*2000*	*2001[b]*	*2002[c]*	*2003[c]*	*2004[c]*
Developed economies of the ESCAP region	2.5	−0.2	−0.9	1.6	1.5	−0.4	−0.4	−0.7	−0.3	0.2
Australia	3.8	4.1	3.0	4.1	3.6	4.5	4.2	2.3	2.4	2.9
Japan	2.4	−0.5	−1.2	1.4	1.4	−0.7	−0.7	−0.9	−0.5	0.0
New Zealand	3.8	2.6	1.9	3.3	2.0	2.6	2.7	2.1	1.8	1.8
Memo:										
Kazakhstan	9.6	13.0	6.3	6.8	7.2	13.5	8.4	6.9	6.7	7.0
Russian Federation	8.3	5.7	3.5	4.0	4.3	20.8	18.6	15.5	13.0	11.0
Uzbekistan	4.0	4.0	2.5	3.0	..	24.9	25.6	25.5	23.1	..

Sources: ESCAP, based on IMF, *International Financial Statistics,* vol. LV, No.1 (January 2002); ADB, *Key Indicators of Developing Asian and Pacific Countries 2001* (Oxford University Press, 2001) and *Asian Development Outlook 2001* (Oxford University Press, 2001); Economist Intelligence Unit, *Country Reports* and *Country Forecasts* (London, 2001 and 2002), various issues; and national sources.

[a] Changes in the consumer price index.

[b] Estimate.

[c] Forecast/target.

[d] Based on data for 28 developing economies representing about 95 per cent of the population of the region (excluding the Central Asian republics); GDP at market prices in United States dollars in 1995 have been used as weights to calculate the regional and subregional growth rates.

[e] The estimates and forecasts for countries relate to fiscal years defined as follows: fiscal year 2001/02 = 2001 for India and the Islamic Republic of Iran; and fiscal year 2000/01 = 2001 for Bangladesh, Nepal and Pakistan.

economies had already introduced fiscal stimulus measures in their 2001 budgets to sustain the 2000 recovery. As the slowdown intensified, fiscal measures were supported by more accommodative monetary policies in the form of lower interest rates in most economies of the region, with only a few minor exceptions. Nevertheless, GDP growth declined sharply in 2001.

As at early March 2002, signs of a global and regional upturn are mixed, although evidence of a rebound in recovery is becoming more discernible. While the majority of the economies in the region are expected to exceed their 2001 GDP growth rates in 2002, the improvement is likely to be modest, about 1.1 percentage points higher in 2002 than in 2001 for the region's developing economies as a whole. Any upturn in the region's developed countries in 2002 would be moderate and restricted to Australia. It is forecast that Japan will experience another contraction in output in 2002.

The global and regional recovery process remains tentative thus far in 2002

The nature of the recovery in 2002 is conditioned by both external and domestic factors. Externally, the overall economic environment in the United States, by and large, remains uncertain despite some positive signs on the horizon, such as improved consumer confidence and an increase in output in the last quarter of 2001. The uncertainty is particularly evident in United States stock markets. However, the Federal Reserve Board has stated that the United States economy was close to a turning point and a moderate recovery was expected in 2002. Japan, is in the throes of yet another recession, the third in the last decade, while the European Union, on present evidence, is unlikely to match its 2001 performance in 2002. Another uncertainty is excessive volatility in energy prices. Domestically, most economies continue to grapple with the inevitable trade-offs involved in running loose fiscal and monetary policies in the short term against the need to maintain sound macroeconomic fundamentals over the medium term. Although low inflation and spare capacity in many parts of the region facilitate the implementation of policy measures to stimulate domestic demand, the downturn in external demand cannot be fully compensated on a sustained basis by domestic measures alone in the short term.

Recent developments and the near-term outlook

Most economies in South-East Asia suffered greatly from the global downturn

Of the various ESCAP subregions, South-East Asia was the most severely affected by the 2001 global slowdown, experiencing a reduction in the aggregate growth rate of more than 4 percentage points. Not only is the subregion particularly vulnerable to external developments on account of the high trade-to-GDP ratios of several economies, but a number of them also have a significant concentration of ICT-related exports, which is the sector that triggered the global slowdown. Intraregional trade failed to provide a cushion as much of it consists of trade in ICT components destined eventually for the United States and Japan. Most economies in the subregion experienced sharply reduced growth, while Singapore's GDP actually contracted in 2001. In addition, softer prices for commodities and energy products intensified the decline in domestic demand in the producing countries. Viet Nam was a notable exception in the subregion and maintained growth at the same pace as that achieved in 2000.

The outlook for South-East Asia in 2002 is directly linked to developments in the global economy. In the short term, the subregion cannot compensate for the loss in external demand entirely through measures to stimulate domestic demand. Moreover, the September 2001 events and their fallout have almost certainly worsened the global outlook, thus necessitating a stronger domestic stimulus than would otherwise have been needed. In addition, in some countries of the subregion, slow progress in the reform and restructuring of the corporate and enterprise sector is likely to hinder the growth of domestic economic activity.

In East and North-East Asia, China remained largely immune to the global slowdown in 2001. Although export growth declined sharply, this was offset by strong domestic demand and public investment expenditure. The country's anticipated accession to WTO also stimulated robust FDI flows in 2001. As a result the GDP growth rate was only marginally below that recorded in 2000, but was still among the highest rates in the ESCAP region. Simultaneously, external reserves had built up to $214 billion by the end of 2001 and were the second highest in the world. In sharp contrast, the Republic of Korea; Hong Kong, China; and Taiwan Province of China were significantly affected by the global downturn, the last two economies actually sliding into a recession. The Republic of Korea's larger domestic market and more diversified exports prevented the economy from contracting in 2001, although there was a considerable rise in unemployment.

Economic expansion remained robust in China, while other economies in East and North-East Asia performed poorly

The outlook remains positive for China in 2002 and, notwithstanding a smaller contribution from net exports, GDP growth is expected to remain strong, driven by rising domestic consumption and investment. With muted inflationary pressures, an expansionary fiscal approach poses few macroeconomic risks in the short term. Growth in the Republic of Korea in 2002 should exceed the 2001 rate as domestic stimulus begins to have a positive effect on output. The outlook for both Hong Kong, China and Taiwan Province of China, however, is directly linked to recovery in the ICT sector, for which most industry experts are forecasting a moderate rebound in the second half of 2002. However, some degree of consolidation within the industry in those economies may be necessary in the interim to enhance profitability, in view of the considerable excess capacity in this sector.

The global slowdown in 2001, combined with continuing domestic constraints, had some effect on the economies of South and South-West Asia, with the notable exception of India and, to a lesser extent, Bangladesh, which saw an increase in the GDP growth rate between 2000 and 2001. India's economy, for example, benefited from a strong performance in agriculture and stable prices, while industrial production tended to remain flat. However, GDP growth, at 5.4 per cent in 2001, exceeded the rate achieved in 2000. Easily the worst affected were Sri Lanka and Turkey, with the latter experiencing a large output contraction. However, Turkey's economic woes were caused entirely by a major domestic financial crisis which led to a massive outflow of capital, collapse of the exchange rate and a huge rise in inflation. The crisis manifested itself in a large fall in industrial production and exports in 2001. Export growth declined virtually throughout the entire subregion. Pakistan, in particular,

Strong growth continued in several economies of South and South-West Asia, with Sri Lanka and Turkey experiencing a significant deterioration in economic performance

was badly affected by the war in Afghanistan, which undermined investor confidence and added to both public and private costs, such as expenditure on refugees and higher premiums and surcharges for war-risk insurance on shipping in the Arabian Sea.

Outlook for 2002 uncertain as a weak global recovery could hinder progress with domestic reform

From the perspective of 2002, South Asian economies in general have relatively low trade-to-GDP ratios. Hence, while the external environment does not have the same impact on overall economic performance as it does elsewhere in the region, a weakening of global growth would constrain economic activities in the subregion to some extent. The lower interest rates are clearly a positive development, although any extra stimulus from the budget needs to be balanced against the need to preserve price stability and foster fiscal consolidation; the latter remains a critical issue, although both India and Sri Lanka are now making good progress with privatization. Slow progress in fiscal consolidation has led to the accumulation of a large burden of domestic debt, which is acting as a major drag on medium-term GDP growth by pre-empting large revenues for debt servicing. Sri Lanka and Turkey are expected to show a significant improvement in GDP growth in 2002 as the 2001 crisis abates and tourism recovers from the September 2001 events. In the Islamic Republic of Iran and Pakistan, higher GDP growth is forecast to follow the ending of drought and recovery of agricultural output.

North and Central Asia remained largely unaffected by the global slowdown, with the Russian Federation growing strongly

Uniquely within the ESCAP region, the Russian Federation and other economies in North and Central Asia remained mostly unaffected by both the global slowdown and the September 2001 events. The momentum of GDP growth, driven by private consumption and exports, was maintained in 2001 despite the softening of energy and some commodity prices. The strong economic performance, in turn, facilitated progress with structural reform and fiscal consolidation through improved revenue collection and expenditure rationalization. In 2001, the aggregate output in the Russian Federation is estimated to rise by an impressive 5 per cent or more although still accompanied by relatively high inflation, following an increase of 7.6 per cent in 2000. Such robust growth helped to sustain the reinvigorated trade flows within CIS. The prospects for 2002 are broadly positive, although the likelihood of softer energy and commodity prices in the event that global economic recovery in 2002 is delayed, or is weaker than anticipated at present, constitutes an element of uncertainty in the near term.

The Pacific island economies were also adversely affected by both the 2001 global downturn and the September 2001 events, although to a somewhat smaller extent than the least developed countries. The lower prices for commodities were the main influence on agricultural performance in those economies, agriculture being the principal domestic economic activity in most parts of the subregion. However, fall-out from the September 2001 events was, by and large, less severe in the subregion as the United States is not a major source of tourists for most of the Pacific island countries; in addition, these countries are perceived as relatively low-risk destinations. Moreover, the economic slowdown in New Zealand was moderate in comparison with that of the United States, and this also helped the Pacific island economies. However, civil disturbances in some countries had a negative bearing on economic and export activities.

Pacific island economies and least developed countries are adversely affected by the impact of the global slowdown through lower commodity prices and some decline in tourism

As is self-evident, the outlook for the subregion remains uncertain. A strong recovery in the United States would generate important spillover effects on global demand, strengthen commodity prices, improve agricul-tural incomes and boost domestic consumption and economic activities more generally. However, in a number of Pacific island countries, GDP performance is equally dependent upon the solution of their civil and political problems.

Many least developed countries were directly affected by both the global slowdown in 2001 and the September 2001 events; the global slowdown had a negative impact on commodity prices and earnings and the September 2001 events on tourism earnings. Most of those countries rely on commodities or tourism, or both, for a major share of GDP. In addition, the weakness in commodity prices and decline in tourism receipts in 2001 widened the current account and fiscal deficits at a time when ODA flows were coming under some additional pressure on account of the urgent humanitarian and reconstruction needs of Afghanistan. The critical issue for the least developed countries in 2002 is thus a significant upturn in the global economy so that increases in external demand for commodities lead to firmer prices, reinforced by higher ODA inflows. With regard to the latter, the overall climate of opinion in the wake of the September 2001 events appears to be more positive than it has been for some time. However, whether this will translate into higher ODA flows in the short term remains to be seen.

Need to enhance ODA flows to least developed countries

The performance of the developed countries of the region was dominated by the continuing weakness of the Japanese economy. Japan experienced its third recession in the last 10 years and unemployment reached its highest level since 1953. Prospects for 2002 remain bleak, indicating another contraction in output. Australia and New Zealand were relatively less affected by the global slowdown. Through a mixture of measures to raise domestic demand, a global upturn and progress with structural reforms, both countries should see growth in 2002 at, or near, the pace achieved in 2001.

Slower growth in New Zealand, while Japan slides into its third recession in 10 years

Policy challenges

Adverse social impact of slow growth in 2002

The dramatic suddenness of the 2001 global slowdown, further aggravated by the events of September 2001, poses a major challenge for all economies in the ESCAP region. Slow growth in 2001 and a hesitant recovery in 2002 will almost certainly have an adverse social impact through higher unemployment and the constrained capacity of Governments to address emerging social problems and alleviate poverty through higher public expenditure. However, a number of countries of the region have some freedom in addressing the emerging issues and problems on account of the benign inflationary environment and comfortable external position in the form of current account surpluses and stabilized levels of foreign debt. Against this background, stronger policy initiatives can be taken to enhance growth in the short run and mitigate the effects of the current slowdown in the medium term. The implications are discussed in the following paragraphs.

Recovery in 2002 is dependent upon strong global growth, although the prospects for each subregion vary considerably

Regional economic recovery in 2002 and beyond is essentially predicated upon a significant improvement in the external environment, supported by appropriate domestic policy measures. However, the varying characteristics of each subregion suggest that policy approaches would need to be conceived in a more nuanced way in order to reflect the differences between and within the various subregions or within a particular group of countries, for instance, the least developed countries.

Higher public spending is not without some risk

At the national level, most Governments would need to put in place measures to preserve or enhance the momentum of growth through counter-cyclical fiscal and monetary policies; the latter would take precedence in cases where public debt was already at a high level. Rebalancing of taxation could also be undertaken so as to improve incentives for production and investment. Privatization provides a useful means to raise resources for increased public expenditure without incurring new debt. Higher public spending could provide important dividends in the form of faster or more equitable growth if carried out within the framework of a prudent, medium-term macroeconomic plan, say, on infrastructure, especially in the rural areas, and on well-targeted social programmes.

It should be emphasized, however, that such a policy approach is not without some degree of risk. In particular, countries need to avoid the debt trap in which debt servicing begins to grow faster than government revenues. Thus, macroeconomic prudence is of critical importance. Low interest rates and low inflation provide some short-term room for policy manoeuvre but would need to be balanced against the longer-term objectives of fiscal consolidation and stabilizing public debt. Another risk is that of creating new spending commitments which may not be sustainable in the long term.

At the same time, Governments should reiterate their commitment to addressing and resolving the many challenges involved in reforming the financial and corporate sectors and to improving transparency and governance. It is a truism that healthy financial systems are a sine qua non for stable, broad-based recovery. Decisive action to deal with the NPL problem and restructure corporate balance sheets requires changes in the socio-economic milieu as much as changes in the law and the availability of additional financial resources. Progress would naturally be difficult and slow in this area, but reform efforts need to be sustained or made more robust, as the case may be.

Need to reiterate the commitment to a reform agenda, in particular to deal decisively with the NPL problem and sustain trade liberalization

In the area of trade, it is imperative that countries avoid taking restrictive measures in the current situation and thus risking a downward spiral in output. In this connection, the onus lies on both developed and developing countries. Indeed, developed countries should accelerate the implementation of their commitments on trade liberalization, especially in textiles and agricultural commodities. Developing countries could increase the flow of trade by enhancing trade facilitation, such as through more streamlined customs clearance procedures. Individual countries could improve their external competitiveness significantly through lower trade transaction costs and better access to market information.

Certain policy initiatives could be promoted at the regional level. The regional perspective on sustainable development, adopted at the High-level Regional Meeting for the World Summit on Sustainable Development, held at Phnom Penh in November 2001, is a good example (see box II.1). Greater regional cooperation can offer a means for economies of the ESCAP region to counter some aspects of the global slowdown. Not all subregions and countries are experiencing the present downturn to a similar degree. China and India are relatively immune, while the economies of Australia, New Zealand and the Republic of Korea are still growing at a reasonable rate. They could therefore provide a useful stimulus to other economies by partially offsetting the decline in external demand from within and outside the region. In this context, the ESCAP region as a whole could move forward with growth-enhancing trade agreements that boost both trade flows and investor confidence; China's intended participation in a free trade arrangement with ASEAN is a case in point.

Potential for greater regional and subregional cooperation

Box II.1. World Summit on Sustainable Development: Asian and Pacific priorities

Ten years have passed since the "Earth Summit", the United Nations Conference on Environment and Development, held at Rio de Janeiro, Brazil, in 1992, when the world community made a commitment, through Agenda 21, to forge a global partnership for sustainable development, a development pathway that took a balanced and integrated approach to environment and development questions.[a] Agenda 21 was a landmark achievement in integrating environmental, economic and social concerns into a single policy framework. The proposals set out in Agenda 21 have been expanded and strengthened at several major United Nations conferences, including the Millennium Summit held in New York in September 2000. However, the commitments alone have proved insufficient in the light of all the action needing to be taken, and the World Summit on Sustainable Development, to be held at Johannesburg, South Africa, in 2002, provides an opportunity to focus on action to achieve sustainable development.

As part of the preparations for the World Summit, the High-Level Regional Meeting for the World Summit on Sustainable Development, organized by ADB, ESCAP, UNDP and UNEP, was held at Phnom Penh in November 2001. It provided perspectives from Asia and the Pacific on the state of progress in the implementation of Agenda 21 and on areas in which further action was required. While some achievements have been made, the majority of the countries in the region have continued to experience a deterioration in environmental quality and ongoing depletion of their natural resources. The Phnom Penh Meeting recognized that the trends in unsustainable development in the region were attributable mainly to poverty, the negative impacts of globalization, heavy debt burdens and the lack of adequate mechanisms for the full participation of stakeholders, including civil society organizations, in decision-making. In order to alleviate poverty, wide-ranging measures are required to promote small enterprises, strengthen micro-financing mechanisms, enhance the role of private sector activities and facilitate the necessary reforms in financial and capital markets. The involvement of stakeholders, particularly non-governmental organizations and women, in the decision-making process was considered to be an imperative in the effective formulation and implementation of policies, and in the follow-up monitoring and evaluation of their impact on sustainable development.

The need to consolidate best practices in various areas, which could enhance the implementation of Agenda 21 in countries of the region, was emphasized. Greater utilization of science and technology could improve production efficiency, mitigate natural disasters, promote better management of natural resources and control pollution. It was also necessary to facilitate the transfer of clean and environmentally sound technologies, particularly clean-coal technology, on favourable terms to developing countries. The use of ICT was advocated for disseminating information on the efficient exploitation of resources and for promoting public efforts and participation in implementing sustainable development. The global partnership between developed and developing countries to support sustainable development initiatives must be reinvigorated and, as an important step towards that objective, developed countries were urged to meet their commitment regarding the ODA target of 0.7 per cent of their combined GNP. The Meeting adopted the Phnom Penh Regional Platform on Sustainable Development for Asia and the Pacific and agreed to submit the Platform to the World Summit on Sustainable Development.

---

[a] Sustainable development is understood as development that meets the needs of the present without compromising the ability of future generations to meet their own needs.

Against this background, reform of the international financial architecture should not wait for international agreement. Some of its elements, such as additional liquidity support and monetary and financial market cooperation, can be implemented just as well at the regional or subregional level. The Chiang Mai Initiative is a pointer for other countries and subregions. Under this initiative, ASEAN members, plus China, Japan and the Republic of Korea, agreed to set up a swap facility to provide liquidity for mutual support in times of need. Within this broad context, one matter merits careful consideration, namely, the role that the substantial reserves of over $800 billion held by countries in the region could play in helping to revive growth in the region over the next year or two.

At the international level too, steps need to be taken to soften the impact of the slowdown on the most vulnerable group of countries, the least developed countries and the Pacific island and the landlocked economies. The enhancement of ODA flows, which are currently equivalent to only 0.22 per cent of the GNP of the developed countries, is an important objective. As an interim measure, the proposal that an explicit share of ODA be earmarked for the least developed countries is worthy of consideration by the donor countries. Simultaneously, the World Bank and regional development institutions should give urgent consideration to speeding up the flow of disbursements to counter the economic slowdown. Another issue of ongoing importance to the least developed countries is the objective of granting duty-free, quota-free market access in developed countries for products originating in least developed countries, as reiterated in the Ministerial Declaration adopted at the WTO Fourth Ministerial Conference, held at Doha, Qatar, in November 2001. There should be more visible progress in this regard in 2002.

Need to soften the impact of the global slowdown on the most vulnerable economies

Furthermore, following the September 2001 events, there is a pressing need to provide assistance to those countries that are experiencing unexpected declines in service receipts, particularly earnings from tourism, simultaneously with higher insurance and security costs. In this regard, the IMF Compensatory Financing Facility, although primarily meant for meeting shortfalls in commodity receipts, could be extended as an option to cover unexpected shortfalls in earnings from services, such as tourism receipts.

Finally, from an overall perspective, it is clear that the content of growth is as important as its pace. All Governments should continue to stress the need to preserve and promote social cohesion, reduce poverty and ensure environmental integrity, which are critical preconditions and parameters for stable, equitable and sustained long-term growth itself. In that connection, chapter III of this *Survey* examines the feasibility of the millennium development goals as set by the United Nations Millennium Summit in September 2000. The flow of ODA from both developed and developing donor countries, and its sectoral priorities and social focus, are the subject of chapter IV of this *Survey.*

Governments should promote social cohesion for sustained long-term growth

DEVELOPING ECONOMIES OF THE ESCAP REGION

Asian least developed countries[1]

Overview and prospects

Economic performance in 2001 was reasonably stable

The least developed countries of Asia did not generally experience the very sharp falls in output seen in some other countries in the region and GDP growth continued in 2001 (figure II.1). The effects of flooding on agriculture were not as damaging as had originally been feared in several countries and industrial growth has held up reasonably well, particularly where hydropower development projects have stimulated construction. Tourism receipts were down in many cases, but the service sector was buoyed up in some countries by increased sales of electricity. However, signs are emerging of a delayed response to the global slowdown and the outlook for GDP growth is less bright in 2002.

Figure II.1. Rates of GDP growth of least developed countries, 1998-2001

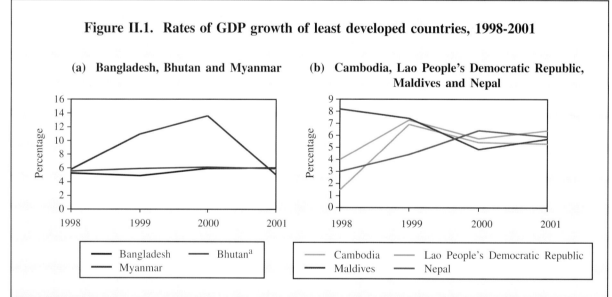

(a) Bangladesh, Bhutan and Myanmar

(b) Cambodia, Lao People's Democratic Republic, Maldives and Nepal

Sources: ESCAP, based on ADB, *Key Indicators of Developing Asian and Pacific Countries 2001* (Oxford University Press, 2001) and *Asian Development Outlook 2001* (Oxford University Press, 2001); and national sources.

Note: Figures for 2001 are estimates.

[a] GDP at factor cost.

---

[1] The Pacific island least developed countries are discussed in a separate section in this chapter.

Consumer prices were stable or declined in most of the Asian least developed countries in 2001 (figure II.2). This was in part a reflection of declining commodity prices on world markets and improvements in the food situation in the countries of South Asia; food prices were generally stable in the South-East Asian least developed countries as well, despite widespread flooding. Some of these countries also benefited from local use of the United States dollar, as this kept import prices down. The outlook as regards inflation, however, is not so encouraging. In the South Asian least developed countries, cost-push pressures could arise from weakening exchange rates due, in turn, to large fiscal deficits or accommodative monetary policy, and increased fuel and utility charges and additional taxes. In South-East Asia, macroeconomic stabilization efforts in Cambodia and the Lao People's Democratic Republic, which have contributed to price stability in recent years, are likely to continue. However, exchange rate depreciation and increases in the prices of petroleum products and electricity will add to inflationary pressures in the medium term.

Price pressures remained weak

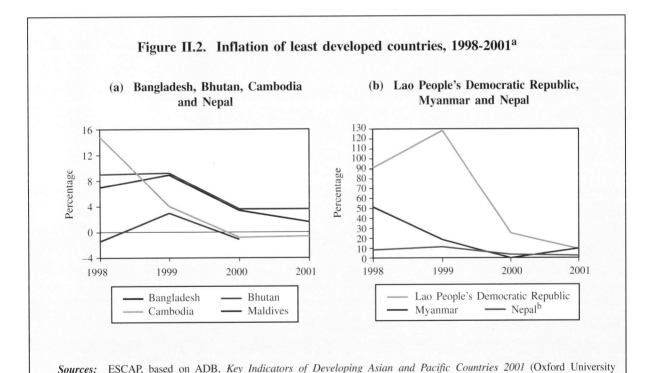

Figure II.2. Inflation of least developed countries, 1998-2001[a]

(a) Bangladesh, Bhutan, Cambodia and Nepal

(b) Lao People's Democratic Republic, Myanmar and Nepal

Sources: ESCAP, based on ADB, *Key Indicators of Developing Asian and Pacific Countries 2001* (Oxford University Press, 2001) and *Asian Development Outlook 2001* (Oxford University Press, 2001); IMF, *International Financial Statistics,* vol. LIX, No. 10 (October 2001); and national sources.

Note: Figures for 2001 are estimates.

[a] Changes in the consumer price index.
[b] National urban consumer price index.

**The global
slowdown affected
some exports**

Merchandise exports from the Asian least developed countries generally grew more slowly, partly as a result of the effects of the global slowdown (figure II.3). Exports of manufactures, particularly ready-made garments, were adversely affected. Service receipts were also down as tourism suffered in many of these least developed countries, especially after the events of 11 September 2001; however, an encouraging sign was the increase in the number of Asian tourists seen in some countries. The import picture (figure II.4) was more mixed, with many countries experiencing a decrease in imports as fewer inputs were needed for the ready-made garment industry.

**FDI flows remained
very low**

Inflows of private capital for investment in the Asian least developed countries have been low. ODA flows remained stable or increased, often quite substantially, in all these countries apart from Bangladesh, where disbursements have slowed, and Myanmar, where such flows have largely been absent for many years. Official reserves remained low in most cases, and the amounts of external debt were much higher in the South-East Asian least developed countries than in South Asia. Myanmar has significant debt arrears; the level of external debt is being carefully monitored in the Lao People's Democratic Republic; and Cambodia has

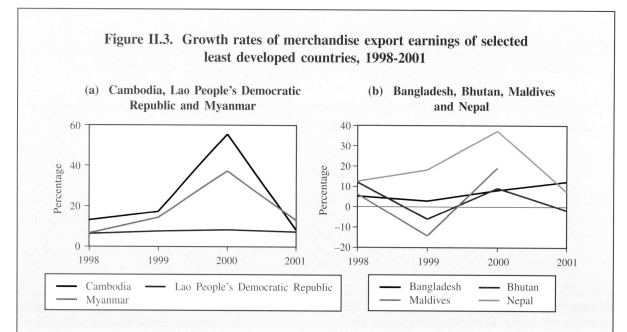

**Figure II.3. Growth rates of merchandise export earnings of selected
least developed countries, 1998-2001**

(a) Cambodia, Lao People's Democratic Republic and Myanmar

(b) Bangladesh, Bhutan, Maldives and Nepal

Sources: IMF, *Direction of Trade Statistics* (CD-ROM), February 2002, *International Financial Statistics* (CD-ROM), January 2002, and web sites <http://www.imf.org/external/np/sec/pr/2001/pr0118.htm> and <http://www.imf.org/external/country/index.htm>, 18 February 2002; ADB, *Asian Development Outlook 2001* (Oxford University Press, 2001); and national sources.

Note: Figures for 2001 for Myanmar are for January-September; figures for Bangladesh, Bhutan and Nepal are for the fiscal year.

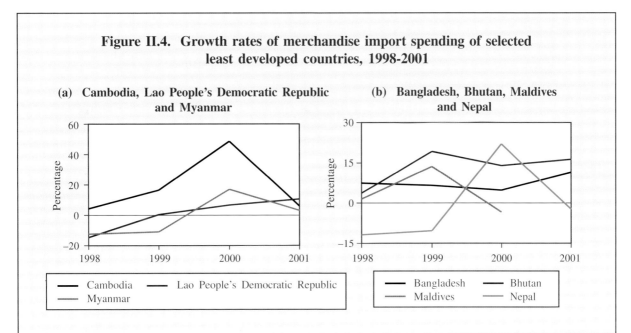

Figure II.4. Growth rates of merchandise import spending of selected least developed countries, 1998-2001

(a) **Cambodia, Lao People's Democratic Republic and Myanmar**

(b) **Bangladesh, Bhutan, Maldives and Nepal**

Sources: IMF, *Direction of Trade Statistics* (CD-ROM), February 2002, *International Financial Statistics* (CD-ROM), January 2002, and web sites <http://www.imf.org/external/np/sec/pr/2001/pr0118.htm> and <http://www.imf.org/external/country/index.htm>, 18 February 2002; ADB, *Asian Development Outlook 2001* (Oxford University Press, 2001); and national sources.

Note: Figures for 2001 for Myanmar are for January-September; figures for Bangladesh, Bhutan and Nepal are for the fiscal year.

completed outstanding bilateral debt rescheduling agreements. National currencies in the South Asian least developed countries showed a downward trend in 2001, in several cases affected by a similar trend in the Indian rupee. Exchange rates were relatively stable in the South-East Asian least developed countries in the first half of 2001, but showed signs of some instability thereafter. Generally however, the outlook for 2002, is for continued currency weakness.

Most of the Asian least developed countries have been grappling with issues related to economic development combined with greater equity. However, Afghanistan will have to confront the huge and pressing tasks of resettlement, rehabilitation and reconstruction for several years to come (see box II.2). Good governance is high on the policy agenda, along with wide-ranging structural reforms, to ensure a sustained focus on poverty alleviation among the least developed countries. This task has been aggravated somewhat by domestic security and stability problems in a number of Asian least developed countries. However, trade liberalization through existing or future membership in WTO provides opportunities for future growth and transformation, especially in an auspicious external environment.

Reforms are high on the policy agenda

43

Box II.2. Rehabilitation and reconstruction of Afghanistan[a]

"By working together, we have every chance of mounting the kind of fully integrated approach to recovery that is needed to help Afghan people to reap the rewards of peace".

– Kofi Annan, Secretary-General of the United Nations (Brussels, December 2001)

The initial conditions and circumstances

Afghanistan, one of the poorest countries in the world, was recognized as a least developed country even prior to the prolonged war and conflict of more than two decades. Its economy is heavily dependent on agriculture, with only a small share in manufacturing. Apart from the devastating war, further damage to the agrarian economy has been caused by drought over the past three years. Out of an estimated population of 25 million, about one fifth are living as refugees in neighbouring Pakistan, the Islamic Republic of Iran and other countries. The bleak socio-economic position of Afghanistan can be seen from the data and information below.[b]

- GDP per capita is less than $200.

- Four out of five people are not literate; the education system has collapsed; and enrolment rates, particularly for girls, are extremely low.

- One in four children dies before the age of 5, half are malnourished and a third of the survivors are orphans.

- The maternal mortality rate is among the highest in the world.

- Adult life expectancy is just 44 years.

- Three out of four persons lack access to safe drinking water.

- Half of the urban housing stock in major cities has been destroyed or damaged.

- Nearly one in 20 is disabled by land mines.

- An abysmal situation with regard to respect for human rights, particularly those of children and women, has existed for decades.

- There is widespread environmental degradation affecting people's livelihood, health and future prospects.

The political transition process

The Afghan Interim Administration, in place since 22 December 2001 following the Bonn Agreement, consists of 30 members presided over by Chairman Hamid Karzai. The Agreement also established a Special Independent Commission for the convening of the Emergency Loya Jirga (assembly of elders), a Central Bank and a Supreme Court. Under the Agreement, the Emergency Loya Jirga is to be convened within six months of the establishment of the Interim Authority and opened by His Majesty Mohammed Zaher, the former King of Afghanistan. The Emergency Loya Jirga will decide on a Transitional Authority, including a broad-based administration, to lead Afghanistan until a fully representative government can be elected through free and fair elections, to be held no later than two years from the date of the convening of the Emergency Loya Jirga. Lastly a Constitutional Loya Jirga, will be convened, within 18 months of the establishment of the Transitional Authority, to adopt a new constitution for Afghanistan.

---

[a] This box is largely based on United Nations, *Immediate and Transitional Assistance Programme for the Afghan People 2002* (New York, January 2002); and ADB, UNDP and the World Bank, *Afghanistan: Preliminary Needs Assessment for Recovery and Reconstruction* (January 2002).

[b] Statistics on Afghanistan's economy have not been published by the Afghan authorities for about a decade and the available data, coming mainly from international sources, are not always consistent or comparable.

The magnitude of the tasks ahead

The successful implementation of any recovery strategy is predicated on durable peace, security and political solutions for the long term.[c] The main responsibilities for ensuring these requirements lie with the Afghans themselves. However, the United Nations and the international community can play an important and indispensable role in the process, in several dimensions. Donor funding requirements for 2002, detailed by the United Nations at the International Conference on Reconstruction Assistance to Afghanistan, held at Tokyo on 21-22 January 2002, amounted to over $1.8 billion for humanitarian assistance, recurrent costs of the Afghan Interim Administration and quick-impact recovery programmes and projects. Joint estimates on reconstruction and rehabilitation made by UNDP, ADB and the World Bank indicate the need for around $5 billion over 2.5 years, $10 billion over 5 years and $15 billion over 10 years. Of the $4.5 billion pledged at the Tokyo Conference by donors for a 5-year period, commitments for the first year were in line with the funds requested by the United Nations. It is important that these pledges should be translated quickly into disbursements to underpin programme and project implementation in a transparent and coordinated manner.

The scope and focus of rebuilding efforts

There is an urgent need for sustained humanitarian assistance, reconstruction and development activities; these have to be implemented concurrently and yield interrelated and mutually reinforcing outcomes. The development approach to be pursued should be rights-based, such as a commitment to promoting and protecting human rights, particularly those of women, children, minorities and returning refugees; other principles integral to this approach include equitable participation, accountability, transparency, non-discrimination and economic and political empowerment. Moreover, the reconstruction strategy could take the form of a rolling plan that could be further developed and refined through the incorporation of experiences and lessons learned from the previous phases of implementation.

The expected return of some 5 million Afghan refugees or internally displaced persons presents a daunting challenge, including in the complex planning and allocation of future resources. The process involves both initial facilitation measures and longer-term support for the returnees and the communities to which they return. To ensure adequate local leadership, participation and ownership, Afghans at various levels have to be involved in all stages of the programmes and projects concerned, from conception to planning and implementation. This is essential not only to maximize a sense of ownership and participation but also to ensure that religious and cultural sensitivities are taken into account adequately in the process. It may be difficult to find expertise inside the country, since a whole generation has had no education and most people with useful skills have left. The very large numbers of skilled Afghans living in refugee camps constitute a pool of human capital on which to draw for the work of reconstruction. Since most women were not engaged in the conflict and had to carry the burden of agricultural work and finding the means of livelihood, their inclusion, following the provision of education and confidence-building, will be particularly important for the rapid development of the country.

The rebuilding and resettlement processes will have to start from almost nothing owing to the absence of basic services and the loss of such key infrastructure as health-care facilities, schools, transport, power and communications. Quick-impact programmes are also needed to meet short-term priorities, especially for higher food production and more extensive food transport and distribution networks. Indeed, agricultural output can potentially meet domestic food requirements as well as provide an exportable surplus. The sector therefore has to play a major role in the economic recovery process, particularly through the spread of labour-intensive, agro-based SMEs. In this connection, mine-clearance activities will not only enhance public safety but also yield valuable acreage for agriculture as well as for the rehabilitation of indispensable rural infrastructure, including irrigation.

---

[c] Economic and social development, in turn, can help to generate support for political stability and peace.

(Continued overleaf)

(Continued from preceding page)

Labour-intensive public works projects will provide job opportunities and on-the-job training, thus facilitating the return of refugees (including entrepreneurs and skilled workers), among other multiplier effects. The creation of adequate employment opportunities is important in another context, namely the reintegration of former combatants as productive participants in the economic reconstruction and recovery of Afghanistan. Key social services such as education and health care will have to be restarted and expanded, with a focus on reaching girls and women. The short-term goals should include increased access to safe drinking water, restoration of the existing power system and rehabilitation of the main road network. To arrest environmental degradation, environmental considerations should be integrated into the planning and development of all projects.

In the medium to long term, a wide range of important institutions have to be set up or reinforced, including central banking authorities, finance, the treasury, the judicial system and statistical services. Effective public administration, transparency and accountability are important conditions for better aid coordination and absorption at the domestic level. At the same time, an enabling environment must be created for private sector development, particularly to attract and utilize productively Afghans living in other countries. Ongoing technical assistance is likely to be required in the foreseeable future to backstop the rehabilitation, reconstruction and development process in Afghanistan. It is hoped that all these efforts will make the Afghanistan of tomorrow different from the Afghanistan of yesterday.

GDP performance

Bangladesh has attained self-sufficiency in food

Economic growth in Bangladesh, where savings and investment rates have been increasing in recent years, remained stable at around 6 per cent in 2001 (table II.2). The country has made great strides in agricultural development in the last five years as a means of poverty alleviation and employment creation as well as to achieve self-sufficiency in food production; it emerged as a producer of surplus foodgrains in 2000. Agricultural production increased by 4 per cent in 2001 but total foodgrain production increased by as much as 7.4 per cent, thus exceeding the year's target. In contrast, the agriculture sector in Bhutan suffered from devastating floods in August 2000 and growth decreased to 2.4 per cent during the year from 3.0 per cent in the previous year. Although the sector continues to provide employment for almost 80 per cent of the population, its share in GDP declined to just over 32 per cent in 2000 from almost 34 per cent a year earlier.

Hydropower underpinned economic activities in Bhutan

GDP growth in Bhutan, which was close to 6 per cent in the last three years, has been driven by the construction sector as major hydropower projects were implemented. These projects, largely financed by transfers from India, have enabled Bhutan to sustain very high rates of investment, well in excess of the savings rate, which has, however, increased in recent years (table II.3). Future growth is expected to remain high as hydropower projects come on stream and electricity sales to India expand. Tourist arrivals in Bhutan increased in 2000, with revenue from tourism rising 5 per cent to almost $10 million, but indications are that there was a fall-off in this sector in 2001. The country is, however,

Table II.2. Selected least developed countries of the ESCAP region: growth rates, 1998-2001

(Percentage)

		Rates of growth			
		Gross domestic product	Agriculture	Industry	Services
Bangladesh	1998	5.2	3.2	8.3	4.8
	1999	4.9	3.2	3.2	5.7
	2000	5.9	6.9	4.8	5.9
	2001	6.0	4.0	9.1	5.9
Bhutan[a]	1998	5.5	1.3	7.7	6.3
	1999	5.9	3.0	12.4	4.5
	2000	6.1	2.4	10.3	5.6
	2001	5.9	..	..	..
Cambodia	1998	1.5	2.5	7.7	−0.2
	1999	6.9	4.8	12.0	5.8
	2000	5.4	−2.7	29.0	3.1
	2001	5.3	4.0	12.5	2.4
Lao People's Democratic Republic	1998	4.0	3.1	9.2	5.5
	1999	7.3	8.2	8.0	6.7
	2000	5.7	5.0	7.6	6.0
	2001	6.4	4.5	10.0	7.0
Maldives	1998	8.2	6.8[b]	16.2	8.8
	1999	7.4	3.4[b]	8.3	8.3
	2000	4.8	−2.3[b]	−0.5	6.4
	2001	5.7	..	..	..
Myanmar	1998	5.8	4.5	6.1	7.0
	1999	10.9	11.5	13.8	9.2
	2000	13.6	..	..	..
	2001	5.0	..	..	..
Nepal	1998	3.0	1.0	2.3	6.5
	1999	4.4	2.7	6.0	5.5
	2000	6.4	5.0	9.1	6.5
	2001	5.9	4.0	5.1	7.9

Sources: ESCAP, based on ADB, *Key Indicators of Developing Asian and Pacific Countries 2001* (Oxford University Press, 2001) and *Asian Development Outlook 2001* (Oxford University Press, 2001); and national sources.

Notes: Figures for 2001 are estimates. Industry comprises mining and quarrying, manufacturing, electricity, gas and power, and construction.

[a] GDP at factor cost.
[b] Including coral and sand mining.

Table II.3. Selected least developed countries of the ESCAP region: ratios of gross domestic savings and investment to GDP, 1998-2001

(Percentage)

	1998	1999	2000	2001
Savings as a percentage of GDP				
Bangladesh	17.3	17.7	17.9	18.8
Bhutan	12.7	13.5	17.2	19.0
Cambodia	5.4	7.3	7.5	7.7
Lao People's Democratic Republic	14.8	16.4	14.6	15.0
Maldives	..	..	..	..
Myanmar	11.8	13.0	..	..
Nepal	13.8	13.6	15.1	16.1
Investment as a percentage of GDP				
Bangladesh	21.6	22.2	23.0	23.6
Bhutan	38.2	43.1	43.8	44.1
Cambodia	12.0	17.0	14.1	14.5
Lao People's Democratic Republic	26.8	23.6	25.1	26.6
Maldives	..	..	..	..
Myanmar	12.4	13.2	..	..
Nepal	24.8	20.5	24.3	25.7

Sources: ESCAP, based on ADB, *Key Indicators of Developing Asian and Pacific Countries 2001* (Oxford University Press, 2001) and *Asian Development Outlook 2001* (Oxford University Press, 2001); and national sources.

Note: Figures for 2001 are estimates.

deliberately trying to keep tourism low so as to limit environmental damage; tourists have to pay $200 a day for food and lodging. Growth in other sectors taken together, including mining and quarrying, manufacturing and electricity, fell to 6 per cent in 2000 from 7 per cent in the previous year. In Bangladesh, industrial output picked up strongly, expanding by over 9 per cent in 2001 from 4 per cent on average in 1999-2000 as a result of rapid growth in the production of cement, cotton cloth, natural gas, paper and steel. However, the effects of the global slowdown, as well as the removal of quotas on exports from some other countries to the United States market, were making themselves felt in the ready-made garment industry. GDP performance in 2002 may be less strong than the solid growth of the last several years (table II.1). In particular, rising international prices for cotton and currency weakness are likely to raise costs and reduce competitiveness in the ready-made garment industry.

Security problems cloud the picture in Nepal

Hydropower is also an important economic stimulus in Nepal, where the completion of new hydropower projects and the production of additional power raised growth in the service sector, notwithstanding the sharp fall in tourism. As a result of the domestic security situation, compounded by the difficult external environment, tourist arrivals were down by almost 21 per cent overall and by one third from India in 2001. GDP expanded by just under 6 per cent in fiscal year 2001, compared with 6.4 per cent in the previous year, reflecting the slowdown in agriculture and industry; the slowdown was quite significant in the industrial sector. Manufacturing was affected by static or declining production of ready-made garments, textiles, woollen carpets and construction materials. Savings and investment rates recovered in 2000-2001 after declining in 1999. However, the medium-term economic outlook depends on the performance of the world economy, and on India in particular, as well as on the resolution of internal security problems; indeed, growth is expected to decline somewhat in 2002 before recovering in subsequent years.

In addition to fishing, tourism has been the economic mainstay of Maldives because of its extensive linkage effects, including with wholesale and retail trade, construction, real estate and transport. GDP growth averaged 7.8 per cent in 1998-1999 but decelerated sharply to just under 5 per cent in 2000 as a result of a broad-based slowdown in output. Although tourist arrivals increased in that year, the average length of stay was shorter, thus limiting tourism revenue growth. GDP was projected to expand by 5.7 per cent owing to a stronger increase in tourism in 2001.

Economic growth in Maldives has been on a lower trend in recent years

Despite the vulnerability of these countries to external shocks, the rate of GDP growth was sustained at 5.3 per cent in Cambodia in 2001 but was higher at 6.4 per cent in the Lao People's Democratic Republic. GDP had originally been forecast to increase by 6 per cent in Cambodia but the marginal decline was attributable to the impact of flooding on agriculture and of the recession in the United States on exports of garments and on tourism. GDP growth in the Lao People's Democratic Republic exceeded earlier estimates and was led by 10 per cent growth in the industrial sector and 7 per cent in the service sector. However, economic activities appear to have decreased significantly in Myanmar with GDP expanding by 5 per cent in 2001 (from almost 11 per cent recorded in 1999 and 13.6 per cent in 2000), which resulted from the effects of adverse weather conditions, such as flooding, on agricultural production, and from weak domestic and external demand. Growth in 2002 is likely to be little changed. The economic outlook in Cambodia and the Lao People's Democratic Republic is likely to be a marginal decrease in GDP growth in 2002 as these economies experience a delayed response to the current slowdown in the world, and in Thailand in particular, followed by a recovery in 2003. The savings rate increased slightly in Cambodia over the period 1999-2001, but remains comparatively very low among the Asian least developed countries. The investment rate in Cambodia, which improved sharply to 17 per cent of GDP in 1999, stabilized at around 14 per cent in the following two years.

Steady economic growth in Cambodia and the Lao People's Democratic Republic

Flooding has affected agriculture in several least developed countries in South-East Asia

The severe floods in Cambodia in September and October 2000 damaged nearly a third of the rice fields and destroyed transport infra-structure and irrigation facilities. The output of the agriculture sector decreased by 2.7 per cent in 2000 but was forecast to expand by 4 per cent in the following year, with rice accounting for nearly one third of total agricultural value added. Rice production was expected to rebound by almost 10 per cent in 2001, after a fall of almost 4 per cent in 2000, as the flood-borne alluvial soil contributed to increased productivity. However, that productivity remained considerably below that achieved by neighbouring countries, partly as a result of inefficient farming techniques and limited irrigation facilities. Forestry production contracted by a third in 2000 following the crackdown on all forms of illegal logging and the decline is expected to continue for some time. The fisheries sector, which derives most of its output from the Tonle Sap lake, grew remarkably in 2001 as the official auction to private individuals of 495,000 hectares of fishing lots was revoked to give the poor better access to common fisheries resources. Flooding in 2000-2001 also affected agriculture in the Lao People's Democratic Republic, causing agricultural output to slow to 4.5 per cent in 2001. In Myanmar, heavy rains during the dry season harvest affected rice production adversely but the output of other crops was not seriously affected. Overall growth in agriculture has also been handicapped by shortages of fertilizer and other inputs. The monopoly of State enterprises in such export crops as rice, rubber, cotton and teak has constrained private sector participation and export growth in Myanmar.

More Asian tourists visit Cambodia

The industrial sector of Cambodia, where output grew 29 per cent in 2000, consists mainly of manufacturing activities (79 per cent), which are largely concentrated in Phnom Penh, and construction (19 per cent). The slowdown in major overseas markets hit garment exports, which account generally for 70 per cent of Cambodia's exports, contributing thus to the sharp decrease in industrial growth to 12.5 per cent in 2001. Construction was expected to expand by 8 per cent in 2001, lower than the 12.6 per cent growth registered in 2000, driven in part by increased government and aid-sponsored capital expenditure. However, the service sector registered modest growth of 2.4 per cent in 2001 and, despite the events of 11 September 2001, tourist arrivals were up 40 per cent year-on-year although they fell by 18 per cent that September. Asian tourists continued to arrive, even though the number of visitors from the United States decreased.

Diverse patterns of industrial production in the Lao People's Democratic Republic and Myanmar

Value added in the manufacturing sector in the Lao People's Democratic Republic comprises mainly food processing, including the production of animal feed, beer, mineral water and rice milling and garment manufacturing. The wood processing industry grew in 2001 but the production of meat, fish, coffee, cigarettes, detergent and construction material remained stagnant or declined. In Myanmar, the manufacturing sector grew rapidly in 2000 as the production of cotton fabrics, cement, edible oils, paper and milled sugar increased in response to the Government's import-substitution strategy. The scope for further industrial expansion may be limited, however, because of slowing domestic and external demand. In addition, power supplies have been erratic, and the increased reliance of manufacturers on imported diesel fuel for generators has raised costs significantly. Other constraints are sluggish domestic investment and FDI and the severe shortage of foreign exchange.

Inflation

In Bangladesh, the inflation rate decelerated significantly in 2000-2001, partly because of the comfortable food supply position following good harvests of cereals and liberal import of consumer goods, and partly because of weak demand (table II.4). Falling prices for commodities such as oil in world markets under the spell of recession also contributed to the decline. Consumer price inflation was 1.6 per cent year-on-year in fiscal year 2001, compared with 3.4 per cent in 2000 and 8.9 per cent in 1999.

Consumer prices stabilized with the comfortable food supply situation in Bangladesh

Table II.4. Selected least developed countries of the ESCAP region: inflation and money supply growth (M2), 1998-2001

(Percentage)

	1998	1999	2000	2001
Inflation[a]				
Bangladesh[b]	7.0	8.9	3.4	1.6
Bhutan[b]	9.0	9.2	3.6	3.6
Cambodia	14.8	4.0	−0.8	−0.6
Lao People's Democratic Republic	91.0	128.5	25.1	9.0
Maldives	−1.4	3.0	−1.1	..
Myanmar	51.5	18.4	−0.1	9.6
Nepal[b,c]	8.4	11.4	3.5	2.4
Money supply growth (M2)				
Bangladesh	11.4	15.5	19.3	14.1[d]
Bhutan	14.0	32.0	17.4	11.1[e]
Cambodia	15.7	17.3	26.9	18.5[d]
Lao People's Democratic Republic	113.3	78.4	46.0	20.0
Maldives	22.8	3.6	4.1	3.8[d]
Myanmar	34.2	29.7	42.4	49.1[f]
Nepal	21.9	20.8	21.8	13.0

Sources: ESCAP, based on ADB, *Key Indicators of Developing Asian and Pacific Countries 2001* (Oxford University Press, 2001), *Asian Development Outlook 2001* (Oxford University Press, 2001) and *Asia Economic Monitor 2001*, December issue (<http.//aric.adb.org>); IMF, *International Financial Statistics,* vol. LV, No. 1 (January 2002); and national sources.

Note: Figures for 2001 are estimates.

[a] Changes in the consumer price index.
[b] Fiscal year.
[c] National urban consumer price index.
[d] January-September.
[e] January-March.
[f] January-June.

Food items, which carry a relative weight of 54.5 per cent in the composite consumer price index, increased by only 0.7 per cent in 2001 compared with 4 per cent and 11.8 per cent respectively in the previous two years. Monetary policy continued to be expansionary in 2001, but the growth in the broad money supply (M2) slowed as a result of reduced government borrowing (table II.4). However, the fiscal deficit widened to 6.9 per cent of GDP in 2001, while interest rates were reduced in October 2001 in a bid to stimulate investment. The large fiscal shortfall, if accompanied by high rates of money supply growth, would be likely to put pressure on the exchange rate and on consumer prices in the coming year.

Monetary expansion in Bhutan reflects inflows of capital

In Bhutan, inflation was steady at 3.6 per cent in both 2000 and 2001, despite some pick-up in prices towards the end of 2000; such overall stability by and large reflected reductions in both food and non-food prices. Large balance-of-payments surpluses have resulted in relatively high rates of monetary expansion in Bhutan in recent years, but credit growth has been sluggish, expanding at around 5 per cent annually. The growth in private sector credit was a reflection of consumer lending, as credit for other purposes was declining. Generally, banks have considerable excess reserves, reflecting the cautious lending culture of the two main commercial banks as well as the lack of investment opportunities. While the Government has avoided borrowing to finance current expenditure, the budget deficit widened to 6 per cent of GDP in 2001 as a result of increased capital spending (financed by transfers mainly from India) associated with the construction of hydropower plants.

Improved food supply slowed inflation in Nepal

In Nepal, despite surging petroleum prices, the improved supply of food products accompanied by reduced monetary growth resulted in a further deceleration of inflation in fiscal year 2001. The national urban consumer price index was only 2.4 per cent higher in 2001, as against an increase of 3.5 per cent the previous year, and was substantially below the 11.4 per cent rise in 1999. A fall in the prices of food and beverages, particularly rice, vegetable oil and ghee, contributed to bringing down the average annual inflation rate to the lowest single-digit level in the last decade. Growth in the broad money supply decelerated in fiscal year 2001, as did private sector credit growth, and in December 2001 the Nepal Rastra Bank lowered cash reserve ratios for commercial banks by an average of 1 per cent and refinancing rates by 1–2 per cent. However, investment is unlikely to post any significant increase while the security situation remains difficult. The spread between lending and borrowing rates at commercial banks is high at 5 per cent, reflecting weakness in the banking system. The budget balance deteriorated in 2001 as revenues fell with the economic slowdown and falling imports; 40 per cent of revenues come from customs duties and import taxes. Expenditure also rose because of the worsening security situation and is likely to remain high, thus putting some pressure on inflation in 2002. Increases in customs duties, taxes and other charges will add to those pressures, but inflation is likely to remain below 5 per cent as a reflection of relative price stability in India.

Falls in the prices of consumer products, such as food, beverages, tobacco, clothing and footwear, resulted in deflation in Maldives in 2000, when prices fell 1.1 per cent as against an increase of 3 per cent in 1999. Fiscal prudence has kept monetary expansion stable on a low trend, growing at an average annual rate of 3.8 per cent in the period 1999-2001. The fiscal deficit as a percentage of GDP remained around 4 per cent in 1999-2000.

In Cambodia, deflation continued in 2001, when consumer prices fell by 0.6 per cent. Prices for food, beverages and tobacco items, which accounted for half of the total goods and services in the consumer basket, fell throughout the year, with the exception of the Khmer New Year in April. However, increased duties on petroleum products and possible depreciation of the riel may lead to higher consumer prices in 2002. Inflation showed signs of accelerating in the Lao People's Democratic Republic, where the estimated annual inflation for fiscal year 2001 reached 9 per cent, and the forecast for subsequent years is even higher. Shortages of basic consumer goods, exchange rate weakness and increases in electricity prices are expected to combine to raise prices. Despite the adverse impact of flooding, which affected both countries in late 2000, rice prices remained little changed owing to large imports of rice and compensatory assistance in kind provided by donors. Government distribution of rice seeds also minimized the impact of the floods on rice production in 2001. Import prices declined owing to the strength of the dollar against the currencies of major suppliers, including Thailand. In both Cambodia and the Lao People's Democratic Republic, the cost of housing, transport and communications rose considerably, owing partly to rising labour costs.

Deflation continued in Cambodia but the outlook is less encouraging

The economy of Cambodia is characterized by a high degree of "dollarization" as a result of the lack of confidence in the domestic currency. Deposits denominated in dollars accounted for nearly 70 per cent of broad money (M2) in 2000, and the total amount of dollars in circulation is estimated to be greater than the broad money supply. Currency and asset substitution limits the effectiveness of monetary policy in Cambodia, and inflation is affected more directly by the depreciation of the riel than by monetary expansion. Broad money growth slowed in 2001 but was still in double digits, accelerating ahead of the elections as fiscal discipline relaxed. However, the riel has been generally stable, contributing to the muted inflationary pressures. Commercial banks continue to be reluctant to lend to the domestic private sector, however, preferring to acquire foreign assets. In the Lao People's Democratic Republic, monetary and credit expansion was tightened considerably in 2001 in an attempt to reduce inflationary pressures, but in that country too the effectiveness of monetary policy is hampered by currency and asset substitution. The budget deficit increased slightly in 2001 but is still considerably lower than the 11 per cent average in 1998-1999.

Currency and asset substitution is a problem common to Cambodia and the Lao People's Democratic Republic

Monetary expansion has been very rapid in Myanmar

In Myanmar, consumer prices were officially estimated as remaining virtually unchanged in 2000 as food prices were stable following the general stability in the exchange rate, improved agricultural performance and the implementation of tax-free markets, which reduced marketing and distribution costs. Large cuts in public expenditure reduced inflationary financing. The inflation rate was expected to average 9.6 per cent in 2001 owing to rising civil service wages, depreciation of the kyat and rising import prices. In addition, broad money (M2) growth accelerated from over 42 per cent in 2000 to nearly 50 per cent in the first half of 2001.

Foreign trade and other external transactions

External trade

Both merchandise exports and imports increased more rapidly in Bangladesh

Bangladesh's export earnings, at $6.4 billion in fiscal year 2001, registered growth of 12.4 per cent compared with 8.2 per cent in the previous year (table II.5). Ready-made garments and hosiery products continued to be the top foreign exchange earners and were responsible for four fifths of total export receipts, but those sectors will be adversely affected by the loss of privileged access to the United States market. Export earnings from leather and tea increased by 30 and 22 per cent respectively. However, exports of frozen shrimp have been hit by weak demand and falling international prices. The total import expenditure of

---

Table II.5. Selected least developed countries of the ESCAP region: merchandise exports and their rates of growth, 1998-2001

	Value *(Millions of US dollars)*	*Exports (f.o.b.)*			
		Annual rate of growth (Percentage)			
	2000	*1998*	*1999*	*2000*	*2001*
Bangladesh[a]	5 752	5.4	2.9	8.2	12.4
Bhutan[a]	114	12.1	−5.9	9.1	−1.8
Cambodia	1 103	13.1	17.4	55.6	8.4[b]
Lao People's Democratic Republic	303	6.4	7.7	8.3	7.4
Maldives	76	3.4	−4.3	19.1	..
Myanmar	1 883	6.6	14.4	37.4	13.1[c]
Nepal[a]	721	12.7	18.2	37.4	7.5

Sources: IMF, *Direction of Trade Statistics* (CD-ROM), February 2002, *International Financial Statistics* (CD-ROM), January 2002 and web sites <http://www.imf.org/external/np/sec/pr/2001/pr0118.htm> and <http://www.imf.org/external/country/index.htm>, 18 February 2002; ADB, *Asian Development Outlook 2001* (Oxford University Press, 2001); and national sources.

[a] Fiscal year.
[b] Estimate.
[c] Figures refer to January-September 2001.

Table II.6. Selected least developed countries of the ESCAP region: merchandise imports and their rates of growth, 1998-2001

	Value (Millions of US dollars)	Imports (c.i.f.)			
		Annual rate of growth (Percentage)			
	2000	1998	1999	2000	2001
Bangladesh[a]	8 403	7.4	6.6	4.8	11.4
Bhutan[a]	185	3.7	19.2	14.0	16.3
Cambodia	1 438	7.4	16.5	48.6	6.0[b]
Lao People's Democratic Republic	477	−14.7	0.3	6.6	10.6
Maldives	388	1.5	13.6	−3.4	..
Myanmar	2 473	−12.4	−11.0	17.0	3.1[c]
Nepal[a]	1 571	−11.8	−10.3	22.0	−2.2

Sources: IMF, *Direction of Trade Statistics* (CD-ROM), February 2002, *International Financial Statistics* (CD-ROM), January 2002 and web sites <http://www.imf.org/external/np/sec/pr/2001/pr0118.htm> and <http://www.imf.org/external/country/index.htm>, 18 February 2002; ADB, *Asian Development Outlook 2001* (Oxford University Press, 2001); and national sources.

[a] Fiscal year.
[b] Estimate.
[c] Figures refer to January-September 2001.

Bangladesh (table II.6) increased 11.4 per cent to $9.4 billion in 2001, compared with import growth of 4.8 per cent in the previous year. Major increases were recorded in imports of capital goods and in inputs for the garment and textile industries, while imports of cement, oil seeds and edible oil declined. The balance on current account was in deficit to the extent of 1.7 per cent of GDP in 2001, and this figure may increase in the medium term (table II.7), in part as the result of a widening deficit in merchandise trade, smaller net services and income receipts, lower official current transfers and lower remittances from migrant workers.

More than 80 per cent of Bhutan's trade flows and 45 per cent of those of Nepal are with India. Bhutan recorded a small decrease (1.8 per cent) in merchandise exports in fiscal year 2001 compared with a 9.1 per cent increase in 2000. Import growth accelerated to 16.3 per cent in fiscal year 2001 from 14 per cent in the preceding year, owing to the high import content in the construction of hydropower plants. Factor service payments also increased. Bhutan will continue to run a trade deficit until its hydropower projects are completed and the export of electricity to India begins. The trade deficit as a percentage of GDP increased from 17 per cent in 2000 to just over 23 per cent in 2001. The average annual current account deficit was around 27 per cent in 2000-2001.

The economies of Bhutan and Nepal are closely linked to the Indian economy

55

Table II.7. Selected least developed countries of the ESCAP region: budget and current account balance as a percentage of GDP, 1998-2001

	1998	*1999*	*2000*	*2001*
Budget balance as a percentage of GDP				
Bangladesh[a]	−4.2	−5.4	−6.1	−6.9
Bhutan	3.0	−0.9	−3.9	−6.0
Cambodia[a]	−6.0	−4.4	−5.7	−6.2
Lao People's Democratic Republic[a]	−11.4	−10.5	−8.5	−8.8
Maldives	−1.9	−4.1	−4.0	..
Myanmar[a]	−0.4	−1.3	−0.5	..
Nepal	−5.9	−5.3	−4.7	−5.8
Current account balance as a percentage of GDP				
Bangladesh	−0.6	−0.9	−[b]	−1.7
Bhutan	−11.7	−24.4	−28.4	−26.8
Cambodia	−8.0	−9.0	−10.2	−9.1
Lao People's Democratic Republic	−10.0	−11.0	−5.4	−6.6
Maldives	−4.5	−11.1	−4.6	..
Myanmar[c]	−0.4	−0.2	..	..
Nepal	−1.5	0.1	−2.3	−1.4

Sources: ESCAP, based on ADB, *Key Indicators of Developing Asian and Pacific Countries 2001* (Oxford University Press, 2001) and *Asian Development Outlook 2001* (Oxford University Press, 2001); IMF, *International Financial Statistics*, vol. LIV, No. 10 (October 2001); and national sources.

Note: Figures for 2001 are estimates.

[a] Excluding grants.
[b] Negligible.
[c] At official exchange rates.

In Nepal, exports grew by 7.5 per cent in fiscal year 2001 as compared with 37.4 per cent in the preceding year. Exports to India grew rapidly in 2000-2001, but slowed in the second half of 2001; vegetable ghee, jute goods, acrylic and polyester yarn and thread, Ayurvedic medicine, copper wire and toothpaste were the main exports. The trade treaty with India, which gives duty-free access to Nepalese exports (except alcohol and tobacco), is currently being renegotiated owing to Indian concerns regarding rules of origin and safeguards. A major "problem product" for India is hydrogenated vegetable oil (vegetable ghee), which is made from palm oil imported from Malaysia that faces negligible duties in Nepal, unlike the heavy duties in India. Imports of palm oil increased 500 per cent in Nepal in fiscal year 2001. Exports of luxury products, such as pashmina shawls, woollen carpets and gold and silver ornaments, to other markets experienced a decline in 2001 as a result of weak demand and consumer environmental concerns in some cases. Exports of ready-made garments slumped after the opening of the United States market, Nepal's main export destination, to African and Caribbean producers.

Total merchandise imports decreased by 2.2 per cent in Nepal in fiscal year 2001, compared with a sharp increase of 22 per cent in the previous year, affected by a tightening of standards for the issuance of letters of credit. Imports from India, in particular transport vehicles, textiles, chemical fertilizers and medicine, increased; however, reduced incentives for smuggling gold to India led to a sharp drop in gold imports. The trade deficit narrowed to 13.6 per cent of GDP and the current account registered a smaller deficit equal to 1.4 per cent of GDP in 2001. Although tourism receipts went down sharply, substantial increases in transfer receipts and grant aid offset the fall. Remittance income, estimated at 10 per cent of GDP, continues to be of major importance.

Official transfers offset the fall in tourism receipts in Nepal

In Maldives, merchandise exports went up by 19 per cent in 2000. Despite falling international prices of fish, the export volume of canned and dried fish increased substantially. Merchandise imports fell by 3.4 per cent in 2000, reflecting the slowdown in the economy. As a result, the trade deficit declined from 45 per cent of GDP in 1999 to 39 per cent in 2000. The current account deficit as a percentage of GDP also fell, notwithstanding the sharp fall in revenues from tourism.

Tourism also suffered in Maldives

Cambodia's major exports are ready-made garments, logs and sawn timber, rubber and fishery products. In 2000, merchandise exports grew by 55 per cent, but the growth rate plunged to a little above 8 per cent in 2001. However, imports of textiles and fabrics for garment factories, oil products and machinery and electrical appliances also faltered to 6 per cent in 2001, after increasing almost 49 per cent in the previous year. Following the signing of an agreement giving Cambodia preferential access to markets in the European Union until 2002 and an increase in the volume quota to the United States in January 2002, garment exports were expected to increase, but competition from China and Viet Nam remains intense. The United States is the destination of 46 per cent of Cambodia's exports, but orders for ready-made garments fell sharply after the events of 11 September 2001, along with tourism. Owing to its low customs duties, Cambodia has become a hub for transit trade in the region, especially with Viet Nam, but such re-exports (of alcohol, tobacco, gold, pulp and paper, electrical appliances and motor vehicles, among other items) have gradually declined since their peak in 1996. Cambodia's current account deficit, excluding official transfers, decreased from 10.2 per cent of GDP in 2000 to 9.1 per cent in 2001.

Trade deficit falls in Cambodia

The growth rate of merchandise exports from the Lao People's Democratic Republic decreased to 7.4 per cent in 2001, from 8.3 per cent in 2000, while that of merchandise imports increased to 10.6 per cent from 6.6 per cent a year earlier. Merchandise exports are dominated by timber and wood products, followed by ready-made garments, hydropower and coffee. The Government would like to diversify exports, as the present reliance on timber and wood products is not environmentally

Timber and wood products dominate exports from the Lao People's Democratic Republic

sustainable. However, limited access to the United States market in the absence of normal trade relations has put a brake on exports of ready-made garments and the United States has moved to place import quotas on textile exports from the Lao People's Democratic Republic. The main import categories of consumer goods are construction and electrical equipment, inputs for the ready-made garment industry, motorcycle parts and petroleum products; Thailand remains an important trading partner. Import growth is likely to continue to outstrip export growth and the trade deficit was expected to reach 11.6 per cent of GDP in 2001, higher than the forecast of 10.2 per cent but still low by historical standards. However, the fall in tourism as a result of domestic security concerns and the global travel slump is likely to reduce service receipts further. The current account deficit widened to 6.6 per cent of GDP in 2001, up from 5.4 per cent in the previous year.

Imports of fuel increased significantly in Myanmar

The growth in merchandise exports from Myanmar, although still on a high trend, was considerably lower in the first nine months of 2001 at just over 13 per cent compared with 37.4 per cent in 2000. A similar deceleration occurred in import growth. There were increased exports of rice, pulses and hardwoods, as well as gas. Imports of fuel have increased significantly as a result of the partial failure of the main hydropower plant and the increased use of diesel generators. However, imports of consumer goods and fertilizer fell sharply and the trade deficit of more than $500 million was 21 per cent lower than in 2000. The reduction in imports, and subsequently the trade deficit, resulted from the rise in the free market exchange rate and from the lower capital imports caused by the slowdown in domestic investment. Import controls were also tightened and strategies adopted to encourage import substitution as well as greater production for export.

Capital inflows, external debt and exchange rates

Donor lending has been slow and private capital inflows low in Bangladesh

Private capital inflows have generally been low in Bangladesh. FDI amounted to $166 million in 2001, 14.4 per cent below the figure for 2000, and any increase in these investment flows will depend on an agreement to permit gas exports. Portfolio investment has been negligible. Donor lending to Bangladesh has been slower than projected as a result of limited reforms, but may now increase with the change in Government. The cumulative total of foreign aid received over the last four years was $5.6 billion as against the projection of $7.7 billion for the fifth five-year plan period. However, external debt outstanding at end-June 2001 was manageable at 31.4 per cent of GDP, compared with 33.5 per cent a year earlier. Debt service amounted to 8.5 per cent of merchandise exports in 2001. Total official reserves, excluding gold, which have been under pressure owing to the widening current account deficit and reduced official capital inflows, amounted to just over $1 billion in October 2001, down from nearly $1.5 billion at the end of 2000. Bangladesh devalued its currency by around 11 per cent against the dollar through two revisions in August 2000 and May 2001 (figure II.5). The taka was devalued again by 1.6 per cent in January 2002, as depreciation of the Indian rupee maintained pressure on the exchange rate.

Capital inflows, mainly in the form of official aid, were more than adequate to support the current account deficit in Nepal, where nearly 60 per cent of development spending is financed by aid. Similarly, increased foreign aid to Bhutan, especially from India, has easily financed the current account deficit and the balance of payments has been in substantial surplus. Official reserves in Bhutan amounted to $282.4 million at the end of December 2001, providing about 16 months of import cover. Total external debt, much of it on concessional terms, increased from 42 per cent

Capital inflows financed the current account deficit comfortably in Nepal

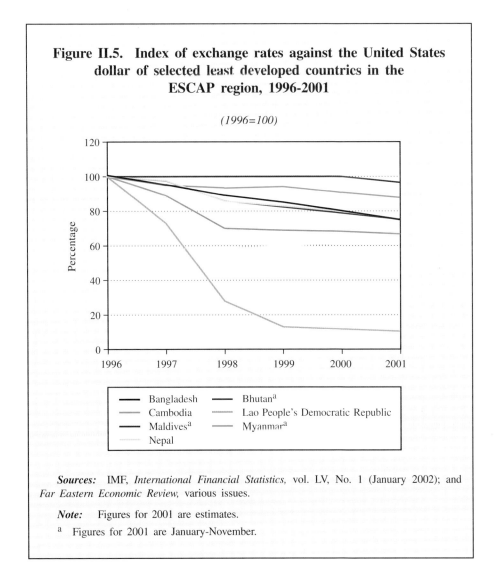

Figure II.5. Index of exchange rates against the United States dollar of selected least developed countries in the ESCAP region, 1996-2001

(1996=100)

Sources: IMF, *International Financial Statistics,* vol. LV, No. 1 (January 2002); and *Far Eastern Economic Review,* various issues.

Note: Figures for 2001 are estimates.

[a] Figures for 2001 are January-November.

of GDP in 2000 to 53 per cent in 2001. More than half of this debt is owed to India, a major source of funding for hydropower projects and other development activities. The debt-service ratio remains low at around 4 per cent of merchandise exports. In Nepal, the outstanding external debt amounted to 49 per cent of GDP in July 2001 and debt servicing has not so far become a critical problem as most of this debt is concessional in nature. The debt-servicing ratio had been growing over the years to reach 10.8 per cent of merchandise exports in 2001. The currencies of both Bhutan and Nepal are pegged at par to the Indian rupee, which circulates freely in both countries. Changes in the values of the Bhutanese ngultrum and the Nepalese rupee are a reflection of exchange rate movements in the Indian rupee. The exchange rate peg has proved beneficial in terms of predictability and convenience, particularly as trade and other links of both countries with India have been very strong.

Maldives has also benefited a great deal from donor assistance, which averaged over 8 per cent of GDP annually during the 1990s. However, foreign exchange reserves at the end of 2000 were only sufficient to pay for 4.3 months of imports of goods and services and total external debt was around 36 per cent of GDP in 2000. The exchange rate, which has been fixed since 1995, was devalued by approximately 8.8 per cent against the dollar in July 2001.

FDI has fallen considerably in Cambodia and Myanmar

In both Cambodia and Myanmar, FDI flows declined from the peaks reached in 1996, from $294 million to an estimated $125 million in 2000 in the case of Cambodia and, even more dramatically, from $2.8 billion to less than $60 million in Myanmar in fiscal year 1999. These flows are likely to have been even lower in 2001 as a result of the regional economic slowdown. Singapore, the United Kingdom, Thailand and Malaysia were among the largest investors in Myanmar, with oil, manufacturing and tourism attracting the most foreign investment. The industrial sector, mainly garment factories, accounted for 40 per cent of total investment approvals in Cambodia, followed by tourism and infrastructure, which accounted for 29 and 26 per cent respectively. Key constraints on private capital flows to Cambodia include inadequate infrastructure, security problems, a weak legal system, shortage of skilled labour and the lack of skilled managers. To remove distortions while protecting revenues, the Government of Cambodia is reviewing incentives provided to investors, as well as taxes.

ODA increased sharply in Cambodia and the Lao People's Democratic Republic

Official aid (including concessional loans) to Cambodia increased significantly, by 36 per cent to $344 million in 2000 from the previous year. Although total external reserves (excluding gold) rose to $569 million at the end of November 2001, or over 13 per cent higher than the end-2000 value, this was sufficient to finance only four months of imports. ODA in the Lao People's Democratic Republic, of which nearly three quarters were grants, was expected to reach $386 million in 2001, an increase of over 16 per cent from the previous year. Gross official international reserves declined by 12 per cent to $124 million at the end of August 2001, after rising steadily in 2000, reflecting the drawing down of reserves through bank financing of the overall budget deficit during the second half of the fiscal year 2000. In contrast, Myanmar's limited access to concessional loans has led to increased reliance on commercial credits, particularly from China, for capital goods imports. However, there was a small increase in aid from Japan in 2001. Official reserves at the end of July 2001 were estimated at $239.5 million, or the equivalent of less than two months of import cover.

The Lao People's Democratic Republic and Myanmar are the only least developed countries in the region that qualify for debt relief under the Heavily Indebted Poor Countries Initiative of the World Bank and IMF (box II.3). However, governance problems have hampered discussions on this initiative. Myanmar's external debt amounted to $5.6 billion in 2000, or slightly lower than the peak of $6 billion reached in 1999. Repayments to ADB and the World Bank were suspended in 1998 and total arrears to those agencies amounted to 40 per cent of external debt in fiscal 1999. However, all bilateral debts have been repaid as the country has focused its debt-servicing efforts on commercial credits. In the Lao People's Democratic Republic, total external debt was equivalent to 73.4 per cent of GDP in 2000, leading to a debt-service ratio of 9.2 per cent of exports of goods and services. In view of its limited debt-servicing capacity, external borrowing is now being closely monitored through the newly established debt-monitoring unit to ensure a sustainable debt burden.

Heavy external debt in the Lao People's Democratic Republic and Myanmar

Despite the external debts incurred over the years, Cambodia's debt burden is considered to be sustainable in terms of the Heavily Indebted Poor Countries Initiative because much of it is concessional. However, the total external debt, over half of which was concessional, amounted to 65.3 per cent of GDP in 2000. The completion of outstanding bilateral rescheduling agreements was expected to allow debt-service payments to remain at less than 5 per cent of goods and services receipts over the medium term.

Exchange rates against the United States dollar in Cambodia and the Lao People's Democratic Republic and in the free market in Myanmar remained relatively stable throughout 2000, in contrast to the significant depreciation of their currencies in recent years. In Cambodia, the official exchange rate adjusts to movements in the flexible parallel market exchange rate with a spread below 1 per cent and remained in the range of 3,800-3,900 riels to the dollar throughout 2000 and the first half of 2001. As in the case of currencies in other countries in the subregion, the

Exchange rate stability in 2000 gave way to greater uncertainty in South-East Asian least developed countries

Box. II.3. Implementation of the Programme of Action of the Third United Nations Conference on the Least Developed Countries

The Programme of Action for the Least Developed Countries for the decade 2001-2010 was adopted at the Third United Nations Conference on the Least Developed Countries, held at Brussels from 14 to 20 May 2001. Subsequently, it was noted in the report of the Secretary-General entitled "Road map towards the implementation of the United Nations Millennium Declaration"[a] that the next steps in support of the 49 least developed countries would include implementing a global version of the European "Everything but arms" trade programme; increasing ODA; fully implementing the enhanced Heavily Indebted Poor Countries Initiative; and pursuing measures to promote the cancellation of official bilateral debt. In addition, the Declaration adopted by the fourth WTO Ministerial Conference, held at Doha, Qatar, in November 2001, urged integration into the WTO work programme of earlier multilateral trade commitments as well as those made at the Third United Nations Conference on the Least Developed Countries. Finally, the agreed draft text of the Monterrey Consensus prepared for the International Conference on Financing for Development scheduled to be held at Monterrey, Mexico, from 18 to 22 March 2002, reaffirmed that ODA to least developed countries should be equivalent to 0.15-0.20 per cent of developed country GNP.

Development assistance and debt relief

ODA to least developed countries grew from 19 to 22 per cent of the aid flow from DAC member countries from 1999 to 2000, compared with 27 per cent in 1989-1990. At its High-level Meeting held in April 2001, DAC agreed to untie ODA to least developed countries to the greatest extent possible as at 1 January 2002, while ensuring adequate ODA flows to those countries as well as reinforcing partner country responsibility for procurement and the ability of the private sector to compete for aid-funded contracts.[b] However, technical cooperation and food aid were an exception, as such untied assistance could present problems for some donors. All in all, untied ODA could amount to some $5.5 billion, or about 70 per cent of all bilateral aid to least developed countries.

The enhanced Heavily Indebted Poor Countries Initiative would help to reduce the debt stock of 22 countries qualifying for debt relief to manageable levels and enable them to access international finance. Nevertheless, it may take those countries several years to meet the required conditions, while several debt-stressed least developed countries are not defined as heavily indebted. DAC member countries have therefore decided to expand the process so as to provide additional debt relief.[c] In particular, the period between the decision and completion points has been compressed and the associated relief provided at an early stage so that it can take effect more quickly. Debt relief under the Initiative, however, represents a very small share of DAC members' annual net ODA, since the total debt relief will be implemented over several years. Lowered repayments to international financial institutions made from debtor countries' own net income derived from other loans and forgiveness or rescheduling of the principal of bilateral ODA loans do not enter ODA data.

The final draft of the Monterrey Consensus reiterated that ODA should comprise 0.7 per cent of developed country GNP and that 0.15-0.20 per cent should be allocated to least developed countries. Donors were also urged to meet their commitments to increase assistance and establish information systems to monitor the use and effectiveness of their ODA. At the same time, it was emphasized that bilateral and multilateral development agencies should take the necessary steps to make their aid programmes more efficient and responsive to the needs of recipient countries, to assist these countries in carrying out further institutional reforms so as to increase transparency and interactive dialogue.

---

[a] A/56/326.

[b] OECD, "Untying aid to the least developed countries", Policy Brief (*OECD Observer*, July 2001).

[c] OECD news release, "ODA steady in 2000; other flows decline", 12 December 2001.

Trade

The implementation of the "Everything but arms" trade initiative from 5 March 2001 and the integration of the development agenda into the Ministerial Declaration adopted by the fourth WTO Ministerial Conference are among the more notable recent events. Under the trade initiative, the European Union accorded duty- and quota-free access for essentially all non-military exports (except sugar, rice and bananas) from the 49 least developed countries. The concession will be maintained for an unlimited period of time and is not subject to periodic renewal, unlike the generalized system of preferences. In view of the difficulties in enforcing rules of origin compliance, the European Union furthermore granted the benefit of a regional cumulation for all exports from Cambodia and the Lao People's Democratic Republic as well as from least developed country members of the South Asian Association for Regional Cooperation.

As from 1 April 2001, some 99 per cent of industrial products (including all textiles and clothing items) from least developed countries can enter Japan duty- and quota-free. The number of items under such treatment would be increased in step with progress in the current WTO round of multilateral trade negotiations and the impact on domestic industry. Meanwhile, a study was carried out by UNCTAD and the Commonwealth Secretariat on the gains to those countries if Canada, Japan and the United States followed the lead of the European Union as regards the "Everything but arms" trade initiative.[d] The results indicate that those countries would benefit from both improved terms of trade and better allocation efficiency, including in structural export diversification. However, ancillary enhancement of the technical and institutional infrastructure in least developed countries would serve to maximize the widened market access thus available. In this context, in the report of the Secretary-General, "Road map towards the implementation of the United Nations Millennium Declaration", other developed countries were urged to follow the lead set by the European Union.

The development dimension of trade was one of the major themes of the Ministerial Declaration adopted by the WTO Ministerial Conference in November 2001. The Declaration urged countries to integrate trade policies into national development policies for poverty reduction, upgrade production and export capabilities and improve the effectiveness of the generalized system of preferences by reducing administrative and procedural complexities. The WTO Subcommittee on Least Developed Countries was therefore requested to design a work programme taking into account the trade issues contained in the Programme of Action of the Third United Nations Conference on the Least Developed Countries. In addition, the Declaration expressed firm commitment to the objective of duty-free, quota-free market access for products originating from least developed countries as well as to the implementation of measures to further widen market access for those exports.

The WTO Ministerial Conference, recognizing that technical assistance and capacity-building were core elements of the development dimension of the multilateral trading system, endorsed the New Strategy for WTO Technical Cooperation for Capacity Building, Growth and Integration. The objectives were to assist least developed countries in adjusting to WTO rules and disciplines, implementing obligations and exercising the rights of membership, including drawing on the benefits of an open, rules-based multilateral trading system. The Declaration noted the need for a coherent policy framework and timetable to ensure effective and coordinated delivery of technical assistance from bilateral donors as well as international and regional intergovernmental institutions. In this connection, the Declaration endorsed the Integrated Framework for Trade-related Technical Assistance to Least Developed Countries as a model for trade development; and development partners were requested to increase their contributions to the Integrated Framework Trust Fund significantly. The European Union, for example, has already committed 49 million euros for trade-related technical assistance and economic development cooperation for the period 2002-2006.

The Declaration was also concerned at the difficult trade issues facing small, vulnerable economies and the need for more speedy and easy procedures for WTO accession negotiations. While several least developed countries have been negotiating for accession, only the Solomon Islands has joined the organization since its establishment in 1995. The European Union has proposed a number of facilitation measures for those countries, although the proposals have yet to be endorsed by other WTO member countries.

---

[d] UNCTAD and Commonwealth Secretariat, *Duty- and Quota-free Market Access for Least Developed Countries: An Analysis of Quad Initiatives* (UNCTAD/DITC/TAB/Misc.7).

(Continued overleaf)

(Continued from preceding page)

Follow-up mechanism

The need for an effective and highly visible follow-up mechanism for coordinating, monitoring and reviewing the implementation of the Programme of Action has been well recognized. The Secretary-General, in his report on the subject to the General Assembly at its fifty-sixth session,[e] proposed the establishment of an Office of the High Representative for the Least Developed Countries, Landlocked Developing Countries and Small Island Developing States to follow up the implementation of the Programme of Action.

------

[e] A/56/645.

riel came under pressure in the third quarter of 2001, but stabilized thereafter. The Government is seeking to maintain the exchange rate at 3,950 riels to the dollar in 2002, but this will depend on a variety of both economic and non-economic factors. In the Lao People's Democratic Republic, the kip depreciated in 2000-2001, in line with the weakening of the Thai baht, increased demand resulting from the year-end budgetary expenditure, and a higher trade deficit. The exchange rate is now managed more flexibly and the margin between the bank and the parallel market rates is to be kept under 2 per cent. The parallel market rate was 9,475 kips to the dollar at the end of February 2002. The market rate in Myanmar, which depreciated significantly in 2001 and reached 750 kyats to the dollar in February 2002, continues to diverge very considerably from the official rate of 6.7 kyats to the dollar. A flexible exchange rate regime which unifies the official exchange rate with the market exchange rate and that for foreign exchange certificates is necessary in order to improve resource allocation and minimize rent-seeking behaviour. The transition to such a regime, however, will require external financing to meet the short-term costs.

Key policy issues

Good governance tops the policy agenda of the Asian least developed countries

Good governance is essential if Governments are to combat poverty, deliver services efficiently and equitably and ensure sustained human development. The donor communities, including multilateral funding agencies, are increasingly giving importance to improving governance and efficiency in the public, corporate and financial sectors and, by extension, to the more effective mobilization and utilization of aid and other resources for development and transformation. To this end, Governments have implemented a series of policy reforms aimed at establishing a strong foundation for long-term economic growth and alleviating poverty. Strengthening and streamlining the public sector is an essential element of those strategies, so that greater resources can be devoted to developing the physical and social infrastructure needed to foster private sector development. Further development of this sector is important for generating employment opportunities, while greater effort is also needed to improve the quality of human resources so that people can take advantage of new opportunities.

Economic growth and poverty alleviation efforts in Bangladesh have been constrained by a large and unprofitable public sector. Multilateral aid agencies have stressed the need for government reforms and privatization of State-owned enterprises and State-run banks. Bangladesh is highly dependent on ODA and such external resources financed 44 per cent of the fiscal deficit in 2000/01. The new Government, which is seen as more committed to reform, has formed a 13-member Administrative Reform Commission, which, has submitted a report containing a total of 137 recommendations for implementation in phases. The Commission touched upon several administrative matters, including issues concerning transparency in public administration, accountability and improvement in the service delivery of autonomous bodies, the establishment of an effective body to stop corruption in all tiers of administration, the reduction of delays in project implementation and the use of modern technology for governance.

The Government of Bhutan has adopted a cautious approach to development, choosing to preserve its traditional culture and pristine environment and improve the health and educational standards of the population, in addition to raising incomes. This policy focus is referred to as increasing "gross national happiness". The country has undertaken major structural reforms, including corporatizing government departments (in telecommunications), privatizing State enterprises (in trade, cement and banking), abolishing State monopolies (petroleum distribution), and putting the legislative framework in place for a modern, market-based economy. The Private Sector Development Committee has been formed, but to date there have been limited signs of private sector growth and development. The country's difficult terrain and limited all-weather transport links, the small local market and limited effective demand are further impediments to private sector development. Such development is becoming a pressing issue as it is proving difficult to generate jobs for a longer-lived and better-educated population which no longer finds subsistence farming attractive. The Government is seeking to limit expatriate employment and to increase spending on developing human resources in the private sector.

Increasing "gross national happiness" is the goal in Bhutan

Poverty remains widespread among subsistence farmers in the rural areas of Nepal

Nepal is another country in which the overwhelming majority of the population relies on subsistence farming and lives in rural areas, where poverty is widespread. Progress in structural reforms has been limited so far, and most loss-making State-owned enterprises have still not been privatized. Donor impatience with the slow pace of implementation is threatening continued support. However, steps have been taken to reform the civil service and develop a comprehensive poverty reduction strategy. Nepal Rastra Bank is implementing a $35 million financial sector reform programme with World Bank support. The two largest banks, one entirely State-owned and the other 41 per cent owned by the State, were technically insolvent and are now being managed by international firms of accountants to turn them around. The independence of the central bank has been increased and it has been given greater supervisory and regulatory authority. Prudential banking norms, on a par with international standards, have been introduced. However, civil disturbances may threaten the stability of the Government, making reforms more difficult to implement and forcing reductions in social spending to accommodate increased security costs.

Cambodia and the Lao People's Democratic Republic have embarked on major reforms

Both Cambodia and the Lao People's Democratic Republic are in receipt of three-year arrangements under the Poverty Reduction and Growth Facility of IMF. Cambodia is still undergoing reconstruction following a lengthy civil turmoil and transition from a centrally planned to a market-based economy. Reforms have so far concentrated on trade, banking, the private sector and public administration. Military demobilization, which has reduced the drain on public finances, and improvements in forestry management have also been important achievements and there was a moratorium on logging beginning on 1 January 2002. However, illegal logging continues to be a problem. Cambodia's Interim Poverty Reduction Strategy Paper recognizes that poverty alleviation depends on the realization of its growth potential, which hinges on political stability and improvements in physical and human resources. Cambodia more than doubled its spending on education between 1998 and 2001 and is committed to increasing this spending even further in 2002. However, weak capacity is seen as constituting a risk to programme implementation, and technical assistance along with donor support and debt relief, are seen as being necessary for success.

The challenge of poverty alleviation is particularly difficult in the Lao People's Democratic Republic

The approach to reforms has been more cautious in the Lao People's Democratic Republic, a landlocked country with a small and dispersed population, 80 per cent of which still live in rural areas. This makes the challenge of poverty alleviation particularly difficult. The focus of the Interim Poverty Reduction Strategy Paper is on macroeconomic stabilization and reform of State-owned commercial banks and enterprises, promotion of the private sector and improvement of public sector finances. VAT is to be introduced in 2003. Technical assistance may also be needed to enhance public expenditure management and transparency in the context of greater decentralization, so as to sharpen the poverty focus. Deepening the financial sector and reducing dependence on agriculture, while ensuring domestic security, are additional challenges.

In contrast, economic policy in Myanmar has been dominated by central planning aimed at import substitution. Agriculture and energy are priority sectors and self-sufficiency in food production is seen to be important for social stability. Market-based reforms may be necessary to sustain growth. Myanmar has reduced its fiscal deficit entirely through cuts in expenditure. As a result, spending on education in Myanmar declined to just 0.6 per cent of GDP in 2001, and that on health fell to 0.2 per cent of GDP. While in principle all citizens have access to free health care in public hospitals, in practice funding levels are inadequate to deliver these services. As a result, privately funded education and health systems have been set up to provide these services to those who can afford to pay. Given Myanmar's infrastructural needs, additional cuts in capital and social spending may lead to lower medium-term growth prospects.

Myanmar continues to effect import substitution but limited resources constrain spending on the social sectors

Bhutan, Cambodia, the Lao People's Democratic Republic and Nepal have yet to accede to WTO; such accession presents both opportunities and challenges and is a key policy issue. Qualifying for this new trading regime calls for further reductions in tariff and tax rates with significant implications not only for the level of protection enjoyed by the domestic industries but also for government revenues. Quotas for garment exports to Canada, the European Union, Norway and the United States will cease when the Multifibre Arrangement is phased out on 1 January 2005. The ready-made garment industry, which has been the largest exporter in some of the least developed countries, will have to face the challenge of surviving in a competitive market. Preparing the least developed countries to join WTO will require vigorous national capacity-building and information dissemination for the necessary awareness creation. In contrast, although Myanmar is a member of both ASEAN and WTO, investment sanctions, the withdrawal of preferential trade privileges and consumer boycotts have dimmed its prospects for using trade effectively as a vehicle for economic growth.

Regional and global trade and economic cooperation present both opportunities and challenges

At the subregional level, the three least developed countries of South-East Asia have doubled efforts to bring their finance, investment, commerce and trade sectors into alignment with ASEAN standards. Trade liberalization, particularly within ASEAN, could have significant benefits for these countries, as preferential access can be used to generate export growth and investment from other countries; this is discussed further in box II.6.

Membership in ASEAN and AFTA gives added impetus to reform efforts

Pacific island economies

Subregional overview and prospects

Weak economic growth in 2001 owing to lower external demand, sluggish agricultural production and civil disturbances in some economies

In common with most other developing subregions of ESCAP, the economic performance of Pacific island economies as a whole weakened or remained weak in 2001, a reflection of lower external demand resulting from the global economic slowdown and several domestic constraints, including sluggish agricultural production and civil disturbances in several economies. Fallout from the September 2001 terrorist attacks in the United States was on balance relatively limited in respect of the Pacific island economies; the United States was an important source of tourists to only a few island economies in the South Pacific. Furthermore, a large number of Pacific islands could be regarded as low-risk destinations, involving equally low-risk travel. Private remittances were important to a large number of island economies and the terrorist-induced sharper slowdown in the United States could affect the flows from Pacific islanders working in Hawaii and on the American west coast to a certain extent. Early estimates indicate a drop of 12 per cent in remittances to Tonga in September and October 2001.

Samoa continued to record impressive growth, with GDP going up by 6.5 per cent in 2001, while Tuvalu gained 5 percentage points in the value of total output during the year. However, the deteriorating law and order situation resulted in a decline (of 3.3 per cent) in aggregate production in Papua New Guinea. GDP contracted further in Solomon Islands; indeed, widespread civil unrest lowered the total output by 23 per cent during the period 1999-2001 (figure II.6). GDP growth rates were relatively low or modest elsewhere in the Pacific island subregion. For example, the economy in Fiji had lost almost 3 percentage points in output in 2000 but the subsequent return to democracy, plus renewed business confidence and higher tourist arrivals, added 1.5 per cent to GDP in the following year.

Agriculture remained the major source of subsistence and cash income for the large majority of the population virtually throughout the Pacific island subregion. Generally, this sector did not perform well for two years in a row (2000 and 2001) in Fiji, Samoa and Solomon Islands; a setback to agricultural output was also recorded by Papua New Guinea, Tonga and Vanuatu for 2001. This adverse development, compounded by lower prices for several major export items, not only weighed heavily on domestic economic activities and services but might also have set back hard-earned progress in poverty eradication in many parts of the island subregion.

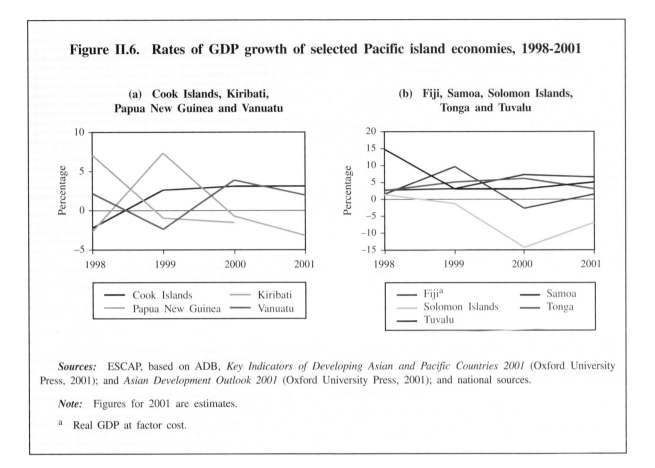

Figure II.6. Rates of GDP growth of selected Pacific island economies, 1998-2001

(a) Cook Islands, Kiribati, Papua New Guinea and Vanuatu

(b) Fiji, Samoa, Solomon Islands, Tonga and Tuvalu

Sources: ESCAP, based on ADB, *Key Indicators of Developing Asian and Pacific Countries 2001* (Oxford University Press, 2001); and *Asian Development Outlook 2001* (Oxford University Press, 2001); and national sources.

Note: Figures for 2001 are estimates.

[a] Real GDP at factor cost.

The behaviour of consumer prices was equally varied among the Pacific island economies (figure II.7). Inflation has been rising in Tonga for a few years and remained at a relatively high level in Papua New Guinea and Solomon Islands in 2001. Price increases were modest elsewhere in the subregion, while Samoa has been experiencing a remarkable degree of price stability for several years. Virtually all Pacific island economies are heavily dependent on imports, mainly, but not exclusively, from Australia, Japan and New Zealand. Weakening exchange rates and, in a number of countries, poor agricultural production and higher food prices were the main cost-push force behind the patterns of inflation observed in the subregion in 2001. With few exceptions, demand factors played a limited role in pulling up prices, as the budget deficits and money supply (M2) growth had been within manageable and modest limits.

Sluggish agricultural production and weakening exchange rates pushed up inflation in most Pacific island economies in 2001

External trade performance was disappointing in some countries of the subregion, with merchandise export earnings falling off in 2001 (figure II.8). This represented the confluence of several factors, including lower world prices and reduced external demand compounded, in several cases, by setbacks to production and export volumes, resulting from widespread

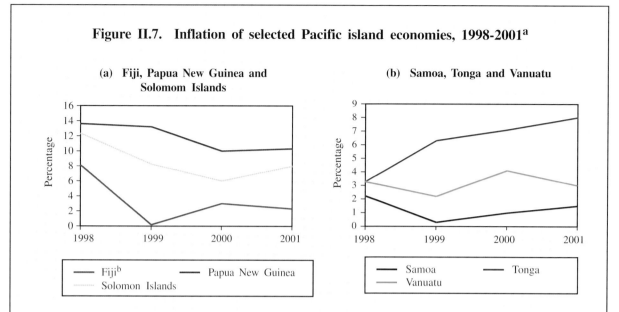

Figure II.7. Inflation of selected Pacific island economies, 1998-2001[a]

(a) Fiji, Papua New Guinea and Solomon Islands

(b) Samoa, Tonga and Vanuatu

Fiji[b]   Papua New Guinea
Solomon Islands

Samoa   Tonga
Vanuatu

Sources: ESCAP, based on ADB, *Key Indicators of Developing Asian and Pacific Countries 2001* (Oxford University Press, 2001); and *Asian Development Outlook 2001* (Oxford University Press, 2001); IMF, *International Financial Statistics,* vol. LIV, No. 10 (October 2001); and national sources.

Note: Figures for 2001 are estimates.

[a] Changes in the consumer price index.
[b] Year-on-year percentage change.

Lower merchandise export earnings in 2001 reflected falling world prices and demand, and setbacks in production and export volumes as a result of civil disorders in some economies

civil disorders, falling ore quality and the approaching exhaustion of oil reserves. Again, Samoa was a notable exception to this overall trend, but the higher export receipts came from a low base since the country's export earnings had contracted by about one quarter in 2000. Expenditure on imports generally mirrored the patterns of export earnings for 2000-2001. Domestic demand was considerably weakened by poorer economic performance and GDP growth, and higher landed prices of imports owing to the exchange rate depreciation in several economies.

Sizeable receipts from tourism and large inflows of private remittances and official transfers eased considerably the shortfalls on the external trade (goods and services) and current accounts of several countries. From the available data, it appears that there were no severe balance-of-payments crises in the island subregion in 2001. The foreign reserve position was stable as a whole, while the service burden on external debt was mostly manageable.

As is to be expected, the economic outlook for the subregion for 2002 remained mixed; as a whole, however, a strong recovery in the United States economy would have important, positive spillover

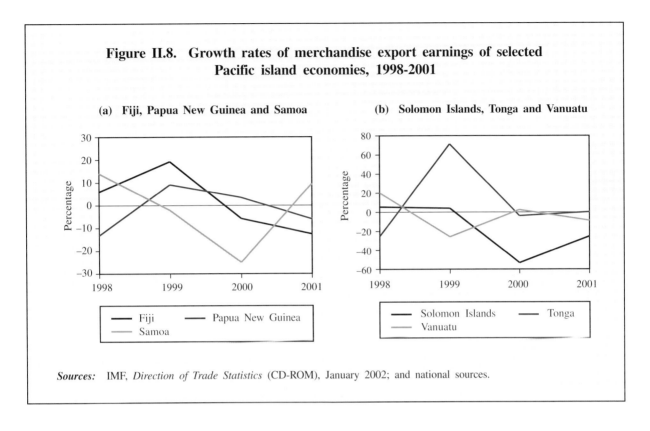

Figure II.8. Growth rates of merchandise export earnings of selected Pacific island economies, 1998-2001

(a) Fiji, Papua New Guinea and Samoa

(b) Solomon Islands, Tonga and Vanuatu

Sources: IMF, *Direction of Trade Statistics* (CD-ROM), January 2002; and national sources.

effects on global demand for goods and services and on the subregion's export performance. Other things being equal, GDP was expected to be more robust, for example, expanding in the range of 2.5 to 5 per cent in Fiji, Samoa, Tonga and Vanuatu. The projected stimulus from external merchandise trade would play an important part in the above scenario. However, such growth would also be driven by a reasonable recovery in tourist arrivals, improved agricultural output and better consumer and investor confidence. All these positive developments, in turn, would depend very much on the elimination or minimization of law and order problems and of other civil disturbances or political uncertainties.

GDP performance

For a variety of reasons of both local and external origin, the recent patterns of economic growth have been rather uneven within Pacific island economies. GDP growth has been low to moderate in recent years and few economies have been able to sustain consistently high rates of expansion in economic activities (table II.8). Largely as a result, there have been some setbacks in per capita income and domestic employment, which have had an impact on the living standards and poverty alleviation efforts. The severe economic crisis in Solomon Islands was noted earlier.

Low economic growth has led to some setbacks in per capita income, domestic employment and poverty alleviation efforts

Table II.8. Selected Pacific island economies: growth rates, 1998-2001

(Percentage)

		Rates of growth			
		Gross domestic product	*Agriculture*	*Industry*	*Services*
Cook Islands	1998	−2.3	2.8	−6.2	−3.4
	1999	2.7	2.5	4.6	2.5
	2000	3.2	..	..	..
	2001	3.2	..	..	..
Fiji[a]	1998	1.4	−7.2	3.1	3.3
	1999	9.7	16.1	9.8	8.0
	2000	−2.8	−1.2	−7.4	−1.1
	2001	1.5	−0.5	−1.8	3.5
Kiribati	1998	7.3	8.1	35.3	7.3
	1999	−1.0	1.0	41.9	−1.0
	2000	−1.6	−1.8	−34.5	−1.6
Papua New Guinea	1998	−2.8	−11.3	9.7	−6.5
	1999	7.6	4.3	5.7	12.4
	2000	−0.8	9.1	−5.4	−4.0
	2001	−3.3	0.9	−6.1	−4.4
Samoa	1998	2.6	7.0	−9.4	7.1
	1999	3.1	−3.5	4.3	5.2
	2000	7.3	1.5	17.0	5.4
	2001	6.5	0.5	10.0	7.0
Solomon Islands	1998	1.3	−4.2	11.4	4.0
	1999	−1.4	−7.2	41.8	−3.6
	2000	−14.5	−16.1	−35.5	−7.2
	2001	−7.0	−10.0	−33.0	0.6
Tonga	1998	2.5	0.3	4.2	7.7
	1999	5.0	−3.1	15.7	6.7
	2000	6.1	9.1	6.3	4.6
	2001	3.0	2.8	8.2	1.2
Tuvalu	1998	14.9	0.7	21.5	16.0
	1999	3.0	..	..	..
	2000	3.0	..	..	..
	2001	5.0	..	..	..
Vanuatu	1998	2.2	9.1	6.7	−0.1
	1999	−2.5	−9.3	5.2	−1.7
	2000	4.0	2.5	8.4	3.7
	2001	2.0	−2.0	3.5	2.5

Sources: ESCAP, based on ADB, *Key Indicators of Developing Asian and Pacific Countries 2001* (Oxford University Press, 2001) and *Asian Development Outlook 2001* (Oxford University Press, 2001); and national sources.

Notes: Figures for 2001 are estimates. Industry comprises mining and quarrying; manufacturing; electricity, gas and power; and construction.

[a] Real GDP at factor cost.

GDP in Papua New Guinea and Vanuatu went up by 0.2-1.4 per cent a year on average over the period 1998-2001. In contrast, economic activities in Samoa have been on an upward trend with GDP gaining almost 6 percentage points a year over the period 1999-2001. However, the rapid expansion in Tonga, averaging over 5.5 per cent annually in 1999-2000, could not be sustained in 2001.

The political coup of May 2000 and the related civil unrest in Fiji led to the loss of market and consumer confidence, a tighter monetary policy approach and other measures to control capital flight, and lower tourist arrivals for the year as a whole. Largely as a result, GDP contracted by 2.8 percentage points in 2000. However, the prolonged political crisis was compounded by the weak performance in agriculture and industry, despite a steady easing of monetary policy from late 2000 through 2001. Domestic credit to the private sector had fallen since May 2000, while aggregate output stagnated and GDP gained only 1.5 per cent in 2001. Among the hardest hit were inward tourism (down by almost 11 percentage points in 2000) and industrial activities (down by over 12 percentage points). In particular, informal sanctions, led largely by the international union movement, resulted in the collapse of garment exports, which had earlier eclipsed sugar exports to become Fiji's second most important export item after tourism services. Garment factory closures and worker lay-offs continued into 2001, along with persistent weaknesses in sugar production and processing (owing to ongoing difficulties in land-lease arrangements) and gold production. All these factors led to a contraction in industrial value added, expected to be 1.8 per cent for the year. The agriculture sector (including fisheries) remained stagnant after a small decline in output had been recorded in 2000. Inward tourism recovered moderately in 2001 but the recovery was not sufficient to provide the needed domestic up-lift, with the result that GDP went up modestly for the year. In that context, mass lay-offs in the tourism and garment industries have led to a degree of hardship and unemployment rarely, if ever, seen in Fiji before. The poor and less well educated in particular have suffered more severely from the consequences.

Growth in output stalled in Fiji owing to the political coup in 2000 and the subsequent loss of market confidence

The economy of Papua New Guinea had recovered strongly in 1999, a performance driven largely by relatively solid growth in the agriculture and service sectors, and renewed industrial strength. It has since been on the decline, with GDP gaining less than 1 per cent in the following year and then falling by 3.3 percentage points in 2001, as against an annual population growth rate of about 2.3 per cent. Among the causal factors and forces were weaknesses in policy management and implementation, some negative repercussions from the structural reform programmes and

Law and order problems among the factors affecting growth in Papua New Guinea

the continued deterioration of law and order. The last factor combined with lower export prices to dampen the output and earnings from Papua New Guinea's main export crops of coffee, copra, cocoa and palm oil. At the same time, weak demand from Asia and a restrictive export tax regime caused a drop in forestry output. The slump in the agriculture sector continued into 2001. Minerals had become a mainstay of the economy, but the diminishing oil reserves in the Southern Highlands contributed to a reduction of about 8 per cent in the mineral sector output for both 2000 and 2001.

Weakened manufacturing, construction and service activities resulted in an overall decline in industrial value added, averaging over 5.7 percentage points annually in 2000-2001, as well as a further deterioration of 4.4 per cent in service sector output in 2001. Indeed, the economic performance of Papua New Guinea was much constrained by the adoption of a tight monetary policy approach in an effort to conserve foreign exchange and abate the depreciation of the kina. Lending rates averaged over 17 per cent in 2000, contributing to a squeeze on private sector credit, which grew by just 3.2 per cent in 2001. Sparked by lower oil prices, among other factors, the kina depreciated again in late 2001, which could lead to renewed monetary tightening.

Higher growth in Samoa driven by the construction and tourism industries

Samoa was the one bright spot within the Pacific island subregion: GDP per capita grew by 23 per cent between 1995 and 2000. Aggregate production, again driven by construction activities and booming services, was expected to gain another 6.5 per cent in 2001. The solid expansion in construction resulted partly from the series of structural reforms and a refocused development strategy in the public sector, and culminated in a number of donor-assisted infrastructure projects and increased investment from the private sector as well. Largely as a result of this, industrial output went up by an average of 13 per cent a year in 2000-2001, a development facilitated by the ready availability of private sector credit, which expanded by 25 per cent in 2000 and was expected to grow by a further 16 per cent in the following year. Meanwhile, higher private remittances from abroad and increased inward tourism served to stimulate commercial activities and other domestic services. Indeed, gross tourism receipts constituted over 17 per cent of GDP in 2000, and the service sector as a whole, which had expanded by over 5 per cent a year in 1999-2000, recorded another solid gain of 7 percentage points in 2001. This sector now contributes 55 per cent of GDP, compared with a relative share of 19 per cent for agriculture (including fishing), whose weak performance in 2001 was not, however, a severe constraint on aggregate domestic economic activities.

The Solomon Islands economy has been badly affected by the political crisis and the associated civil unrest and widespread disruption which began in 1999. In particular, GDP plummeted by 14.5 per cent in 2000 and was expected to go down by another 7 percentage points in the following year, despite the peace agreement reached in 2000. Domestic activities in agriculture, forestry and fisheries were severely affected by the civil disturbances, with output going down by an annual average of over 11 per cent in the period 1999-2001. In turn, this served to dampen industrial activities, which contracted by over a third in each of the years 2000 and 2001. Cutbacks in new bank lending in an environment of increasing risk were a compounding constraint. In particular, domestic credit to the private sector fell by more than a fifth in 2001 and the higher risk premium on debt was reflected in the sharp widening of the interest rate margin; while the average deposit rates were reduced from 3.0 to 0.7 per cent from 2000 to 2001, the average lending rates were relatively stable, at the high level of just over 15 per cent, in 2001.

A large contraction in the Solomon Islands economy as a result of the political crisis

Fish products and palm oil were the Solomon Islands' second and third biggest exports after forestry products. Palm oil processing ceased in 1999. Solomon Taiyo Ltd. ceased its fishing and fish processing operations in 2000, but resumed its activities in mid-2001 following nationalization. Copra and cocoa production, already low in the first half of 2000, was halved as a result of the insolvency of the Commodities Export Marketing Authority towards the end of 2000. However, the Authority's operations were restarted late in 2001 through a rescue package underwritten by Taiwan Province of China. Forestry operations, although considerably disrupted, remained the only source of growth in the commercial sector.

The economy of Tonga had expanded strongly in 1999-2000, with GDP expansion averaging over 5.5 per cent each year. This owed much to large inflows of private remittances from Tongans working abroad; such resources not only accounted for the bulk of foreign exchange earnings but also sustained a considerable portion of consumption expenditure in the country. Another economic stimulus came from agriculture and, to a much lesser extent, industrial production. The agriculture sector, by and large, had performed better than many others in the Pacific island subregion thanks to various measures to improve the (export) marketing of agricultural produce as well as to diversify its composition (from squash to water melons, root crops, fruit and vegetables). The growth process was facilitated by a commensurate credit expansion, by 13 per cent in 1999 and 18 per cent in 2000, to the private sector, mostly for industrial and commercial purposes. Strong GDP growth, however, was not sustainable in 2001 and aggregate output was expected to go up by 3 percentage

Reduced economic growth for Tonga and Vanuatu in 2001

points, reflecting a sharp decline in agricultural output, from over 9 per cent to below 3 per cent from 2000 to 2001. In addition, the service sector continue to decline; growth in local value added fell continuously from almost 8 per cent in 1998 to just over 1 per cent in 2001. Another factor was the grounding of Royal Tonga Airlines' only jet used on international routes, while inward tourism was further reduced by the fallout from the 11 September 2001 terrorist attacks; the United States was Tonga's second biggest tourist market.

Vanuatu was another island country whose economic performance was not keeping up with the population growth rate of 2.6 per cent; in particular, aggregate output went up by less than 1.5 per cent a year over the period 1998-2001. Economic activities decelerated noticeably, and GDP growth fell from 4 to 2 per cent from 2000 to 2001. In spite of a more accommodating monetary policy approach, domestic credit expanded marginally (by less than 1 per cent) in 2000, while the average borrowing rates remained high, at over 13 per cent, as against 13.5 per cent in 2000. Services constituted about 70 per cent of GDP; this sector was underpinned by tourism and, to a lesser extent, the provision of financial services. Strong growth in inward tourism and the associated multiplier effects led to the sharp upturn in Vanuatu's GDP in 2000. However, the growth momentum could not be sustained in the following year, when there was a considerable deceleration in the output of industry and services and a contraction of 2 per cent in agriculture. Lower world prices for copra, the most important agricultural commodity in Vanuatu and a principal source of cash income for the rural community, led to a continued fall in its production in both 2000 and 2001.

Inflation

Inflation remained at relatively high levels in Papua New Guinea and Solomon Islands in 2001

Two trends in consumer prices were discernible in the Pacific island subregion. Inflation was on an upward trend in Tonga, while it remained at a relatively high level in Papua New Guinea and Solomon Islands in absolute terms. However, increases in consumer prices were moderate elsewhere, including Fiji, Samoa and Vanuatu (table II.9). Papua New Guinea has recorded double-digit inflation for several years; consumer prices were higher by about 10 per cent in 2000 and 2001, despite modest increases in the money supply (M2), low levels of fiscal deficits as a proportion of GDP and weak demand in consequence of economic contraction. The economy was highly dependent on imported consumer and producer goods, and the depreciation of the kina by 8 per cent against the Australian dollar in 2001 pushed up the landed costs of imports. In addition, there were the lagged effects of higher oil prices in 2000.

Table II.9. Selected Pacific island economies: inflation and money supply growth (M2), 1998-2001

(Percentage)

	1998	*1999*	*2000*	*2001*
Inflation[a]				
Fiji[b]	8.1	0.2	3.0	2.3
Papua New Guinea	13.6	13.2	10.0	10.3
Samoa	2.2	0.3	1.0	1.5
Solomon Islands	12.3	8.3	6.0	8.0
Tonga	3.3	6.3	7.1	8.0
Vanuatu	3.3	2.2	4.1	3.0
Money supply growth (M2)				
Fiji	−0.3	14.2	−2.1	−1.4[c]
Papua New Guinea	2.5	9.2	5.0	2.1[c]
Samoa	2.5	15.7	16.3	13.8[c]
Solomon Islands	2.5	7.0	−0.7[c]	..
Tonga	14.7	11.9	18.8	15.5[c]
Vanuatu	12.6	−9.2	5.5	11.6[c]

Sources: ESCAP, based on ADB, *Key Indicators of Developing Asian and Pacific Countries 2001* (Oxford University Press, 2001) and *Asian Development Outlook 2001* (Oxford University Press, 2001); IMF, *International Financial Statistics*, vol. LV, No. 1 (January 2002); and national sources.

Note: Figures for 2001 are estimates.

[a] Changes in the consumer price index.
[b] Year-on-year percentage change.
[c] January-September.

Inflation in Solomon Islands showed a downward trend during the period 1998-2000 but picked up again in the following year, rising from 6 to 8 per cent in 2001, despite the ongoing contraction in economic activities totalling more than 21 per cent in 2000-2001. This reversal was attributable to the ongoing shortages in the production and marketing of essential goods (including foodstuffs), resulting from the civil disturbances, and to the higher cost of imports. There were large deficits in the external current account, which deteriorated from a surplus of almost 9 per cent of GDP in 1999 to a deficit of 18 per cent in 2000 and a further deficit of 8 per cent in 2001 (table II.10). Such a high degree of external imbalance, in turn, was a reflection of the rising level of aggregate absorption, with the fiscal deficit going up from less than 4 per cent of GDP in 1999 to an average of 7 per cent in 2000-2001. The upward trend of inflation in Tonga, from 3.3 to 8 per cent between 1998 and 2001, was in part attributable to a weaker exchange rate, which depreciated by 8 per cent up to November 2001 against the Australian dollar; imports from Australia and New Zealand dominate Tonga's consumption.

Table II.10. Selected Pacific island economies: budget and current account balance as a percentage of GDP, 1998-2001

(Percentage)

	1998	1999	2000	2001
Budget balance as a percentage of GDP				
Fiji	5.1	−0.2	−3.0	−6.0
Papua New Guinea	−1.6	−2.6	−1.9	−1.4
Samoa[a]	2.1	0.3	−0.7	−2.3
Solomon Islands[a]	−1.6	−3.9	−5.0	−8.8
Tonga[a]	−4.3	−1.4	−0.9	−0.5
Vanuatu	−6.7	−0.9	−7.4	−2.5
Current account balance as a percentage of GDP				
Fiji	−3.5	−2.4	−1.1	−0.7
Papua New Guinea	−0.5	4.0	8.6	9.4
Samoa	9.6	−8.3	−5.6	−11.4
Solomon Islands	2.7	8.8	−18.1	−8.1
Tonga	−11.8	−3.8	−6.9	−4.3
Vanuatu	2.0	−5.5	4.8	5.8

Sources: ESCAP, based on ADB, *Key Indicators of Developing Asian and Pacific Countries 2001* (Oxford University Press, 2001) and *Asian Development Outlook 2001* (Oxford University Press, 2001); IMF, *International Financial Statistics*, vol. LIV, No. 10 (October 2001); and national sources.

Note: Figures for 2001 are estimates.

[a] Excluding grants.

Consumer prices went up moderately in other Pacific island economies in 2001

The available data for other Pacific island economies provided a different picture. In Fiji, inflation went down from 3 per cent in 2000 to an estimated 2.3 per cent for the following year. Poor GDP performance and the ensuing weak domestic demand helped to contain pressures on consumer prices, despite the impact of higher world prices on energy products. Another stabilizing influence was money supply (M2) growth, and the current account deficits were, by and large, marginal. The exchange rate was relatively stable and, despite the collapse in exports after the political coup, there was no great pressure to devalue the Fijian dollar; there was a corresponding collapse in import demand as well. It is worth noting the one-off effect on consumer prices of the legal dispute over the removal of VAT on a number of food items made by the previous Government.

Samoa enjoyed remarkable price stability among Pacific island economies, inflation being contained within the narrow range of 0.3 to 1.5 per cent during the period 1999-2001. Such enviable stability signified a new era of responsible fiscal and monetary management which, in turn, was manifested in relatively stable exchange rates. The budget shortfall as a proportion of GDP was modest, while the current account deficit, although relatively high, was sustainable in view of the healthy level of foreign reserves of $51 million in 2001, or almost five months of import cover, as at November 2001. The modest increase in consumer prices in 2001 was largely due to higher prices for food and some energy products; however, inflation was projected to be around 2 per cent or less in the medium term. Vanuatu was another island country with relatively stable prices. The flow-on effects of higher prices for imported energy products contributed to an inflation rate of over 4 per cent in 2000. Pressures on consumer prices moderated in the following year along with a much lower budget deficit at 2.5 per cent of GDP, compared with over 7 per cent in 2000, and appreciation of the vatu against the Australian dollar by 7 per cent in 2001. Domestic consumption is import-intensive in Vanuatu and Australia supplies nearly half of its imports.

Foreign trade and other external transactions

International trade presented a dismal picture in 2001, with setbacks of varying degrees of seriousness in merchandise export earnings virtually throughout the Pacific island subregion (table II.11). Export values declined in Fiji, Papua New Guinea, Solomon Islands and Vanuatu. Samoa recorded an increase of under 10 per cent in trade earnings but this was not sufficient to compensate for a contraction of 25 per cent in 2000. Tonga's exports also went down by about 4 per cent

Slight improvements in trade deficits for some Pacific island economies in 2001

Table II.11. Selected Pacific island economies: merchandise exports and their rates of growth, 1998-2001

| | *Value (Millions of US dollars)* | *Exports (f.o.b.)* | | | |
| | | *Annual rate of growth (Percentage)* | | | |
	2000	*1998*	*1999*	*2000*	*2001*
Fiji	572	6.0	19.3	−5.7	−12.5
Papua New Guinea	2 024	−13.2	9.2	3.5	−6.0
Samoa	14	4.0	−2.1	−25.0	9.5
Solomon Islands	69	5.6	4.0	−53.2	−25.3
Tonga	12	−25.5	71.5	−3.7	0.1
Vanuatu	26	20.2	−26.0	2.5	−8.8

Sources: IMF, *Direction of Trade Statistics* (CD-ROM), January 2002; and national sources.

in that year, but remained unchanged in 2001. The patterns of import spending (figure II.9) followed a roughly similar trend to that of export receipts in 2000-2001, although the rates of compression of import expenditure were generally less pronounced than those associated with export earnings.

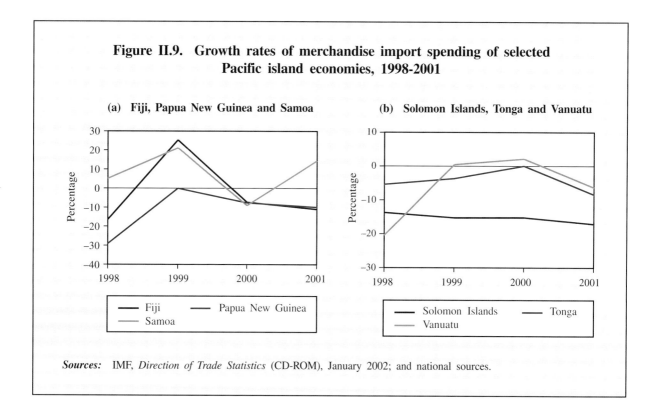

Figure II.9. Growth rates of merchandise import spending of selected Pacific island economies, 1998-2001

(a) Fiji, Papua New Guinea and Samoa

(b) Solomon Islands, Tonga and Vanuatu

Sources: IMF, *Direction of Trade Statistics* (CD-ROM), January 2002; and national sources.

Lower oil production led to a decline in export receipts in Papua New Guinea in 2001

Papua New Guinea is by far the largest trader in the subregion; its exports constituted 44 per cent of GDP in 2000. Merchandise exports, which had recovered and expanded strongly (by over 9 percentage points) in 1999, have been on a declining trend since then, despite favourable prices for several commodities; their value rose by only 3.5 per cent (to $2 billion) in 2000 and then contracted by 6 per cent in the following year. The value of mineral exports, equivalent to 77 per cent of the total trade earnings, was dominated by oil and gold, both of which suffered from lower export prices and volume in 2001, the lower volume being due to reserve depletion. Oil production was down by about 16.5 per cent in 2001 compared with the previous year's level. Exports of forestry products were stagnant and, in volume terms, remained at half of the levels traded prior to the financial and economic crisis in East and South-East Asia. Earnings on agricultural exports also declined, as a result of lower prices received for the main export crops such as coffee, cocoa, palm oil and copra. The coffee industry, once the dominant export activity and the main source of cash income for rural Papua New Guineans, has been on a gradual decline largely because of law and order problems.

Spending on merchandise imports, which had amounted to around $1 billion in 2000, fell and was almost 8 per cent lower; it dropped by another 10 per cent in 2001 (table II.12). In fact, import expenditure had contracted every year since 1998, in part a reflection of economic and structural adjustment problems in Papua New Guinea. However, the trade surplus, over $1 billion (or almost 29 per cent of GDP) in 2000, was expected to rise to over 31 per cent as a result of a sharper fall-off in import value in 2001. The deficit on the external services was also smaller, while the current account surplus, at $0.3 billion (or almost 9 per cent of GDP) in 2000, would remain at around 9-10 per cent as a result of a greater surplus on the trade account for 2001. The deficit in the external capital account trebled to $184 million in 2000, mainly owing to increased loan repayments from the Government and from minerals companies. However, the current account surpluses were much larger than the capital account shortfalls, resulting in a balance-of-payments surplus of $130 million in 2000 and about $162 million in 2001. International reserves had dropped to $90 million in June 1999, contributing to the steep slide of the exchange rate of the kina (figure II.10). The reserves were successfully rebuilt to over $300 million (or four months of import cover) in 2001. External debt had fallen to 68 per cent of GDP in 2000, with a debt-service burden of 11 per cent of GDP.

Table II.12. Selected Pacific island economies: merchandise imports and their rates of growth, 1998-2001

	Value (Millions of US dollars)	Imports (c.i.f.) Annual rate of growth (Percentage)			
	2000	1998	1999	2000	2001
Fiji	833	−16.5	25.3	−7.3	−11.0
Papua New Guinea	999	−29.2	−0.1	−7.7	−9.9
Samoa	105	5.1	21.2	−9.0	14.4
Solomon Islands	92	−13.7	−15.3	−15.2	−17.1
Tonga	61	−5.4	−3.7	0.0	−8.4
Vanuatu	78	−20.4	0.4	2.1	−6.3

Sources: IMF, *Direction of Trade Statistics* (CD-ROM), January 2002; and national sources.

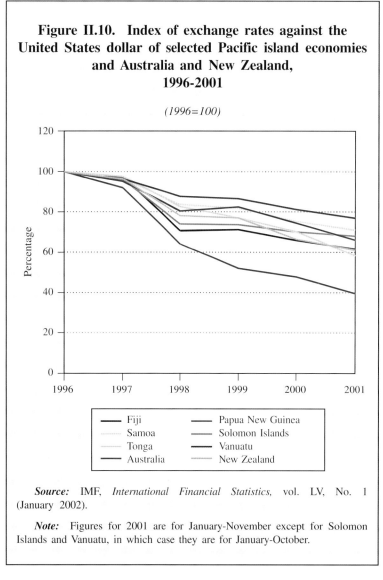

Figure II.10. Index of exchange rates against the United States dollar of selected Pacific island economies and Australia and New Zealand, 1996-2001

(1996=100)

Fiji — Papua New Guinea
Samoa — Solomon Islands
Tonga — Vanuatu
Australia — New Zealand

Source: IMF, *International Financial Statistics,* vol. LV, No. 1 (January 2002).

Note: Figures for 2001 are for January-November except for Solomon Islands and Vanuatu, in which case they are for January-October.

Merchandise export earnings by Fiji, another large trader in the Pacific, fell by almost 6 per cent (to $0.6 billion) in 2000 and by a further 12.5 per cent in the following year. The two main export items, garments and sugar, were affected by informal sanctions led by the trade union movement in the aftermath of the political coup and the subsequent losses of markets, including in Australia and New Zealand. The sugar industry was in difficulty over land-lease arrangements, which had an adverse impact on crop planting and hence on sugarcane harvesting and processing. Total cane production for the 2001 season amounted to 2.8 million tons, yielding just over 293,000 tons of sugar, a sharp decline by 26 and 14 per cent compared with the respective output levels in the 2000 season. Such minor export commodities as gold, timber and copra did not perform well for a variety of reasons, including declining ore quality, weak orders and low export prices. However, exports of fresh fish were expected to do better as a result of secure

Lower export earnings in Fiji owing to a sharp fall in garment and sugar production

markets in Asia and the United States. In an effort to boost the depressed export sector, a new export credit scheme was introduced in July 2001 to ensure the on-lending to exporters of a minimum of 5 per cent of the amount of deposits in commercial banks.

Tourism-dominated service exports which, as a whole, had fallen by almost 21 percentage points in 2000, recovered strongly to an expected growth rate of 8 per cent in the following year. The tourism industry had been hit particularly hard by the political and civil disturbances; visitor arrivals dropped to around half of the initial projections for the second half of 2000, leading to a total loss of 28 per cent in visitor numbers for the whole year. While some of these losses were recouped in 2001, it may take several years for tourism to recover fully in the light of the damage to Fiji's reputation, especially in Australia and New Zealand. Moreover, imports were also on a downward trend, so that the merchandise trade deficit remained relatively unchanged at around 16 per cent of GDP in both 2000 and 2001.

The current account deficit went down to around 1 percentage point of GDP in 2000-2001. Strict capital controls implemented after the coup were gradually eased in 2001 along with the stability of foreign exchange reserves, which went down slightly from $420 to $390 million from the end of 2000 to the end of 2001; the latter figure was sufficient to cover four months of imports of goods and services. Fiji's external debt, dominated by public sector obligations, remained relatively low at under 10 per cent of GDP, with an external debt-servicing burden of 2 per cent of GDP.

Merchandise export earnings in other parts of the Pacific island subregion, although critical to the economies concerned, were relatively small in absolute value (in the range of $12 to $70 million in 2000). Exceptionally, exports from Samoa rose by just under 10 per cent in 2001, from a contraction of about a quarter (to $14 million), owing to poor earnings on fish exports in the previous year. The closure of the coconut oil mill affected exports of coconut oil in 2000, but processing was to recommence in 2002. There is now considerable scope for Samoa to attract further investment and boost exports in the garment industry.

Generally, however, Samoa continued to experience a substantial trade deficit, which was expected to reach $105 million, equivalent to 44 per cent of GDP, for 2001; higher import spending by over 14 percentage points was fuelled by increased domestic investment. Tourism brought in some $40 million in both 2000 and 2001, nearly three times the merchandise export value. Private inward remittances went up by 9 per cent to reach $45 million in 2000, thus continuing to underpin growth in private consumption and investment expenditure. The overall current account deficit had dropped to under 6 per cent of GDP in 2000 but was expected to expand to over 11 per cent with the sharp increase in imports of goods and services in 2001. However, the external capital account surplus was expected to rise from 6 to 10 percentage points of GDP from 2000 to 2001, an improvement led largely by higher inflows of official finance for public investment projects. There was a small surplus (0.4 per cent of GDP) in the overall balance of payments in 2000 and a projected deficit of 1.3 per cent for the following year. Nevertheless, Samoa's foreign exchange reserves remained strong, amounting to $51 million (or about five months of import cover) as at November 2001. Total external debt went down from over 100 per cent of GDP in the early 1990s to less than 64 per cent currently; the debt-service burden was rather light, at just over 2 percentage points of aggregate output.

Substantial trade deficit and strong foreign reserve position in Samoa in 2001

*Solomon Islands'
merchandise
exports registered a
severe setback*

In Solomon Islands, the export base was collapsing; widespread civil unrest contributed to a deep contraction in earnings of over half (to $69 million) in 2000 and a further drop of one quarter during the ensuing year. Gold mining operations ceased in mid-2000, causing a fall of almost three quarters in export earnings, while the closure of the Solomon Taiyo Ltd. operations resulted in a drop of over three quarters in the value of fisheries exports. Copra and cocoa exports were halved in 2000 as a result of the civil unrest and the insolvency of the Commodities Export Marketing Authority towards the end of 2000. The value of merchandise exports in 2001, at just one third of the 1999 level, was thus the lowest in two decades. The prospects for any significant upswing in merchandise exports are not encouraging in the short term. The Gold Ridge mine and palm oil plantations had suffered extensive damage, while a positive push from the resumption of export fisheries in 2001 would probably not be sizeable until at least 2002. The lingering business uncertainties in the country constituted another constraint.

Solomon Islands had enjoyed sizeable merchandise trade surpluses which, in 1999, had stood at 14 per cent of GDP. The export collapse has since transformed this surplus into a substantial deficit of over 9-10 per cent of GDP over 2000-2001. The external current account balance followed a similar pattern; a surplus of around 9 per cent of GDP in 1999 turned into a deficit of 18 per cent in the following year and, owing largely to lower service imports and higher aid transfers, to 8 per cent in 2001. There had been some capital flight in 1999 but capital controls and higher ODA helped to turn a deficit of $19 million into a capital account surplus of $22 million from 1999 to 2000; the surplus was expected to be higher in 2001. Nevertheless, the overall balance of payments was in a shortfall, amounting to $19 million (or 27 per cent of export earnings) in 2000. Foreign exchange reserves continued to fall, so that they amounted to less than $20 million (around two months of import cover) towards the middle of 2001; they have been rebuilt moderately since. External debt accounted for more than 70 per cent of GDP, although the debt-service burden was relatively low at under 4 per cent of GDP.

*Inward remittances
in 2000 twice the
value of exports of
goods and services
in Tonga*

Earnings by Tonga on merchandise exports fell by almost 4 per cent (to $12 million) in 2000 and remained stagnant (in dollar terms) in the following year. Some three quarters of such earnings came from squash and fish, whose exports, as well as those of niche-market roots crops, fruit and vegetables, strengthened somewhat in 2001. Merchandise exports, equivalent to over 8 percentage points of GDP, were small compared with expenditure on imports which, although declining steadily from the late 1990s, amounted to some $56 million in 2001. The trade deficit in goods and services, at just over one third of

GDP in 2000, was funded largely from inward transfers, mostly of a private nature. Such resources netted Tonga $43 million in 2000, equal to 27 per cent of GDP, or twice the value of the exports of goods and services.

The overall current account deficit was expected to improve slightly from about 7 per cent to just over 4 per cent of GDP from 2000 to 2001. However, failed investments overseas from the Tonga Trust Fund could have an impact on the transfer account in the short to medium term. Surpluses on the external capital accounts were expected to rise from $0.2 to $4 million (or just below 3 per cent of GDP) from 2000 to 2001. However, the overall balance of payments was in deficit, amounting to the equivalent of 7 per cent of GDP in 2000 and 1.5 per cent of GDP in 2001. Foreign reserves, which had recovered to $15 million by the end of 2000, fell back to $11 million (or just over two months of merchandise import cover) in 2001. Tonga's external debt-service burden was manageably light, at just over 2 per cent of GDP for a total debt equivalent to almost two fifths of GDP in 2000.

Merchandise exports from Vanuatu, which had grown just slightly to reach $26 million in 2000, contracted by almost 9 per cent in the following year. The principal export commodity, copra, was suffering from low external prices, although a new coconut oil mill was expected to add more value to that export production activity. Other important export items, notably beef, timber and kava, also faced weak external demand. Similarly, merchandise imports grew modestly (just 2 per cent in 2000), despite higher world oil prices and an increase in the capital imports needed for public infrastructure projects. Import spending, however, dropped by over 6 per cent in 2001, largely as a result of lower economic activities and consumption in Vanuatu during the year.

Vanuatu's large trade deficit in 2001 offset by a substantial surplus on service trade

The large trade deficit of some 22-23 percentage points of GDP was more than offset by the substantial surpluses on the service trade, which averaged over 29 per cent of GDP in 2000 and 2001. Exported services went up by 13 per cent to $129 million, of which about $56 million came from tourism receipts in 2000; in comparison, merchandise exports earned $26 million in the same year. Service exports would be down slightly in 2001, in part as a result of the appreciation by 7 per cent of the vatu against the Australian dollar and its cost-push impact on tourists from Australia, which was the origin of two thirds of all holiday visitors to Vanuatu. Surpluses in the external current account, in the range of 5-6 per cent of GDP over 2000-2001, were generally more than sufficient to cover shortfalls in the external capital account of $11 million (or just under 5 per cent of GDP) and an expected lower deficit of $9 million for the following year. The overall balance of payments showed a small surplus of just over $1 million in 2000 and an expected surplus of over $4 million in 2001. Foreign reserves of $30 million in the second half of 2001 were enough for five months of import cover. External debt reached just 28 per cent of GDP in 2001, involving servicing commitments of around $1.5-1.7 million over 2000-2001.

Key policy issues

Pacific island economies face many challenges in their development efforts

Pacific island economies face many daunting challenges in sustaining the ongoing process of economic and social development, and not just because of their great isolation from the main trade and investment partners and the often huge dispersal within their own internal boundaries. There are other special needs inherent in economies small in size and with limited human and physical endowments, a narrow resource and production base and a fragile ecology. In several of these economies, inward private remittances from migrants and migrant workers have helped to sustain domestic consumption and investment. But there are trade-offs, too, in the patterns and policies of human resources development, and in the provision of social welfare and safety nets, especially for the resident population and their skills base. Most Pacific island economies have also been the destination of comparatively large amounts of ODA in per capita terms. The general concern is not just with aid fatigue, a phenomenon which can perhaps be read from the declining trend in ODA flows worldwide, especially in the 1990s (discussed in chapter IV of this *Survey*); there are also such ever-pressing issues as effective aid coordination and absorption.

GDP growth has not been satisfactory

In the 1990s in particular, a large number of Pacific island economies implemented a series of economic and structural adjustments and reforms to enhance domestic economic efficiency and flexibility, especially of the private sector. However, GDP growth has not been satisfactory virtually throughout the whole subregion in recent years, as reviewed earlier, not least in relation to the need for job creation commensurate with the number of new labour force entrants and, more generally, for ongoing poverty reduction and human development. Other matters of concern are the rising aspirations and popular demand for improved services in an environment of dwindling resources at the disposal of "leaner and meaner", or downsized, Governments.

Globalization poses more challenges for Pacific island economies

The effective and innovative management of change in small and remote island economies is rendered even more complicated in two other dimensions, which may be complementary but nevertheless require policy and institutional measures and directions of a largely dissimilar nature. One concerns the timely and cost-effective responses to the diverse impulses and imperatives, in particular the higher and more frequent volatility, and the ripple effects and contagion associated with globaliza-tion and regionalization. The highly adverse impact of the financial and economic crisis in East and South-East Asia on several island economies is an illustration of this. The other dimension relates to island countries' own efforts to integrate better into the new economy; this is an economy driven increasingly by rapid advances in ICTs and characterized by new and innovative forms and modalities of industrial organization and management, including by the multiplying nexus and networks of supply and production at both the global and regional levels made possible by the speedy progress of ICTs themselves.

Capacity-building and ongoing learning to achieve enhanced effi-ciency and competitiveness, at both the domestic and external levels, and in production as well as in the process of continuous structural diversifica-tion, is a pressing issue in the subregion. This applies especially in view of the gradual erosion of preferential treatment long accorded to Pacific island economies and of the more intensified competition faced by Pacific island economies; such competition is a result of the upward trends in the liberalization of trade and investment and other financial flows, including through WTO, and other regional and subregional arrangements. A related problem in this context is the recent blacklisting by the Financial Action Task Force on Money Laundering (set up by the Group of Seven in 1989) of several island economies in the Pacific as being non-cooperative in the global fight against money laundering.

Capacity-building and ongoing learning a pressing issue in the Pacific island subregion

It is thus encouraging that many Pacific island economies, with the help of subregional organizations such as the Pacific Islands Forum Secretariat, have been working actively together on many issues of common interest and concern, such as in combating money laundering activities, raising international awareness concerning their vulnerability to global warming and enhancing intrasubregional and extrasubregional trade and investment flows. The endorsement of the Pacific Agreement on Closer Economic Relations and the Pacific Island Countries Trade Agree-ment by Pacific island leaders at the thirty-second meeting of the Pacific Islands Forum, held in Nauru in August 2001, is a concrete example of such cooperation. Both agreements provide a basis for increasing regional and subregional integration and a means to ensure more effective prepara-tion of their economies to respond better to the push and pull forces of globalization. These agreements will come into force once they have been ratified by a sufficient number of signatory States.

Various subregional cooperative initiatives to address common issues

Effective and sustainable external integration is dependent on domestic policy reform and economic restructuring as an ongoing undertaking, and is not a one-off exercise. In turn, good governance is indispensable in this context because reform and restructuring are not free of costs, pain and dislocation. As indicated earlier, profound

Good governance is indispensable for sustained and equitable growth

damage has been caused to the economic base and the social fabric of several Pacific island economies by civil unrest, law and order problems and political disturbances and uncertainties. This emphasizes the need for the formulation of national strategies to promote good governance.

The necessary readjustments and rebuilding of political, social and economic policies and institutions can be a relatively long-term process. Nevertheless, such rehabilitation and reconstruction remain a prerequisite for the restoration of domestic and external market perceptions and sentiments in the economies concerned and more generally in the subregion itself.

Poor and uneven GDP performance has an impact on poverty and poverty alleviation efforts

An acute and chronic lack of reliable, comparable and up-to-date data and micro-level information makes it difficult to gauge the changing patterns and levels of poverty in the Pacific island subregion. From cursory observations drawn from the pace and direction of economic growth and structural transformation in the subregion, poverty may have been on the rise in the second half of the 1990s (box II.4). Aggregate output in several island economies in recent years has not increased sufficiently faster than the rate of population growth to permit any noticeable improvement in per capita incomes and standards of living. The patterns of GDP expansion themselves have also been relatively uneven; boom-and-bust conditions create adjustment problems, with costly implications for poverty alleviation and reduction efforts. Whether temporary or more lasting in nature, mass lay-offs and retrenchment of workers, wage freezes, arrears in payments and so on have contributed to unemployment, hardship and poverty not often seen before in several Pacific island economies. Furthermore, the social and economic conditions and positions of many persons have been greatly affected and eroded by widespread civil disturbances and political unrest, social tensions and persistent problems in law and order enforcement. The serious disruptions in transport and marketing have been particularly severe for those living in the rural areas and working on plantations; their principal means of cash earnings are through small-scale commercial agriculture and fisheries or plantation employment.

Extreme poverty may have been moderated by traditional access to land

Extreme rural poverty may have been moderated by universal access to land by the majority of the people in most Pacific island economies, the so-called "subsistence affluence" phenomenon. Commercial agriculture itself has been an important source of monetary earnings for a very large number of people, through small-scale cash cropping or plantation work. However, a matter of persisting concern is the fact that the agriculture sector has not performed consistently well in most parts of the subregion in recent years. Concerted efforts have been made to improve

Box II.4. Economic performance and living standards in Guam, the Marshall Islands and New Caledonia

The absence of reliable data makes it difficult to determine the extent of poverty in many Pacific island economies. However, poverty levels may be on the rise and standards of living on the decline, given the poor and uneven economic performance in several parts of the subregion in recent years. On average, expansion in aggregate output was insufficient to keep up, or barely kept pace, with the rate of population growth in a large number of Pacific islands. In fact, GDP contracted by an annual average of 5 per cent in the Marshall Islands and 0.8 per cent in the Federated States of Micronesia during the period 1996-2000; in comparison, the population grew by an annual average of 1.5 and 1.9 per cent respectively during the same period. A similar trend was observed in Guam and New Caledonia in the period 1996-2000; Guam experienced an annual contraction of 2.3 per cent in aggregate output, while New Caledonia's GDP remained virtually unchanged. The average population growth was 2.3 per cent a year in Guam and 1.7 per cent in New Caledonia. All these patterns imply some stagnancy or reduction in the standard of living and, by implication, a rise in unemployment and disguised unemployment. Outmigration helps to relieve some pressures from the labour market, but this option is either not open to all island economies in need, or not at the rate and volume required.

In fact, Guam, with a per capita GDP of $16,575, which is slightly lower than that of New Caledonia ($16,973), has seen higher levels of poverty in recent years. According to the United States Census Bureau, the percentage of people living below the poverty level in Guam increased from 14 per cent in 1990 to 23 per cent in 2000. There has also been a rise in the percentage of single-mother households, about 1 in 14 households in 1990 and 1 in 10 a decade later. An allocation of $26 million was made in fiscal year 2001 for temporary assistance to needy families; however, owing to resource constraints, funding for fiscal year 2002 was reduced to $16 million. This could mean a reduction of about 57 per cent in the temporary assistance for welfare recipients, unless additional or supplementary resources are forthcoming.

The Guam economy was in a buoyant state in the early 1990s but this could not be sustained and output, for example, declined by 2 per cent in 1998 and by another 10 per cent in 1999 before expanding again by 2 percentage points in 2000. However, the economy was not expected to expand in 2001. Tourism is the central pillar of economic activities in Guam, and Japan has been by far the dominant source of tourists; Japanese visitors averaged more than 1 million, or four fifths of the total number of visitor arrivals, annually during the period 1995-2000. However, as a result of the feeble economic performance in Japan, the higher unemployment level and the lower yen exchange rate, any significant increase in tourist arrivals from Japan is unlikely. The economic downturn in the United States has been another compounding factor in the economic difficulties facing the Guam economy in 2001 and perhaps in part of 2002 as well.

productivity and to foster the viable diversification of crops. However, progress appears to have been slow, thus contributing to the urban migration of people in search of more rewarding employment and other opportunities. This has added further pressures on the already over-stretched infrastructure and services in urban areas, creating social tensions and other problems. Furthermore, there now seems to be a new generation of people born and raised in urban centres who are largely displaced from their traditional entitlements to land in their villages of origin. The need to generate adequate, gainful job opportunities is self-evident and, in this context, the promotion of activities and services of an informal nature merits reconsideration.

North and Central Asia

Subregional overview and prospects

Driven by consumption and exports, robust economic growth and concerted reforms continued in 2001

The terrorist attacks in the United States of America in September 2001, and related events in the aftermath, greatly compounded the many challenges to the world and regional economies in the wake of the economic slowdown among most of the developed countries, evident since early 2001. Generally, however, countries of North and Central Asia continued the recovery process which had been under way for the three preceding years. The rates of economic expansion in all except two of those economies were in the range of 5-16 per cent (figure II.11), making

Figure II.11. Rates of GDP growth of North and Central Asian economies, 1998-2001

(a) Armenia, Tajikistan and Turkmenistan

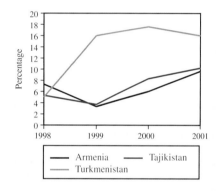

(b) Azerbaijan, Kazakhstan and Kyrgyzstan

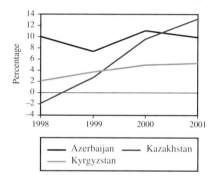

(c) Georgia, Russian Federation and Uzbekistan

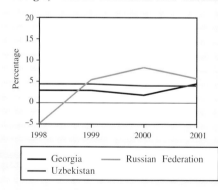

Sources: ESCAP, based on Economic Commission for Europe, *Economic Survey of Europe 2000, No. 1* (United Nations publication, Sales No. E.00.II.E.12) and *No. 2/3* (United Nations publication, Sales No. E.00.II.E.28); web site of the Interstate Statistical Committee of the Commonwealth of Independent States; and Economist Intelligence Unit, *Country Reports* (London, 2001), various issues.

Note: Figures for 2001 are estimates.

them among the fastest-growing in the world in 2001. Such growth was driven by increased levels of private domestic consumption and exports, the latter being boosted by higher prices for oil and other primary commodities, on which most of the subregion was heavily dependent. In fact, for the first time since the break-up of the Union of Soviet Socialist Republics in 1991, most countries of North and Central Asia were experiencing a strong or high rate of economic growth, considerable price stability, more balanced budgets, large trade surpluses and, in several cases, rising external reserves in 2000-2001.

The strong economic performance, in turn, facilitated concerted efforts in policy and structural reforms in North and Central Asia. In particular, more comprehensive tax codes and some simplification of and reduction in corporate income, personal income and VAT rates were introduced in 2001 as part of the ongoing reform process towards a more hospitable and transparent fiscal environment. In addition, improved revenue collection and expenditure rationalization contributed to a more balanced or a surplus budget (instead of an initially projected deficit) in several economies, including Kazakhstan, Kyrgyzstan, the Russian Federation and Tajikistan.

Lower oil prices from the last quarter of 2001 and the difficulties ensuing from the terrorist attacks in September 2001 were not expected to have a strong negative impact on the economic prospects of the economies of the subregion as a whole in 2002. Import dependence was rather low, as several of those economies were able to rely on gas or coal as a substitute. Furthermore, the three net oil exporters, Azerbaijan, Kazakhstan and the Russian Federation, were comparatively less vulnerable to low oil prices than other oil-producing economies elsewhere, as they had accumulated sufficient foreign exchange reserves during the previous two years, when there had been steep rises in oil prices. Stabilization funds were set up in Kazakhstan and the Russian Federation to help to cushion the impact of the fall in world oil prices. In support of OPEC efforts to stabilize oil prices, oil exports from the Russian Federation were reduced by 50,000 barrels a day in December 2001 and by 150,000 barrels a day in January 2002.

Good prospects for strong growth in 2002

Despite the lower international prices for oil and gas, GDP growth in North and Central Asia was expected to remain solid in 2002, given the expected improvements in the economic performance of the major industrial economies and the sustained growth expected in the Russian Federation itself. Indeed, some economies could be expected to benefit, directly and indirectly, from the economic and social reconstruction in, and the more normal relationships with, Afghanistan.

Robust economic expansion of 12 per cent was projected in Turkmenistan; around 7 per cent in Azerbaijan, Kazakhstan and Tajikistan; and 3-6 per cent in Armenia, Georgia, Kyrgyzstan and the Russian Federation. Again, the growth momentum would be driven by the oil/gas and other export-oriented industrial sectors in many of the economies of the subregion. However, agriculture was also expected to be the main contributor to such growth in Tajikistan and Uzbekistan. Those two countries and Turkmenistan have common borders with Afghanistan and could thus be expected to have increased access to world markets for their energy resources through new gas and oil pipelines via Afghanistan.

On the other side, the pace of expansion appeared to have slowed somewhat in several areas of the subregion in the later part of 2001. In addition, according to estimates from the European Bank for Reconstruction and Development, real GDP remained 30 per cent below the 1989 level in absolute terms. Uzbekistan was the only country which could be expected in 2001 to reach the GDP level of 1989. In addition, during the first decade after the formation of CIS, intraregional trade was less vigorous than expected. It fell from $8.6 billion at the beginning of the 1990s and recovered to $8.2 billion in 2000. This was largely due to a less favourable economic performance during parts of that first decade of systemic transition and greater competition among countries of the subregion exporting basically similar items (box II.5). Nevertheless, sustained growth in the Russian Federation, being the dominant economy in the subregion, could be expected to raise intra-CIS trade flows, as in the case of the Russian Federation's increased demand (by 25 per cent) for exports from other economies of the subregion in 2001.

GDP performance

Growth rates in 2001 were among the highest in the world

In general, the economic situation was better than originally expected in North and Central Asia (table II.13). It is striking that the GDP of Turkmenistan expanded by 16 per cent, which was a sustained, solid outcome driven by booming hydrocarbons exports and capital investment. Double-digit growth in the output of industries (about 15 per cent in 2001) and agriculture (13 per cent in the first nine months of 2001) was behind the 10 per cent growth rate in Tajikistan in 2001. Meanwhile, GDP growth rates in the Russian Federation and Kyrgyzstan, for example, were respectively estimated at 5.7 and 5.3 per cent in 2001, compared with an earlier projection of about 4 per cent in both economies. As regards the other economies of the subregion, economic expansion in 2001 was estimated at 13 per cent in Kazakhstan, 9.6 per cent in Armenia, 4.5 per cent in Georgia and 4 per cent in Uzbekistan.

A common denominator behind the highly positive economic trends was rising domestic demand, which served to boost, or keep at high levels, industrial production in most parts of the subregion (except for one economy) in 2001 (table II.13). In particular, Armenia saw the opening of several new export-oriented factories in 2001, including enterprises in the IT sector, with a commensurate increase in job creation and opportunities in the country. Higher industrial production in Turkmenistan (by 9.3 per cent in the first nine months of 2001) was due to the implementation of a

Box II.5. Ten years of market-based transition in North and Central Asia

The subregion comprises 9 out of 12 member countries of CIS, which was created after the break-up of the Union of Soviet Socialist Republics in December 1991. Since then all 9 subregional economies have been in the process of transition from a centrally planned to a market-oriented economic system. The process has been both complex and painful. It involved the adoption of fundamentally different policies; the creation of an entirely new set of institutions, including independent banking and financial systems; the introduction of national currencies; and a complete reorientation of economic incentive structures and approaches to economic management. The consequent policy and institutional reforms have been wide-ranging and have entailed significant costs and dislocation in transition, including a substantial contraction of output and the associated decline in income and employment; high rates of inflation; and greater vulnerability to external swings and shocks.

Indeed, during the 1990s, the economies in transition in North and Central Asia were plunged into a long-lasting recession of 5 or 6 years, with economic stabilization and recovery gaining momentum only from the second half of the decade. In the process, they lost about half of their GDP, compared with the 1989 level. However, the stabilization and recovery processes were then interrupted by the ripple effects of the 1998 financial crisis in the Russian Federation. Nevertheless, considerable and hard-earned achievements have been made on the transition path. Hyperinflation, recorded across the subregion during the period 1992-1995, was largely a result of consumer price liberalization and the monetization of large fiscal deficits. It had led to a complete breakdown of monetary exchange until it was effectively contained in 1997-1998, when formerly triple-digit price increases became more manageable at lower double-digit levels. Such stabilization reflected, in turn, notable progress in organizational, institutional, structural and policy adjustments and reforms among North and Central Asian economies. For example, measures to reorient the financial and banking sectors aimed at encouraging domestic savings and investment included the establishment of a two-tier banking system with independent central banking authorities; the removal of interest rate control so as to allow greater market determination of interest rates; improvements in the functioning of different types of financial institutions; and strengthening of the legal and regulatory frameworks. Such measures were then complemented by the gradual liberalization of the external current accounts, more flexible exchange rates and the participation of foreign financial companies in the domestic market.

North and Central Asian economies have also reformed their tax policies and tax administration, although some have been more successful in this than others. The eroding traditional tax bases, plus extensive tax exemptions and evasions, contributed significantly to the large budget deficits in all subregional economies in the early 1990s. In fact, the persistent budget shortfalls constituted one of the most intractable problems for most of those countries. Subsequently, new tax laws have been adopted to bring about a tax structure that was in greater conformity with the requirements of a market-based economic system. Much progress has also been achieved in reforming tax policies, especially in the elimination of export taxes and excess wage taxes. However, there has been mixed progress in the introduction of VAT, excise tax and personal income tax regimes and in the simplification of the rate structure within various tax categories. Relatively more limited progress has been achieved in the introduction of new accounting systems and standards, the elimination of exemptions and the effective taxation of small businesses and the agriculture sector. Tax administration reform in most parts of North and Central Asia has focused on the enactment of tax administration legislation consistent with the new tax structure. Reform measures have included management and organizational changes and adjustments, the development of systems and procedures and the enforcement and determination of the scope of non-compliance.

Collectively, the North and Central Asian economies have a rather large and growing market, with an area of more than 21 million km^2 (about 96 per cent of the total territory of CIS) and consisting of 218 million people (almost 77 per cent of the total population of CIS). However, the geographical and economic characteristics of this group of countries differ widely. Seven countries of the subregion are landlocked. In terms of size, Armenia is the smallest country, with 30,000 km^2 of surface area, whereas the Russian Federation has a vast territory of 17 million km^2. The size of the population ranges from 3.8 million in Armenia to more than 145 million in the Russian Federation. The second most populous economy of the subregion is Uzbekistan, with a population of about 25 million, followed by Kazakhstan with 15 million and Azerbaijan with 8 million. There are also considerable differences in natural resource endowments among the subregional economies. The natural resource base of Armenia, Georgia, Kyrgyzstan and Tajikistan is modest compared with that of other economies such as Azerbaijan, Kazakhstan, the Russian Federation, Turkmenistan and Uzbekistan; these countries have substantial hydrocarbon deposits, the

(Continued overleaf)

93

(Continued from preceding page)

exploitation of which accounts for their principal export earnings and prospects. The subregion has some competitive advantages in agricultural products and can be self-sufficient in food. In addition, the people of the subregion possess a high level of education and scientific and technical skills.

The natural outcome of the geographical proximity of the economies of North and Central Asia and progress in subregional integration efforts would be that it could help to restore and revitalize their significant economic complementarities. Economic cooperation is also a prerequisite for their economic and social development. The integration process among the CIS countries was initiated in 1993 with the signing of an agreement on the creation of an economic union to form a common economic space. However, progress has been slow as such close integration would require many actions, including the establishment of a common central bank and a single supranational currency; a common macroeconomic and fiscal position; common agreements with regard to the unimpeded movement of goods, labour, scientific and technical expertise, and capital; and a joint budget for common needs, preferably financed through a single taxation system. In order to improve the forms and mechanisms of subregional economic integration, four countries of Central Asia (Kazakhstan, Kyrgyzstan, Tajikistan and Uzbekistan) formed the Central Asian Economic Community in 1994; this was then replaced by the Central Asian Cooperation Organization in December 2001. Three Central Asian economies, Kazakhstan, Kyrgyzstan and Tajikistan, with Belarus and the Russian Federation were also member States of the CIS Customs Union, which was upgraded to become the Eurasian Economic Community in October 2000.

The existing intercountry cooperation initiatives in North and Central Asia, however, still require firm political commitment on the part of the cooperating countries. It is also important that political commitment be concretized through the required administrative, policy and other follow-up measures. The implication is that the cooperating countries themselves have to institute a host of actions to realize the potential benefits that cooperation within North and Central Asia could entail.

massive construction programme covering about 300 new projects. The volume and value of oil output were higher in Azerbaijan (by 5.4 per cent in the first nine months of 2001), largely in response to export demand. In contrast, however, industrial production fell by more than 1 per cent in Georgia in 2001, owing to the delays in the privatization process and weak investment.

Reform-driven increases in agricultural output despite extended drought

Agriculture, another important pillar of many economies in North and Central Asia, grew strongly in several economies despite the second consecutive year of severe drought in most parts of the subregion. The increases ranged from under 7 per cent in Kyrgyzstan (reaching 1.75 million tons of grain in 2001) to over 16 per cent in Kazakhstan (reaching 18 million tons of grain in 2001). The Russian Federation sustained another record grain harvest of 83 billion tons in 2001, up from 65 and 55 million tons respectively in the previous two years. Agricultural output also recorded strong growth in Armenia and, to a much lesser extent, in Georgia, despite some difficulties in providing seeds and other inputs for the harvest of 2001; this was due in part to difficulties caused by the drought.

To a considerable extent, the higher agricultural output and productivity in North and Central Asia were attributable to the introduction of a system of long-term leasing of agricultural land; efforts to improve yields; more stable fuel supplies; and greater financial and market-based incentives for agricultural workers. In the Russian Federation, for example, there was more investment in agriculture as well as better management of

Table II.13. North and Central Asian economies: growth rates, 1998-2001

(Percentage)

		Rates of growth		
		Gross domestic product	*Gross agricultural output*	*Gross industrial output*
Armenia	1998	7.3	13.1	−2.1
	1999	3.3	1.0	5.2
	2000	6.0	2.0	6.4
	2001	9.6	11.8[a]	3.8
Azerbaijan	1998	10.0	6.0	2.2
	1999	7.4	7.0	3.6
	2000	11.1	12.0	6.9
	2001	9.9	11.0	5.1
Georgia	1998	2.9	−10.0	−1.8
	1999	2.9	8.0	5.0
	2000	1.8	15.0	11.0
	2001	4.5	6.2[a]	−1.1
Kazakhstan	1998	−1.9	−19.0	−2.4
	1999	2.7	28.0	2.7
	2000	9.6	−4.0	14.6
	2001	13.0	16.9	13.5
Kyrgyzstan	1998	2.1	2.9	5.3
	1999	3.7	8.0	−4.0
	2000	5.0	4.0	7.0
	2001	5.3	6.8	5.4
Russian Federation	1998	−4.9	−13.2	−5.2
	1999	5.4	4.0	8.1
	2000	8.3	7.0	9.0
	2001	5.7	7.4[a]	4.9
Tajikistan	1998	5.3	6.0	8.2
	1999	3.7	3.0	5.6
	2000	8.3	12.0	10.3
	2001	10.2	13.0[a]	14.8
Turkmenistan	1998	5.0	24.4	0.2
	1999	16.0	26.0	15.0
	2000	17.6	..	25.0
	2001	16.0	..	9.3[a]
Uzbekistan	1998	4.4	4.0	3.6
	1999	4.4	6.0	6.1
	2000	4.0	−1.0	6.4
	2001	4.0	7.7[b]	7.6[a]

Sources: ESCAP, based on Economic Commission for Europe, *Economic Survey of Europe 2000, No. 1* (United Nations publication, Sales No. E.00.II.E.12) and *No. 2/3* (United Nations publication, Sales No. E.00.II.E.28); web site of the Interstate Statistical Committee of the Commonwealth of Independent States; and Economist Intelligence Unit, *Country Reports* (London, 2001), various issues.

Note: Figures for 2001 are estimates.

[a] January-September.
[b] January-June.

land use. A new Land Code approved in September 2001 introduced a system of market-based transactions in agriculture, including the buying and selling of small parcels of land. A programme to break up collective farms and redistribute land in the agricultural sector was introduced in Azerbaijan in 2001.

Inflation

Inflation was higher than expected in some economies

Movements in consumer prices provided a mixed picture in North and Central Asia in 2001 (figure II.12). Inflation has remained a matter of concern to the Governments of many countries of the subregion owing to its impact on their fiscal commitments and on the burden of foreign debt

Figure II.12. Inflation of North and Central Asian economies, 1998-2001[a]

(a) Armenia, Azerbaijan and Georgia

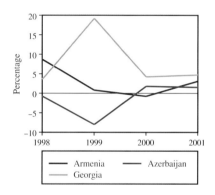

(b) Kazakhstan, Kyrgyzstan and Russian Federation

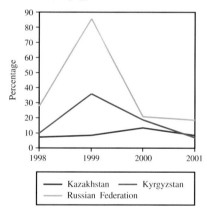

(c) Tajikistan, Turkmenistan and Uzbekistan

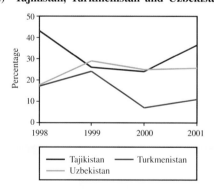

Sources: ESCAP, based on Economic Commission for Europe, *Economic Survey of Europe 2000, No. 1* (United Nations publication, Sales No. E.00.II.E.12), *No. 2/3* (United Nations publication, Sales No. E.00.II.E.28) and *Economic Survey of Europe 2001, No. 1* (United Nations publication, Sales No. E.01.II.E.14); web site of the Interstate Statistical Committee of the Commonwealth of Independent States; and Economist Intelligence Unit, *Country Reports* (London, 2001), various issues.

[a] Percentage changes in the consumer price index.

service payments. In the last four years, for example, the budget deficits expanded or remained relatively high in several economies of the subregion as a result of higher public spending to compensate in part for rising prices and costs as well as poor revenue collection (table II.14). Price increases were in excess of the forecasts, or remained high, in several economies in 2001 (table II.15). In the Russian Federation, for example, higher prices for its main exports and food, tariffs and charges on various services, and money supply growth, contributed to an expected inflation rate of around 19 per cent, compared with the limit of 12-14 per cent established in the 2001 budget. Among the common factors pushing up consumer prices in other economies, including Tajikistan and Uzbekistan were increases in public-sector (minimum) wages and pensions (by some 40 per cent); higher prices for food owing to shortages caused by the droughts in Tajikistan in 2000-2001; and rising prices for and charges on bread, gasoline and public transport in Uzbekistan in October 2001. Average consumer price inflation was thus estimated to reach almost 37 per cent in Tajikistan; it was in excess of 25 per cent in Uzbekistan.

Table II.14. North and Central Asian economies: budget balance as a percentage of GDP, 1998-2001

(Percentage)

	1998	1999	2000	2001
Armenia	−3.7	−5.2	−4.8	−5.7[a]
Azerbaijan	−2.0	−2.8	−1.9	−2.0
Georgia	..	..	..	−4.0
Kazakhstan	−4.2	−3.5	−0.1	1 4
Kyrgyzstan	−3.0	−2.5	−2.6	1.0
Russian Federation	−4.9	−1.4	2.3	1.4
Tajikistan	−3.8	−3.1	−0.6	1.4[b]
Turkmenistan	−2.6	0.9	0.4	−1.2[c]
Uzbekistan	−2.3	−3.2	−3.9	−3.6

Sources: ESCAP, *Economic and Social Survey of Asia and the Pacific 2001* (United Nations publication, Sales No. E.01.II.F.18); and Economist Intelligence Unit, *Country Reports* (London, 2001), various issues.

Note: Figures for 2001 are estimates.

[a] January-June.
[b] January-July.
[c] January-October.

Most other economies of the subregion, however, experienced much lower or falling rates of inflation in 2001, owing in part to subdued pressure on prices in the past few years and, in several cases, a tight monetary policy stance. Consumer prices in Azerbaijan, which had not risen above 2 per cent for the previous four years, fell further to

... and lower in others

Table II.15. North and Central Asian economies: inflation, 1998-2001[a]

(Percentage)

	1998	1999	2000	2001
Armenia	8.7	0.8	−0.8	3.1
Azerbaijan	−0.8	−8.0	1.8	1.5
Georgia	3.6	19.2	4.2	4.7
Kazakhstan	7.3	8.4	13.5	8.4
Kyrgyzstan	10.0	35.9	18.7	6.9
Russian Federation	27.8	85.7	20.8	18.6[b]
Tajikistan	43.1	26.0	24.0	36.5
Turkmenistan	17.2	24.1	7.0	11.0
Uzbekistan	17.8	29.0	24.9	25.6

Sources: ESCAP, based on Economic Commission for Europe, *Economic Survey of Europe 2000, No. 1* (United Nations publication, Sales No. E.00.II.E.12), *No. 2/3* (United Nations publication, Sales No. E.00.II.E.28), and *Economic Survey of Europe 2001, No. 1* (United Nations publication, Sales No. E.01.II.E.14); web site of the Interstate Statistical Committee of the Commonwealth of Independent States; and Economist Intelligence Unit, *Country Reports* (London, 2001), various issues.

Note: Figures for 2001 are estimates.

[a] Percentage changes in the consumer price index.

[b] December 2000 to December 2001.

1.8 per cent in 2000 and 1.5 per cent in 2001. In Georgia, inflation was expected to rise marginally, from 4.2 to 4.7 per cent, in 2000-2001, largely because of higher prices for utilities, food and energy. Kazakhstan was able to reduce its inflation rate from 13.5 to 8.4 per cent between 2000 and 2001, despite higher prices for consumer goods, especially bread. Lower import prices for energy products and stable currency exchange rates helped to lower price increases in Kyrgyzstan to 6.9 per cent in 2001, from about 19 per cent in 2000.

Foreign trade and other external transactions

External trade

High trade turnover and surpluses

North and Central Asia as a whole continued to record considerable trade expansion. However, the growth rates of earnings were noticeably lower than the substantial increases experienced in 2000 (figure II.13). The total value of the foreign trade of the Russian Federation, at $129.5 billion in the first 11 months of 2001, was more than 5 per cent higher than during the same period in 2000. Export earnings remained stagnant at $92.5 billion but import spending went up by 22 per cent to almost $37 billion (figure II.14), primarily on

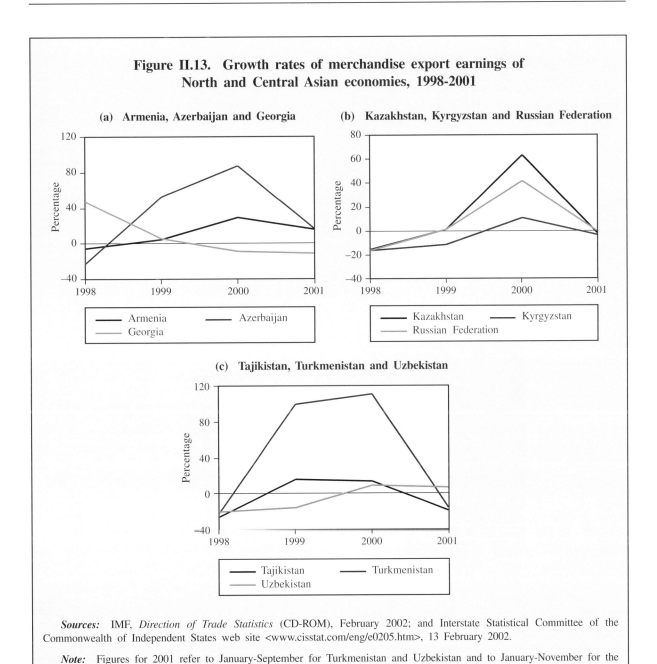

**Figure II.13. Growth rates of merchandise export earnings of
North and Central Asian economies, 1998-2001**

(a) **Armenia, Azerbaijan and Georgia**

(b) **Kazakhstan, Kyrgyzstan and Russian Federation**

(c) **Tajikistan, Turkmenistan and Uzbekistan**

Sources: IMF, *Direction of Trade Statistics* (CD-ROM), February 2002; and Interstate Statistical Committee of the Commonwealth of Independent States web site <www.cisstat.com/eng/e0205.htm>, 13 February 2002.

Note: Figures for 2001 refer to January-September for Turkmenistan and Uzbekistan and to January-November for the other countries.

account of lower prices for the principal export commodities and higher import volumes brought about by the industrial revival, especially for imported machinery and equipment (tables II.16 and II.17). The geographic structure of the foreign trade of the Russian Federation remained largely unchanged, with the European Union and CIS accounting for 35 and 14 per cent respectively of the total turnover of foreign trade.

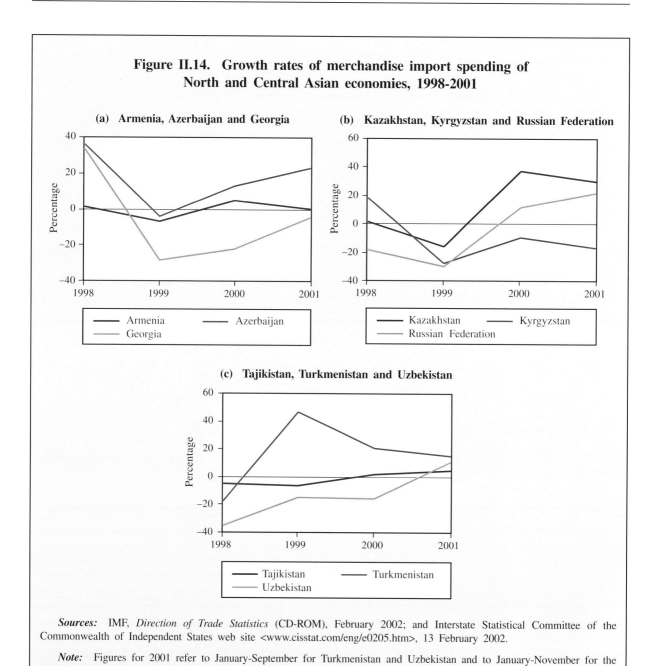

Figure II.14. Growth rates of merchandise import spending of North and Central Asian economies, 1998-2001

(a) Armenia, Azerbaijan and Georgia

(b) Kazakhstan, Kyrgyzstan and Russian Federation

(c) Tajikistan, Turkmenistan and Uzbekistan

Sources: IMF, *Direction of Trade Statistics* (CD-ROM), February 2002; and Interstate Statistical Committee of the Commonwealth of Independent States web site <www.cisstat.com/eng/e0205.htm>, 13 February 2002.

Note: Figures for 2001 refer to January-September for Turkmenistan and Uzbekistan and to January-November for the other countries.

The trade surplus of the Russian Federation was expected to be smaller in 2001 than the substantial level of $69 billion recorded in 2000. The current account surplus, although smaller, was projected to be almost 12 per cent of GDP in 2001 (table II.18). Underpinned by such a favourable level of foreign reserves, the country repaid the first international bond of $1 billion issued in 1996, reduced its external debt in 2001 and raised the funds needed to meet its future debt repayments, which will

Table II.16. North and Central Asian economies: merchandise exports and their rates of growth, 1998-2001

	Value (Millions of US dollars)	Exports (f.o.b.)			
		Annual rate of growth (Percentage)			
	2000	1998	1999	2000	2001 Jan.-Nov.
Armenia	300	−5.3	5.1	29.7	15.5
Azerbaijan	1 745	−22.3	53.1	87.8	17.6
Georgia	330	47.1	6.4	−8.4	−10.5
Kazakhstan	9 138	−15.2	1.6	63.2	−2.2
Kyrgyzstan	502	−15.8	−11.6	10.6	−3.7
Russian Federation	102 998	−16.1	1.5	42.2	−0.1
Tajikistan	784	−25.7	15.4	13.9	−18.5
Turkmenistan	2 505	−21.0	100.0	111.0	−15.5[a]
Uzbekistan	2 130	−20.2	−15.5	9.0	7.1[a]

Sources: IMF, *Direction of Trade Statistics* (CD-ROM), February 2002; and Interstate Statistical Committee of the Commonwealth of Independent States web site <www.cisstat.com/eng/e0205.htm>, 13 February 2002.

[a] January-September 2001.

peak in 2002-2003. Repayments of the debt outstanding to IMF were made ahead of schedule and to the level that would remove the Russian Federation from the list of major IMF debtors. As a result, its sovereign credit ratings were raised by the main international rating agencies, thus enhancing its attractiveness to foreign investors considerably, a striking turnaround from the financial crisis, with considerable international repercussions, of 1998.

The CIS countries, in particular the Russian Federation, remained the main trading partners for most countries in North and Central Asia. Turkmenistan's trade surplus of $87 million in the first eight months of 2001 was attributed to the increased export of hydrocarbons to the CIS countries. Those economies also accounted for about 57 per cent of the total trade turnover and 78 per cent of the total import expenditure of Tajikistan in the first 11 months of 2001. Its export earnings were expected to be smaller in 2001 as a slump in cotton and aluminium prices offset an increase in export volumes. At the same time, higher import expenditure (by more than 4 per cent in the first 11 months of 2001) was due to higher grain imports to meet consumption requirements and high energy prices. In the first 11 months of 2001, intra-CIS exports from Kazakhstan rose by 11 percentage points to reach 30 per cent of total exports, while the share of CIS countries in Kazakhstan's imports

Subregional trade mostly CIS-oriented

Table II.17. North and Central Asian economies: merchandise imports and their rates of growth, 1998-2001

	Value (Millions of US dollars)	Imports (c.i.f.)			
		Annual rate of growth (Percentage)			
	2000	*1998*	*1999*	*2000*	*2001 Jan.-Nov.*
Armenia	885	1.2	−6.6	5.0	0.1
Azerbaijan	1 172	36.0	−3.8	13.2	23.4
Georgia	704	34.3	−28.0	−21.8	−3.9
Kazakhstan	5 052	1.6	−15.7	37.0	29.9
Kyrgyzstan	554	18.6	−27.4	−9.2	−16.4
Russian Federation	33 853	−18.1	−29.5	11.8	22.2
Tajikistan	675	−5.2	−6.7	1.8	4.4
Turkmenistan	1 788	−17.9	46.8	20.9	15.1[a]
Uzbekistan	2 111	−35.2	−14.7	−15.8	11.2[a]

Sources: IMF, *Direction of Trade Statistics* (CD-ROM), February 2002; and Interstate Statistical Committee of the Commonwealth of Independent States web site <www.cisstat.com/eng/e0205.htm>, 13 February 2002.

[a] January-September 2001.

remained at the same level of 52 per cent. During the first nine months of 2001 in Uzbekistan, export earnings grew by more than 7 per cent as a result of increased cotton sales to the Russian Federation. However, the expansion in imports (by 11 per cent in value) was attributed largely to the increased expenditure for machinery and other capital goods from non-CIS countries.

Persistent trade deficits in Armenia and Georgia

In the first 11 months of 2001, non-CIS economies accounted for the bulk, about 90 per cent of Azerbaijan's exports, compared with 87 per cent in the corresponding period of 2000. Such exports were dominated by energy products such as crude oil and gas condensate; Azerbaijan was one of the main suppliers of energy resources to Georgia, whose higher bill for imported oil and gas resulted in a trade deficit of $344 million in the first 11 months of 2001. Armenia recorded a trade deficit of $483 million in the same period, despite stagnant import expenditure. However, the policy of import compression pursued in Kyrgyzstan over the period 1998-2001 resulted in the first small trade surplus of just over $25 million in the first 11 months of 2001, with imports declining to $415 million, compared with $496 million in the first 11 months of 2000. Consumer goods, food and machinery inputs to develop the non-gold industrial sector were the main import items, while gold and electricity were the largest sources of export revenue.

Table II.18. North and Central Asian economies: current account balance as a percentage of GDP, 1998-2001

(Percentage)

	1998	1999	2000	2001
Armenia	−21.3	−16.6	−14.7	−13.4
Azerbaijan	−30.7	−13.3	−3.4	−5.4
Georgia	−11.4	−6.9	−5.6	−8.2
Kazakhstan	−5.5	−1.4	5.9	−4.5
Kyrgyzstan	−23.2	−15.1	−7.7	−3.5
Russian Federation	0.3	13.4	18.4	11.7
Tajikistan	−9.1	1.6	−6.3	−7.8
Turkmenistan	−33.0	−26.0	2.3	−3.7
Uzbekistan	−0.7	−1.0	−0.3	−1.9

Sources: ESCAP, *Economic and Social Survey of Asia and the Pacific 2001* (United Nations publication, Sales No. E.01.II.F.18); Economic Commission for Europe, *Economic Survey of Europe 2001, No. 1* (United Nations publication, Sales No. E.01.II.E.14); and Economist Intelligence Unit, *Country Reports* (London, 2001), various issues.

Note: Figures for 2001 are estimates.

Exchange rate developments

Given the volatility of the currency and financial markets, effective management of the exchange rate remained important in North and Central Asia, a subregion under market-based economic transition and heavily dependent on exports and external resources. The Russian Federation, for example, had run a huge trade surplus (as indicated earlier) owing to high oil and other commodity prices in the previous two years. The expanded monetary base contributed to rising domestic prices and appreciation of the rouble, whose floating exchange rate then depreciated slightly (from 28.9 roubles to the dollar in April 2001 to more than 30 to the dollar in December 2001) along with lower oil prices and a trade surplus. Kazakhstan depreciated the tenge exchange rate from 88 to just under 148 to the dollar between April and September 2001 to keep its exports competitive, among other reasons (figure II.15).

The national currencies of Armenia and Georgia fell only marginally, with the Georgian lari registering the lowest-ever rate of depreciation (from 2.08 to 2.10 to the dollar). The currencies of Azerbaijan, Kyrgyzstan and Tajikistan were relatively stable in 2001 owing to strong economic growth and tight monetary policies. A large inflow of hard currency from gas exports helped to stabilize the exchange rate of the manat in Turkmenistan, although the multiple exchange rate system remained in place in 2001. Uzbekistan introduced a number of policy

Relatively stable exchange rates in 2001 compared with earlier years

103

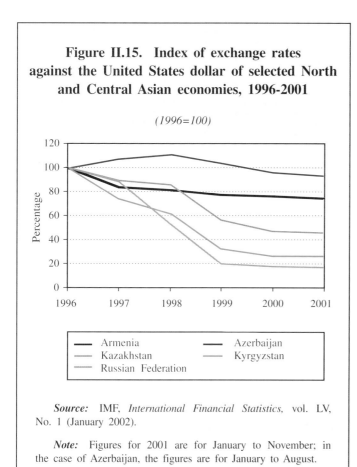

Figure II.15. Index of exchange rates against the United States dollar of selected North and Central Asian economies, 1996-2001

(1996=100)

— Armenia
— Kazakhstan
— Russian Federation
— Azerbaijan
— Kyrgyzstan

Source: IMF, *International Financial Statistics,* vol. LV, No. 1 (January 2002).

Note: Figures for 2001 are for January to November; in the case of Azerbaijan, the figures are for January to August.

measures to relax currency control for both foreign investors and national businesses in 2001 in order to liberalize the foreign currency market gradually. Among these were the introduction of a new exchange rate for exporters and foreign investors, the abolition of tax on repatriated hard-currency earnings and the exemption of SMEs from the surrender rate. While foreign investors could convert their profit from Uzbek soms into the hard currencies at the new exchange rate without paying the 5 per cent commission, exporters still had to sell a minimum of 50 per cent of their hard-currency earnings to the Government; Uzbekistan thus continued to rely on the multiple exchange rate system, and the exchange rate of the som was adjusted downwards from 433.7 to 680.9 to the dollar in November 2001, so as to better reflect the rates in the so-called parallel market as well as to boost exports. However, the som did not become fully convertible in 2001, as had been planned.

Ongoing trade reforms

Further trade liberalization for WTO accession

Countries in North and Central Asia continued to pursue further trade liberalization measures in 2001 in order to join WTO, with the ensuing enlarged access to global trade and financial markets that such accession was expected to bring about in the long run. The Russian Federation, for example, introduced a new set of draft laws on customs, protectionism, import tariffs and State subsidies to industry and agriculture; additional amendments to the tax and customs codes were made to align the existing legislation with WTO standards and requirements. At the same time, the further reforms in the banking sector required by WTO were also implemented for accession purposes, as well as to enable the domestic banks to stand up to foreign competition and serve as engines of economic growth. Concerted efforts were also made in other countries of the subregion with regard to accession to WTO. One of the main difficulties for Kazakhstan was the downward adjustment of local tariffs on commodities to bring them into line with those set by WTO. Several elements in the legal framework and regulatory environment of Armenia were being amended or modified for the same process and purpose.

Key policy issues

The reform agenda in the countries of North and Central Asia remained extensive, encompassing both policy and structural elements. A variety of measures were implemented in 2000-2001 to stimulate investment in countries of the subregion; among these were the restoration and maintenance of macroeconomic and financial stability; the simplification of taxes and customs duties; the provision of better fiscal incentives; and the adjustment of other regulations to ensure greater transparency and conformity with international business norms. As was to be expected, however, the reform process was far from complete; among the most important items on the reform agenda were the ongoing improvements in the investment and business climate and in external debt management, and the deepening of structural adjustments and further social sector reforms.

An extensive agenda for continued reform

Foreign investment

Kazakhstan and the Russian Federation remained by far the major recipients of FDI in 2001; the Russian Federation received almost $2.9 billion in the first nine months of 2001, or about the same (year on year) as the 2000 level. Kazakhstan was the host economy for $1.2 billion in 2000 and FDI inflows rose by just over $0.9 billion in the first quarter of 2001. The improved credit ratings of the Russian Federation, in consequence of timely debt repayments, were noted earlier. In addition, a new law to crack down on money laundering was adopted in 2001 to bring the current legislation closer to international standards. Kazakhstan experienced a significant improvement in its external liquidity; it was also accorded higher credit ratings on sovereign debt and the successful capital amnesty programme induced a return flow of some $480 million in June July 2001.

Higher inflows to some economies

Typically, however, FDI inflows remained comparatively low and volatile in several other countries of the subregion. In net terms, for example, such investment accounted for 2.6 per cent of the GDP of Azerbaijan in 2000 and about 9 per cent of total investment in Turkmenistan in the first half of 2001. In this context, the economic strategy of Turkmenistan over 2000-2010 had envisaged extensive State-led investment to be supported by foreign resource inflows and hard-currency earnings from increased gas exports. The manufacturing industry was to be expanded through the implementation of import-substituting industrialization, while the modernization of domestic infrastructure was expected to improve the generation and distribution of electricity to meet the growing demand from the industrial sector.

... but FDI remained small in most parts of the subregion

FDI flows to Azerbaijan declined on a year-on-year basis by 76 per cent in the first quarter of 2001 and those to Armenia (at about $51 million) fell off by 36 per cent in the first half of 2001. Armenia had made considerable progress in stabilizing its economy in the previous five years, when GDP had grown by an average of 4-5 per cent. However, it remained heavily dependent on external resources, including foreign aid, owing to low levels of tax collection and a high incidence of poverty. Another area of concern was the need to improve corporate governance in order to create a business environment that would be more attractive to foreign investors. Given the advantage of the country's highly skilled workforce, high-tech and high value-added activities, such as diamond cutting and IT, tourism, metallurgy and food processing, could provide future opportunities for foreign investors in Armenia. In the past two years, FDI inflows fell in Kyrgyzstan (by 20 per cent), owing in part to high (bureaucratic) transaction costs and inadequate legislation to protect investors' interests. Tajikistan was expected to attract about $20 million in FDI in 2001, or one third lower than the level in 2000.

Foreign debt

High and, often, rising debt stock

External debt management remained another issue of considerable policy concern in North and Central Asia. Foreign resources were needed not just to stimulate more broad-based economic growth but also to underwrite and backstop reforms in the State sectors, including pension and social security systems, housing and health care, and State enterprises. The external debt stock, which had increased in all countries of the subregion, except one, in the past several years, was over 200 per cent of export earnings in Tajikistan and Turkmenistan in 1998 and in Kazakhstan in 1999. The debt-to-exports ratio in Kazakhstan fell sharply to 37 per cent in 2000 but remained high in Tajikistan and Turkmenistan in 2001. In Kyrgyzstan, foreign debt (estimated at $1.4 billion in September 2001) was equivalent to 98 per cent of GDP. However, external debt was expected to be cut by almost one half (from 137 to 72 per cent of GDP between 2000 and 2010) owing to increased exports, new FDI and the development of the communications, energy and tourism sectors.

Debt reduction and rescheduling arrangements made in several countries

Strong economic growth in Tajikistan in 2001 owed much to a strengthened fiscal system and effective and extensive structural reforms in agriculture. However, sustained growth was likely to be constrained somewhat by weak governance and the external debt burden. A debt-reduction strategy was being developed and implemented with assistance from IMF, its main components being better monitoring of the debt burden, greater resource mobilization and expenditure streamlining through budgetary measures, the ongoing restructuring of bilateral debt and the encouragement of debt-for-equity swaps. In addition, part of the proceeds from privatization would be set aside for debt reduction. The foreign debt of Georgia to the Paris Club totalled $922 million in 2001. However, the proceeds for debt reduction from the privatization programme were lower than expected, with the result that agreement on the rescheduling (particularly of debt related to the energy sector) had to be reached with the main international creditors; the rescheduling was for a period of 15 years and payment would begin in 3 years. The total foreign debt of Armenia was largely the same, $840 million in 2000 and $839 million in the first half of 2001. Azerbaijan had a low ratio of external debt to exports in 2001.

Structural reform

Another key policy priority in North and Central Asia has been embodied in a wide-ranging programme of industrial restructuring and privatization of natural monopolies designed to introduce free-market prices and greater competition into sectors where the Government continued to play a leading role. In particular, the unified system of electric power generation in the Russian Federation was expected to be split up, through privatization, into five or seven competing electricity generation companies while the State-backed gas giant, Gazprom, was to be divided into separate production and transport units. More generally, the ongoing reform of communal services and utilities in the Russian Federation envisaged the redistribution of subsidies from the inefficient providers of heat, power and housing to poor families. It was expected to be the most difficult step in reform undertaken since the liberalization of consumer prices in January 1992 and the subsequent period of hyperinflation in the country.

Concerted efforts made in restructuring natural monopolies but with mixed results

International tenders were called to privatize four electricity distribution networks in Armenia in 2001, although the transactions were not finalized owing to the excessively restrictive conditions set for the tenders. This had implications for the release of some IMF credit, which was contingent on the successful completion of this component of the privatization programme. Partly as a result of this, the fiscal deficit amounted to over 5 per cent of GDP in 2001. Concerted efforts were also made in Georgia to expedite privatization and create favourable tax conditions so as to boost small businesses for greater employment generation, including in the industrial sector, in 2001. Nevertheless, owing to the lack of interest from foreign companies, privatization revenue had been lower than anticipated in the budget and there was also a concurrent fiscal revenue shortfall. This contributed to a postponement of IMF credit disbursement to help to bridge the budget deficit, estimated at 4 per cent of GDP in 2001.

Elsewhere in North and Central Asia, the strong economic growth and low inflation in Azerbaijan reflected the ongoing structural reform process, improved governance and the abolition of subsidies to the inefficient energy sector. Indeed, the private sector had started to play a leading role in agriculture with the sale of 96 per cent of State-owned and collective farms and their assets in 2001. During the year, Kazakhstan successfully completed the first phase of its strategic plan for the period 1999-2030, an achievement facilitated by the buoyant oil and gas sector and increased capacity of new pipelines, plus improved agricultural performance through the introduction of further market-based reforms.

Ongoing reform of State-owned enterprises in industry and agriculture alongside the promotion of private business, and small enterprises in particular

However, high levels of inter-enterprise payment arrears and debt persisted as a result of inadequate industrial restructuring, including within the State-owned enterprise sector. Attention was also to be directed to the social sphere to ensure the creation of more jobs, lower the incidence of poverty and increase social benefits.

Kyrgyzstan remained vulnerable to external shocks, as privatization and the restructuring of State-owned enterprises had slowed since the completion of its privatization programme on small-scale enterprises. In 2001, the State-owned electricity company was restructured and split into a number of joint-stock companies for domestic and external distribution and sale of the energy. Among other priorities were the restoration and maintenance of macroeconomic and price stability, continuing administrative reform, external debt reduction, the development of the small business sector and the provision of support to small towns for employment generation and poverty reduction. Meanwhile, Tajikistan completed its privatization programme for SMEs and embarked on the disposal of large State-owned enterprises. Uzbekistan made moderate progress with privatization in 2001.

Short- and long-term remedial measures for the adverse social consequences of economic transition

An important social issue concerned living standards, which had declined in virtually all parts of the subregion as a result of the adverse ripple effects of the transition process, including a substantial reduction in real wages and increased unemployment and under-employment. Indeed, unemployment remained high in Armenia, Georgia and the Russian Federation in the middle of 2001, whereas unemployment rates varied from just over 1 per cent of the workforce in Azerbaijan to some 4 per cent in Kazakhstan. Consequently, countries of North and Central Asia were classified, in the UNDP *Human Development Report 2001,* as having a medium human development index. The Russian Federation was ranked fifty-fifth out of 162 countries in terms of income, health care, life expectancy and education level, while the others were placed between Armenia (ranked seventy second) and Tajikistan (ranked hundred and third).

In the above context, a 10-year strategic plan, as well as a medium-term plan (up to 2004), for the social and economic development of the Russian Federation were adopted in 2001. The projected increases in per capita incomes would boost the country's middle class from 20-25 to 50-55 per cent of the population and would reduce the proportion of people living in poverty considerably. The increase in the size of the middle class was expected to be driven by the development of small business enterprises; measures have already been initiated to reduce taxes and red tape and simplify tax regulations and payment methods so as to expand the small business sector in the country. In Kyrgyzstan, a 3-year poverty reduction strategy was approved as the initial phase of a 10-year programme which envisaged a real annual GDP growth rate of 5 per cent, and a reduction in the number of persons living in poverty in the country by one half.

South and South-West Asia

Subregional overview and prospects

The rates of GDP growth declined in most subregional economies in 2001, India being the only exception (figure II.16).[2] This less favourable trend in economic performance in the subregion reflected the combined impact of a variety of conditions and forces which became less conducive to sustained expansion. The external factors included a slowing world economy, lower prices for energy products, the aftermath of the terrorist attacks in the United States and severe capital outflows. Poorer agricultural production and civil unrest were also contributing factors in some economies. The net result was an economic slowdown which was particularly sharp in Turkey and, to a much lesser extent, in Sri Lanka in 2001. The slowdown was modest in the Islamic Republic of Iran (half a percentage point) and Pakistan (just over 1 percentage point).

Aggregate output slowed and contracted, except in India

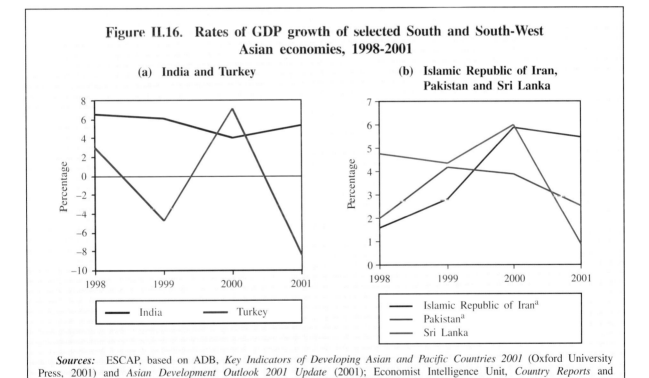

Figure II.16. Rates of GDP growth of selected South and South-West Asian economies, 1998-2001

(a) India and Turkey

(b) Islamic Republic of Iran, Pakistan and Sri Lanka

Sources: ESCAP, based on ADB, *Key Indicators of Developing Asian and Pacific Countries 2001* (Oxford University Press, 2001) and *Asian Development Outlook 2001 Update* (2001); Economist Intelligence Unit, *Country Reports* and *Country Forecasts* (London, 2001), various issues; and national sources.

Note: Figures for 2001 are estimates.

[a] Real GDP at factor cost.

---

[2] The least developed countries of the subregion, i.e. Bangladesh, Bhutan, Nepal and Maldives are discussed under the Asian least developed countries section of the chapter.

Exceptionally, however, economic expansion was sustained in India with a substantial increase in GDP growth, from 4.0 per cent in 2000 to 5.4 per cent in 2001.

Agriculture and agro-based exports have played an important role in income and employment generation, and hence poverty reduction, in most parts of South and South-West Asia; relative and absolute poverty was heavily concentrated in the rural sectors of the subregion. Lower external demand resulted in falling prices and reduced export earnings for several commodities and agricultural products in 2001. At the same time, the agriculture sector in most subregional economies remained susceptible to the vagaries of weather, thus exposing aggregate production and employment and, by implication, poverty reduction efforts and achievements to uncontrollable and unpredictable exogenous forces, including through the forward linkages of agriculture to industries and services.

Inflation on an upward trend and at double-digit rates in several countries

Inflation was another matter of some concern in 2001 (figure II.17). Consumer prices went up across the region and, in addition, the rate of increase was at the double-digit level in the Islamic Republic of Iran and Sri Lanka (in the range of 12-13 per cent) and Turkey (65 per cent). Inflation, however, remained moderate in absolute terms in India and

Figure II.17. Inflation of selected South and South-West Asian economies, 1998-2001[a]

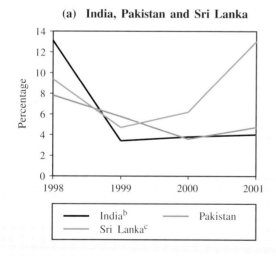

(a) India, Pakistan and Sri Lanka

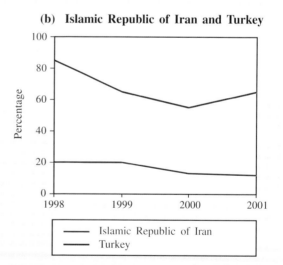

(b) Islamic Republic of Iran and Turkey

Sources: ESCAP, based on ADB, *Key Indicators of Developing Asian and Pacific Countries 2001* (Oxford University Press, 2001); IMF, *International Financial Statistics,* vol. LIV, No. 10 (October 2001); Economist Intelligence Unit, *Country Reports* and *Country Profiles* (London, 2001), various issues; and national sources.

Note: Figures for 2001 are estimates.

[a]   Changes in the consumer price index.
[b]   Consumer price index for industrial workers.
[c]   Colombo only.

Pakistan (around 4-5 per cent). As can be expected, such movements in prices embodied the interactive influences of both cost-push and demand-pull factors.

Several currencies suffered from a large depreciation, with the Turkish lira losing almost half of its exchange value relative to the dollar early in 2001; the rates of depreciation were in the range of 18-20 per cent in Pakistan and Sri Lanka. Other factors included the lagged effects from earlier adjustments in the prices and charges for energy and other basic services in several countries. Money supply (M2) expanded sharply in Turkey and, to a much lesser extent, in the Islamic Republic of Iran; this was mainly a reflection of the economic crisis in Turkey and large external surpluses and higher foreign reserves in the Islamic Republic of Iran. Another factor behind the revealed trends in inflation was the persistence, virtually across the subregion, of relatively large budget deficits and the associated debt-service burdens and other implications for resource allocations. These will be discussed at some length in connection with an examination of major policy issues in South and South-West Asia.

Poorer trade performance was an important factor that dampened aggregate economic activities in the subregion in 2001, a development which provided a sharp contrast to the vibrant expansion in exports and imports a year earlier (figures II.18 and II.19). India, the Islamic Republic of Iran and Sri Lanka in particular experienced a comparatively

Sharp falls in export earnings and import spending in most subregional economies

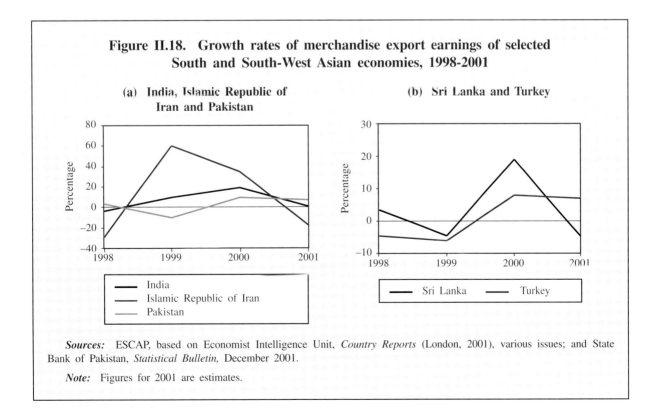

Figure II.18. Growth rates of merchandise export earnings of selected South and South-West Asian economies, 1998-2001

(a) India, Islamic Republic of Iran and Pakistan

(b) Sri Lanka and Turkey

Sources: ESCAP, based on Economist Intelligence Unit, *Country Reports* (London, 2001), various issues; and State Bank of Pakistan, *Statistical Bulletin,* December 2001.

Note: Figures for 2001 are estimates.

large decline or contraction in export earnings attributable to a less auspicious exogenous environment, among other factors. Of the three countries, the Islamic Republic of Iran, a large net oil exporter, experienced the most sizeable reduction in export receipts. Mirroring the trends in GDP and exports, the rates of import spending also decelerated, although much less sharply, in most parts of the subregion. In Turkey, the value of imports was estimated to have contracted sharply by over a quarter in 2001. As a whole, deficits on the trade account improved in several subregional economies, as did the current account balance. Turkey recorded a substantial outflow of capital, while in India there was a turnaround in both FDI and portfolio investment. Pakistan received debt relief from the Paris Club of creditors, while Sri Lanka and Turkey were granted loan packages by IMF for stabilization and adjustment purposes.

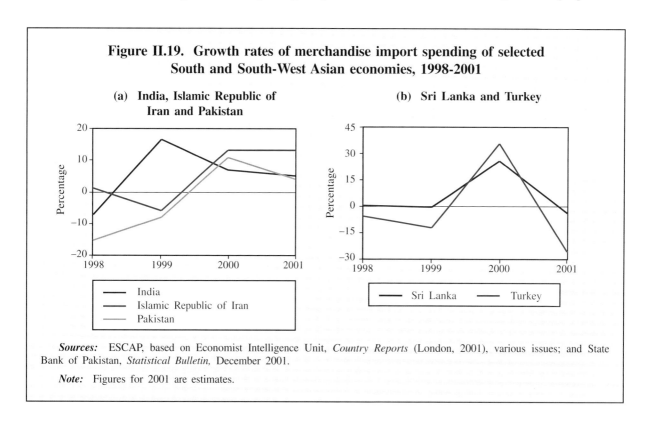

Figure II.19. Growth rates of merchandise import spending of selected South and South-West Asian economies, 1998-2001

(a) India, Islamic Republic of Iran and Pakistan

(b) Sri Lanka and Turkey

Sources: ESCAP, based on Economist Intelligence Unit, *Country Reports* (London, 2001), various issues; and State Bank of Pakistan, *Statistical Bulletin,* December 2001.

Note: Figures for 2001 are estimates.

Reasonable prospects for improved economic performance in most parts of the subregion

The economic outlook for any significant uplift in GDP growth in South and South-West Asia remains uncertain. However, in the absence of a major external or domestic shock, and assuming some recovery among the industrialized countries during the second half of 2002, economic performance could be expected to improve in several subregional countries, not least because of a low initial base in 2001. Another gain in aggregate production would be likely in India, with GDP expanding by about 6 per cent in 2002. Among other stimuli, exports could be expected to recover strongly along with a modest upturn in industrial production, driven by easier liquidity and lower interest rates, moderate crude oil prices, a rise in rural income and increased public spending on physical infrastructure. A higher growth trend in the medium term would be feasible through a sustained pace of fiscal adjustments combined with the implementation of second-generation economic reforms. Higher rates of both public and private sector savings and investment rates, and larger capital inflows for investment purposes, would provide the needed resources for ongoing structural upgrading and diversification and hence for greater sustainability in income and employment expansion and in poverty reduction efforts.

Sri Lanka, Turkey and, to a much lesser extent, Pakistan, did not perform well in 2001 and therefore, GDP growth could be expected to improve measurably in the following year. A rebound in Pakistan's agricultural output, which contracted by 2.5 per cent in 2001, a sustained performance in exports and manufacturing and a less constraining debt-service burden could push up aggregate output by 4 per cent in 2002, via various direct and indirect channels. Nevertheless, the economic picture could be clouded by adverse developments of an exogenous nature, including those relating to domestic and external security and political conditions. There was a contraction in agricultural output (of 2 percentage points) in Sri Lanka in 2001, and a recovery in that sector as well as in merchandise exports would constitute a strong stimulus to domestic economic activities. By and large, GDP growth is expected to be considerably higher in 2002, in spite of uncertainties as regards civil unrest and its adverse ripple effects on tourism and on investor perceptions and confidence. Turkey's GDP is forecast to expand by 2 per cent in 2002, compared with a crisis-induced contraction of over 8 per cent in the previous year. Such recovery is to be facilitated by better or improved domestic and international conditions and circumstances, especially given the expected recovery in global demand and renewed market and consumer confidence resulting from continued commitment to the IMF-backed reform programme.

... especially with a rebound in agricultural output and export earnings

In the Islamic Republic of Iran, GDP growth is targeted at 6.5 per cent for 2002. However, there are several downside risks. First, the prospects for any quick and sharp recovery of oil prices to the upper range of the $22-$26 price band are by no means clear-cut, in spite of the current restraints in OPEC oil supplies. Second, any noticeable recovery in the United States and other OECD economies is generally not expected before the middle of the year; the growth impulses on oil demand can thus be somewhat offset by lower oil requirements in this period.

GDP performance

The slowing global economy and other less auspicious external conditions had an adverse impact on economic and export performance across the board in the subregion, especially in activities and services relating to manufacturing, IT and inward tourism. The terrorist attacks in the United States and the conflict in Afghanistan contributed to heightened security concerns and some restrictions on shipping movements through the Gulf, as well as higher air and sea transport freight rates and insurance

Despite a less favourable external environment, gains in the agriculture and service sectors underpinned India's growth momentum

113

surcharges on most goods and services. Nevertheless, the growth momentum in India was effectively maintained by a significant gain in agricultural
production, from –0.2 per cent in 2000 to 5.7 per cent in 2001 as well as a
sustained rate of capital formation. In particular, the output of food grain
went up from 196 in 2000 to 207 million tons in 2001.

At the same time, the service sector remained vibrant, reflecting
the direct and multiplying effects of higher agricultural production and
procurement activities in a bumper crop year. Growth in that sector's
value added, at 6.5 per cent in 2001, was significantly higher than in
the previous year (table II.19). However, there was a sharp deceleration

Table II.19. Selected South and South-West Asian economies: growth rates, 1998-2001

(Percentage)

| | | Rates of growth | | | |
		Gross domestic product	Agriculture	Industry	Services
India	1998	6.5	6.2	3.7	8.3
	1999	6.1	1.3	4.9	9.5
	2000	4.0	–0.2	6.3	4.8
	2001	5.4	5.7	3.3	6.5
Iran (Islamic Republic of)[a, b]	1998	1.6	8.1	2.1	–0.9
	1999	2.8	–5.6	2.3	4.5
	2000	5.9	3.8	9.1	5.0
	2001	5.5	5.3	5.2	7.2
Pakistan[a]	1998	2.0	4.5	0.3	1.6
	1999	4.2	1.9	4.7	–0.3
	2000	3.9	6.1	0.2	4.6
	2001	2.6	–2.5	4.2	4.5
Sri Lanka	1998	4.7	2.5	5.9	5.1
	1999	4.3	4.5	4.8	4.0
	2000	6.0	1.8	7.5	7.0
	2001	0.9	–2.0	2.1	1.3
Turkey	1998	3.1	8.4	1.8	2.6
	1999	–4.7	–4.6	–6.3	–3.5
	2000	7.1	4.1	5.6	9.5
	2001	–8.4	–2.0	–6.0	–11.5

Sources: ESCAP, based on ADB, *Key Indicators of Developing Asian and Pacific Countries 2001* (Oxford University Press, 2001) and *Asian Development Outlook 2001 Update* (2001); Economist Intelligence Unit, *Country Reports* (London, 2001), various issues; and national sources.

Notes: Figures for 2001 are estimates. Industry comprises mining and quarrying; manufacturing; electricity, gas and power; and construction.

[a] Real GDP at factor cost.
[b] Industry comprises oil; mining and manufacturing; water, power and gas; and construction.

(of almost 3 percentage points) in industrial growth, including in automobiles, cement, metal and engineering. Among other factors, this was due to the inherent lags in industrial restructuring and in cyclical business adjustments, and high transaction costs, including those pertaining to interest rates and energy prices. Indeed, interest rates had become positive in real terms and this contributed to strong growth in bank deposits. In order to boost bank lending and economic activities, in late October 2001 the Reserve Bank of India reduced the bank rate from 7 to 6.5 per cent and lowered the cash reserve ratio in phases from 7.5 to 5.5 per cent.

There was a marginal decline in economic performance in the Islamic Republic of Iran, from 5.9 per cent in 2000 to 5.5 per cent in 2001 and somewhat greater decrease in Pakistan from 3.9 to 2.6 per cent in the same period. The Islamic Republic of Iran was heavily dependent on energy-based industries, and oil prices and export volume were lower, owing to both reduced external demand and production cuts in support of OPEC efforts to stabilize world oil prices (for example, from 3.9 million barrels daily in November 2000 to 3.4 million in September 2001). Largely as a result, earnings on oil exports and the current account surplus fell off significantly in 2001. Pakistan had to endure a very bad drought, and agricultural production contracted by 2.5 per cent in 2001, compared with a healthy expansion of over 6 per cent in the previous year. However, there were offsetting gains in industrial value added (by over 4 percentage points) and a sustained rate of strong expansion in the service sector in 2001. There was, in particular, sizeable growth in large-scale manufacturing with the coming on stream of a number of new plants in automobiles, refined petroleum products and fertilizers.

Lower export prices and earnings, weather-induced setbacks to agriculture and renewed civil unrest dampened economic activities in several other subregional economies

Economic performance deteriorated more sharply in Sri Lanka and Turkey, however. Sri Lanka had achieved a substantial gain of 6 per cent in GDP in 2000, but the growth rate was about 1 per cent in the following year, a reverse attributable to several external and domestic factors. The sharp decline in export demand, and hence earnings, was compounded by weak agricultural production, renewed civil unrest and the associated loss of consumer and investor confidence. In particular, lower capital formation reduced the investment-to-GDP ratio by almost 2 percentage points in 2001 (table II.20). Poorer performance was evident across the board, with value added from the industry and service sectors registering relatively steep fall-offs, to around 1-2 per cent in 2001, compared with an expansion of about 7 per cent a year earlier. The agriculture sector had not grown well in 2000; however, it contracted by 2 per cent in the following year owing, inter alia, to the weather-induced decline of almost 14 per cent (to 1.53 million tons) in the harvest of the main rice crop.

Table II.20. Selected South and South-West Asian economies: ratios of gross domestic savings and investment to GDP, 1998-2001

(Percentage)

	1998	1999	2000	2001
Savings as a percentage of GDP				
India	21.7	23.2	23.4	23.0
Iran (Islamic Republic of)	25.5	25.4	28.5	29.0
Pakistan	15.5	12.3	15.2	14.4
Sri Lanka	19.2	19.5	17.3	17.2
Turkey	22.7	19.9	17.7	..
Investment as a percentage of GDP				
India	22.7	24.3	24.0	24.2
Iran (Islamic Republic of)	24.7	26.0	26.5	27.0
Pakistan	17.1	15.0	15.0	14.7
Sri Lanka	25.2	27.2	27.9	26.0
Turkey	23.7	22.3	24.0	..

Sources: ESCAP, based on ADB, *Key Indicators of Developing Asian and Pacific Countries 2001* (Oxford University Press, 2001) and *Asian Development Outlook 2001* (Oxford University Press, 2001); and national sources.

Note: Figures for 2001 are estimates.

Turkey was facing an economic crisis, causing a sharp contraction in total output

Turkey's GDP fell by over 8 per cent in 2001, an economic crisis triggered and exacerbated by a combination of both supply- and demand-side shocks. The deterioration in macroeconomic fundamentals and the consequent uncertain outlook, especially as regards inflation and the exchange rate, caused a severe loss of consumer and investor confidence, including a massive capital flight on account of the perceived delays and slowdowns in structural reform. The Turkish lira was floated and this resulted in a nominal devaluation of about 100 per cent over the year, leading to higher import costs and more upward pressure on consumer prices. Efforts were also made to pursue a tighter fiscal and monetary policy stance, in part to contain the rising budget shortfall, which had been equivalent to 16.5 per cent of GDP in 2001. This led to reduced credit availability and continued high interest rates. Private consumption was adversely affected by inflation-driven losses in real wages and earnings leading, in turn, to an all-round contraction of demand for consumer durables and non-durables. In particular, output from both the industrial and service sectors was lower by 6 and over 11 per cent respectively in 2001. At the same time, there was a fall of 2 per cent in agricultural production, as a result of inadequate rainfall.

Inflation

Inflation picked up virtually throughout South and South-West Asia in 2001 (table II.21). Turkey had been able to stabilize consumer prices somewhat, with the result that inflation fell steadily from almost 85 per cent in 1998 to 55 per cent in 2000. Consumer prices, however, rose by 65 per cent in 2001 reflecting, among other things, cost-push forces, the substantial devaluation of the lira and the flow-on upward pressure on costs, wages and prices. All these were reflected, in part, by the expanding budget deficit (as a percentage of GDP) and money supply (M2). M2 for example, grew by over 64 per cent in the first quarter of 2001, compared with 40 per cent for the previous year as a whole. On advice from IMF, Turkey adopted a formal approach to targeting inflation towards the end of 2001 and a new law was passed to guarantee the independence of the central banking authorities, a prerequisite for that shift. The base money target remained the nominal anchor for

Another adverse development was the double-digit rate of price increases in several parts of the subregion on account of strong cost-push and demand-pull factors

Table II.21. Selected South and South-West Asian economies: inflation and money supply growth (M2), 1998-2001

(Percentage)

	1998	1999	2000	2001
Inflation[a]				
India[b]	13.1	3.4	3.7	4.2
Iran (Islamic Republic of)	20.0	20.1	12.6	12.0
Pakistan	7.8	5.7	3.6	4.7
Sri Lanka[c]	9.4	4.7	6.2	13.0
Turkey	84.6	64.9	54.9	65.0
Money supply growth (M2)				
India	18.2	17.2	15.2	14.1[d]
Iran (Islamic Republic of)	20.4	21.5	22.4	30.6[d]
Pakistan	7.9	4.3	12.1	11.0[e]
Sri Lanka	9.6	13.3	12.8	11.7[e]
Turkey	89.7	98.3	40.0	64.2[e]

Sources: ESCAP, based on ADB, *Key Indicators of Developing Asian and Pacific Countries 2001* (Oxford University Press, 2001); IMF, *International Financial Statistics*, vol. LIV, No 10 (October 2001); Economist Intelligence Unit, *Country Reports* and *Country Forecasts* (London, 2001), various issues; and national sources.

Notes: Figures for 2001 are estimates.

[a] Changes in consumer price index.
[b] Consumer price index for industrial workers.
[c] Colombo only.
[d] January-June.
[e] January-March.

controlling inflation, with interest rates to be adjusted in accordance with data on actual inflation movements. Funding of the fiscal deficit and the bank requirements for liquidity would thus be kept under strict check, while another trade-off related to discretionary interventions in the foreign exchange market; those would be limited to smoothing operations in support of a stable lira exchange rate.

Consumer prices were on a downward trend in the Islamic Republic of Iran, although inflation remained at a high level in absolute terms, averaging 20 per cent a year in 1998-1999 and about 12 per cent a year in the following biennium. Among the major cost-push factors were higher administered prices of several commodities and services. At the same time, strong earnings from oil exports contributed to a substantial surplus in the external current accounts, over 6 per cent in 1999 and around 10 per cent in 2000 (table II.22). That solid improvement fed through to the domestic economy and boosted both private and government consumption demand. In particular, money supply (M2) had expanded at about 21 per cent a year in the Islamic Republic of Iran over

---

Table II.22. Selected South and South-West Asian economies: budget and current account balance as a percentage of GDP, 1998-2001

(Percentage)

	1998	1999	2000	2001
Budget balance as a percentage of GDP				
India	–5.1	–5.4	–5.7	–5.7
Iran (Islamic Republic of)[a]	–2.2	–0.2	–0.2[b]	–0.2
Pakistan	–7.7	–6.1	–6.5	–5.3
Sri Lanka	–8.5	–6.9	–9.5	–8.5
Turkey	–7.1	–11.6	–10.5	–16.5
Current account balance as a percentage of GDP				
India	–0.9	–1.0	–0.6	–1.2
Iran (Islamic Republic of)	–1.1	6.1	9.9	4.9
Pakistan	–2.9	–3.9	–1.7	1.6
Sri Lanka	–1.4	–3.6	–6.5	–2.5
Turkey	1.0	–0.7	–4.8	1.8

Sources: ESCAP, based on ADB, *Key Indicators of Developing Asian and Pacific Countries 2001* (Oxford University Press, 2001); IMF, *International Financial Statistics*, vol. LIV, No. 10 (October 2001); Economist Intelligence Unit, *Country Reports* and *Country Forecasts* (London, 2001), various issues; and national sources.

Note: Figures for 2001 are estimates.

[a] Excluding grants.

[b] If the Oil Stabilization Fund was taken into account as a component of government revenue, the budget would be in surplus, equivalent to 8.6 per cent of GDP.

the period 1998-2000; money supply growth went up further to over 30 per cent in the first half of 2001. Among the various measures aimed at neutralizing excess liquidity and containing demand-push inflationary pressure was the introduction of government-backed bonds yielding an interest rate of 17 per cent. Attractive bonds were also issued by the Electricity Development Organization to raise funds for 14 new power projects.

Consumer prices had been on an upward trend in Sri Lanka; inflation had been less than 5 per cent in 1999 but accelerated to reach an expected 13 per cent in 2001. There had been cost-push pressure in higher food prices as well as higher import costs; the latter reflected increases in import duties and currency depreciation (about 18 per cent relative to the dollar) in 2001. The lagged impact from upward adjustments in the administered prices of energy, including electricity and gas, made itself felt in the following year. A surge in government spending and increasing instability in the foreign-exchange market (due in part to the widened trade deficit and falling reserves) had taken place in Sri Lanka in 2000. Monetary policy was thus tightened significantly, with the indicative rate being raised an unprecedented eight times in 2000. The prime lending rate stood at 22 per cent in May 2001, compared with 15.9 per cent in May 2000 and an average of 14-15 per cent during the period 1997-1999. Domestic production and GDP growth (less than 1 percentage point) deteriorated noticeably in 2001. However, the upward trend in inflation and a fairly high fiscal deficit reduced considerably the scope for monetary easing to boost economic activities during the year.

Consumer prices rose somewhat in India and Pakistan although, in absolute terms and comparatively, inflation in those countries was clearly modest within the subregion. This was a remarkable achievement, as increases in consumer prices had effectively been contained within the narrow and low range of 3-6 per cent over the previous three years in both countries. Such price stability, in turn, was attributable to modest money supply (M2) growth, relatively stable fiscal absorption (as a percentage of GDP) and moderate increases in the administered prices of essential commodities as well as adequate supplies of other items of mass consumption. In particular, the basic intent of monetary policies in India was to restrain inflation to around 5 per cent while sustaining overall GDP growth in the range of 5.5-6 per cent. In the face of a distinct moderation of inflation in the later part of 2001, the thrust of monetary policy was to ensure an adequate flow of credits to the productive sectors of the economy. Pakistan applied tight fiscal restraints which effectively helped to lower the fiscal deficit (and inflationary pressure) by over 1 percentage point of GDP in 2000-2001. In addition, the State Bank of Pakistan followed a relatively restrictive monetary policy to limit inflationary

Inflation, although rising, was comparatively modest in absolute terms in India and Pakistan

pressure as well as to stabilize the exchange rate; the local currency depreciated by almost 20 per cent relative to the dollar in 2001. A trade-off was higher interest rates, with the weighted average lending rate rising from 12.9 per cent in June 2000 to around 14 per cent in early 2001, and their restrictive impact on domestic economic activities and hence GDP growth for the year.

Foreign trade and other external transactions

External trade

Vibrant trade gains in 2000 became muted, with steep fall-offs in the rates of export expansion in most parts of the subregion

The improved trade performance of the subregional economies in 2000 could not be maintained in the following year (except in the case of Turkey), when there was comparatively lower growth in both export earnings and import spending (tables II.23 and II.24). In particular, export receipts contracted in the Islamic Republic of Iran (by over 17 per cent) and in Sri Lanka (by almost 5 per cent) in 2001. In Sri Lanka, garment exports, which accounted for about half of the merchandise trade earnings fell by over 1 per cent (to $815 million) in 2001. At the same time, the closure of refineries cut earnings on petroleum exports by over one third. Exports of footwear, diamonds and chemical products were also lower, by 8-15 per cent. In 2000, oil had accounted for some 85 per cent of export earnings by the Islamic Republic of Iran. In the following year, the

Table II.23. Selected South and South-West Asian economies: merchandise exports and their rates of growth, 1998-2001

| | Value (Millions of US dollars) | Exports (f.o.b.) | | | |
| | | Annual rate of growth (Percentage) | | | |
	2000	1998	1999	2000	2001
India[a]	44 894	−3.9	9.5	19.6	1.0
Iran (Islamic Republic of)[a]	28 345	−28.6	60.3	34.8	−17.4
Pakistan[b]	8 570	3.5	−9.7	9.9	7.6
Sri Lanka[a]	5 463	3.6	−4.6	19.1	−4.8
Turkey[a]	31 700	−4.4	−6.1	8.1	6.9

Sources: ESCAP, based on Economist Intelligence Unit, *Country Reports* (London, 2001), various issues; and State Bank of Pakistan, *Statistical Bulletin*, December 2001.

[a] Figures for 2001 are estimates.
[b] Fiscal year.

country experienced lower export prices, value and volume, which were attributable, in turn, to falling external demand and OPEC-mandated cuts of over 13 per cent in production quotas. Consequently, there was a lower trade surplus and the current account surplus was cut by half, to around 5 per cent of GDP, in 2001.

The rate of export earnings growth declined sharply in India, from almost 20 per cent in 2000 to about 1 per cent in 2001. Export performance was adversely affected almost across the board. In particular, garments and textiles have traditionally been a major foreign exchange earner for many countries, including India. Their exports faltered as a result of the external economic slowdown and demand contraction in the developed region. In addition, the bursting technology bubble led to a steep fall in external demand for IT products, including software. Such exports were expected to bring in $7.7 billion, compared with an earlier projection of $8.3 billion. Companies in the United States accounted for some two thirds of the total value of export orders from India. In this context, India has made concerted efforts (including aggressive marketing and trade promotion measures) to diversify trade relationships in favour of other Asian and non-traditional countries. Indian software firms, for example, have begun to explore new markets in South America and Europe so as to be less vulnerable to business cycle downturns in the OECD countries.

Table II.24. Selected South and South-West Asian economies: merchandise imports and their rates of growth, 1998-2001

	Value *(Millions of US dollars)*	Imports (c.i.f.)			
		Annual rate of growth (Percentage)			
	2000	*1998*	*1999*	*2000*	*2001*
India[a]	59 264	−7.1	16.5	7.0	5.0
Iran (Islamic Republic of)[a]	15 207	1.2	−6.0	13.2	13.1
Pakistan[b]	10 311	−15.3	−7.8	10.8	4.1
Sri Lanka[a]	6 647	0.7	−0.4	25.6	−3.7
Turkey[a]	54 000	−5.6	−12.3	35.8	−25.9

Sources: ESCAP, based on Economist Intelligence Unit, *Country Reports* (London, 2001), various issues; and State Bank of Pakistan, *Statistical Bulletin*, December 2001.

[a] Figures for 2001 are estimates.
[b] Fiscal year.

Pakistan and Turkey managed to sustain their export momentum, although the rates of growth in earnings declined somewhat, from about 10 per cent in 2000 to under 8 per cent in 2001 in Pakistan and from 8 to 7 per cent in Turkey in the same period. Such traditional items as rice, raw cotton, leather and non-traditional products (for example, chemicals and pharmaceuticals) continued to spearhead Pakistan's export receipts. Cotton products, for example, contributed over $2.1 billion, and rice over $0.5 billion, to the total export value of $9.2 billion in 2001. Turkey recorded strong earnings in automobiles and parts, textiles and garments, and agricultural products, driven in part by the steep devaluation of the local currency. That helped to sustain the rate of export expansion, which was slightly lower than in 2000.

Import expenditure was also declining, so that the trade deficits and current account balance tended to improve somewhat

As noted earlier, the patterns of import spending generally reflected the unfavourable trends in export earnings or economic performance in the subregion. The Islamic Republic of Iran was an exception: facilitated by the substantial current account surpluses in the two previous years, the rates of import expenditure remained largely the same, at around 13 per cent, in 2000-2001. Outlays on imports became more subdued elsewhere in South and South-West Asia as a result of the less vibrant performance of the industrial or service sectors, demand compression measures as part of the domestic stabilization and restructuring package and lower growth in exports themselves. These diverse patterns of export receipts and import spending combined to result in an improved trade deficit position in some countries (for example, Pakistan and Sri Lanka) and a worsened position in others, including India, which recorded a higher current account deficit of just over 1 per cent of GDP in 2001. The current account balance remained or became positive in the Islamic Republic of Iran, Pakistan and Turkey. Sri Lanka, however, managed to lower its current account deficit appreciably, by 4 percentage points of GDP in 2000-2001.

Capital flows and exchange rates

Capital outflows and sharp depreciations in the local exchange rate being experienced in several economies

Despite the global economic slowdown, the net inflows of external capital in India remained stable at $8.5 billion owing, in part, to the turnaround in both FDI and portfolio investment. The country's foreign exchange reserves increased to $46.6 billion (equivalent to nine months of imports) at the end of 2001, despite a higher deficit in the current account. There was, however, only a modest depreciation of just over 4 per cent in the exchange rate of the Indian rupee relative to the dollar (figure II.20). Pakistan and Turkey experienced a decline in FDI, and a sizeable outflow from the equity and debt markets, among other adverse developments. However, a larger trade surplus and greater inward remittances contributed to a current account surplus in Pakistan in 2001. The country's foreign exchange position strengthened significantly as a result of the debt-relief package from the Paris Club. External reserves went up from $1.4 to $4.8 billion between the end of June 2000 and the end of December 2001. Nevertheless, the local currency lost just over 20 per cent of its value relative to the dollar between June 2000 and July 2001. A similar currency depreciation (of just under 18 per cent) was recorded in Sri Lanka, but the Turkish lira lost half of its value against the dollar. Both countries received emergency assistance from IMF, $133 million for Sri Lanka and $3.8 billion for Turkey.

Lower earnings from oil exports by the Islamic Republic of Iran accounted for the smaller, but still very healthy, surplus on its current account (equivalent to 4.9 per cent of GDP) in 2001. A solid foreign exchange position was sustained, with external reserves amounting to $12.6 billion, or 8.4 months of imports, in 2000. The country, however, continued to rely on a dual exchange rate system, one for official transactions at the fixed rate of Rls 1,750 per dollar, and the floating Tehran Stock Exchange rate of about Rls 8,000 per dollar in 2001. The latter rate, which had remained more or less at the same level as in 2000, was to be used for all private and public sector transactions by the beginning of 2002.

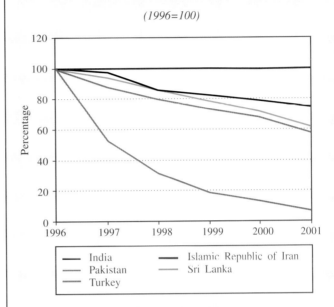

Figure II.20. Index of exchange rates against the United States dollar of selected South and South-West Asian economies, 1996-2001

(1996=100)

Sources: IMF, *International Financial Statistics*, vol. LV, No. 1 (January 2002); and *Far Eastern Economic Review*, various issues.

Note: Figures for 2001 are estimates. In the case of the Islamic Republic of Iran, the figures are for January to November.

Foreign debt

Concerted efforts continued to be made by subregional economies in 2001 to improve their external debt situation. India has made considerable achievements in reducing short-term debt and increasing non-debt-creating capital inflows. As a result, the level of external indebtedness, consisting of short- and long-term liabilities on government and non-government accounts, was reduced to about 20 per cent of GDP in 2001, compared with about 23 per cent in 1998; it is expected to remain at that level in the future. The ratio of debt servicing to gross receipts of the external current account also went down, from 35 to just over 10 per cent, between 1990 and 2001.

Notable achievements by India in reducing the external debt service burden; Pakistan successful in debt-rescheduling negotiations; Turkey receiving emergency assistance from IMF

Pakistan faced a serious external debt situation in 2001, with the debt-to-GDP ratio standing at over 44 per cent. However, it was successful in debt-rescheduling negotiations with creditors both within and outside the Paris Club. In consequence, the debt-service ratio was brought down from 20 per cent of export earnings in 1999 to 17.5 per cent in 2001. Continuous and heavy foreign borrowings by the public and private sectors in Turkey had led to a steady increase in external debt, which, at over $117 billion at the end of fiscal year 2000, was equivalent to 56 per cent of GDP. About half of that debt was incurred by the private sector, which had been a major source of debt accumulation since 1996, a trend facilitated by the liberalization of current and capital account transactions since 1989. By comparison, over 90 per cent of external debt was government-owned or government-guaranteed in Sri Lanka.

Key policy issues

The persistence of relatively large budget deficits is a common concern

A wide range of issues emerged in various subregional economies in 2001. These covered the need for ongoing rejuvenation of the agriculture sector in Pakistan through, for example, extending the irrigation network, improving commodities marketing and encouraging crop diversification. In India, the issues were the design and implementation of a judicious programme of second-generation reform of policies and structures, including those of a macroeconomic nature. Another set of issues concerned policy and regulatory efforts to enhance the functioning of the money and capital markets as well as to improve financial and corporate sector governance, especially in terms of greater transparency, accountability and prudence. Some of these issues were examined in the *Survey 2001.*[3]

The following discussion focuses on another policy issue which has been plaguing most countries in South and South-West Asia for quite some time, namely, the persistence of relatively large budget deficits. These ranged between 10 and 16 per cent of GDP for Turkey, 8 and 9 per cent in Sri Lanka to 5 and 6 per cent in India and Pakistan in 2000-2001 (table II.22). The pressing imperative to reduce the budget shortfall within the subregion has been mediated though a combination of integrated strategies and measures for expenditure rationalization, the widening and deepening of the tax base and effective debt management.

Excess fiscal absorption is an important source of domestic imbalances and expenditure constraints owing to the rising debt-service burden

Revenue shortfalls have been a major cause of macroeconomic imbalances in South and South-West Asia in the last decade. In addition, the persistent mismatch between revenue mobilization and growing expenditure requirements, if accompanied by a balance tilted towards non-productive fiscal outlays, would compound the overall budget imbalances further. The subsequent increases in public debt would crowd out the

---

[3] See *Survey 2001*, pp. 86-87.

private sector if government bills and bonds had to be absorbed by domestic financial institutions from their deposit-based resource. This could prove counterproductive from the perspective of the economy as a whole. Moreover, higher and rising debt-service burdens could reduce the flexibility in public sector resource allocations and render future commitments in fiscal spending more difficult and uncertain. They could also encroach upon outlays largely oriented to poverty alleviation and social capital formation, which are principal sources of domestic economic equity and future stimuli of growth and employment.

Public debt stock as a percentage of GDP in Turkey, at 29 per cent in 2000, was expected to more than double by the end of 2001. The debt-to-GDP ratio was similarly high, at just over 51 per cent in Pakistan and 83 per cent in India during the same year. As a result, interest payments alone absorbed 56 per cent of the total budget revenue of Turkey in 2000, and 39 per cent in Pakistan in 2001, and up to 70 per cent of total net tax revenue for India in 2001.

Concerted efforts have been made to lower the budget shortfall in the subregion. The taxation structure and tax administration systems have been improved, while the one-off privatization of State enterprises (especially the loss-making units) yielded important amounts of non-tax revenue while reducing the level of the public subsidies involved. The divestment programme in India, for example, is expected to yield some $2.5 billion in 2001, of which 60 per cent is to be allocated to the Public Sector Undertakings and the remainder to the budget. Receipts from privatization in Sri Lanka returned some $90 million up to August 2001. Another important revenue source has been mobilized through the imposition and strengthening of the VAT system in several countries of the subregion. Attempts have also been made to streamline and rationalize public spending so as to raise its relevance to, and maximize its impact on, various target groups. For example, a series of measures have been implemented to reduce market-distorting subsidies and rationalize user charges, including those on public utilities and on other items of mass consumption. Self-funding schemes and operations in social security and social protection have also been encouraged so as to reduce public sector liabilities and financial exposure.

Wide-ranging and ongoing remedial measures to broaden and deepen the tax base, ...

A number of pertinent policy measures carried out to address the budget deficits are briefly reviewed below to illustrate some of the efforts made to deal with this issue in countries of the subregion. In India, for example, the range of structural reforms for deficit reduction announced in the 2001 budget included phased adjustments in food and fertilizer subsidies and a further rationalization of the excise duty structure on manufacturing products to include a VAT component of 16 per cent in favour of the central Government. A disinvestment programme worth Rs 120 billion (or $2.5 billion, equivalent to 0.5 per cent of GDP) was also to be implemented; of this amount, Rs 70 billion (around $1.5 billion)

... and rationalize and streamline public spending, including through privatization and divestment programmes

were earmarked for restructuring assistance to the Public Sector Under-takings. Moreover, efforts would be made to rationalize power tariffs, restructure the State Electricity Boards (which have been making huge losses) and dismantle the administered price mechanisms for petroleum products by the end of March 2002. For medium-term management of the fiscal deficit, the Fiscal Responsibility and Budget Management Act, 2000 was introduced in parliament with the main aim of putting a cap on the fiscal deficit, government borrowings and the total stock of public debt. In the recently presented budget for 2002, the fiscal deficit has been estimated at 5.3 per cent of GDP which is somewhat lower than 2001. The deficit on the current account of the budget was thus expected to be eliminated completely within the next five years.

In the Islamic Republic of Iran, oil-based receipts were booming, while non-oil revenue was sluggish owing to underperformance in the mobilization of income taxation and profit transfers from public sector enterprises. Remedial measures included improved tax administration through the establishment of a large taxpayer unit and the pending introduction of VAT as a means to widen the tax base. In Pakistan, efforts have also been focused on broadening the tax base, improving tax compliance, minimizing the level of corruption, streamlining tax laws and strengthening tax administration. In particular, the introduction of a two-tier agricultural income tax and the broadening and streamlining of the General Sales Tax would help to enlarge the tax base. The launching of a tax survey resulted in the issue of 187,000 new national tax numbers, of which almost 72 per cent belonged to persons who had never registered before. This broadened tax base has perhaps been the most important element of the tax reform, which would also serve to develop a tax culture in the country. Moreover, the wealth tax was abolished at the federal level and several taxes at the provincial level, as part of the overall tax reform package, while greater assistance to taxpayers was expected through the establishment of the office of the Federal Tax Ombudsman. At the same time, the recommendations made in two key reports, one dealing with the strengthening of tax administration and the other with new and simplified income tax laws, were under active consideration with a view to phased-in implementation by the Government.

In Sri Lanka, the VAT system was being expanded, various fiscal concessions (reduction or elimination of tax rates) rationalized and the tax administration strengthened. The privatization of State-owned enterprises has been given emphasis as a means of generating non-tax revenue. A substantial cut in military expenditure, further privatization of State-owned enterprises and (public-sector) wage moderation were being proposed under a new reform programme for enhanced fiscal restraint in Turkey. In addition, the elimination of certain subsidies, increases in VAT rates and higher social security contributions were also being implemented to reduce the fiscal shortfalls.

South-East Asia

Subregional overview and prospects

The past year has been difficult for most of South-East Asia[4] with the growth momentum from the rapid post-1997 crisis recovery having dissipated and the biting effects of the global slowdown being felt from the second half of 2000. GDP performance deteriorated throughout the subregion in 2001; the setback was particularly severe in Malaysia, where total output expanded by less than 1 percentage point, and Singapore, which registered one of its very few contractions in domestic production (figure II.21). Countries with the greatest reliance on exports of electronics and electrical products to Japan and the United States were the hardest hit. However, lower commodity prices, particularly for agricultural products and hydrocarbons, and weakness in private domestic demand in some countries were other dampening factors. There was, however, some offsetting impact from the fiscal stimulus packages introduced in several countries, including Malaysia, Singapore and Thailand.

Growth faltered along with weak global demand and the cyclical downsizing in the electronics industry

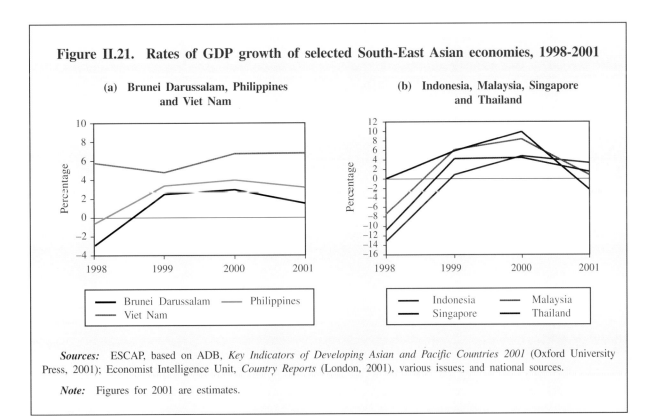

Figure II.21. Rates of GDP growth of selected South-East Asian economies, 1998-2001

(a) **Brunei Darussalam, Philippines and Viet Nam**

(b) **Indonesia, Malaysia, Singapore and Thailand**

Sources: ESCAP, based on ADB, *Key Indicators of Developing Asian and Pacific Countries 2001* (Oxford University Press, 2001); Economist Intelligence Unit, *Country Reports* (London, 2001), various issues; and national sources.

Note: Figures for 2001 are estimates.

---

[4] The least developed countries of the subregion (Cambodia, Lao People's Democratic Republic and Myanmar) are discussed in the Asian least developed countries section of this chapter.

Exceptionally, output growth was sustained by Viet Nam (almost 7 per cent in 2001), but declined somewhat in Indonesia and the Philippines. Among the underpinning forces in these countries were strong private consumption, complemented by investment that was facilitated by low interest rates, generally good out-turns in industrial and service activities and, in the case of Indonesia, better agricultural production. The immediate effects of the 11 September 2001 events on the subregional economies were not entirely clear, but tourism was badly hit and some countries lost export orders because of security concerns.

Economic prospects for 2002 depend on an export revival and sustained domestic demand

Higher GDP growth in 2002 can be expected for most economies in South-East Asia, in part because they will be starting from a low or reduced level of economic activities. The width and depth of this process will depend heavily on clear signs of a strong economic upturn, particularly in the United States and the European Union. These signs were still largely unclear in the early months of 2002, while the economic contraction in Japan seems likely to continue, as discussed in chapter I of this *Survey*. Economic activity in the subregion in the first half of the year will therefore depend to a large extent on the vibrancy of domestic demand and, by implication, investment spending from either the private or the public sector. A vigorous upturn in export earnings, if it materialized, would provide a complementary stimulus to growth from the second half of the year. In this context, the electronics cycle as well as the business cycle in the United States appear to be bottoming out.

Indonesia and Thailand, in particular, will need faster growth to sustain debt and corporate restructuring arising from the 1997 crisis and, as in the Philippines, to reduce unemployment and poverty further. However, GDP growth in the coming year is expected to be only slightly faster, at 4-4.5 per cent in the Philippines, 3.5-4 per cent in Indonesia and 2-3 per cent in Thailand. In Viet Nam, strong output growth is likely to be maintained in 2002, even though external demand may continue to be depressed. Public investment is set to grow at double-digit rates, while private investment is expected to continue responding to improved incentives, including the recent passage of a constitutional amendment by the National Assembly in December 2001 calling for equal treatment for the private sector. FDI flows will also continue to be high as three projects in the energy sector which have already been approved come on stream.

Inflation and the outlook for consumer prices generally benign

Inflation was on a downward trend or stabilized at low levels of between 1 and 2 per cent in most South-East Asian countries in 2001, except Indonesia, the Philippines and Viet Nam (figure II.22). Consumer prices remained virtually unchanged in Viet Nam, following deflation of almost 2 per cent in 2000. Indonesia had been able to cut inflation deeply, from over 20 per cent to less than 4 per cent from 1999 to 2000. However, consumer prices picked up considerably in 2001, rising by about 11 percentage points, on account of the relatively sharp upward adjustments in the costs of several items of mass consumption and some

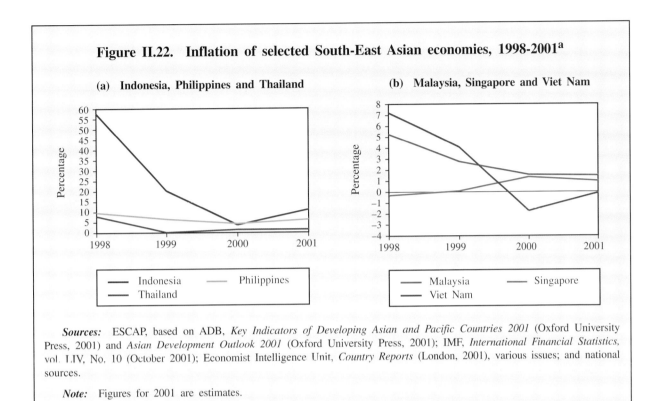

Figure II.22. Inflation of selected South-East Asian economies, 1998-2001[a]

(a) Indonesia, Philippines and Thailand

(b) Malaysia, Singapore and Viet Nam

Sources: ESCAP, based on ADB, *Key Indicators of Developing Asian and Pacific Countries 2001* (Oxford University Press, 2001) and *Asian Development Outlook 2001* (Oxford University Press, 2001); IMF, *International Financial Statistics,* vol. LIV, No. 10 (October 2001); Economist Intelligence Unit, *Country Reports* (London, 2001), various issues; and national sources.

Note: Figures for 2001 are estimates.

[a] Changes in the consumer price index.

depreciation of the local currency. There was also an inflationary upturn in the Philippines, although the pace of change was comparatively modest. Generally, the outlook for inflation remains benign as demand pressures are unlikely to exceed the margins of spare capacity in the near future and labour market conditions remain soft.

The trade picture in 2001 was disappointing in South-East Asia, a subregion heavily dependent on trade and external finance. The rates of export expansion went down quite steeply in all of the subregion and import expenditure followed basically the same pattern in several subregional countries (figures II.23 and II.24). This was a trend driven not only by declining consumer confidence and domestic investment, and the associated lower import levels, but also by the high import content of such major export sectors as electrical goods and electronics, and textiles and garments. The external trade and current account balances remained positive, but narrowed considerably in most countries. Inflows of FDI appeared to have revived and net portfolio investment to have increased, although there were some offsetting outflows of resident capital in a few countries. In particular, countries which tapped international capital markets in 2001 met with considerable success, an encouraging sign of the return of confidence to the subregion. In this context, the stock of official reserves was on the rise or stable in most parts of South-East Asia. Exchange rates were

Despite the downturn in trade performance, confidence appears to have returned to the region

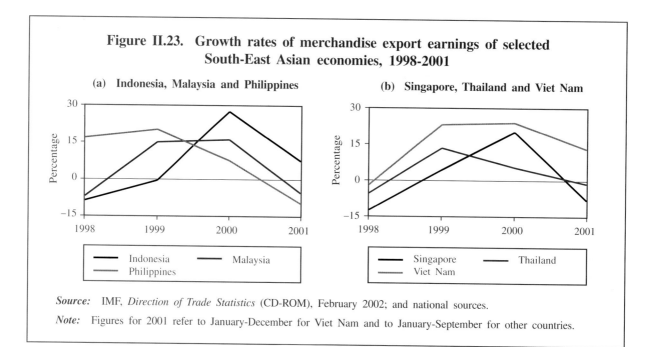

Figure II.23. Growth rates of merchandise export earnings of selected South-East Asian economies, 1998-2001

(a) Indonesia, Malaysia and Philippines

(b) Singapore, Thailand and Viet Nam

Source: IMF, *Direction of Trade Statistics* (CD-ROM), February 2002; and national sources.

Note: Figures for 2001 refer to January-December for Viet Nam and to January-September for other countries.

relatively stable following brief periods of instability during the year, notably after 11 September 2001. Most countries were operating on a managed float or a pegged system. However, the ongoing weakness of the yen and its spill-over effects have introduced a major element of uncertainty in the near-term outlook for exchange rates in the subregion.

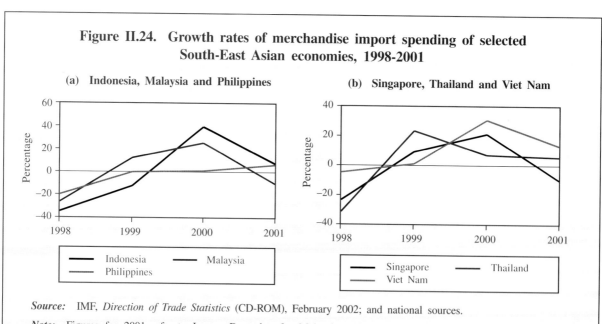

Figure II.24. Growth rates of merchandise import spending of selected South-East Asian economies, 1998-2001

(a) Indonesia, Malaysia and Philippines

(b) Singapore, Thailand and Viet Nam

Source: IMF, *Direction of Trade Statistics* (CD-ROM), February 2002; and national sources.

Note: Figures for 2001 refer to January-December for Malaysia and Viet Nam and to January-September for other countries.

There were some common themes running through the issues facing policy makers in the subregion, among which were maintaining the good progress made on poverty reduction so far, in the face of the economic slowdown and its adverse effects on living standards, and diversifying the economic base and reducing reliance on the exports of a narrow range of products (e.g. hydrocarbons and electronics). Moving up the value added scale by improving human resources and productivity is a task upon which several Governments have embarked. Developing capital markets and tourism are other areas attracting interest. Market diversification, where possible, is also an important goal. No country has gone back on trade liberalization; the ASEAN Free Trade Area was realized at the beginning of 2002, and is to be expanded to include China within ten years (box II.6). Negotiations are proceeding with Japan and the Republic of Korea. Many countries are exploring trade agreements with non-ASEAN partners. Another major policy issue is the outstanding agenda on corporate and financial restructuring, which has circumscribed policy-making and deflected Governments from their poverty reduction goals.

Poverty reduction, economic diversification and continued reform and restructuring were among the major policy issues

GDP growth performance

The global slowdown affected most countries in South-East Asia in 2001, with the exception of Viet Nam (table II.25). The economic setback was particularly severe in Singapore; its GDP recorded the fastest rate of expansion (10 per cent) within the subregion in 2000, but contracted by over 2 percentage points in the following year, a recession termed the worst since independence 37 years earlier. The unprecedented speed and depth of the decline reflected Singapore's growing reliance on the electronics sector, which accounted for over half of its manufacturing output and nearly three fifths of its non-oil domestic exports in 2000. In addition, lower consumer confidence and the consequent decline in private consumption expenditure of nearly 2 per cent year-on-year in the third quarter of 2001 were compounded by a fall in tourist arrivals of over 2 per cent in the first 11 months of 2001, compared with a 10 percentage point increase in the same period of the previous year. Reduced onward travel to other destinations was partially responsible for this. Entrepot trade and transport were also dragged down by the regional downturn. Malaysia also registered a sharp drop in industrial value added, from an expansion of over 15 per cent in 2000 to a reduction of over 3 per cent in 2001. Largely as a result, GDP growth was significantly weakened to 0.4 per cent in 2001, compared with the robust rate of over 8 per cent in the previous year.

Lower export demand and weaker commodity prices had an adverse impact on domestic economic activities in several countries ...

However, there was a brighter note: the business cycle could be bottoming out along with signs of a revival in electronics. In Singapore, for example, electronics-related exports fell at a slower rate in the last two months of 2001 and some producers reported increased orders. GDP also went up by 4.3 per cent over the last two quarters of the year, although it contracted by 7 percentage points year-on-year in the fourth quarter of 2001. Official forecasts for GDP growth were revised upwards to 1-3

Box II.6. The ASEAN Free Trade Area

AFTA was established in 1992 to realize an integrated market of 500 million people. The six original signatories of the Agreement on the Common Effective Preferential Tariff Scheme for the ASEAN Free Trade Area, Brunei Darussalam, Indonesia, Malaysia, the Philippines, Singapore and Thailand, agreed to bring down tariffs on a wide range of manufactured and processed agricultural goods traded within ASEAN, and meeting a 40 per cent ASEAN content requirement, to 0-5 per cent within a 15-year period commencing on 1 January 1993. The deadline for implementation was brought forward repeatedly and those countries realized AFTA formally on 1 January 2002, albeit with some flexibility. Of the remaining members of ASEAN, Viet Nam is expected to realize AFTA by 2006, the Lao People's Democratic Republic and Myanmar by 2008 and Cambodia by 2010.

The key instrument under the Common Effective Preferential Tariff (CEPT) scheme is the inclusion list, containing all tariff lines scheduled for tariff reduction. By the beginning of 2002, 96.2 per cent of the products on the inclusion lists of the six original members had tariffs in the 0-5 per cent range. However, Brunei Darussalam exercised flexibility on 16 items, Indonesia on 66, Malaysia on 922, the Philippines on 199 and Thailand on 472. The tariffs on those items (constituting 3.8 per cent of the inclusion list total) will meet the tariff reduction requirement by the beginning of 2003. In addition to the inclusion list, the temporary exclusion list contains items due to be transferred to the inclusion list and the sensitive list contains unprocessed agricultural products that are to be phased into the CEPT scheme by 2010 for the original members and by 2015 for the new members. Finally, the general exclusion list contains items (representing 1.09 per cent of all tariff lines in ASEAN) permanently excluded from the CEPT scheme for reasons of national security, protection of human, animal or plant life or health, and artistic, historic or archeological value.

The current average tariff on goods traded under AFTA is approximately 3.8 per cent. Eventually, all import duties within AFTA are to be eliminated, by 2010 for the six original members and by 2015 for the new members, and quantitative restrictions and non-tariff barriers will also be eliminated. At the fifteenth meeting of the AFTA Council, held at Hanoi on 14 September 2001, the six original members agreed to eliminate duties on 60 per cent of the items on the inclusion list by 2003, while the new members agreed to maximize the number of tariff lines in the 0-5 per cent range and expand the number with zero tariffs. Viet Nam will have zero tariffs on 35.37 per cent of the items on the inclusion list by 2006, the Lao People's Democratic Republic on 87.6 per cent and Myanmar on 3.9 per cent of the items by 2008 and Cambodia on 7.64 per cent of the items by 2010. The Council also endorsed the indicative list of ICT products under article 6 of the e-ASEAN Framework Agreement on which duties and non-tariff barriers are to be eliminated in three tranches (2003, 2004 and 2005 for the six original members and 2008, 2009 and 2010 for the new members).

At the same meeting of the Council, it was agreed that the ASEAN Integration System of Preferences, under which the six original members committed themselves to extending tariff preferences unilaterally to the new members on products proposed by them, would be implemented on a bilateral and voluntary basis. Several other steps are being taken by ASEAN to integrate subregional trade. Attention has focused on trade facilitation in the area of customs, for which the ASEAN Harmonized Tariff Nomenclature has been adopted, and on the elimination of technical barriers to trade. The Mutual Recognition Arrangement for Telecommunications Equipment has been put in place, and negotiations are proceeding on cosmetics, pharmaceuticals and electrical and electronic products. National standards are to be aligned with international standards for 20 priority product groups, representing some of the most widely traded products in the subregion, and other standards are to be harmonized. A dispute settlement mechanism, largely patterned after the WTO Dispute Settlement Understanding, and covering all economic agreements, has been adopted. Finally, a Protocol allowing countries faced with real difficulties to delay the transfer of products on the temporary exclusion list for a limited time, or to suspend concessions on products already transferred to the inclusion list, has also been agreed.

The realization of AFTA has not prevented ASEAN from exploring closer integration with other countries in the region. A free trade agreement between ASEAN and China is to be implemented within 10 years, with special and differential treatment as well as flexibility for the newer ASEAN members. Similar agreements with Japan and the Republic of Korea are under study. A framework to link ASEAN and Australia and New Zealand under the Closer Economic Relationship Agreement has also been endorsed and a work programme for its implementation approved.

As a result of the successful implementation of the CEPT scheme, trade among ASEAN countries grew at an average annual rate of 11.6 per cent between 1993 and 2000. Interregional exports accounted for over 23 per cent of total ASEAN exports in 2000. In general, intra-ASEAN trade has been expanding at a faster rate than total trade, although the 1997/98 financial and economic crisis and the recent economic slowdown have tended to obscure the picture.

Source: ASEAN secretariat and its web site <www.aseansec.org>

Table II.25. Selected South-East Asian economies: growth rates, 1998-2001

(Percentage)

		Rates of growth			
		Gross domestic product	Agriculture	Industry	Services
Brunei Darussalam	1998	–2.9	2.4	–11.2	6.8
	1999	2.5	–0.1	3.2	1.7
	2000	3.0	..	..	..
	2001	1.5	..	..	..
Indonesia	1998	–13.1	–1.3	–14.0	–16.5
	1999	0.8	2.7	2.2	–1.0
	2000	4.8	1.7	5.2	5.3
	2001	3.3	2.0	3.5	3.3
Malaysia	1998	–7.4	–2.8	–10.6	–5.0
	1999	6.1	0.4	8.5	5.0
	2000	8.3	0.6	15.3	3.1
	2001	0.4	1.5	–3.5	4.4
Philippines	1998	–0.6	–6.4	–2.1	3.4
	1999	3.4	6.5	0.9	4.1
	2000	4.0	3.3	3.9	4.4
	2001	3.4	2.9[a]	2.1[a]	4.0[a]
Singapore	1998	0.1	–6.9	0.6	–0.2
	1999	5.9	–1.1	7.1	5.2
	2000	9.9	–1.5	10.2	9.8
	2001	–2.0	–1.7	–9.5	–0.1
Thailand	1998	–10.8	–3.2	–13.3	–9.9
	1999	4.2	2.7	9.5	–0.1
	2000	4.4	2.7	5.1	4.1
	2001	1.5	1.9	0.9	1.6
Viet Nam	1998	5.8	3.5	8.3	5.1
	1999	4.8	5.2	7.7	2.3
	2000	6.8	4.0	10.1	5.6
	2001	6.8	2.7	10.4	6.1

Sources: ESCAP, based on ADB, *Key Indicators of Developing Asian and Pacific Countries 2001* (Oxford University Press, 2001); Economist Intelligence Unit, *Country Reports* (London, 2001), various issues; and national sources.

Notes: Figures for 2001 are estimates. Industry comprises mining and quarrying; manufacturing; electricity, gas and power; and construction.

[a] January-September.

per cent in 2002. Business conditions in Malaysia appear to have stabilized at the end of 2001 and aggregate production was expected to go up by 3.2 per cent in 2002, a turnaround to be driven by the implementation of several development projects in the first half of the year, followed by a recovery in exports. Malaysia was one of the countries to introduce fiscal stimulus packages to deal with the downturn (box II.7). Falling

Box II.7. Public spending as a counter-cyclical stimulus

Public spending played a major role in sustaining domestic demand in several South-East Asian economies, such as Malaysia, Singapore, Thailand and Viet Nam. In Malaysia, two additional stimulus packages of M$ 3 billion and M$ 4.3 billion, introduced in March and September 2001 respectively, widened the projected fiscal deficit to 6.6 per cent of GDP (see table II.30). These packages had a pro-poor and pro-education focus and were designed to revive construction and agriculture in particular. Among other things, about 1 billion ringgit were allocated for selected rural and urban development projects. Computer laboratories were to be established and 10,000 degree and diploma holders given temporary allowances to learn IT, mathematics and languages. Workers' contributions to the Employees Provident Fund were reduced by 2 per cent for one year, while the current rate of welfare payments was doubled. Growth in private consumption expenditure, which had slowed considerably, revived somewhat in the second half of the year in response to the fiscal stimulus. As is commonly the problem elsewhere, however, disbursements for capital projects have not been made as fast as had been anticipated.

Fiscal policy has generally been conservative in Singapore, where a budget surplus is the norm. In addition, the country's small size and openness tend to dissipate the positive multiplier effects from standard pump-priming measures. To combat falling domestic and external demand, however, two off-budget stimulus packages, amounting, in total, to 8.6 per cent of GDP, were announced in July and October. Their implementation was expected to lead to a budget deficit equivalent to 2 per cent of GDP by the end of 2001, as against an average surplus of almost 3 percentage points in each of the previous three years. The stimulus packages were designed to improve the competitiveness of domestic firms, particulary SMEs, and to increase job training. Improvements to the main university campuses and the construction of new polyclinics and hospitals were among over 100 infrastructure projects earmarked for accelerated implementation. Notably, through the newly introduced "Singapore Shares" scheme, citizens (especially those on lower incomes) are to receive shares that will pay a guaranteed annual dividend plus a bonus in those years when the economy does well, thus giving them a direct stake in its performance.

To stimulate economic growth in Viet Nam, the programmed budget deficit went up from 4.5 to 6.1 per cent of GDP from 2000 to 2001. However, the actual deficit is likely to be 1 percentage point lower than the targeted level, thanks to an unexpected surge in crude oil revenues in the first half of the year and the slower implementation of structural reforms and capital projects.

In Thailand, the new Government's expansionary fiscal policy had a pro-poor and pro-rural focus mediated through, among other measures, the introduction of a village development fund, a health fund and farmers' debt relief. A fiscal reserve fund of 58 billion baht (about 1 per cent of GDP) was set aside for use in case the upturn in exports did not occur in 2002. Deficit spending is programmed to be 3.6 per cent of GDP in the current fiscal year, but owing in part to underspending in the first nine months of the year, public investment was not expected to grow much in 2001. Meanwhile, the projected increase of 2 per cent in public consumption was much less than the 6.5 per cent growth in the previous year. As a result, the main impact of the fiscal stimulus is likely to be felt in 2002. Public debt, expected to rise to 65 per cent of GDP in 2002, is to be financed primarily by domestic borrowing. Any increase in foreign borrowings is being capped at $1 billion; government foreign debt currently stands at $32 billion, out of a total external debt of $72 billion.

Budgetary problems have served to limit the scope for fiscal pump-priming in Indonesia and the Philippines. Government expenditure in Indonesia is not likely to be a sustainable source of growth stimulus for some time to come. Public sector debt (53 per cent of which is external) ballooned to around 95 per cent of GDP in Indonesia in 2001. The projected budget deficit of 3.7 per cent of GDP in 2001 overshot to 6 per cent at mid-year as a result of additional outlays due to higher interest rates and a weaker currency. Interest payments alone accounted for over 30 per cent of government recurrent spending, and principal repayments, another 7 per cent. This added burden necessitated the adoption of supplementary measures in June 2001 to ensure a return to the original projected level and also to compensate the poor for higher fuel prices. A lower budget shortfall of 2.5 per cent of GDP has been set as a target for 2002 and this entails a considerable reduction in both routine and development spending; in particular, fuel subsidies will fall and electricity prices rise further (so as to reduce losses by the State-owned electricity company). The final outcomes will depend on the feasibility of various assumptions underlying the forecast budget shortfall, especially those concerning the economy, oil revenues and receipts from asset sales by the Indonesian Bank Restructuring Agency and from privatization.

The deteriorating external environment has contributed to lower tax revenues than originally expected in the Philippines, which is also struggling with the legacy of large deficits left by the previous Government. The current policy is to restore fiscal discipline so that the longer-term goal of poverty reduction is not jeopardized by reduced spending on infrastructure in the short term. The budget is to be balanced by 2006 through greater tax effort and improved tax administration; this commitment was reiterated in the National Socio-economic Pact signed on 10 December 2001 by members of the Government and leaders of business, labour and civil society. Meanwhile, helped by lower disbursements and declining interest payments, the target government deficit at the national level was lower than forecast: 4 per cent of GDP at the end of December 2001 as against the programmed 4.2 per cent and down from the actual 4.1 per cent in 2000. Central government debt, which had increased to almost two thirds of GDP in 2000, had fallen to 62.5 per cent by June 2001.

demand and prices for energy products also played a role in the declining rate of output expansion in Brunei Darussalam and Malaysia as they reduced oil and gas production and exports. In Brunei Darussalam, for example, oil production had increased substantially in 2000 to take advantage of higher prices for hydrocarbons, which constituted about half of its GDP in that year, when growth reached 3 per cent; this growth rate was halved in 2001.

In Viet Nam, value added in agriculture felt the negative effects of lower rice prices, and the country's remarkable success in expanding coffee, cashew and pepper production rebounded somewhat as the prices of those commodities fell. At the same time, the adverse impact of the global slowdown was transmitted through lower export expansion. Nevertheless, the country posted the fastest rate of GDP growth, at almost 7 per cent, in the subregion in 2001, largely the same rate as had been achieved in the previous year. This strong performance was sustained through vibrant industrial growth, over 10 per cent annually, and service activities during the last two years. Industrial sector performance was relatively broad-based and motor bicycles and automotive products were among the fastest-growing in 2001.

... but in Viet Nam high growth was sustained by vibrant industrial and services activities

Investment spending continued to grow strongly, by over 4 percentage points during the period 1999-2001, to reach 31.4 per cent of GDP in 2001 (table II.26). This investment rate was almost the highest in South-East Asia, just marginally below that of Singapore. It was facilitated by low interest rates and driven by a large increase in the number of SMEs (following the implementation of the new Enterprise Law in 2000) and higher FDI inflows (in response to amendments to the Law on Investment to improve the business environment climate).

Overall GDP held up well in Indonesia and the Philippines, increasing by over 3 per cent in 2001. Indonesia registered a slowdown in manufacturing and export growth, partly as a result of weakened external demand and falling commodity prices, especially for energy products, palm oil and timber. Indonesia has only a small reliance on electronics

Agriculture and services were significant stimuli in Indonesia and the Philippines

135

Table II.26. Selected South-East Asian economies: ratios of gross domestic savings and investment to GDP, 1998-2001

(Percentage)

	1998	1999	2000	2001
Savings as a percentage of GDP				
Indonesia	26.5	20.2	25.7	24.4
Malaysia	48.7	47.3	46.7	44.7
Philippines	12.4	14.3	16.5	16.7
Singapore	50.6	49.9	50.7	51.9
Thailand	35.0	32.6	32.5	34.5
Viet Nam	21.5	24.6	27.0	25.9
Investment as a percentage of GDP				
Indonesia	16.8	12.2	17.9	15.0
Malaysia	26.7	22.3	26.8	25.0
Philippines	20.3	18.8	17.8	18.2
Singapore	32.6	32.4	31.3	32.0
Thailand	20.3	19.9	22.7	26.1
Viet Nam	29.0	27.6	29.5	31.4

Sources: ESCAP, based on ADB, *Key Indicators of Developing Asian and Pacific Countries 2001* (Oxford University Press, 2001) and *Asian Development Outlook 2001* (Oxford University Press, 2001); and national sources.

Note: Figures for 2001 are estimates.

exports and strong domestic demand helped to underpin output in agriculture and services, specifically utilities, transport and communications. Private consumption appears to have been fuelled by inflationary expectations and informal sector growth. Investment spending was down as a proportion of GDP in 2001 and its upturn will depend on the business climate and market confidence, which picked up briefly after the installation of the new Government in August 2001. Further, FDI inflows have not revived in Indonesia, as has been the case in some other subregional countries.

In the Philippines, electronics and electrical products comprised three fifths of the country's exports, 30 per cent of which went to the United States. However, industry constituted just under 31 per cent of domestic output in 2000, compared with a relative share of 53 and 17 per cent for services and agriculture respectively. These two sectors largely underpinned the GDP growth of 3-4 per cent over 2000-2001. Livestock (especially poultry) and fisheries performed well within the agriculture sector, while strong service activities were driven by transport and communications. Personal incomes and private consumption were further sustained by falling interest rates, which also helped investment spending, and by migrant workers' inward remittances, which picked up significantly in the latter half of the year after an earlier decline. All these compensated in part for a sharp decline in export earnings to moderate GDP growth from 4 to 3.4 per cent from 2000 to 2001.

In Thailand, there was a decline in GDP growth, to around 1.5 per cent in 2001. Export earnings had gone up relatively modestly in 2000 but declined in 2001 partly as a result of the global economic slowdown; agricultural production also suffered from falling prices for rice and prawns, among other items. Growth in the service sector, which accounted for over 49 per cent of GDP in 2000, went down noticeably from over 4 per cent to less than 2 per cent from 2000 to 2001. A strong increase was displayed by transport and communications, particularly telecommunications. However, tourist arrivals increased at a slower rate, of just over 7 per cent in the first nine months of 2001, compared with almost 11 per cent in the previous year, as these were affected by the economic slowdown in major external markets. The tourism industry was further disrupted by the 11 September 2001 events, although subsequent signs of a recovery emerged towards the end of the year as tourists switched destinations from other countries in the subregion (such as Indonesia, Malaysia and the Philippines) to Thailand.

The industrial sector, with a relative GDP share of almost 42 per cent, did not perform well; among the dampening factors were the unfavourable external environment and the still incomplete bank and corporate restructuring process. Indeed, growth in industrial value added declined from over 9 per cent to less than 1 per cent between 1999 and 2001, thus keeping capacity utilization rates low (averaging just over 53 per cent for the first nine months of 2001). Private consumption had shown signs of reviving in the first half of the year and lower interest rates stimulated spending, particularly on transport equipment. However, the momentum was not sustained and annual growth in consumption was estimated to have declined from 4.3 per cent to around 2.5 per cent from 2000 to 2001.

More subdued economic activities in Thailand

Inflation

Consumer prices stabilized at relatively low rates in Malaysia, Singapore and Thailand in 2001, but accelerated sharply in Indonesia and less so in the Philippines. Viet Nam was the only subregional country to experience deflation, which continued from the previous year (table II.27). Currencies in the subregion have generally stabilized, while excess production capacity and weakness in labour markets will help to contain demand-pull price pressures, at least at the early stages of the recovery process. However, there have been recent increases in freight rates, insurance premiums and surcharges and other transport costs, and this may generate some pressure on prices in the coming year.

Inflation was mixed with prices on the rise in some countries

Table II.27. Selected South-East Asian economies: inflation and money supply growth (M2), 1998-2001

(Percentage)

	1998	1999	2000	2001
Inflation[a]				
Indonesia	57.7	20.5	3.7	11.1
Malaysia	5.3	2.8	1.6	1.5
Philippines	9.7	6.7	4.4	6.3
Singapore	−0.3	0.1	1.4	1.0
Thailand	8.1	0.2	1.6	1.6
Viet Nam	7.2	4.1	−1.7	−0.1
Money supply growth (M2)				
Indonesia	62.3	11.9	15.6	16.3[b]
Malaysia	1.5	13.7	5.2	3.9
Philippines	8.6	16.9	8.1	11.8[b]
Singapore	30.2	8.5	−2.0	5.0[c]
Thailand	9.7	5.4	3.4	4.4[c]
Viet Nam	23.5	66.4	35.4	23.0

Sources: ESCAP, based on ADB, *Key Indicators of Developing Asian and Pacific Countries 2001* (Oxford University Press, 2001) and *Asian Development Outlook 2001* (Oxford University Press, 2001); IMF, *International Financial Statistics,* vol. LIV, No. 10 (October 2001); Economist Intelligence Unit, *Country Reports* (London, 2001), various issues; and national sources.

Note: Figures for 2001 are estimates.

[a] Changes in the consumer price index.
[b] January-June.
[c] January-September.

Indonesia had registered a steep cut in inflation, from over 20 per cent to below 4 per cent from 1999 to 2000, but consumer prices went up strongly in 2001, by over 11 per cent, as a result of the weakening rupiah, rising fuel prices and a pick-up in money supply (M2) growth. Interest rates were raised in September, but Bank Indonesia was reluctant to raise them further so as not to undermine the position of banks holding fixed-rate Bank Indonesia Certificates as part of their recapitalization as well as to keep the government debt-servicing burden down. At the same time, the weakness of the currency precludes an early reduction in interest rates. Increasing inflation in effect lowered interest rates in real terms, thus stimulating consumer credit and demand. Inflation is targeted at 9 per cent for 2002, but may be higher.

The Philippines experienced a pick-up in prices, from 4.4 in 2000 to 6.3 per cent in 2001. Higher prices for food and other items of mass consumption and recurrent weaknesses in the exchange rates were among the cost-push forces. Monetary conditions were eased during the year, the overnight borrowing and lending rates having been cut by a cumulative total of almost 725 basis points since December 2000, when interest rates were at very high levels to counter the depreciation in the peso during the political crisis (figure II.25). However, episodes of currency depreciation, notably in the third quarter, have forced temporary reversals of this monetary stance. The behaviour of prices in the coming year will continue to reflect the peso exchange rate, which may weaken if imports increase faster than exports in the coming economic upturn. In this context, the central banking authorities have adopted inflation targeting from January 2002 (postponed from a year earlier), the target range being 5-6 per cent in 2002, with a further reduction of 0.5 per cent planned for 2003.

Consumer prices remained stable at low levels, in the range of 1-1.6 per cent, in Malaysia, Singapore and Thailand in 2001. Weaknesses in the external environment and domestic demand, and more intensified competition at the retail level, were among the common denominators behind such price stability. In addition, cost pressures were further reduced with lower interest rates. Producer prices in Singapore have fallen on account of weak demand, despite a slight depreciation of the Singapore dollar and some increases in unit labour costs, by 5.5 per cent in the first nine months of 2001; the latter was due to a steeper fall in production than in employment, which caused labour productivity to suffer, especially in manufacturing. Inflation stood at only 1 per cent in 2001, down from 1.4 per cent in the previous year.

In Malaysia, producer prices and capacity utilization have been falling since the end of 2000. Inflation had been on a downward trend from 5.3 to 1.6 per cent from 1998 to 2000 but eased marginally to 1.5 per cent in 2001. Consumer prices in Thailand rose by about 1.6 per cent annually in both 2000 and 2001, although the rate of change slowed as the economy

Figure II.25. Index of exchange rates against the United States dollar of selected South-East Asian economies, 1996-2001

(1996=100)

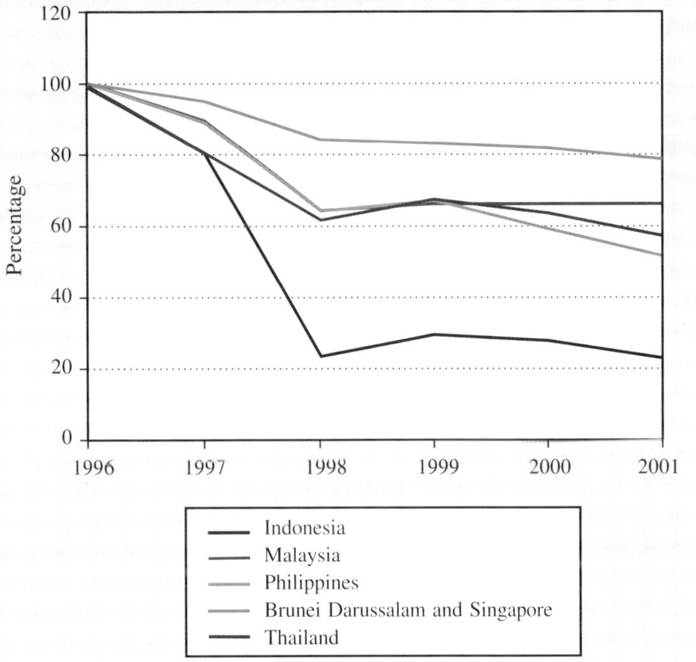

Legend:
- Indonesia
- Malaysia
- Philippines
- Brunei Darussalam and Singapore
- Thailand

Sources: IMF, *International Financial Statistics,* vol. LV, No. 1 (January 2002); and *Far Eastern Economic Review,* various issues.

Notes: Figures for 2001 are estimates. The currency of Brunei Darussalam is set at par with the Singapore dollar.

Demand weakness has contained inflation in Malaysia, Singapore and Thailand ...

weakened, oil prices fell and the baht appreciated somewhat in the later part of 2001. The Bank of Thailand's benchmark 14-day repurchase rate had been raised (by 1 percentage point) to 2.5 per cent in July 2001 to prevent further depreciation of the baht and reduce capital outflows. The rate was cut by 25 basis points in December 2001 and again in January 2002 (to stand at 2 per cent) as a result of negligible price pressures and concerns about the economy, as well as a stronger external position.

... but deflation continued in Viet Nam despite strong economic expansion

Consumer prices, which had fallen by 1.7 per cent in Viet Nam in 2000, continued to be lower in the first half of 2001. However, non-food prices began to rise in July as the dong depreciated, and there was a sharp increase in the price of rice at the end of the year. The base monthly interest rate was reduced slightly, from 0.75 per cent set in August 2000 to 0.70 and 0.60 per cent respectively in April and October 2001. Some cost-push pressures may be felt in the coming year as a result of strong domestic demand, the phasing-out of fuel and electricity subsidies and any weakness in the dong exchange rate.

Foreign trade and other external transactions

Trade

Merchandise export earnings had gone up strongly in South-East Asian countries (except the Philippines and Thailand) in 2000, but the rates of export expansion fell off throughout the subregion in the following year; the setbacks were particularly sharp in Indonesia, Malaysia, the Philippines and Singapore (tables II.28 and II.29). The main causes of

Table II.28. Selected South-East Asian economies: merchandise exports and their rates of growth, 1998-2001

	Value (Millions of US dollars)	Exports (f.o.b.)			
		Annual rate of growth (Percentage)			
	2000	1998	1999	2000	2001 Jan.-Sep.
Indonesia	62 103	−8.6	−0.4	27.6	7.6
Malaysia	98 153	−6.9	15.1	16.1	−10.4
Philippines	38 207	16.9	20.3	7.7	−9.6
Singapore	137 932	−12.3	4.4	20.2	−8.0
Thailand	65 160	−5.3	13.4	5.4	−1.3
Viet Nam	14 308	−1.9	23.2	24.0	13.1[a]

Sources: IMF, *Direction of Trade Statistics* (CD-ROM), February 2002; and national sources.

[a] January-December 2001.

this adverse trend included reduced demand in major export markets (the European Union, Japan and the United States) and within the subregion itself. Spending on merchandise imports was also declining, as fewer imported inputs were needed owing to cutbacks in export-oriented production.

Oil and gas exports, which had expanded by nearly 50 per cent in Brunei Darussalam and Indonesia in 2000, remained flat in 2001 as a result of lower hydrocarbon prices, which, in turn, reflected the global economic slowdown as well as some buyer concerns in the aftermath of the 11 September 2001 events. In addition, non-oil exports from Indonesia were considerably lower, by over $2 billion in the first three quarters of 2001. As a net result, the country's export earnings were up by 9 per cent during the period January-August 2001, compared with the previous year's increase of almost 28 per cent.

Oil and gas exports were flat for Brunei Darussalam and Indonesia, but Malaysia and Singapore were badly hit by the electronics downturn

The downturn in electronics was the principal factor causing Malaysia's export earnings to fall by over 10 per cent in 2001, compared with the expansion in the previous year of over 16 per cent; however, lower prices for other commodities, such as palm oil, tin and forestry products, also played their part in dampening earnings. Similarly, Singapore experienced a decline in exports, estimated at 8 per cent for January-September 2001, as against a sharp rise of one fifth in the previous year. Exports of electronic products for 2001 were down by almost 21 per cent, and earnings on non-electronics by 2 per cent. In terms of markets, there was a significant drop in exports to the European

Table II.29. Selected South-East Asian economies: merchandise imports and their rates of growth, 1998-2001

	Value (Millions of US dollars)	*Imports (c.i.f.)*			
		Annual rate of growth (Percentage)			
	2000	*1998*	*1999*	*2000*	*2001 Jan.-Sep.*
Indonesia	33 511	−34.4	−12.2	39.6	7.8
Malaysia	82 195	−26.2	12.3	25.5	−9.9[a]
Philippines	31 694	−19.8	−0.1	1.0	6.5
Singapore	134 630	−23.4	9.3	21.2	−9.9
Thailand	56 915	−31.4	23.4	7.0	5.5
Viet Nam	13 680	−4.8	1.1	30.8	13.2[a]

Sources: IMF, *Direction of Trade Statistics* (CD-ROM), February 2002; and national sources.

[a] January-December 2001.

Union, Malaysia, Taiwan Province of China and the United States. In contrast, the Chinese market held up reasonably well, registering growth of 10 per cent in 2001 (down from over 24 per cent during the previous year). In both Singapore and Malaysia, falling demand for intermediate inputs and capital goods was behind the slump in imports. The trade performance of the Philippines in 2001 deteriorated not just as a result of the steep electronics slump: exports of garments were also hit hard by the slowdown in the United States. Service exports were down significantly, the tourism sector in particular being affected by concerns over security in addition to the overall negative economic environment.

Price competition is intensifying for some Thai exports

The value of total exports from Thailand, down by 1.3 per cent during the period January-September 2001, was expected to decline further in 2001 as a whole. The decline occurred almost across the board and in all markets except China, where exports of poultry, cassava and canned seafood did well. In general, high-tech electronic and telecommunications products were adversely affected by the global economic slowdown, but labour-intensive products such as garments suffered from intensified price competition from China, Indonesia and Viet Nam. Jewellery and ornaments, however, performed strongly. Growth in import spending remained comparatively strong although the rate was lower primarily as a result of reduced demand for intermediate inputs, particularly for electronics products. However, imports of capital goods increased.

Merchandise export earnings in Viet Nam expanded by 13 per cent during 2001, a much slower rate than the 24 per cent increase recorded in 2000. This was a reflection of the slowdown in the country's principal export markets, Japan, Malaysia, the Republic of Korea, Singapore and Taiwan Province of China. Export revenues were also hit by lower prices for oil and agricultural commodities. Merchandise imports also slowed, to just over 13 per cent, as fewer inputs were needed for export-oriented industries such as textiles and garments and electronics; at the same time, private consumption weakened.

Capital inflows, external debt and exchange rates

Foreign direct investment and net portfolio flows were positive

External current account balances remained positive in 2001, except in the case of Viet Nam, even though they declined as a percentage of GDP from the levels of the previous year. An exception was Singapore, where the positive balance went up further to almost 28 per cent of GDP (table II.30). An encouraging feature in 2001 was that FDI and net inflows of portfolio investment were generally positive. Inward FDI rose significantly in Viet Nam along with the brightened outlook for exports

Table II.30. Selected South-East Asian economies: budget and current account balance as a percentage of GDP, 1998-2001

	1998	*1999*	*2000*	*2001*
Budget balance as a percentage of GDP				
Indonesia[a]	−3.7	−2.3	−4.8	−3.7
Malaysia[a]	−1.8	−3.2	−5.8	−6.6
Philippines	−1.9	−3.8	−4.1	−4.0
Singapore[a]	2.5	2.6	3.5	−2.0
Thailand[a]	−2.8	−3.3	−2.2	−3.6
Viet Nam[b]	−2.6	−2.8	−3.0	−5.1
Current account balance as a percentage of GDP				
Indonesia	4.3	4.1	5.1	2.8
Malaysia	13.1	16.0	10.5	6.9
Philippines	2.4	10.4	12.2	4.5
Singapore	24.6	25.9	23.6	27.7
Thailand	12.7	10.2	7.7	4.5
Viet Nam	−1.0	4.3	0.7	−0.1

Sources: ESCAP, based on ADB, *Key Indicators of Developing Asian and Pacific Countries 2001* (Oxford University Press, 2001) and *Asian Development Outlook 2001* (Oxford University Press, 2001); IMF, *International Financial Statistics*, vol. LIV, No. 10 (October 2001); Economist Intelligence Unit, *Country Reports* (London, 2001), various issues; and national sources.

Note: Figures for 2001 are estimates.

[a] Excluding grants.
[b] Excluding grants and including onlending.

emanating from the implementation of a bilateral trade agreement with the United States. In the first half of the year, Malaysia received some M$ 4 billion of FDI, which was increasingly directed to the service sector. Net inflows of portfolio investment were also on the rise in the first half of the year but declined subsequently. However, the gradual removal of capital controls introduced in the aftermath of the 1997 financial crisis has apparently not had a marked effect on capital movements.

The Philippines also recorded inflows of both FDI and net portfolio capital, but there was a large net outflow from residents' investments abroad and reduced trade credits. This category is receiving greater scrutiny in connection with concerns over money laundering. In Thailand, there was a small surplus on the private capital account owing to reductions in foreign debt repayments and commercial banks' holdings of foreign assets, even though the outflows of portfolio capital increased. FDI (much of it directed to the retail sector) was sluggish at $1.9 billion in the first three quarters of 2001 as against $3 billion for 2000 as a whole. However, there was a large deficit on the public capital account as the Bank of Thailand repaid its outstanding credits to IMF. Outflows on the capital and financial accounts from Singapore reflected net repatriation of portfolio investments and the shifting of assets of domestic banks to Asian Currency Units offshore. Private capital outflows were also experienced by Indonesia owing to political uncertainties and the continuing lack of market confidence. Moreover, official capital inflows have slowed partly because projects related to the 1997 crisis are coming to an end and partly because some delays in implementing reforms have led to delays in disbursements.

Official reserves increased or remained stable ...

Official reserves were up and relatively stable in South-East Asia, where most currencies had generally stabilized by the end of 2001. However, there were some periods of exchange rate instability in that year notably in the aftermath of 11 September 2001. Those countries that have tapped international capital markets have met with success, and this augurs well for the return of confidence in the subregion. Malaysia's foreign reserves had increased to almost $31 billion (or five months of retained imports) by the end of December 2001, a contributing factor being the successful global issue in July of government bonds worth $1 billion. The total external debt, at 47 per cent of GDP (of which around one fifth was short-term) in mid-2001, required a debt-service equivalent to just under 6 per cent of exports. The external payments position was also comfortable in Thailand, where the total external debt outstanding (around one fifth short-term) was estimated at $72 billion at the end of 2001. Moreover, the rise in international reserves to $32 billion was helped by a successful yen-denominated bond issue. In Singapore, official foreign reserves stood at a very substantial $73 billion in the third quarter of 2001.

... in spite of some significant increases in the balance-of-payments deficit

The deficit in the Philippines' balance of payments widened from $0.6 billion (in 2000) to $1.3 billion in the first nine months of 2001. Nevertheless, gross international reserves had risen to almost $16 billion by the end of December 2001, partly on account of proceeds from government bond issues and loan drawdowns. The positive investor sentiment induced a further global bond flotation for $500 million in January 2002, a level that was oversubscribed. International reserves were equivalent to almost five months of imports and 130 per cent of the country's short-term foreign liabilities on a residual maturity basis. The service payments on external debt, which stood at 64 per cent of GDP at the end of 2001, constituted just under 11 per cent of exports. Although this figure is manageable, the Government hopes to reduce external borrowings for deficit financing in 2002 and intends to rely heavily on concessional project and programme lending from multilateral organizations.

Much of Viet Nam's external debt (43 per cent of GDP) is also in the form of ODA loans, and debt service in 2001 is estimated to be equivalent to about 10 per cent of total exports. Gross official reserves, projected to increase to $3.6 billion at the end of 2001, were equal to about 2.5 months of imports. By comparison, Indonesia is in a more vulnerable position, as total external debt had risen to 97 per cent of GDP by mid-2001. Notwithstanding the balance-of-payments weakness, official reserves have been generally stable and amounted to around $29 billion at the end of September 2001. Nevertheless, sovereign credit ratings were downgraded (by Standard and Poor's) in 2001, once for long-term debt in rupiah (to B-) and twice for long-term foreign currency debt (to CCC). The floating rupiah, which appreciated briefly in August against the dollar with the change in Government, depreciated again and was almost 22 per cent lower on average in 2001 compared to the previous year. The Philippine peso also came under a great deal of pressure in the first eight months of the year, owing to the deterioration in the balance of payments and political instability. This contributed in part to the postponed introduction of inflation targeting by the central banking authorities by one year to January 2002. The peso lost about 15 per cent in exchange value relative to the dollar in 2001.

The Bank of Thailand had been targeting inflation, but the policy focus was apparently switched to the exchange rate and international reserves in July 2001 when interest rates were raised. This move was intended both to encourage residents to hold local currency assets and to discourage capital outflows. Subsequently, the baht strengthened towards the end of 2001 as a result of interest rate arbitrage, falling oil prices, the "Samurai" bond issue and a successful sale of shares in a State-owned oil company. Interest rates were cut by a total of 50 basis points in December 2001 and January 2002, as noted previously. The baht is expected to remain basically stable, trading in the range of 43-45 baht to the dollar; the average depreciation was just under 11 per cent in 2001.

Diverse movements in the exchange rate of subregional currencies with the Thai baht and Malaysian ringgit strengthening while other currencies weakened

The Malaysian ringgit, pegged at M$ 3.8 to the dollar, has appreciated in line with the dollar against other major currencies inside and outside the subregion. Given the healthy level of reserves and low inflation, the return to a more flexible ringgit is likely to be deferred to a time when the global economic outlook and international financial markets are more settled. The trade-weighted exchange rate of the Singapore dollar appreciated modestly at the start of 2001, but this trend was halted as the economic climate worsened in the second half of the year. There was greater flexibility in managing the exchange rate following the events of 11 September 2001, although more settled international markets led to the return of a narrower band in January 2002. As a whole, the Singapore dollar went down slightly against several major currencies in 2001, including by about 4 per cent against the dollar. Brunei Darussalam operates a currency board system, and the local currency, fully convertible at par with the Singapore dollar, also depreciated in 2001. The dong in Viet Nam, relatively stable until May 2001, fell in value by about 4 per cent against the dollar during the year, following the adoption by the central banking authorities of a more flexible approach to the management of the crawling peg against the dollar, and a reduction in foreign currency surrender requirements to 40 per cent from 50 per cent. The greater willingness to let the dong depreciate in line with similar movements in the regional currencies helped to maintain export competitiveness, although the debt-service burden may rise in the process.

Key policy issues

Poverty and vulnerability are likely to have increased in parts of the subregion

Labour markets have proved to be fairly flexible in South-East Asia, with little increase in measured unemployment rates as a result of production cutbacks and the deterioration in economic performance. However, there has been a greater adjustment in money wages. Some disguised unemployment and underemployment are likely to exist in the subregion and, notwithstanding the lack of recent statistics on poverty, the living standards for lower income groups are likely to have been adversely affected during the recent economic setback through either job losses or reduced real incomes (see chapter III of this *Survey*).

The informal economy and agriculture gain importance as a source of employment in Indonesia and the Philippines

Measured unemployment, which remains at around 6 per cent of the labour force, appears to have increased little in Indonesia, with real wages bearing the brunt of supply-demand imbalances. The informal sector appears to have absorbed a considerable number of the workers losing formal-sector jobs, but underemployment and disguised unemployment may still be a problem. In this context, agriculture still accounts for more than half of the employment of the working population, while in other informal sector occupations, especially services, self-employed and unpaid family workers play an important role. To absorb new entrants into the labour force, estimated to grow at approximately 2 per cent a year, aggregate output has to expand by 6 per cent annually, and even higher if unemployment is to be reduced further, but GDP growth has not approached this figure in the past few years. Recent estimates indicate that 18 per cent of the population was living below the national poverty line in 1999, as compared with 11 per cent before the 1997 crisis.

In the Philippines, agriculture accounted for over half of total employment in 2001. The unemployment rate in the first three quarters of 2001 averaged 11.6 per cent, slightly higher than the rate of 11.5 per cent for the same period in the previous year. However, it declined in 2001, reaching 10.1 per cent in the third quarter, mainly as a result of an increase of 11.4 per cent in agricultural employment, owing to improved weather conditions. Continuing low productivity in agriculture, however, will hinder attempts at long-lasting poverty reduction in rural areas. Recent economic performance has been relatively modest, while annual population growth has been around 2.2 per cent. The available estimates indicate that 39.4 per cent of the population were living below the national poverty line in 2000.

The average unemployment rate in Thailand increased to 4.1 per cent in the first half of 2001 from 3.6 per cent a year earlier, but recent data suggest that it fell in the second half of the year. New jobs have been created primarily in services, but employment in agriculture declined as a result of falling commodity prices and flooding. Aggregate output expanded by less than 2 per cent a year on average during the period 1998-2001, and the estimated proportion of the population living below the national poverty line went up noticeably during the post-crisis period, from 11.4 to 15.9 per cent between 1996 and 1999. It is apparent that poverty is re-emerging as one of Thailand's more serious problems. Nevertheless, family self-reliance and community-based support systems have helped to alleviate the depth and spread of poverty in Thailand to some extent.

Family and community ties help to alleviate poverty in Thailand

The creation of new enterprises and increased investment following the implementation of reform measures in Viet Nam are estimated to have generated some 1.4 million jobs in 2001, while there are about 1.2-1.3 million new entrants into the labour force each year. The urban unemployment rate declined slightly to 6.3 per cent from the previous year, but underemployment and disguised unemployment are thought to exist in a number of sectors; in particular, around 8.5 million people are estimated to be not fully employed in rural areas. According to a report on human development funded by UNDP, Viet Nam was able to cut the incidence of poverty by a third between the mid-1980s and 2000, one of the fastest rates on record for any developing country. However, poverty remains concentrated in rural areas, where 90 per cent of the poor live; in 1998, 45 per cent of the rural population were under the poverty line, as against 9 per cent of the urban population.

New enterprises generate more jobs in Viet Nam

Many countries in the subregion are grappling with issues connected to diversifying production so as to avoid excessive reliance on a narrow range of industries and export markets (box II.8). Tourism is an industry which has also been of great importance in many parts of South-East Asia. In Malaysia, it received additional incentives in the 2002 budget. Brunei Darussalam has also been promoting tourism and tourist

Tourism is attracting more attention

Box II.8. Diversification and structural upgrading to add value

Diversification of output and markets and the consequent economic restructuring is an important policy issue for economies in the subregion, and elsewhere in the world for that matter. Brunei Darussalam remains heavily dependent on the hydrocarbon sector and although the relative contribution to domestic output of non-oil activities increased during the 1990s, this trend has been reversed recently. The recent fall in oil prices and the electronics downturn have highlighted problems with the export-led growth strategy that had been so successful in the past in several countries, including Malaysia, the Philippines and Singapore. In particular, over three fifths of Malaysia's gross exports in 2000 comprised electrical and electronic goods, of which electronic circuits alone accounted for about a quarter. Over half of the country's exports are destined for Japan, Singapore and the United States; exports to Japan and Singapore often constitute inputs in the manufacture of goods to be shipped to the United States market. Similar degrees of export specialization or geographical concentration of export trade flows are evident in several other subregional countries, such as the Philippines, Singapore and Thailand. However, the attractiveness of some of these economies as a base for producing less sophisticated products requiring limited labour skills, because of standardized technologies, may be gradually eroded as a result of the rising costs of labour, land and infrastructure services, combined with the impact of China's accession to WTO.

As a response, Malaysia is committed to moving up the value added scale in shifting more resources to higher-value ICT products. An indication of this strategic reorientation can be seen in the increasing emphasis being given to education and to improving ICT technical skills and infrastructure in the 2002 budget, plus the fiscal stimulus packages announced in 2001; spending on education jumped 50 per cent in the stimulus packages alone. Economic policy in Singapore has also been driven for several years by the need to reduce its vulnerability to the electronics cycle; the rapid technological obsolescence in the industry; and job losses through corporate relocation to lower-cost countries. China, with its huge domestic market and lower labour costs, is pulling low-skill jobs and investment away from Singapore as well as from other economies in East and South-East Asia. Singapore has been shifting towards services as well as moving up the value added scale within electronics and in sophisticated manufacturing generally. Indeed, the share of services in GDP expanded from three fifths to 67 per cent between 1980 and 2000. Recently, however, the country's entrepot trade and transportation services have come under threat from an expansion in these activities in neighbouring countries. Within the electronics industry itself, restructuring has resulted in the emergence of such products as communications and computing and data processing equipment at the expense of semiconductors. In manufacturing as a whole, chemicals and chemical products have become the second most important industry; pharmaceutical and biopharmaceutical items, for example, had a 90 per cent local value added content in 1999.

Another aspect of policy is to shift away from a capital-intensive to a knowledge-intensive economy and to position Singapore as a regional hub not only for transnational corporations (in activities such as product design and development) but also for networks of SMEs in the region. In this context, the need to foster a culture of entrepreneurship and innovation is well recognized, and so is the importance of expanding the local supply of services, such as health care, education, consulting and engineering, for which regional demand is growing. Indeed, such knowledge- and entrepreneurship-driven structural transformation is given added weight by the slippage in Singapore's high ranking, from 2 in 2000 to 4 in 2001, in the competitiveness index of 75 countries compiled by the World Economic Forum. The relative economic dominance of Government-linked companies and the skills composition of the labour force may have to evolve as appropriate; in particular, only 35 per cent of Singaporean workers had post-secondary education or higher in 1999. As in Malaysia, investment in human capital was an important component in the off-budget fiscal stimulus package announced in October 2001.

The "Big Three", the United States, Japan and the European Union, have long been the main trade partners of most subregional economies; their importance as major export markets is likely to remain so in the foreseeable future. The realization of the ASEAN Free Trade Area among the six traditional member countries from the beginning of 2002 will boost intra-ASEAN trade, but will bring with it the need to improve productivity and competitiveness as well. Several countries have also been turning their attention to other markets, and Singapore, in particular, has been exploring and pursuing bilateral free trade agreements with countries outside ASEAN, such as Chile, China, Japan, Mexico and New Zealand. China, apart from being a competitor in third markets, has agreed to negotiate and enter into a free trade arrangement with ASEAN within ten years. In recent years, it has been an important source of counter-cyclical demand for export products of the subregion, and India may also offer some degree of shock-absorbing demand.

Brunei Darussalam and Malaysia are hoping to develop their capital markets as a way to initiate and ensure structural diversification. Brunei Darussalam is aiming to become an offshore Islamic financial centre and has stated its intention to open its own capital market and begin issuing Islamic government bonds of different maturities denominated in both the local currency and the dollar. In this connection, the Brunei International Financial Centre, opened in July 2000, is attracting interest with the first foreign bank and mutual fund opening offices there; other applications are in the pipeline. The establishment of the Centre is part of Brunei Darussalam's plan to position itself in the ongoing globalization of financial and commercial services, including through the creation, with Bahrain, Indonesia, Malaysia and Saudi Arabia, of an International Islamic Money Market. International capital markets were tapped for the first time by Brunei Darussalam in November 2001 with a five-year syndicated loan for $250 million (to finance non-oil sector and defence projects). Plans to issue a five-year bond instead were dropped owing to financial uncertainties, but the country still intends to seek a sovereign rating in the near future.

In Malaysia, the Capital Market Master Plan was unveiled in February 2001 with the aim of creating an internationally competitive and efficient market capable of supporting the country's capital and investment needs. A single exchange and a single clearing house are to be established. The plan, to be implemented in three phases over 10 years, envisages an initial period during which a pool of highly skilled professionals will be created and investor awareness increased. This will be followed by the encouragement of greater domestic competition, leading to increased deregulation and the participation of foreign institutions. Altogether, there are 6 objectives, linked to 24 strategic initiatives and 152 recommendations. At the beginning of September 2001, 20 per cent of the recommendations included in phase 1 (2001-2003) had been completed, wholly or partially; among these was the formalization by Bank Negara Malaysia of guidelines on bank regulation and supervision.

arrivals did increase to some extent with the "Visit Brunei Year 2001" promotion before slumping following the terrorist attacks in the United States. However, the country will receive a boost from its selection as the host country for the 2002 "Visit ASEAN Campaign". The promotion of intra-ASEAN tourism has gained momentum, but some rethinking of strategies may be required to attract ASEAN tourists and cater for their tastes. Governments of some countries will have to address security and governance concerns before tourism can return to pre-11 September 2001 levels. Some environmental issues will also need to be addressed, which may require subregional cooperation (box II.9). Moreover, the flow of tourists, particularly from Europe and the United States but also within ASEAN itself, tends to be cyclical, in line with global and regional economic conditions. In this connection, Thailand is seeking to attract more tourists from China, India, the Middle East and South Africa to help to iron out some of the fluctuations in tourism revenues.

The current economic downturn came when several countries were still dealing with an unfinished agenda of corporate and financial restructuring, thus making the task even more difficult to complete. The issue of fiscal stimulus and sustainability was discussed earlier (box II.7), and monetary policy has become less effective as a tool of macroeconomic stabilization, with fragile balance sheets making banks reluctant to lend. GDP has not returned to pre-crisis levels in the two countries worst

The corporate and financial restructuring agenda is unfinished and bank solvency is fragile in Indonesia

---

Box II.9. South-East Asian countries join forces to fight haze

Environmental issues not only have global or national dimensions: there are problems that require a regional response. The smoke haze problem affecting parts of the South-East Asian subregion in recent years, for instance, shows how subregional cooperation among neighbouring countries can address the problem. The ASEAN Regional Haze Action Plan was adopted in December 1997 as a response to the smoke haze, which, in that year, was the most extensive in ASEAN's history, affecting millions of people in the region, particularly in Brunei Darussalam, Indonesia, Malaysia and Singapore. The Action Plan called for specific measures:

- To prevent land and forest fires through better management policies and enforcement and intensified public education programmes

- To establish operational mechanisms to monitor land and forest fires

- To strengthen land and forest firefighting capabilities in the region

Malaysia is spearheading and coordinating work on preventive measures; Singapore, on monitoring measures; and Indonesia, on strengthening firefighting capabilities.

In a review of the Action Plan during the ASEAN Ministerial Meeting on Haze, held at Kuching, Malaysia, in February 1998, ASEAN member countries agreed to implement the firefighting component in East Kalimantan. This calls for the fortification of national and subregional firefighting capabilities through a complete inventory of the land and forest firefighting capabilities in each country, and the identification of resources that could be used subregionally. Reports and satellite photos from the ASEAN Specialized Meteorological Centre in Singapore on the extent of haze on the island of Borneo and in neighbouring areas, and on developing "hot spots", were presented. The Centre's data were made accessible to all ASEAN countries through the Internet and will strengthen the region's early-warning system for peat and forest fires. A public education campaign was launched on the haze hazard and its prevention through the mass media and people's local committees.

At the more recent sixth Informal ASEAN Ministerial Meeting on the Environment, held at Phnom Penh in May 2001, further preparedness measures were adopted subregionally. These included the development of fire suppression mobilization plans, the monitoring of land and forest fires and transboundary haze, and preventive measures to promote the zero-burning policy and strengthen law enforcement efforts. Indonesia enforced a new regulation in February 2001 which included enforcement measures to control open burning, and took court action against a number of plantation companies which had undertaken open burning.

Subsequent experience has shown that there are difficulties in implementing the zero-burning policy at the field level, particularly for the local communities whose livelihood is related with the practice. At the Twelfth Meeting of the ASEAN Senior Officials on the Environment, held in Brunei Darussalam in August 2001, ASEAN member countries agreed to work towards banning all forms of open burning as a long-term strategy within the period of the south-westerly monsoon, especially during the months of July to September. As a short-to-medium term strategy, the Meeting also agreed to continue the development of guidelines and techniques for the controlled burning method.

affected by the 1997 crisis, Indonesia and Thailand. Indonesia, in particular, has had to weather the present global slowdown largely on the strength of private domestic demand. While bank recapitalization has been largely completed, NPLs (excluding those transferred to the Indonesian Bank Restructuring Agency) still constitute around 16 per cent of total bank loans. Bank solvency is fragile, posing a threat to the future fiscal position. Bank assets are dominated by government bonds and

Bank Indonesia Certificates, which are rarely traded; their face value is probably larger than the market value, so that capital adequacy is probably overstated. The second phase of restructuring, involving the sale of assets held by the Agency, is proceeding slowly; only around 6 per cent of the NPLs purchased had been disposed of by September 2001. Debts have been restructured in approximately 7 per cent of NPLs, reflecting the slow pace of corporate restructuring, although the speed picked up in 2001. The privatization of State-owned enterprises, which are also mired in difficulties, has been limited.

NPLs in the Thai banking system comprised just under 13 per cent of total loans in September 2001, substantially below the ratio of nearly 18 per cent at the end of December 2000. The decline was mainly due to the transfer of NPLs to the Thai Asset Management Corporation established in June 2001 with extraordinary legal powers to consolidate the management of NPLs of domestic financial institutions and to expedite corporate restructuring. The Corporation is to take over NPLs worth almost 1,240 billion baht, of which 89 per cent are from State banks, with the aim of reducing NPLs to 10 per cent of all loans. Loan restructuring is proceeding slowly, however, and the delay has been attributed partly to inefficient back-office operations and partly to caution being exercised by officials from both the Corporation and the creditor banks involved in the restructuring process to avoid the risk of future legal challenges.

The Thai Asset Management Corporation has been established

The privatization programme, under which 18 State-owned enterprises were to be privatized by the end of 2003, has not proceeded as quickly as expected, partly because of the poor economic environment but also because of the desire to limit foreign ownership of shares and to maintain control over management. In recent months, however, the Government has decided to attract foreign investment by relaxing limits on share ownership and by offering a permanent 67 per cent reduction in corporate tax to foreign companies establishing their headquarters in Thailand. The successful sale of shares in the Petroleum Authority of Thailand (PTT), a State-owned oil company, towards the end of 2001 has led to the acceleration of privatization plans.

Financial and corporate restructuring is proceeding well in Malaysia. Following the bank merger programme initiated by Bank Negara Malaysia in 2000, 51 out of 54 banks have now been consolidated into 10 banking groups. Bank balance sheets have improved significantly; the core capital adequacy ratio was steady at 10.6 per cent (well above the Basel minimum of 8 per cent) and NPLs of the banking system had declined to 8 per cent by November 2001. Of the 10 banks into which Danamodal, the bank recapitalization agency, had injected capital following the 1997 crisis, 7 have now repaid the agency, which is

Malaysia has made good progress on restructuring

expected to be wound up in 2003. Danaharta, the asset management corporation, which had acquired 40.5 per cent of NPLs of the banking system, has managed to dispose of 85 per cent of these, with an average asset recovery rate of 57 per cent. The Corporate Debt Restructuring Committee, which had received applications involving a total of M$ 56.4 billion, had resolved approximately 52 per cent of this amount by November 2001.

Non-performing loans are increasing owing to the slowdown in the Philippines

Unlike other subregional countries, the Philippine Government did not set up an asset management corporation to help in bank restructuring. The growth in the number of NPLs during the recent economic slowdown has led to renewed calls for the establishment of such a corporation, but fiscal constraints and concerns over moral hazard (endorsed by IMF) have led to the Government relying on the private sector to find solutions to the problem. In this context, under a deal worth about $1 billion signed with Lehman Brothers in January 2002, the investment bank would acquire mortgages, foreclosed real estate and NPLs from State housing agencies and financial institutions; it would then dispose of them and use the proceeds to finance mass housing projects. Capital adequacy ratios for the banking system as a whole stood at 16.8 per cent in February 2001, well above the Basel standard of 8 per cent, and new risk-based capital adequacy requirements were also introduced by the central banking authorities in June. Generally, the banking system is on a sounder footing than in several other countries in the subregion, although costs are high and profitability is low.

Reforming State-owned enterprises is the key to reducing non-performing loans in Viet Nam

The privatization of State-owned enterprises has met with some resistance from both employees and managers in Viet Nam. Reform of this enterprise sector is needed, not only to improve domestic efficiency and competitiveness but also to ensure fiscal sustainability and to free resources for poverty reduction. Enterprise reform is also part and parcel of the restructuring of State-owned commercial banks, although the process has been proceeding more slowly than planned. The State Bank of Viet Nam has encouraged credit growth in the past to boost invest- ment, and much of this lending has come from State-owned commercial banks to unproductive State-owned enterprises. Many of the loans are now non-performing, although estimates of the magnitude involved vary widely. Credit growth has been tightened following the agreements with IMF and the World Bank to improve the management of credit risk by the banking system and speed up banking reform. The establishment of a steering board to oversee bank reforms and the announcement in October 2001 of the creation of an asset management corporation to deal with NPLs of State-owned commercial banks are indicative of the Government's commitment to enterprise and banking reform and restruc- turing.

East and North-East Asia

Subregional overview and prospects

The newly industrialized economies in this subregion, the Republic of Korea and Hong Kong, China, experienced a sharp deterioration in GDP performance in 2001. The adverse external environment, caused by the synchronized global economic slowdown and compounded by the September 2001 terrorist attacks on the United States, reduced business confidence, and growth of consumer spending and exports. By and large, aggregate output remained stagnant in Mongolia. In sharp contrast, China again posted robust GDP growth, which, at 7.3 per cent for 2001, was the highest among economies of the ESCAP region, except those in North and Central Asia (figure II.26). In particular, both Hong Kong, China, and the Republic of Korea were hit hard by the sharp fall in external demand for high-technology products, especially ICT items, and this in turn, contributed, to a significant decline in industrial production and exports. The vibrant economic activities in China were largely driven by domestic factors which offset considerably the decline in export expansion in 2001. Nevertheless, the ongoing reform of State-owned enterprises in China and the current restructuring of the financial and corporate sector in the

The Republic of Korea and Hong Kong, China, hit by the global downturn but economic activities remained robust in China

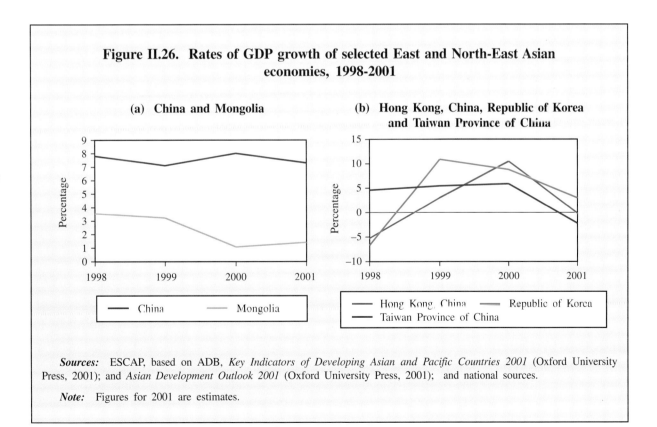

Figure II.26. Rates of GDP growth of selected East and North-East Asian economies, 1998-2001

(a) China and Mongolia

(b) Hong Kong, China, Republic of Korea and Taiwan Province of China

Sources: ESCAP, based on ADB, *Key Indicators of Developing Asian and Pacific Countries 2001* (Oxford University Press, 2001); and *Asian Development Outlook 2001* (Oxford University Press, 2001); and national sources.

Note: Figures for 2001 are estimates.

Republic of Korea put added pressure on the employment situation, with some adverse impact on consumer confidence and on domestic efforts to alleviate domestic poverty and protect social welfare.

Deflation pressures in Hong Kong, China, and low inflation in other economies, except Mongolia

Inflation in the subregion generally remained in check in 2001 (figure II.27). Hong Kong, China, continued to experience falling consumer prices, although at a slower pace. Inflation stayed at very low levels in China in 2000-2001. In the Republic of Korea, it rose slightly to about 3 per cent in 2001 because of the higher costs of utilities and a variety of services. In Mongolia, inflation went down to less than 9 per cent in 2001, compared with almost 12 per cent in the previous year, thanks in part to lower energy prices and stable meat prices. Only marginal changes, either way, are expected in the behaviour of consumer prices in the subregion in 2002.

Figure II.27. Inflation of selected East and North-East Asian economies, 1998-2001[a]

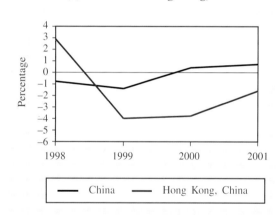

(a) China and Hong Kong, China

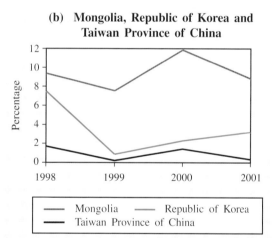

(b) Mongolia, Republic of Korea and Taiwan Province of China

Sources: ESCAP, based on ADB, *Key Indicators of Developing Asian and Pacific Countries 2001* (Oxford University Press, 2001) and *Asian Development Outlook 2001* (Oxford University Press, 2001); IMF, *International Financial Statistics*, vol. LIV, No. 10 (October 2001); and national sources.

Note: Figures for 2001 are estimates.

[a] Changes in the consumer price index.

Setback to trade in most parts of East and North-East Asia

Merchandise trade performance deteriorated virtually throughout the subregion in 2001. A high rate of export expansion continued in Mongolia, although merchandise imports fell by about half (figures II.28 and II.29). The Republic of Korea and Hong Kong, China, experienced the most severe setback in export earnings, from strong expansion in 2000 to a contraction during the first three quarters of the following

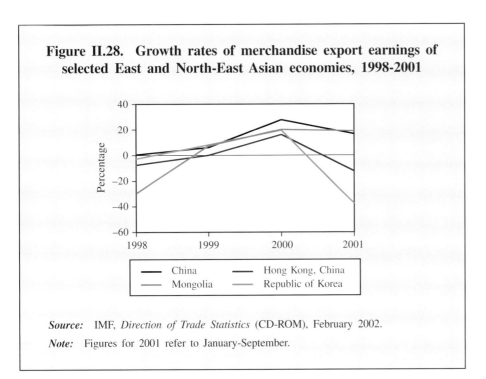

Figure II.28. Growth rates of merchandise export earnings of selected East and North-East Asian economies, 1998-2001

Source: IMF, *Direction of Trade Statistics* (CD-ROM), February 2002.

Note: Figures for 2001 refer to January-September.

year of 38 per cent in the Republic of Korea and 12 per cent in Hong Kong, China. As was the situation elsewhere in South-East Asia, ICT products were particularly hard hit by the lower external demand. China's export earnings continued to grow strongly, although at a slower pace of 17 per cent in the first nine months of 2001. Mongolia was able to sustain similarly vibrant growth in exports for both 2000 and three quarters of 2001; however, the growth rates of import spending went down sharply throughout the subregional economies. There was a surplus on the trade account of both China and the Republic of Korea. A surplus on the current account was achieved by China, Hong Kong, China, and the Republic of Korea. The foreign exchange reserves of those three economies totalled over $420 billion as at October 2001.

The economic prospects in the subregion in 2002 are likely to improve because of a low initial base in 2001 or, in the case of China, to remain good. Certainly most subregional economies would gain from a solid recovery of the United States economy beginning in the second half of 2002; at present, an upturn is widely anticipated, although its strength remains uncertain. The impact will be both direct, including through improved export earnings and indirect, through a variety of positive spillover effects on consumer and business confidence, and through a stock market rebound as well. An additional push to the recovery process or to the pattern of sustained growth in the subregion is also

Modest recovery of growth and trade expected in 2002

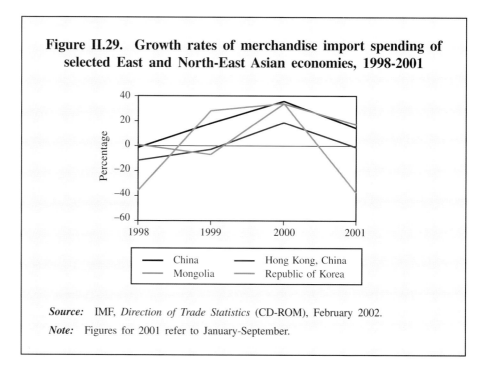

Figure II.29. Growth rates of merchandise import spending of selected East and North-East Asian economies, 1998-2001

Source: IMF, *Direction of Trade Statistics* (CD-ROM), February 2002.

Note: Figures for 2001 refer to January-September.

expected from the ongoing effects of the expansionary policy in 2001. However, there are a number of downside risks associated with, among other things, the feeble performance of the Japanese economy and the volatility of financial markets and, in particular, the financial ripple effects emanating from economic problems in some emerging markets. All in all, aggregate output in Hong Kong, China is expected to expand by 1 percentage point and in the Republic of Korea by 4 percentage points while in China it is expected to go up by 7 per cent in 2002.

GDP performance

Strong growth in China and stagnation in Hong Kong, China

Economic growth in East and North-East Asia slowed in 2001 largely because of unfavourable external conditions; China constituted a striking exception, and GDP expansion was marginal in Mongolia. The Republic of Korea and Hong Kong, China, were among the newly industrialized economies severely hit by the global slowdown, especially the sharp decline in external demand for high-technology products. Only China maintained its steady, high growth path from the time of the 1997-1998 financial and economic crisis in East and South-East Asia through to the current slowdown. Its GDP expanded at a relatively stable rate of between 7 and 8 per cent during the period 1998-2001, giving an enviable annual increase of 7.6 per cent on average during this period (table II.31). Although China is less vulnerable to shocks in the high-technology sector,

Table II.31. Selected East and North-East Asian economies: growth rates, 1998-2001

(Percentage)

		Rates of growth			
		Gross domestic product	*Agriculture*	*Industry*	*Services*
China	1998	7.8	3.5	9.2	7.7
	1999	7.1	2.8	8.1	7.5
	2000	8.0	2.4	9.6	7.8
	2001	7.3	2.6	9.3	7.1
Hong Kong, China	1998	−5.3	..	..	..
	1999	3.0	..	..	..
	2000	10.5	..	..	..
	2001	−0.2	..	..	..
Mongolia	1998	3.5	6.4	3.9	0.3
	1999	3.2	4.2	0.9	3.5
	2000	1.1	−16.8	7.8	17.0
	2001	1.4	..	..	..
Republic of Korea	1998	−6.7	−6.6	−7.5	−6.0
	1999	10.9	5.4	12.8	9.9
	2000	8.8	0.1	11.3	7.6
	2001	3.0	0.7[a]	2.2[a]	3.3[a]

Sources: ESCAP, based on ADB, *Key Indicators of Developing Asian and Pacific Countries 2001* (Oxford University Press, 2001) and *Asian Development Outlook 2001* (Oxford University Press, 2001); and national sources.

Notes: Figures for 2001 are estimates. Industry comprises mining and quarrying; manufacturing; electricity, gas and power; and construction.

[a] Growth rates for three quarters.

it was not totally immune to the slowdown in the industrialized countries. As demand contracted in China's top five export markets, the United States, Japan, the Republic of Korea, Germany, and Hong Kong, China, the growth of export earnings, although still strong, was on a declining course. Facing the deteriorating external environment, China implemented strong expansionary policies, including higher spending on infrastructure development projects and on property upgrading. Facilitated by housing policy reform and low interest rates on bank lending, investment in the property sector was soaring, thus contributing, in part, to rising domestic demand in 2001. Consumer and business confidence was also boosted with China's entry into WTO, the selection of China as the host of the 2008 Olympic Games and the granting of higher wages for civil servants.

All those factors contributed to sustained strong growth in output from both the industrial and service sectors. In fact, industrial value added went up consistently fast, by an annual average of just over 9 per cent during the period 1998-2001; the corresponding figure for the service sector was 7.5 per cent. Aggregate capital formation notched up another percentage point of GDP to 37.5 per cent in 2001, while the already high rate of savings was maintained at 39.5 per cent during the same year (table II.32). Nevertheless, one of the major challenges for China is to foster more private enterprises and to sustain the restructuring of State-owned enterprises. While the latter will enhance private sector participation and development, the trade-offs involved may be higher unemployment, at least in the short term, and lower private consumption. Inward FDI jumped in 1996 and remained at a high level, averaging almost $42 billion annually during the period 1996-2000, and there is some evidence that foreign-funded enterprises have a better performance record than State-owned enterprises. Thus, greater job creation could be mediated through policy measures in support of the expansion of foreign-funded enterprises as part and parcel of the process of private sector development in China. Agricultural growth has been maintained at a respectable rate, averaging about 2.8 per cent annually during the period 1998-2001. The quality of agricultural products was also improving, and there have been large grain exports in recent years. With China as a WTO member, some market-oriented adjustments in agricultural protection will be necessary.

Table II.32. Selected East and North-East Asian economies: ratios of gross domestic savings and investment to GDP, 1998-2001

(Percentage)

	1998	*1999*	*2000*	*2001*
Savings as a percentage of GDP				
China	41.3	39.7	39.2	39.5
Hong Kong, China	30.8	32.2	33.0	32.7
Mongolia	18.5	20.0	19.0	21.0
Republic of Korea	34.4	33.5	32.5	32.6
Investment as a percentage of GDP				
China	37.7	37.2	36.9	37.5
Hong Kong, China	29.7	25.0	27.6	26.2
Mongolia	25.0	27.0	26.0	25.0
Republic of Korea	21.2	26.7	28.7	29.0

Sources: ESCAP, based on ADB, *Key Indicators of Developing Asian and Pacific Countries 2001* (Oxford University Press, 2001) and *Asian Development Outlook 2001* (Oxford University Press, 2001); and national sources.

Note: Figures for 2001 are estimates.

Hong Kong, China, was the worst affected by the global downturn among the subregional economies, with GDP remaining virtually unchanged in 2001 after strong expansion of over 10 per cent during the previous year. Sharp declines were recorded for both exports and domestic demand, despite a higher budget deficit amounting to 4.5 per cent of GDP in 2001, compared with less than 1 per cent the year before. In particular, lower private demand reflected falling consumer confidence, plunging tourist arrivals, weakening retail sales, rising unemployment and a faltering construction business. Furthermore, stagnant property and stock markets contributed to a decline (of about 1.4 percentage points) in total investment equivalent to 26.2 per cent of GDP in 2001. Capital formation is not likely to pick up in the near term, at least until exports of goods and services are on the upswing along with the global economic recovery expected towards the second half of 2002.

Economic activities in Mongolia were strong, with GDP growing by around 3.4 per cent a year in 1998-1999. However, total output slumped in 2000 and the recovery was subdued, with GDP expanding by just 1.4 per cent in the following year. Although agricultural production accounted for about a third of GDP, Mongolia is not self-sufficient in food, and agricultural activities are highly vulnerable to severe weather conditions and other shocks. The output of meat and meat products was adversely affected by severe weather conditions and foot-and-mouth disease in 2001.

Mongolia experienced a marginal improvement in output ...

In 2001, the Republic of Korea experienced the worst economic downturn since the financial and economic crisis of 1997-1998. The subsequent economic turnaround was speedy and significant; GDP expanded by almost 11 per cent in 1999 and economic activities were sustained at a relatively high level during the following year. However, total output went up by only about 3 per cent in 2001, when private consumption became stagnant and, along with a steep decline in export earnings, investment contracted during the first three quarters of the year. Weakened demand from the country's major export markets for such products as electronics and electrical machinery led to a drop in industrial production and dampened business confidence across the board until the third quarter of 2001. Instability in financial markets was another compounding factor; the collapse of several investment trust companies in the wake of the Daewoo group's bankruptcy heightened financial uncertainties and credit conditions became tight, further constraining investment. Government policies became strongly expansionary; interest rates were lower and the budget deficit went up to 2 per cent of GDP in 2001, compared with a surplus position of 1.3 per cent in the previous year (table II.33). The policy stimulus began to take effect at the beginning of the fourth quarter of 2001, when business confidence,

... while the Republic of Korea suffered a steep drop in GDP growth

159

Table II.33. Selected East and North-East Asian economies: budget and current account balance as a percentage of GDP, 1998-2001

	1998	*1999*	*2000*	*2001*
Budget balance[a] as a percentage of GDP				
China	−1.2	−2.1	−2.8	−2.3
Hong Kong, China	−1.8	0.8	−0.9	−4.5
Mongolia	−14.3	−12.2	−6.8	−7.3
Republic of Korea	−4.2	−2.7	1.3	−2.0
Current account balance as a percentage of GDP				
China	3.1	1.6	1.5	1.0
Hong Kong, China	2.4	7.3	5.4	2.8
Mongolia	−13.2	−13.7	−17.2	−16.7
Republic of Korea	12.7	6.0	2.4	3.0

Sources: ESCAP, based on ADB, *Key Indicators of Developing Asian and Pacific Countries 2001* (Oxford University Press, 2001) and *Asian Development Outlook 2001* (Oxford University Press, 2001); IMF, *International Financial Statistics*, vol. LIV, No. 10 (October 2001); Economist Intelligence Unit, *Country Forecast: South Korea* (London, December 2001); and national sources.

Note: Figures for 2001 are estimates.

[a] Excluding grants.

retail sales and construction investment were revitalized and regained momentum. Other confidence-raising factors included the forthcoming 2002 World Cup Soccer games (co-hosted by Japan and the Republic of Korea) and the 14th Asian Games (hosted by the Republic of Korea). Some leading indicators are showing a mild recovery of economic activities in the Republic of Korea, although any sustained upturn in manufacturing and the associated investment in machinery and equipment necessary for regained strong growth, as was the pattern in 1999-2000, would depend heavily on a robust recovery in external economic conditions.

Inflation

Consumer prices were muted in most parts of the subregion in 2000-2001 (table II.34). The exception was Mongolia, where inflation had been very high, averaging, for example, 50 per cent annually during the period 1995-1997. Tight fiscal and monetary policies helped to bring the rate of increase in consumer prices to the single-digit level in 1998 and 1999. Higher prices on energy and food products contributed to higher

Table II.34. Selected East and North-East Asian economies: inflation and money supply growth (M2), 1998-2001

(Percentage)

	1998	1999	2000	2001
Inflation[a]				
China	−0.8	−1.4	0.4	0.7
Hong Kong, China	2.9	−4.0	−3.8	−1.6
Mongolia	9.4	7.5	11.8	8.8
Republic of Korea	7.5	0.8	2.3	3.2
Money supply growth (M2)				
China	15.3	14.7	12.3	13.8[b]
Hong Kong, China	11.8	8.1	8.8	9.3
Mongolia	−1.7	31.6	17.6	23.0[c]
Republic of Korea	27.0	27.4	25.4	14.5[c]

Sources: ESCAP, based on ADB, *Key Indicators of Developing Asian and Pacific Countries 2001* (Oxford University Press, 2001) and *Asian Development Outlook 2001* (Oxford University Press, 2001); IMF, *International Financial Statistics*, vol. LV, No. 1 (January 2002); and national sources.

Note: Figures for 2001 are estimates.

[a] Changes in the consumer price index.
[b] January-September.
[c] January-June.

inflation, of almost 12 per cent, in 2000, although the trend was reversed with lower and more stable oil and meat prices in 2001. Inflation was again down to the single-digit level, at 9 per cent, during that year; it is expected to be lower (about 6 per cent) in 2002, but this will again depend very much on weather conditions, such as winter temperature and rainfall.

Consumer prices in China remained very stable, rising by less than 0.6 per cent on average in 2000-2001. China had experienced some deflation when prices fell by just over 1 per cent a year in 1998-1999, a reflection of oversupply of several consumer items, excess capacity, lower export growth and weak consumer demand; the latter was attributable in part to the fear of job loss. Some of these factors continued to operate over the years 2000-2001. Strong agricultural production over the past several years helped to keep food prices low. There were, however, higher charges for housing and services in 2001. All these cost-push pressures contributed to the positive, but highly marginal, increase in consumer prices during the year.

Muted consumer prices in China and Hong Kong, China, still under deflationary pressures

Consumer prices in Hong Kong, China, fell consecutively in recent years, although deflation levelled from 4 per cent in 1999 to 1.6 per cent two years later. Among the causal factors were lower property rentals as a result of the deteriorating housing market, a fall in retail prices caused by strong competition at the retail level, and cheaper costs of imports owing to the relatively strong local currency, which had a fixed peg to the strong United States dollar. Some mild deflation is expected in 2002, given the current economic downturn, the sharp contraction in current-year exports, the pegged exchange rate and the underlying trends in consumer prices over the last three years.

Prices edged upwards in the Republic of Korea

Inflation was well under control in the Republic of Korea after the 1997-1998 crisis, despite a high rate of money supply (M2) growth in 1999-2000. Consumer prices went up by less than 1 percentage point in 1999 and inflation was modest in absolute terms, although it was apparently on an upward trend in the following two years, amounting to just over 3 per cent in 2001. There were higher costs of utilities and medical services but demand-pull pressures were relatively weak, reflecting lower growth of wage rates, stable prices for raw and intermediate materials (such as crude oil and natural gas) and reduced economic activities more generally. The central banking authorities expect inflation to remain largely at the same level in the coming year.

Foreign trade and other external transactions

Falling export growth in the Republic of Korea

Merchandise trade performance deteriorated virtually throughout the subregion; only Mongolia was able to maintain a high rate of export expansion, although that of merchandise imports fell by about half (table II.35 and II.36). The Republic of Korea and Hong Kong, China, experienced the most severe setback in export earnings, from an expansion of one fifth (to $171.8 billion) in 2000 to a contraction of 38 per cent during the first three quarters of the following year in the case of the Republic of Korea. ICT products, which accounted for about a fifth of the Republic of Korea's export value, were hard hit by lower external demand; in particular, lower receipts from semiconductors and personal computers were responsible for about 70 per cent of the export contraction in 2001. The decline would have been more serious without some offsetting gains in the so-called "traditional industry" export products, such as passenger cars and marine vessels, a development underpinned by an enhanced reputation and increased specialization in niche markets. There was an equally sharp contraction in import spending, by just over 37 per cent during the first three quarters of

Table II.35. Selected East and North-East Asian economies: merchandise exports and their rates of growth, 1998-2001

	Value (Millions of US dollars)	*Exports (f.o.b.)*			
		Annual rate of growth (Percentage)			
	2000	*1998*	*1999*	*2000*	*2001 Jan.-Sep.*
China	249 195	0.5	6.1	27.8	16.6
Hong Kong, China	201 871	−7.5	0.1	16.2	−12.4
Republic of Korea	171 826	−2.7	8.2	19.6	−37.9
Mongolia	409	−29.8	7.4	20.3	19.0

Source: IMF, *Direction of Trade Statistics* (CD-ROM), February 2002.

2001, compared with the previous year's expansion of 34 per cent. This contributed to a trade surplus for the year, while the current account surplus rose marginally from 2.4 per cent of GDP in 2000 to 3 per cent of GDP in 2001. Both the trade and current accounts were expected to be in surplus in 2002.

Table II.36. Selected East and North-East Asian economies: merchandise imports and their rates of growth, 1998-2001

	Value (Millions of US dollars)	*Imports (c.i.f.)*			
		Annual rate of growth (Percentage)			
	2000	*1998*	*1999*	*2000*	*2001 Jan.-Sep.*
China	225 096	−1.3	18.0	35.8	14.2
Hong Kong, China	213 183	−11.5	−2.7	18.7	−1.0
Republic of Korea	160 479	−35.6	28.2	34.0	−37.5
Mongolia	588	0.9	-6.9	33.6	17.1

Source: IMF, *Direction of Trade Statistics* (CD-ROM), February 2002

China's entry into WTO expected to boost trade and FDI in China and Hong Kong, China

Earnings on merchandise exports by Hong Kong, China, which had expanded by 16 per cent (to $201.9 billion) in 2000, were also on the decline; the earnings were down by just over 12 per cent in the first nine months of 2001 owing to sharply reduced revenue from electrical appliances, office machinery and professional equipment. Import expenditure rose by almost 19 per cent (to $213 billion) in 2000 but remained more or less stagnant during the first three quarters of the following year. The merchandise trade deficit widened somewhat but, owing to higher earnings on a wide range of services, the current account is expected to post a surplus of 2.8 per cent of GDP in 2001, or about half the figure for the previous year.

In China, the merchandise trade performance in 2000-2001 showed that both export earnings and import spending remained on a high trend, although at a declining rate. Export value went up substantially, by about 28 per cent (to $249 billion) in 2000, and continued to grow by a considerable margin of 17 per cent in the first nine months of the following year. The value of foreign trade has expanded at the average rate of 15 per cent annually for the 22 years ending in 2000. In fact, China has become the seventh biggest trading country in the world, with a ratio of trade to GDP of just over 9 per cent in 1978 and 44 per cent in 2000. Its recent entry into WTO is expected to boost trade and investment activities, especially FDI and imports capital goods, as part and parcel of the ongoing process of global and regional integration. Indeed, the three most important export markets of China are the United States, Japan and Hong Kong, China, which together contributed about 55 per cent of China's export earnings. The top four export product groups, mechanical and electrical products, electric and electronic products, garments and clothing accessories, and computer and telecommunications equipment, accounted for almost nine tenths of the total export value as at September 2001.

Strong export earnings by Mongolia, but large trade and current account deficits

Mongolia's recent trade performance improved significantly, with merchandise export earnings expanding by almost a fifth annually 2000-2001. The main trading partners are China and the Russian Federation, and the main export items are copper and cashmere. However, total export value was comparatively modest, at $409 million in 2000. Expenditure on imports ballooned in 2000, in part owing to higher oil prices, but moderated considerably to rise by about 17 percentage points during the first three quarters of 2001. Mongolia experienced considerable deficits in its trade and current accounts, the latter averaging about 17 per cent of GDP for both 2000 and 2001.

Along with the global economic slowdown, the level of net private capital flows to the emerging markets in the region, China, India, Indonesia, Malaysia, the Philippines, the Republic of Korea and Thailand, fell by almost a third, from $67 billion to just over $44 billion, in 2000 and 2001. However, FDI flows to China in 2001 remained strong, reflecting in part such positive factors as the country's entry into WTO and the "Olympics 2008" effect. Net FDI inflows, which amounted to $37.5 billion in 2000, are expected to reach some $40 billion in the following year; this is equivalent to about 9 per cent of gross fixed investment in China. The country has been the largest FDI host for years and accounted for almost a fifth of all FDI flows among developing economies in 2000. China's savings rate is also among the highest in the world, hovering between 39 and 41 per cent during the period 1998-2001. Hong Kong, China, ranked second as an FDI recipient among developing economies in 2000, with a relative share of 16 per cent, although the flows have been rather volatile over the last few years. Net FDI is expected to rise to $10 billion in 2001, equivalent to 24 per cent of the gross fixed investment in 2001, from $1.4 billion in the previous year. Portfolio investment in Hong Kong, China, is expected to decline in 2001, reflecting the weakness of the economy.

FDI is expected to increase in China; Hong Kong, China; and Mongolia

FDI in Mongolia is on a rising trend, reaching $40 million in 2000 compared with $30 million in the previous year and $19 million in 1998. However, the net FDI flows into the Republic of Korea are expected to decline to $1.2 billion in 2001 (or about 1 per cent of gross fixed investment) from $4.3 billion in 2000 (or just over 3 per cent). FDI had been promoted as a means to overcome the financial crisis of 1997-1998 and the net inflow had peaked at just over $5.0 billion in 1999 from $0.7 billion in 1998. The Republic of Korea was the sixth largest FDI host among the developing economies in 2000 (after China; Hong Kong, China; Brazil; Argentina and Mexico) The flow of portfolio investment to the Republic of Korea was volatile in 2001, reflecting the economic uncertainties in the economy. Its net amount was around $12 billion in 2000, almost three times larger than the net FDI. Portfolio investment is expected to increase again along with the domestic economic recovery in 2002.

As a whole, the foreign reserve position of the three largest subregional economies was reasonably comfortable. As at October 2001, China is estimated to have accumulated foreign reserves totalling more than $206.5 billion, or about 1.5 times the level of its external debt; such debt had declined steadily, from 15 per cent of GDP in 1999 to an estimated 12 per cent in 2001. The amount of foreign exchange reserves was also equivalent to about 10 months of import spending. The level of reserves in Hong Kong, China, was $113.1 as at October 2001 and in the Republic of Korea, it was $101.6. The external debt of the Republic of

Substantial foreign reserves among the major subregional economies

Korea has been on a declining trend since the 1997-1998 financial crisis, amounting to $120.3 billion as at November 2001 compared with $131.7 billion at the end of 2000. The ratio of short-term external debt to foreign exchange reserves, which had been as high as 63.3 per cent in 1998, went down to just under 50 per cent as at December 2000 and 40 per cent as at November 2001. The local currencies in both Mongolia and the Republic of Korea depreciated somewhat against the United States dollar, the won reflecting in part weakened domestic economic conditions and the weakening Japanese yen in 2001. However, China, and Hong Kong, China, maintained their pegged rate of foreign exchange with the dollar (figure II.30).

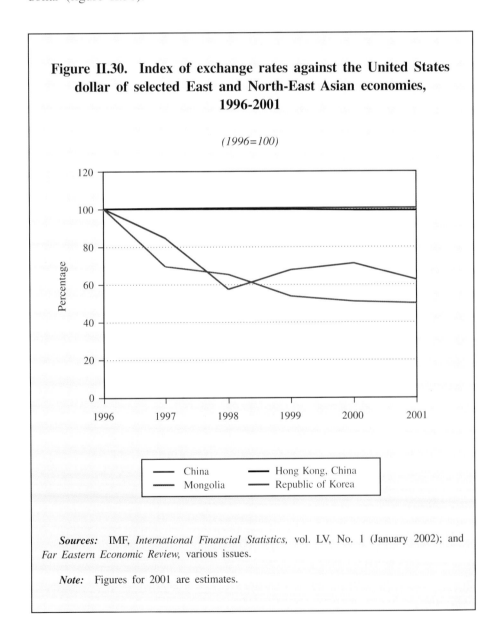

Figure II.30. Index of exchange rates against the United States dollar of selected East and North-East Asian economies, 1996-2001

(1996=100)

Sources: IMF, *International Financial Statistics,* vol. LV, No. 1 (January 2002); and *Far Eastern Economic Review,* various issues.

Note: Figures for 2001 are estimates.

Key policy issues

The economies in East and North-East Asia share a number of common policy issues in economic reform and restructuring. A key issue in China is the reform of State-owned enterprises and the financial sector as many of those enterprises were highly indebted and operating at a loss thus adding NPLs to the domestic banking system. Among the policy responses were debt-for-equity swaps, privatization, reducing the workforce of the enterprises and the closure of non-viable enterprises. Although the profitability of State-owned enterprises as a whole improved somewhat in the first half of 2001, concerns about rising unemployment and the adverse external environment were among the constraints on the restructuring process. Furthermore, the State banks' financial situation is still heavily dependent on the performance of the State-owned enterprises and progress in financial sector reform is also dependent on the pace of enterprise restructuring. In the process of financial and State-owned enterprise sector restructuring, a considerable number of NPLs have been transferred to asset management companies thus lowering the NPL ratio to 29 per cent at the end of 2000, from 39 per cent at the end of 1999. However, the comparatively high NPL ratio is another constraint on the financial situation of the banking sector. In addition, the possible areas for strengthening of the legal infrastructure include a framework that can handle speedily defaults or delays on payment, bankruptcy procedures, manipulation of stock prices, false financial reporting and breaches of contract.

China needs to improve the efficiency of its State-owned enterprises

Since 1997 the Government of China has pursued a policy of "reducing employment and increasing efficiency" and the number of employees of State-owned enterprises decreased by 26 per cent, from 110 million in 1997 to 81 million in 2000. The unemployment rate, based on registered unemployment in the urban areas, is estimated to be 3.6 per cent in 2001, compared with 3.1 per cent in 2000. Concerted efforts have been made to provide laid-off workers from the enterprise sector with alternative employment opportunities in labour-intensive activities, including through the development of more service business and non-State firms. The very high savings rate in China, noted earlier, and the low levels of public debt (under 12 per cent of GNP) can help to facilitate the process, especially if the financial sector can be both deepened and widened to ensure effective and flexible resource mobilization and intermediation. However, the unemployment problem is expected to remain a key issue for policy attention at least in the short to medium terms, especially with more intensifying competition from external producers in the wake of China's entry into WTO. In this context, the social safety nets needs to be strengthened, although programmes for the unemployed already exist.

The current pension system only covers urban workers, and adequate provisions would need to be made to cater for the growing ageing population in the country.

Rising unemployment in Hong Kong, China

Unemployment in Hong Kong, China, fell steadily in 2000 but, as is the case elsewhere in the subregion, the unemployment rate has been rising since early 2001, with the seasonally adjusted rate standing at 5.3 per cent in September 2001, compared with 4.5 per cent in the first quarter of the year. This trend is expected to continue until the first half of 2002, especially as the new graduates start to enter the workforce. The economy of Hong Kong, China, would need to be even more flexible, knowledge-based and focused on high value added activities through continuous education, training and skills upgrading, especially with China's entry into WTO. The sudden economic downturn and the associated revenue shortfalls, and increased public expenditure, resulted in a considerable increase in the budget deficit, to 4.5 per cent of GDP during fiscal year 2001 compared with less than 1 percentage point in the previous year. In this context, the needs of an ageing population and the associated demand for greater public spending on health care and on social welfare and safety nets will put added pressure on government resources in the longer term. Facing an increasingly competitive financial industry, Hong Kong, China, also needs to upgrade its infrastructure in order to sustain an efficient and secure financial environment, strengthen financial risk management and monitoring capabilities, develop new products and services, such as a credit reference service, and introduce deposit insurance schemes that involve minimum moral hazard risks.

Mongolia in transition towards a market economy

Mongolia, which has been in transition towards a market-based economy, has made remarkable progress in reducing fiscal deficits and bringing down inflation in recent years. For example, inflation averaged 50 per cent annually during the period 1995-1997, compared with an average of less than 10 per cent a year in the following four years. The budget shortfall was also contained at around 6-7 per cent of GDP in 2000-2001 relative to over 12 per cent a year during the previous biennium. The current account deficit, however, remained at a high and rising level in 2000-2001. Larger inflows of ODA and FDI would relieve the pressures from this deficit, as would better export performance and diversification in combination with more streamlined import spending. There is also no sustainable substitute for greater domestic resource mobilization, again in combination with concerted efforts to rationalize and streamline public expenditure so as to further improve its relevance and impact in line with national development priorities. In this context, the granting of subsidies to public enterprises would need to be carefully reviewed along with policy measures to speed up the privatization process and encourage greater private sector participation in economic activities.

The Republic of Korea has made considerable progress in financial sector restructuring, including strengthened profitability, improved recapitalization and lower NPL ratios. Most of the needed improvements were made within the "hardware" institutional and regulator framework, while several elements in the "software" of the financial system, such as risk management, credit analysis, lending practices and financial system monitoring, require further development and strengthening for greater resilience and efficiency. The base of skilled human resources and managerial expertise needs to be both deepened and widened in order to maximize the potential within the reformed and reinforced financial industry. The privatization and sale of Government-owned banks and investment and trust companies will be a challenging task for the Republic of Korea in 2002.

Considerable progress in financial sector restructuring in the Republic of Korea

The corporate sector of the Republic of Korea is still highly vulnerable to external shocks; its exports are heavily concentrated in ICT products such as semiconductors and consumer and office electronics equipment. Although the overall level of corporate debt has declined and corporate profitability risen, a large segment of the corporate sector is still not able to cover and service borrowing costs from its own cash flows. Many firms therefore have to engage in operational restructuring, that is, closing non-profitable operations and concentrating on their core business activities in order to sharpen their international and domestic competitiveness and maintain their financial stability. However, the promotion of greater market discipline, improved corporate governance (including enhanced accountability and transparency in management, and better protection of minority shareholders' rights), and revamped insolvency laws and bankruptcy procedures would contribute to the corporate restructuring and strengthening processes. The successful sale of Daewoo Motor Co. and Hynix Semiconductor Inc. are expected to reduce market uncertainties, thus facilitating progress in corporate restructuring; Daewoo used to be one of the "Big Three" car manufacturers and Hynix the world's third largest computer-chip manufacturer.

The corporate sector needs to improve its competitiveness and profitability

The elderly dependency ratio is rising relatively rapidly in the Republic of Korea relative to other OECD countries. This has long-term implications for social welfare and social protection since the current National Pension Scheme is projected to be financially inadequate to meet future (funding) commitments. The current health care system also requires major revamping to enable it to meet future financial needs and provide better service.

DEVELOPED COUNTRIES OF THE REGION

Australia, Japan and New Zealand

Overview and prospects

The external slowdown had an adverse impact in 2001 and domestic stimulus measures proved insufficient

Notwithstanding their diverse structural characteristics, economic growth in the developed countries of the region slowed from 2000 to 2001. While external factors were primarily responsible for this weakened performance, domestic influences also played a part, particularly in Japan. The sharp decline in world demand came with dramatic suddenness in the later part of 2000 and continued unabated in 2001, thus reducing the contribution of net exports to output in all three countries. This did not apply to Australia which actually saw growth accelerate in 2001. In New Zealand, measures to stimulate domestic demand were not able to offset the externally generated contraction fully, so that GDP growth fell off by 1.2 percentage points; Japan slipped into its third economic recession within the last decade (figure II.31).

As discussed in chapter I of this *Survey,* the global slowdown originated in the United States and, in the initial stages, was largely concentrated in the ICT sector; it was therefore expected that the overall setback might be both shallow and short-lived. However, the consequent spillovers included higher unemployment and losses in business and consumer confidence, which were compounded by the terrorist attacks in September 2001. The generalized global downturn resulted in a reversal of export and output growth and higher unemployment in Japan and several of the economies of East and South-East Asia. These economies account for most of the trade flows of the ESCAP region, effectively intensifying the global slowdown. Given the speed and spread of the external slowdown, domestic activities could not be fully protected through conventional measures to stimulate domestic demand. On the positive side, GDP growth in Australia and New Zealand was still in excess of the OECD average of 2.0 per cent in 2001, although the same cannot be said for Japan.

Figure II.31. Rates of GDP growth of developed countries in the ESCAP region, 1998-2001

Australia, Japan and New Zealand

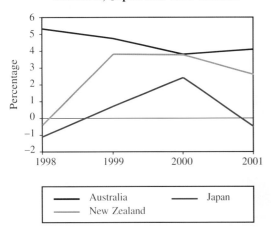

Sources: ESCAP, based on IMF, *International Financial Statistics,* vol. LIV, No. 10 (October 2001) and *World Economic Outlook* (Washington, December 2001); and Economist Intelligence Unit, *Country Forecasts* (London, 2001), various issues.

Note: Figures for 2001 are estimates.

Economic performance in all three countries hinges primarily on an improvement in the external environment combined with the impact of the fiscal and monetary policy easing that has already taken place (table II.37), plus any additional measures that might be taken in 2002. With regard to the global economy, current forecasts suggest only a marginal increase in output growth in 2002. However, the outcome for the three economies in 2002 is likely to be driven more by a recovery of growth in the United States than global developments, given their trading patterns and other external links. In this connection, the United States economy is not expected to display vibrancy until the second half of 2002, with GDP growth for the full year registering perhaps a modest decline compared with 2001. Aggregate output in Australia and New Zealand would therefore probably remain flat or expand slightly, while the economic contraction in Japan is expected to continue in 2002.

Uncertain prospects for 2002

The need to minimize rising unemployment and preserve consumer and investor confidence, via a combination of fiscal and monetary easing with structural reforms, is a major policy challenge in all three countries. Economic performance in Japan has been heavily weighed down by the legacy of the asset bubble collapse of the 1980s and the limited progress in meaningful reform of the domestic corporate and financial sectors. Consumer confidence has been sapped by successive downturns following short-lived recoveries in output. Indeed, a chronic phase of deflation persisted during the period 1999-2001, although the weakness of the yen in recent months might nudge prices upwards somewhat (figure II.32).

Major policy challenges ahead

Table II.37. Developed countries of the ESCAP region: budget and current account balance as a percentage of GDP, 1998-2001

(Percentage)

	1998	1999	2000	2001[a]
Budget balance as a percentage of GDP				
Australia[b, c]	0.3	0.8	0.9	0.5
Japan[c]	−4.5	−6.8	−7.9	−7.2
New Zealand[c]	1.0	0.4	0.6	0.7
Current account balance as a percentage of GDP				
Australia	−5.0	−5.9	−4.1	−1.9
Japan	3.1	2.4	2.5	1.8
New Zealand	−4.0	−6.5	−5.4	−2.0

Sources: ESCAP, based on IMF, *International Financial Statistics,* vol. LIV, No. 10 (October 2001) and *World Economic Outlook* (Washington, October 2001 and December 2001); and Economist Intelligence Unit, *Country Forecasts* (London, 2001), various issues.

[a] Estimate.
[b] Data exclude net advances (primarily privatization receipts and net policy-related lending).
[c] General government fiscal balance.

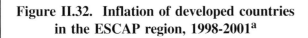

Figure II.32. Inflation of developed countries in the ESCAP region, 1998-2001ᵃ

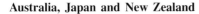

Australia, Japan and New Zealand

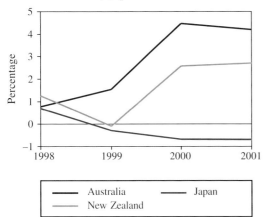

Sources: ESCAP, based on IMF, *International Financial Statistics*, vol. LIV, No. 10 (October 2001) and *World Economic Outlook* (Washington, December 2001); and Economist Intelligence Unit, *Country Forecasts* (London, 2001), various issues.

Note: Figures for 2001 are estimates.

ᵃ Percentage changes in the consumer price index.

Given the large excess capacity in domestic industry, however, deflationary trends are unlikely to be reversed in the short term. More recently, growing doubts have emerged about the long-term sustainability of the public debt, making economic policy formulation an unusually complex exercise. All things considered, a self-sustaining economic recovery is likely to prove elusive for some time in Japan.

In Australia, a certain amount of reform fatigue is apparent in the important areas of taxation, labour market practices and welfare policies. The Government's avowed reluctance to entertain budget deficits could reduce the scope for further fiscal stimulus in the event that the world economy were to prove weaker than anticipated at present. In addition, the scope for significant cuts in interest rates appears limited, with inflation running near the top of the Reserve Bank's target range and the Australian dollar tending to lose ground vis-à-vis the United States dollar as well as on a trade-weighted basis.

The fiscal situation in New Zealand, while somewhat easier than that in Australia, is likely to deteriorate as growth slows in the coming months. Unexpected demands on the State coffers, such as the bailout of Air New Zealand, have reduced room for fiscal manoeuvre in the short term. Monetary easing has been extended close to its prudential limits following the 11 September 2001 events; further easing could put pressure on the exchange rate of the New Zealand dollar. Given its high trade-to-GDP ratio, New Zealand's economic fortunes are thus primarily dependent upon an upturn in the global economy, particularly in the economies of Australia, Japan and the United States. These countries account for half of New Zealand's exports and are also an important source of tourist arrivals; the tourism industry is a significant source of employment and foreign earnings for the New Zealand economy.

GDP performance

Japanese GDP contraction driven by low consumer and business confidence

A buoyant world economy strengthened economic activity in Japan, with GDP growing by 2.4 per cent in 2000 (table II.38). The expansion, however, was not broad-based as it was led primarily by a spurt in business investment and net exports. Consumer expenditure remained

Table II.38. Developed countries of the ESCAP region: rates of economic growth and inflation, 1998-2001

(Percentage)

	1998	1999	2000	2001[a]
GDP growth rates				
Australia	5.3	4.7	3.8	4.1
Japan	−1.1	0.7	2.4	−0.5
New Zealand	−0.4	3.8	3.8	2.6
Inflation[b]				
Australia	0.8	1.5	4.5	4.2
Japan	0.7	−0.3	−0.7	−0.7
New Zealand	1.3	−0.1	2.6	2.7

Sources: ESCAP, based on IMF, *International Financial Statistics,* vol. LIV, No. 10 (October 2001) and *World Economic Outlook* (Washington, October 2001 and December 2001); and Economist Intelligence Unit, *Country Forecasts* (London, 2001), various issues.

[a] Estimate.
[b] Percentage changes in the consumer price index.

weak, as in 1999, and the economy stalled sharply towards the end of 2000 and at the beginning of 2001 as export growth came to an abrupt end and the ICT investment bubble burst. Compounding the adverse knock-on effects was the collapse of corporate profits to virtually zero in the first quarter of 2001, and most new business investment plans were suspended or cancelled as a consequence.

Consumer and business confidence in Japan has been severely undermined in the last few years by the continuing uncertainties regarding bank and corporate restructuring and their implications for job prospects and domestic demand. Unemployment had reached 5.6 per cent by the end of 2001 and was expected to rise further as companies were forced to restructure in order to survive. Consumer demand could thus remain stagnant into the foreseeable future, with little or no growth in real earnings and chronic uncertainties on the horizon. Another complicating factor against this backdrop is the emerging doubt about the viability of the public debt burden following the implementation of a series of sizeable, but largely ineffective, fiscal stimulus packages. The decline in nominal GDP is perhaps unprecedented in historical terms; by the end of 2002, aggregate output would be 5.4 per cent smaller than in 1997.

Most observers believe that there have not been adequate policy initiatives to deal decisively with the highly complex problems being experienced by the Japanese economy. Cutbacks in investment and falling consumer confidence have been further intensified as a result of stagnant private demand, flagging exports, continuing deflationary pressures and the inexorable compulsion on the financial system to reduce lending to weaker enterprises. More generally, business sentiment was also undermined by an acceleration in the relocation of production facilities abroad, particularly to China in anticipation of its accession to WTO. Meanwhile, the new fiscal stimulus package to be introduced early in 2002 is unlikely to have much of an impact given the dire state of public finances, among other reasons.

Deflation nullified monetary easing

The ongoing deflation has had a strong, perhaps decisive, influence on the Japanese economy in the last three years. There can be few worse combinations for indebted Japanese companies than falling prices and stagnant growth in real output. If present trends continue, downward pressures on prices could be higher in 2002. Thus, for more than two years, these companies will have had to service their loans with ever-falling revenues, and price levels in 2002 could well be lower than those in 1998. Deflation has thus perversely raised the real value of debt for both households and corporations in Japan, drastically weakening corporate balance sheets and, by raising the level of real interest rates, has largely nullified the effectiveness of monetary easing.

Australian growth robust in 2001

In contrast to the rest of the ESCAP region, Australia recorded fairly robust growth in 2001. The country enjoyed its ninth year of continuous expansion, the longest since the 1960s. Output gains during this period averaged just over 4 per cent, comparing very favourably with the performance of other OECD countries. The economy declined from the fourth quarter of 2000 and into 2001 in tandem with the global downturn. However, full year growth in 2001 was higher than in 2000, driven by strong household consumption and private capital spending. There was a fall off in net export earnings, which went up by just over 1 per cent in the first three quarters of 2001, compared with almost 13 per cent in the comparable period of 2000. At the same time, domestic problems such as higher energy prices had a negative impact on household consumption, while the weakening United States economy served to dampen the business climate and lower investment spending. The goods and services tax, introduced on 1 July 2000, created a strong incentive to carry out housing investment in the first half of the year, to be followed inevitably by a sharp decline in the second half. As a result of these negative impulses, industrial production was slightly down on a year-on-year basis by the latter part of 2001, while unemployment had risen marginally from 6.3 to 6.7 per cent in December 2001.

Strong productivity growth underpinned Australian economic performance

Australia's impressive economic performance, particularly over the last five years, and the relatively limited impact of the 2001 downturn, thus far at any rate, can be attributed to strong productivity growth, a close parallel to similar trends in the United States. Some recent research results indicate that about half of the labour productivity can be explained by capital deepening, and around two thirds of capital deepening can be attributed to ICT-related expenditure. Comparatively, such spending has had as large a qualitative impact as that in the United States and is actually well above the average for OECD countries. The investment-driven diffusion of ICT, and the sizeable positive externalities associated with it, should continue to yield benefits on an economy-wide basis, once the downturn ends. It also explains the limited impact of the 2001 slowdown in the country.

After rising rather strongly in 2000, inflation flattened out somewhat in 2001. Movements in energy prices were the principal factor behind both the increase and the subsequent improvement in consumer prices during those two years. Changes in the tax regime, including the new goods and services tax, also contributed in part to the upward pressure on prices, estimated to be equivalent to an annualized 2.5 percentage points between June 2000 and June 2001. Flooding in parts of the country early in 2001 raised fruit and vegetable prices sharply, but the increases were reversed as supplies returned to normal. The outlook for inflation is mostly benign, as the effects of the new tax system will have gone out of the index after June 2001. Other positive elements include more affordable energy prices and moderate growth in labour earnings owing to a slight increase in unemployment. The only question mark in the above context is a seemingly persistent weakness in the exchange rate of the Australian dollar.

Modest price pressures

Despite the global slowdown, economic activities remained buoyant in the country in 2001, with GDP expanding at a rate faster than that in OECD economies. This strong performance was primarily driven by government spending and net exports, plus a robust increase in non-residential fixed investment in agriculture, especially in certain new downstream activities in forestry and fishing. The global slowdown had a somewhat delayed effect on New Zealand and was felt only through faltering business confidence in the aftermath of the 11 September 2001 events in the United States.

New Zealand's economy showed good growth in 2001

The relatively good economic performance of New Zealand was achieved with monetary stability. Consumer prices rose by around 2.6 per cent a year over 2000-2001, despite a falling local currency and much higher energy prices in 2000. It thus appears that higher import prices have been absorbed by shrinking margins at the wholesale and retail trade levels. However, this process cannot be sustained indefinitely and the weaker exchange rate, if it persists, would have a negative impact on the price situation at some stage. There is a policy dilemma in this connection: the depreciation has been instrumental in stimulating exports and keeping out imports. There are trade-offs involved, however; stimulating exports and maintaining price stability may not be achievable within the same policy matrix.

... and with stable prices

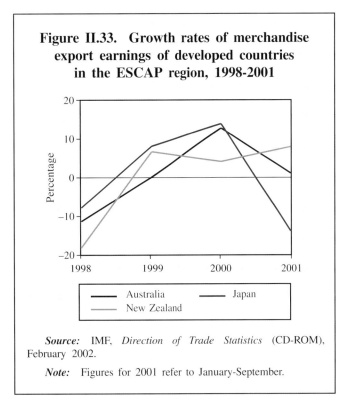

Figure II.33. Growth rates of merchandise export earnings of developed countries in the ESCAP region, 1998-2001

Australia — Japan —
New Zealand —

Source: IMF, *Direction of Trade Statistics* (CD-ROM), February 2002.

Note: Figures for 2001 refer to January-September.

Foreign trade and other external transactions

Foreign trade (as a proportion of GDP) plays a relatively limited role in the economy of Japan compared with other developed countries, and a much smaller part compared with the relative share of trade in the developing countries of the ESCAP region. However, its absolute magnitude is substantial, equivalent to over $800 billion annually in export and import value, and therefore the pattern of Japanese trade has a huge significance for Japan's trading partners, especially the developing countries of the ESCAP region. More specifically, Japan is the world's second largest importer and exporter of ICT components and products and its trade pattern over the last two years is largely a reflection of the global electronics cycle (figures II.33 and II.34). The buoyant electronics markets underpinned external demand for Japanese ICT products and overall exports rose by 14 per cent in 2000. World demand tapered off in the last quarter of 2000 and declined sharply in the first three quarters of 2001, causing a contraction of nearly 14 per cent in export earnings.

Narrowing current account surplus in Japan ...

... with import penetration expanding

Imports followed a broadly similar pattern, rising strongly in 1999 and 2000 and falling in 2001. However, a new feature of Japanese foreign trade is the rapid increase in the import penetration of consumer goods. Consequently, the trade surplus declined from 3 to 2 per cent of GDP over the period 1998-2001. With services being in broad balance, the current account surplus has also narrowed, although a strong increase in investment income pushed the current account surplus back above 2.5 per cent of GDP in the first half of 2001. The outcome for the whole year is likely to be lower again, at under 2 per cent of GDP. Japan should nevertheless continue to be a significant provider of global investment funds on a net basis into the foreseeable future, despite the recent narrowing of the current account surplus. Notably, the external reserves of Japan had reached nearly $397 billion in November 2001, the highest in the world.

Trade within the ESCAP region on the rise

The strong expansion of Japanese trade with the Asian and Pacific countries was another feature in 2000, when exports to the region went up by over 28 per cent and imports by 29 per cent. This intraregional dynamism in trade stood in sharp contrast to the more modest growth in trade with the United States and the European Union. More significant, around two fifths of Japanese exports currently go to the Asian and Pacific region, which is the source of a roughly similar proportion of Japanese imports. Such intraregional trade is the clearest manifestation of the "componentization" of the electronics industry in East and South-East Asia, often via Japanese FDI. While such trading links have given Asian economies a high and growing share in a rapidly expanding sector of manufacturing, they have at the same time accentuated their vulnerability to external cyclical forces. The product cycle of electronics tends to be significantly more volatile than that of traditional manufactured goods, as revealed by the crisis of 1997 and the upturn of 1999 and 2000. Consequently, a substantial slowdown in capital investment by corporations would tend to have

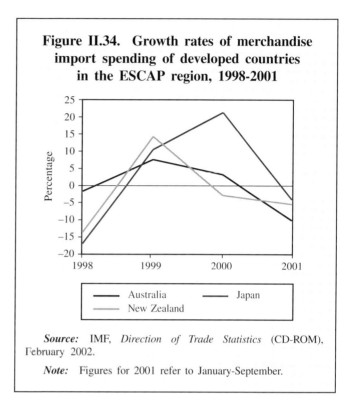

Figure II.34. Growth rates of merchandise import spending of developed countries in the ESCAP region, 1998-2001

Source: IMF, *Direction of Trade Statistics* (CD-ROM), February 2002.

Note: Figures for 2001 refer to January-September.

disproportionately large effects on trade in electronic products as well as on related activities among the suppliers concerned, and vice versa.

A high rate of export expansion, by almost 13 per cent in 2000, and lower growth in import spending, at just over 3 per cent (tables II.39 and II.40) contributed to a smaller deficit of 2 per cent of GDP in the external current account; the comparable figure was at the high

Lower current account deficit in Australia ...

Table II.39. Developed countries of the ESCAP region: merchandise exports and their rates of growth, 1998-2001

	Value (Millions of US dollars)	Exports (f.o.b.)			
		Annual rate of growth (Percentage)			
	2000	1998	1999	2000	2001 Jan.-Sep.
Australia	63 128	−11.3	0.1	12.7	1.1
Japan	477 323	−7.9	8.1	13.9	−13.9
New Zealand	12 712	−18.1	6.7	4.1	7.9

Source: IMF, *Direction of Trade Statistics* (CD-ROM), February 2002.

level of 5-6 per cent as recently as 1998-1999. The Australian export performance in the last three years reflects higher earnings from both traditional exports (i.e. coal, meat, metals, wheat and wool) and non-traditional items, including the so-called elaborately transformed manu-factures, and services. Imports continue to cover a wide range of items, with expenditure on capital goods displaying one of the highest rates of growth. Approximately 33 per cent of Australian imports are currently sourced from the ESCAP region, compared with around one-fifth in 1997.

Table II.40. **Developed countries of the ESCAP region: merchandise imports and their rates of growth, 1998-2001**

| | Value (Millions of US dollars) | Imports (c.i.f.) | | | |
| | | Annual rate of growth (Percentage) | | | |
	2000	1998	1999	2000	2001 Jan.-Sep.
Australia	74 265	−1.7	7.6	3.3	−10.1
Japan	377 152	−17.0	10.5	21.4	−4.0
New Zealand	13 971	−13.6	14.3	−2.8	−5.4

Source: IMF, *Direction of Trade Statistics* (CD-ROM), February 2002.

... as the debt-servicing burden declined

Notwithstanding the persistent current account deficits, Australia's net foreign debt stood at about 49 per cent of GDP, or close to $170 billion, in 2001. Benefiting from lower interest rates, however, the debt-service ratio went down from over 9.5 to 9.1 per cent of foreign exchange earnings from 2000 to 2001. At that level and with a declin-ing current account deficit, external debt is no longer considered an issue of significance. Nevertheless, prolonged weakness in the Australian dollar exchange rate would in effect raise the debt-service burden in local currency, with possible negative implications for the holders of such debt (figure II.35).

New Zealand's current account deficit also shrank

The pattern of New Zealand's foreign trade in 2000 and 2001 displayed a striking resemblance to the experience of Australia. Exports went up in 2000, though less strongly than in Australia, and imports fell, thus narrowing the current account deficit by more than 3 percentage points of GDP. Contrary to trends elsewhere, export growth actually picked up in the first three quarters of 2001, while imports continued to decline. The current account deficit fell to 2 per cent of GDP, compared

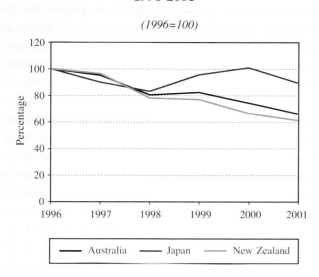

Figure II.35. Index of exchange rates against the United States dollar of developed countries in the ESCAP region, 1996-2001

(1996=100)

Sources: IMF, *International Financial Statistics,* vol. LV, No. 1 (January 2002); and *Far Eastern Economic Review,* various issues.

Note: Figures for 2001 are estimates.

with 6.5 per cent in 1999. Unlike Australia, however, New Zealand's exports are still predominantly traditional in nature (e.g. dairy, meat, forestry and fisheries products) and this explains the lagged response of New Zealand's exports to the 2001 global slowdown. Standing at over 50 per cent of GDP in 2001, foreign trade plays a much bigger role in the economy of New Zealand than in Australia. Trade with the Asian and Pacific region accounts for around one third of the total and thus economic activity in New Zealand is closely linked to trading performance in general and to trade with the ESCAP region in particular. However, New Zealand's exports are primarily traditional consumer goods and therefore the downside risks are likely to be limited over the short term.

Key policy issues

Among the major policy issues confronting all three countries is the need to counter the sharp and rather sudden deterioration in the external environment in 2001, a setback which could well linger into much of 2002. The decline in GDP growth, if it persists, would bring a host of economic and social problems in its wake. In particular, as public

Australia and New Zealand faced with cyclical downturns

finances come under pressure and unemployment rises, Governments have to grapple with, and reconcile, difficult policy trade-offs, for example stimulating growth through fiscal and monetary measures without putting at risk macroeconomic, and especially price stability. At the micro level, a slowdown often calls into question the functioning of product and labour markets; the viability of particular activities and hence the related human resource skills; the reallocation of resources from slow-moving to more dynamic sectors; and the provision of social protection to the more vulnerable sections of the community, such as the unemployed and older persons.

Serious structural impediments to growth to be addressed by Japan

While Australia and New Zealand have had to grapple primarily with a cyclical downturn, Japan has had to manage a far more serious set of policy issues, in particular, a range of long-term, structural impediments to growth that have had an adverse impact on domestic economic performance over the last decade. In real terms, GDP expanded by barely 1.75 per cent a year in the 1990s, down considerably from an annual average of 4 per cent a decade earlier. Moreover, such a comparatively modest economic performance has major implications for the ESCAP region as a whole, given Japan's crucial role as a market and as a source of both FDI and financial resources for many regional economies. The following paragraphs contain a brief discussion of the principal policy issues facing the three countries.

... as it experiences another economic contraction ...

In Japan, successive cyclical downturns have been superimposed upon structural deficiencies, so that the economy has simply lurched from one setback to another over the last decade. There have been three recessions in the last 10 years, and negative GDP growth in 2001 was expected to persist into 2002. A number of different hypotheses have been advanced to explain the persistence of the economic problems in Japan. The roots undoubtedly lie in the bursting of the asset price bubble in the 1980s and the ensuing massive losses of personal and corporate wealth in the 1990s. The financial sector both contributed to the excesses of the 1980s and suffered subsequently from the chronic weakness of the economy in the 1990s. It magnified each phase considerably in the process. In the 1980s, for example, there were massive increases in bank lending, operating both directly and through a self-reinforcing cycle with rising prices on land (the main collateral for bank lending) and stocks (a component of bank capital). However, the process then operated in reverse with the bursting of the asset price bubble, forcing under-capitalized banks to stop lending, while collapsing land values left many loans devoid of adequate security and effectively non-performing. This process, in turn, largely nullified the impact of expansionary monetary policies as households and corporations were unable to respond to the lower interest rates.

An addendum to the above hypothesis relates to the rather static pattern of productivity growth in Japan, especially in services. An overvalued exchange rate gravely weakened corporate balance sheets and significantly reduced productivity-enhancing investment in the early to mid-1990s. In this connection, it has been argued that the introduction of new technologies is strongly conditioned by the prospects for future demand for them, and any perceived demand insufficiency, say, for services, would result in delays by corporations in introducing new technology. Japan has become the victim of a liquidity trap along with falling profit rates; with nominal interest rates being close to zero and with the emerging deflationary pressures, real interest rates have become too high for corporations to be able to borrow and invest (table II.41). As a result, economic activities have become stuck in a low- or no-growth mode, despite the succession of fiscal packages implemented in the 1990s.

... low consumer confidence and poor productivity growth undermining economic performance and posing new policy challenges

Table II.41. Developed countries of the ESCAP region: short-term interest rates and money supply growth (M2), 1998-2001

(Percentage)

	1998	*1999*	*2000*	*2001[a]*
Short-term interest rates				
Australia	4.7	5.8	6.2	4.2
Japan	0.5	0.2	0.5	0.02
New Zealand	7.3	4.8	6.5	6.2
Money supply growth (M2)				
Australia	8.4	11.7	3.8	8.6[b]
Japan	4.1	3.4	1.1	1.6[b]
New Zealand	14.6	7.8	0.9	13.7[b]

Sources: ESCAP, based on IMF, *International Financial Statistics,* vol. LIV, No. 10 (October 2001); OECD, *OECD Economic Outlook,* No. 70 (December 2001); and Economist Intelligence Unit, *Country Forecasts* (London, 2001), various issues.

[a] Estimate.

[b] January-June.

There has been renewed emphasis on the critical need to bring about sustained recovery in Japan over the medium term, with the economy faltering yet again in 2000 and 2001. For its part, the new Government has unequivocally accepted the reform agenda. It has recognized the pressing reasons for structural reforms to raise productivity growth in the economy in addition to the need to address the question of fiscal consolidation in a credible and realistic manner over the next few years. Among the principal items on the reform agenda are the problems of an insolvent banking sector. There has also been considerable debate about the conduct of monetary policy and what might be an appropriate exchange rate for the yen so as to aid the recovery process. Evidently, however, there are no easy options or shortcuts.

Massive NPL problems and demanding structural reforms

There is general agreement that the most urgent need is for the Japanese authorities to develop a package of reforms in the banking sector in combination with the removal of structural impediments to growth. The impediments include high levels of corporate debt, the lack of consolidation of small businesses and the absence of market forces and competition in the provision of health and nursing care, social welfare and education. Greater flexibility in the labour market and stimulating business start-ups, including through changes in the regulatory regime, are other complementary measures in support of the reform process.

Estimates vary widely as to the true extent of the NPL problem. In April 2001, for example, Japan's Financial Services Agency put NPLs at about 25 per cent of GDP. Thus, it seems unrealistic to assume that a problem of this magnitude can be eradicated within three years, as has been suggested. Nevertheless, the ongoing failure to tackle the NPL problem has led to a series of downgrades of Japanese banks and corporations by international credit rating agencies, setbacks that have in effect nullified the stimulus that was supposed to have been provided by easier monetary conditions. It has also caused a net outflow of yen-denominated assets, primarily as a result of concerns about the solvency of the Japanese banking system. These concerns weakened the yen exchange rate sharply in the later part of 2001 and early in 2002. As of late February 2002, for example, the yen-dollar rate had reached 134, compared with 118 a year earlier, equivalent to a depreciation of around 13 per cent. The yen volatility will inevitably have implications and ripple effects for other economies in the region.

The Australian economy to expand moderately in 2002

In Australia, GDP growth is expected to ease in 2002 to around 3 per cent or over, without the emergence of any significant domestic imbalances; in this context, the underlying inflation is low but the potential inflationary consequences of a weakening exchange rate constitute a downside risk. The range of structural reforms undertaken in recent years has made Australia well prepared to cope with adverse external shocks. Labour market flexibility has improved considerably in recent years, while better industrial relations have been complemented by the introduction of more active job search facilities, which has aided labour mobility. These measures have been reinforced by initiatives to strengthen the economy's innovative capacity, especially in services and in the creation of new jobs. The functioning of product markets has been enhanced by the removal of restrictions on competition that were either accepted or implicit in long-standing legislation and practices in the country.

The tax reform package of 2000 has aided fiscal consolidation by broadening the tax base; it has enhanced productivity as well by the elimination of differential taxation for labour and capital and the abolition of restrictive practices. Some items in the reform programme, such as a new framework for superannuation and the reduction of relatively high personal tax rates, could be delayed as a result of the current slowdown. However, such delays should have no material impact on economic performance in the country. All in all, Australia should be able to see out the current slowdown relatively unscathed and, when it ends, resume the high growth path of the last few years. All this reflects and is predicated on a combination of continued macroeconomic stability, the rapid implementation of structural reforms and greater emphasis on sustaining growth through higher long-term productivity.

New Zealand has weathered the turbulence of the last few years relatively well and, contrary to what tended to happen in the past, high levels of fiscal deficit and inflation have been successfully avoided. Nonetheless, recent economic performance has fallen short of expectations and certain vulnerabilities remain. The economy is still heavily dependent on traditional agricultural commodities and thus remains strongly exposed to swings in international commodity prices over which it has little control. Although the current account deficit went down sharply in 2001, New Zealand has had a relatively low savings rate, making it dependent upon foreign capital to maintain investment levels. It is therefore vulnerable to swings and shifts in investor sentiment, changes largely unrelated to any domestic events or developments within New Zealand. Furthermore, compared with Australia, overall productivity remains low on account of low economies of scale, the protection given to agriculture in other OECD economies and persistent weakness in New Zealand's terms of trade.

New Zealand must boost productivity through investment in education ...

On the plus side, New Zealand has established, with prudent macroeconomic policies, a positive framework for improving savings and investment, thus boosting productivity in the future. The current slowdown could delay progress in these areas to some extent, but the country's competitive position has strengthened considerably following the exchange rate depreciation; market growth could be quite robust with the expected global recovery in late 2002. At the same time, it would be unrealistic to overlook the disadvantages of New Zealand's small size, geographical isolation and relatively limited resource endowment, particularly labour skills. Investment in education and retraining is thus a key priority for the future.

... to counter the disadvantages of its small size

THE FEASIBILITY OF ACHIEVING THE MILLENNIUM DEVELOPMENT GOALS IN ASIA AND THE PACIFIC

INTRODUCTION AND OVERVIEW

World conferences and summits held by the United Nations during the 1990s adopted many goals for sustainable economic and social development. Building on those, in June 2000, the United Nations, the World Bank, IMF and OECD jointly endorsed a set of international development targets for all countries in the world (see box III.1). Those targets became the foundation of the millennium development goals.

The United Nations Millennium Declaration, unanimously adopted at the Millennium Summit held in New York from 6 to 8 September 2000, contains a large number of objectives and goals, mostly qualitative in nature, urging action by countries and other stakeholders.[1] However, there are a number of quantitative goals for which deadlines have been set for achievement through collective action.

The millennium development goals cover all major areas related to the well-being of people, including extreme poverty, education, health, gender equality and the environment. These are interlinked, and efforts to achieve one goal will have positive spillover effects on several others. For example, the achievement of the targets on education, particularly female education, serve to underpin poverty alleviation, better nutrition and family health, improved environment and so forth.

The report of the Secretary-General entitled "Road map towards the implementation of the United Nations Millennium Declaration"[2] elaborated on the goals. In that document, 1990 was established as the relevant base year for comparison; the targets were made more specific and indicators defined to monitor them. The goals, with their targets and indicators, are reproduced in table III.1.

The United Nations Millennium Declaration addresses vast challenges being faced by mankind and provides a policy agenda, as encapsulated in the millennium development goals

---

[1] General Assembly resolution 55/2 of 8 September 2000, paras. 19 and 20.

[2] A/56/326.

Box III.1. Background of the millennium development goals: global conferences and international development targets

During the 1990s, a number of United Nations world conferences and summits were held, including the following:

- World Summit for Children, New York, 1990
- World Conference on Education for All: Meeting Basic Learning Needs, Jomtien, Thailand, 1990
- United Nations Conference on Environment and Development, Rio de Janeiro, Brazil, 1992
- International Conference on Nutrition, Rome, 1992
- World Conference on Human Rights, Vienna, 1993
- International Conference on Population and Development, Cairo, 1994
- Fourth World Conference on Women, Beijing, 1995
- World Summit for Social Development, Copenhagen, 1995
- World Food Summit, Rome, 1996
- United Nations Conference on Human Settlements (Habitat II), Istanbul, 1996

The World Summit for Social Development is briefly reviewed below to illustrate the foundation of the millennium development goals.

World Summit for Social Development

The World Summit for Social Development, held at Copenhagen in March 1995, was the first major United Nations conference specifically devoted to social development issues. It adopted the Copenhagen Declaration and Programme of Action, which drew extensively on the recommendations of earlier conferences, particularly the United Nations Conference on Environment and Development and the International Conference on Population and Development. The Declaration and Programme of Action also benefited from the preparatory work for the Fourth World Conference on Women and the United Nations Conference on Human Settlements (Habitat II). The Copenhagen Declaration contains 10 commitments made by world leaders to:[a]

- Eradicate absolute poverty by a target date to be set by each country
- Support full employment as a basic policy goal
- Promote social integration based on the enhancement and protection of all human rights
- Achieve equality and equity between women and men
- Accelerate the development of Africa and the least developed countries
- Ensure that structural adjustment programmes include social development goals
- Increase resources allocated to social development
- Create an economic, political, social, cultural and legal environment that will enable people to achieve social development
- Attain universal and equitable access to education and primary health care
- Strengthen cooperation for social development through the United Nations

The Programme of Action outlines policies, actions and measures to implement the commitments enunciated in the Declaration. It makes countries responsible for defining time-bound goals and targets for eradicating absolute poverty, reducing unemployment and enhancing social integration, within their own national context. The Programme of Action also contains some time-bound goals and actions.

---

[a] United Nations, World Summit for Social Development, *The Copenhagen Declaration and Programme of Action* (New York, 1995), p. vii.

International development targets

Building on the world conferences and summits of the 1990s, the international development targets listed below, address some of the many dimensions of poverty and their effects on people's lives.[b]

(1)   Halve between 1990 and 2015, the proportion of people living in extreme poverty

(2)   Enrol all children in primary school by 2015

(3)   Make progress towards gender equality and empowering women by eliminating gender disparities in primary and secondary education by 2005

(4)   Reduce infant and child mortality rates by two thirds between 1990 and 2015

(5)   Reduce maternal mortality ratios by three quarters between 1990 and 2015

(6)   Provide access for all who need reproductive health services by 2015

(7)   Implement national strategies for sustainable development by 2005 so as to reverse the loss of environmental resources by 2015

---

[b]   All international development targets, except those on infant mortality and reproductive health services, are covered by the millennium development goals. However, infant mortality is a part of the indicators for monitoring the target on the under-5 mortality rate, whereas reproductive health services are included among the selected indicators for monitoring the goal on HIV/AIDS and other major diseases. The millennium development goals have additional targets (not covered by international development targets) on hunger, safe drinking water, gender equality for higher education (not just secondary education), HIV/AIDS and other major diseases, and improved lives for slum dwellers.

Conceptual and empirical issues encountered in monitoring the implementation of the millennium development goals

It is obvious that, in the absence of the relevant data and information, particularly consistent time-series data, progress in the implementation of the goals cannot be monitored at all. In addition, if some data are available but not reliable or comparable, definite conclusions cannot be drawn; for example, if there are wide differences in data on the same indicator as reported from different sources. Moreover, data may be available for some goals and not others and their coverage may also be limited. Lastly, the non-availability or limited availability of data for the benchmark year 1990 poses yet another set of problems. Cross-sectional data on indicators may not be comparable across countries as a result of the inevitable differences in definitions and methodologies. This limits the practicability and feasibility not only of country comparisons but also of aggregation at the subregional and regional levels.

Bearing these qualifications in mind, a preliminary assessment was made of the feasibility of achieving certain goals, the results of which are reported below. The selected goals pertain to the eradication of extreme poverty and hunger, the achievement of universal primary education, the promotion of gender equality and the empowerment of women, reduction of child mortality and improvement of maternal health.

- The eradication of extreme poverty is the overarching millennium development goal, and the target is to halve the proportion of people with a daily income less than one dollar (in terms of purchasing power parity) between 1990 and 2015. Based on

Table III.1. Millennium development goals, targets and indicators

Goals and targets	*Indicators*
Goal 1. Eradicate extreme poverty and hunger	
Target 1. Halve, between 1990 and 2015, the proportion of people whose income is less than one dollar a day	1. Proportion of population below one dollar per day
	2. Poverty gap ratio (incidence x depth of poverty)
	3. Share of poorest quintile in national consumption
Target 2. Halve, between 1990 and 2015, the proportion of people who suffer from hunger	4. Prevalence of underweight children (under 5 years of age)
	5. Proportion of population below minimum level of dietary energy consumption
Goal 2. Achieve universal primary education	
Target 3. Ensure that, by 2015, children everywhere, boys and girls alike, will be able to complete a full course of primary schooling	6. Net enrolment ratio in primary education
	7. Proportion of pupils starting grade 1 who reach grade 5
	8. Literacy rate of 15-24-year-olds
Goal 3. Promote gender equality and empower women	
Target 4. Eliminate gender disparity in primary and secondary education, preferably by 2005, and to all levels of education no later than 2015	9. Ratio of girls to boys in primary, secondary and tertiary education
	10. Ratio of literate females to males among 15-to-24-year-olds
	11. Share of women in wage employment in the non-agricultural sector
	12. Proportion of seats held by women in national parliament
Goal 4. Reduce child mortality	
Target 5. Reduce by two thirds, between 1990 and 2015, the under-5 mortality rate	13. Under-5 mortality rate
	14. Infant mortality rate
	15. Proportion of 1-year-old children immunized against measles
Goal 5. Improve maternal health	
Target 6. Reduce by three quarters, between 1990 and 2015, the maternal mortality ratio	16. Maternal mortality ratio
	17. Proportion of births attended by skilled health personnel
Goal 6. Combat HIV/AIDS, malaria and other diseases	
Target 7. Have halted by 2015 and begun to reverse the spread of HIV/AIDS	18. HIV prevalence among 15-to-24-year-old pregnant women
	19. Contraceptive prevalence rate
	20. Number of children orphaned by HIV/AIDS
Target 8. Have halted by 2015 and begun to reverse the incidence of malaria and other major diseases	21. Prevalence and death rates associated with malaria
	22. Proportion of population in malaria risk areas using effective malaria prevention and treatment measures
	23. Prevalence and death rates associated with tuberculosis
	24. Proportion of tuberculosis cases detected and cured under directly observed short course of treatment

(Continued on next page)

Table III.1 *(continued)*

Goals and targets	Indicators
Goal 7. Ensure environmental sustainability[a]	
Target 9. Integrate the principles of sustainable development into country policies and programmes and reverse the loss of environmental resources	25. Proportion of land area covered by forest 26. Land area protected to maintain biological diversity 27. GDP per unit of energy use (as proxy for energy efficiency) 28. Carbon dioxide emissions (per capita) [Plus two figures of global atmospheric pollution: ozone depletion and the accumulation of global warming gases]
Target 10. Halve by 2015 the proportion of people without sustainable access to safe drinking water	29. Proportion of population with sustainable access to an improved water source
Target 11. Have achieved a significant improvement in the lives of at least 100 million slum dwellers by 2020	30. Proportion of people with access to improved sanitation 31. Proportion of people with access to secure tenure *[Urban/rural disaggregation of several of the above indicators may be relevant for monitoring improvement in the lives of slum dwellers]*
Goal 8. Develop a global partnership for development[a]	
Target 12. Develop further an open, rule-based, predictable, non-discriminatory trading and financial system Includes a commitment to good governance, development, and poverty reduction – both nationally and internationally	*[Some of the indicators listed below will be monitored separately for the least developed countries (LDCs), Africa, landlocked countries and small island developing States]* **Official development assistance**
Target 13. Address the special needs of the least developed countries Includes: tariff- and quota-free access for least developed countries' exports; enhanced programme of debt relief for heavily indebted poor countries (HIPCs) and cancellation of official bilateral debt; and more generous ODA for countries committed to poverty reduction	32. Net ODA as percentage of OECD/Development Assistance Committee donors' gross national product (targets of 0.7 per cent in total and 0.15 per cent for LDCs) 33. Proportion of ODA to basic social services (basic education, primary health care, nutrition, safe water and sanitation) 34. Proportion of ODA that is untied 35. Proportion of ODA for environment in small island developing States 36. Proportion of ODA for transport sector in landlocked countries
Target 14. Address the special needs of landlocked countries and small island developing States (through the Programme of Action for the Sustainable Development of Small Island Developing States and the outcome of the twenty-second special session of the General Assembly)	**Market access** 37. Proportion of exports (by value and excluding arms) admitted free of duties and quotas 38. Average tariffs and quotas on agricultural products and textiles and clothing

(Continued on next page)

189

Table III.1   *(continued)*

Goals and targets	Indicators
Target 15. Deal comprehensively with the debt problems of developing countries through national and international measures in order to make debt sustainable in the long term	39. Domestic and export agricultural subsidies in OECD countries 40. Proportion of ODA provided to help to build trade capacity **Debt sustainability** 41. Proportion of official bilateral HIPC debt cancelled 42. Debt service as a percentage of exports of goods and services 43. Proportion of ODA provided as debt relief 44. Number of countries reaching HIPC decision and completion points
Target 16. In cooperation with developing countries, develop and implement strategies for decent and productive work for youth	45. Unemployment rate of 15-to-24-year-olds
Target 17. In cooperation with pharmaceutical companies, provide access to affordable essential drugs in developing countries	46. Proportion of population with access to affordable essential drugs on a sustainable basis
Target 18. In cooperation with the private sector, make available the benefits of new technologies, especially information and communications	47. Telephone lines per 1,000 people 48. Personal computers per 1,000 people *[Other indicators to be decided]*

Source: United Nations, "Road map towards the implementation of the United Nations Millenium Declarartion", report of the Secretary-General (A/56/326).

a   The selection of indicators for goals 7 and 8 is subject to further refinement.

Achievement of some millennium development goals is possible given concerted efforts made to sustain ongoing progress thus far

past trends, the achievement of this target for the ESCAP region as a whole may be possible,[3] especially given the sustained performance of East Asia (mainly China) and South-East Asia. However, South Asia and individual countries in other subregions (such as Cambodia and Papua New Guinea) may not be able to attain the target. The current global downturn, if prolonged, could pose a downside risk to maintaining past successes in poverty reduction.

---

[3]   Time-series data on the incidence of poverty are available for only a small number of countries.

- With regard to hunger, the target is to halve, between 1990 and 2015, the proportion of people who suffer from hunger. Owing to the lack of reliable consistent time-series data, a definitive statement cannot be made on the possibility of the achievement of the target for hunger and undernourishment.

- Universal primary education for boys and girls appears on target for achievement by 2015, based on current evidence.

- In terms of gender equality and empowerment of women, the current gender disparity in primary and secondary education is to be removed, preferably by 2005, and at all levels of education, no later than 2015. Slow progress in South Asia and in some countries in other subregions may render it difficult to realize this goal.

- As to child mortality, the target is to reduce the under-5 mortality rate by two thirds between 1990 and 2015. For the ESCAP region as a whole, progress thus far seems slower than desired, so that the achievement of this goal could be doubtful if current trends persist.

- With regard to maternal health, the target is to reduce the maternal mortality ratio by three quarters between 1990 and 2015. There is a lack of reliable time-series data for measuring the progress on the achievement of the target, making it very difficult to predict the outcome for this goal.

In order to draw pertinent policy lessons, a more rigorous analysis is needed of the main determinants in success stories as well as the root causes of the slow progress made by many countries in realizing the set of goals and targets.[4] Some strategies for achieving the targets are outlined in this chapter, and in-depth, follow-up reviews and analyses are required. However, a major effort has to be made by a large number of countries in the collection of reliable and consistent time-series data, as mentioned earlier. There is an additional significant requirement: suitably disaggregated data do not exist in many countries to enable the needed assessment of whether the achievement of a goal at the national level is accompanied by the fulfilment of the same target in all domestic regions or for all income groups within the country. Comprehensive and periodic data collection and storage and retrieval constitute a time-consuming and expensive undertaking. In this connection and as appropriate, countries should be encouraged and assisted, inter alia, through capacity-building of their statistical departments and exchange of hands on experience on a subregional and regional basis.

---

[4] ESCAP and UNDP plan to bring out a joint detailed report, towards the end of 2002, on the implementation status of the millennium development goals in the ESCAP region, along with an in-depth analysis of policy issues related to the achievement of the targets. A similar report is planned for 2004.

IMPLEMENTATION STATUS OF SELECTED MILLENNIUM DEVELOPMENT GOALS

Goal 1. Eradication of extreme poverty and hunger

The overarching goal is halving extreme poverty between 1990 and 2015

Extreme poverty is the major problem facing many developing countries of the ESCAP region, and the first target for its reduction is to halve the proportion of people with a daily income of less than one dollar between 1990 and 2015 (see table III.1). The primary indicator for this target is the headcount index, giving the percentage of the population with a daily income or consumption below one dollar per capita.[5] The poverty gap ratio and the share of the poorest quintile in national income/consumption are suggested as secondary indicators.

The dollar poverty line is defined in terms of purchasing power parity to allow cross-country comparison of poverty estimates.[6] Some estimates based on this definition of the poverty line are given in table III.2.

The incidence of extreme poverty in East Asia, South-East Asia and the Pacific declined rapidly during the 1990s, from 28 to 15 per cent between 1990 and 1998. On this trend-line basis and given sustained efforts, the goal of halving poverty between 1990 and 2015 would be

---

Table III.2. Incidence of extreme poverty by subregion, 1990-1998

	Percentage of the population living on less than one dollar a day			
	1990	*1993*	*1996*	*1998*
East Asia, South-East Asia and the Pacific	27.6	25.2	14.9	15.3
(Excluding China:	18.5	15.9	10.0	11.3)
South Asia	44.0	42.4	42.3	40.0
Eastern Europe and Central Asia	1.6	4.0	5.1	5.1
Asia and the Pacific	34.3	–	–	25.6

Source: ESCAP based on World Bank, *World Development Report 2000/2001: Attacking Poverty* (New York, Oxford University Press, 2000), p. 23. Aggregate data for Asia and the Pacific, covering East Asia, South-East Asia and the Pacific plus South Asia, have been derived by the ESCAP secretariat.

---

[5] A primary indicator is most directly and closely associated with the target. The secondary indicators, less directly associated with the target, are used for gathering supporting evidence. If data on the primary indicator are not available, these secondary indicators become proxy indicators for monitoring progress.

[6] More precisely, the poverty line is $1.08 per capita a day at 1993 purchasing power parity. For the many limitations of the poverty estimates, see Angus Deaton, "Counting the world's poor: problems and possible solutions", *World Bank Research Observer*, vol. 16, No. 2 (fall 2001); see also the comments on the paper by Martin Ravallion and T.N. Srinivasan in the same issue.

within reach in East Asia and South-East Asia. Progress in poverty reduction in South Asia has been slow, only 4 percentage points over the same period, and thus achievement of the above target remains doubtful. Eastern Europe and Central Asia had very low poverty rates in the pre-transition period.[7] Subsequently, those rates showed rapid increases in most of the 1990s, especially in several countries in Central Asia, which face great difficulties and thus have little chance of achieving the goal of halving poverty with 1990 as the base year.

For Asia and the Pacific as a whole, the incidence of poverty fell from 34.3 to 25.6 per cent between 1990 and 1998, or about 9 percentage points in eight years (table III.2). The target of halving poverty by 2015 would be met if this figure dropped to around 17 per cent, or by another 9 points in 17 years (see figure III.1). Thus, on the basis of past trends, the ESCAP region as a whole may be able to attain the target, even though some subregions and individual countries may not do so. In addition, the incidence of poverty increased in some countries after the 1997 financial

Building on past progress, the poverty reduction target for the region as a whole can be achieved through a sustained, concerted and focused effort

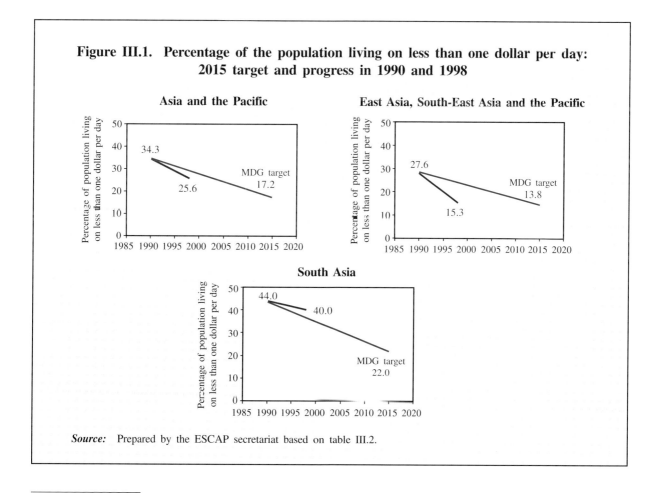

Figure III.1. Percentage of the population living on less than one dollar per day: 2015 target and progress in 1990 and 1998

Source: Prepared by the ESCAP secretariat based on table III.2.

---

[7] Separate data for the Central Asian subregion are not available.

and economic crisis in East Asia and South-East Asia. Some lost ground was subsequently regained in those two subregions, although the current global downturn, if it persisted, could set back or delay the process of poverty reduction among the developing countries of the ESCAP region.

The available poverty data based on the one dollar a day poverty line, which are much more limited at the country level, show that China, Indonesia, Malaysia, Thailand and Viet Nam had achieved the target of halving extreme poverty for all practical purposes by 2000 (table III.3). Cambodia, the Lao People's Democratic Republic and the Philippines are making good progress towards achieving the target in 2015; it is note-worthy that the rates of poverty in the first two countries were among the highest in the region in 1990. The rate of poverty reduction in India between 1990 and 1997 was slow and that in Papua New Guinea had fallen by half between 1990 and 1996 before rising and then stabilizing at around 17 per cent in the late 1990s. The lack of sufficient data makes it difficult to draw any concrete conclusions as regards, for example, Bangladesh, Kazakhstan, Mongolia, Nepal, Pakistan and Sri Lanka. In sum, out of the 16 countries in table III.3, about half may not be able to achieve the poverty reduction goal.

Table III.3. Percentage of the population below the one dollar poverty line in selected countries, 1990-2000

	1990	1991	1992	1993	1994	1995	1996	1997	1998	1999	2000
Bangladesh	..	..	35.9	..	..	..	29.1	..	..	..	..
Cambodia	48.3	..	..	..	..	..	36.7	..	38.7	36.7	34.0
China	31.3	..	..	29.4	..	..	17.2	..	17.1	17.4	16.5
India	46.6	..	51.1	..	45.1	47.1	46.2	44.2	..	..	..
Indonesia	20.6	..	..	14.8	..	..	7.8	..	..	12.0	8.0
Kazakhstan	..	..	..	1.1	..	..	1.5	..	..	..	..
Lao People's Democratic Republic	53.0	..	48.8	..	..	..	41.3	38.4	37.4	33.6	31.5
Malaysia	0.5	..	0.0	..	..	0.0	0.0	0.0	0.0	0.0	0.0
Mongolia	..	..	..	..	..	13.9	..	..	..	..	..
Nepal	..	..	..	..	..	37.7	..	..	..	..	..
Pakistan	47.8	..	..	33.9	..	..	31.0	..	..	..	..
Papua New Guinea	23.7	..	..	..	..	..	11.7	15.1	17.2	16.2	17.5
Philippines	19.1	19.8	..	..	18.4	..	14.8	12.1	14.6	13.7	12.7
Sri Lanka	3.8	..	..	..	..	6.6	..	..	..	..	..
Thailand	12.5	..	6.0	..	..	..	2.2	..	3.9	4.3	3.5
Viet Nam	50.8	..	..	39.8	..	..	23.1	..	15.0	12.6	9.1

Source: World Bank, *East Asia Update: Regional Overview,* March and October 2001; and World Bank web page "Global poverty monitoring", at <http://www.worldbank.org/research/povmonitor/index.htm>, 30 October 2001.

Note: A number of countries (such as Afghanistan and Myanmar) which may have a high incidence of poverty are not included in the table due to lack of data.

Data on country-specific poverty lines are not comparable owing to differences in baseline, coverage and methodology, among other things. Poverty estimates are not available on a periodic or regular basis. Those available on country-specific poverty lines from 1990 onwards are reported in table III.4.[8] It is clear that China and Malaysia achieved the target of halving poverty within the last decade while Viet Nam has made good progress to date. However, Indonesia, the

Many countries in the region have their own poverty lines

Table III.4. Percentage of the population below the national poverty line in selected countries, 1990-2000

	1990	1991	1992	1993	1994	1995	1996	1997	1998	1999	2000
Armenia	18.0[a]	..	..	..	..	..	..	..	..	55.0	..
Azerbaijan	33.0[a]	..	..	..	..	62.0	..	..	..	..	..
Bangladesh	47.8[b]	..	42.7	..	..	..	36.0	..	..	..	34.0
Cambodia	..	..	..	..	39.0	..	..	36.1	..	..	..
China	9.4	..	..	..	..	7.1	6.7	5.4	4.6	3.7	..
Georgia	16.0[a]	..	..	..	..	..	..	..	..	60.0	..
India	38.9[a]	..	..	..	36.0	..	..	..	..	26.1	..
Indonesia	15.1	..	..	13.7	..	..	11.3	..	..	18.2	..
Kazakhstan	..	..	..	..	..	..	34.6	43.0	43.4	34.5	31.8
Kyrgyzstan	37.0[a]	..	..	40.0	..	..	..	51.0	..	55.0	..
Malaysia	17.1[b]	..	..	13.4	..	9.6	..	6.8	..	8.1	..
Mongolia	..	..	17.0	24.0	..	36.3	..	..	35.6	..	..
Nepal	41.4[c]	..	..	..	..	..	42.0	..	..	..	..
Pakistan	..	22.1	..	22.4	29.3	..	..	31.0	..	32.6	33.5
Philippines	..	45.3	..	..	40.6	..	..	36.8	..	..	39.4
Republic of Korea	8.4[a]	..	..	8.2	..	..	7.0	..	..	..	..
Sri Lanka	..	33.0	..	..	..	..	39.2	..	..	..	..
Tajikistan	59.0[a]	..	..	..	..	..	..	..	..	83.0	..
Thailand	27.2	..	23.2	..	16.3	..	11.4	..	13.0	15.9	..
Viet Nam	..	..	..	58.2	..	..	..	..	37.4	..	32.0

Sources: ESCAP, *Growth with Equity: Policy Lessons from the Experiences of Selected Asian Countries* (United Nations publication, Sales No. E.00.II.F.14); ADB, country papers prepared for the Inception Workshop on Building a Poverty Database, held at Manila in July-August 2001; World Bank, *World Development Report 2000/2001: Attacking Poverty* (New York, Oxford University Press, 2001); IMF and World Bank, *Poverty Reduction, Growth and Debt Sustainability in Low-income CIS Countries* (Washington, 2002); and national sources.

Notes: Poverty estimates are based on country-specific poverty lines, expressed in national currencies. Many countries have more than one such poverty line, and efforts have been made to include consistent time-series data on the incidence of poverty. Note in the previous table is also applicable here.

[a] 1988.
[b] 1989.
[c] 1985.

---

[8] Many countries have more than one poverty line. The national poverty line with the longest time-series estimates has been relied upon for the sake of consistency.

Philippines and Thailand recorded higher levels of country-specific poverty estimates in the wake of the 1997 economic crisis. South Asia as a whole has not experienced satisfactory progress, with poverty being on the rise in Nepal, Pakistan and Sri Lanka. However, there was apparently a rapid decline in poverty in India between 1994 and 1999. Poverty increased rapidly in Armenia, Azerbaijan, Georgia, Kyrgyzstan and Tajikistan.

Achievement of a goal at the national level does not necessarily imply similar success in different regions or among different groups of people within a country

Different regions of countries can exhibit diverse poverty levels and trends, a pattern of uneven regional development seen particularly in many large countries (for example, China, India and Indonesia). Data based on national poverty lines, available for 12 countries, indicate a higher incidence of poverty in rural than in urban areas in nine countries (annex table III.1). Urban poverty also declined faster than rural poverty in the majority of cases. Despite rapid urbanization, the overwhelming majority of the population still live in rural areas in a large number of developing countries of the ESCAP region. Thus, a rapid reduction in rural poverty can help to achieve the millennium development goal at the national level while enhancing overall equity in distribution and access in the countries concerned.

There are insufficient regional data on the poverty gap ratio and the income share of the poorest quintile as an indicator of relative poverty

The headcount index shows the percentage of the population below the poverty line but does not reveal the depth of such poverty, that is, how poor the poor actually are. The poverty gap ratio is a recommended secondary indicator. Poverty gap is defined as the total income needed to bring the poor up to the poverty line, thereby eliminating poverty. A meaningful discussion on the patterns and movements of this gap, and hence ratio, is not possible as the relevant data are available for only a small number of countries in the region.

The income share of the poorest quintile reveals the income position of the lowest 20 per cent income group as compared with the rest of the population. This indicator gives the income or consumption share of the lowest 20 per cent of the population. An increase in this share indicates an improvement in the relative position of this group and, a priori, a reduction in the incidence of poverty. However, the headcount index is influenced not only by the distribution of income but also by the average income of the population. Thus, in a growing economy, the incidence of poverty can fall despite a decline in the income share of the poorest quintile, and vice versa. In the case of growing average income, however, an increase in the income share of the poorest quintile will have a larger impact on poverty reduction, a situation that can be termed "pro-poor growth". This indicator is useful for analytical purposes, even though there is no target set for it.

Data on the relative shares of the lowest quintile of income or consumption distribution are reported for selected countries and periods in annex table III.2. These shares are not comparable across countries as they are a mixture of income and consumption ratios. In particular, income shares are usually lower than the corresponding consumption shares, so that countries for which consumption shares are reported will appear more egalitarian than those for which income shares are presented.

The income/consumption shares of the poorest 20 per cent of the population remained virtually unchanged over time in Indonesia and the Republic of Korea, while they fell in 8 out of 11 countries reported in annex table III.2. This means that the reduction in poverty, if any, in those countries was largely the result of income growth. The income/ consumption share of the lowest quintile increased in Pakistan, whereas the incidence of poverty declined on the basis of the one dollar poverty line but rose on the basis of the national poverty line, illustrating how different poverty lines can lead to widely divergent results.

The second target of the millennium development goal is to halve, between 1990 and 2015, the proportion of people suffering from hunger. The prevalence of underweight children (below 5 years of age) and the proportion of the population with dietary energy consumption below a minimum level are two recommended indicators for monitoring purposes. Malnutrition and hunger are closely associated with poverty, in that the people so affected lack adequate resources to buy the amount of food necessary for a healthy and active life. The poverty line of one dollar a day relates to extreme poverty, so that people with consumption levels below this line are likely to be undernourished.

Eliminating hunger is also part of the goal

The physical growth of children is commonly used to indicate the nutritional status of the entire community. This is because children, especially those under 5 years of age, represent the most vulnerable segment of the population from a nutritional standpoint. Thus, the underweight children indicator measures the proportion of underweight children below 5 years of age as a percentage of the population of children in this age group. A child is underweight if his or her weight is less than minus two standard deviations from the median weight for his/ her age group in the United States. Some may not agree with the United States as the reference population being used.

Data on underweight children indicate that over 40 per cent of the children were underweight in most South Asian countries in 1990; the rate was over 60 per cent in Bangladesh and India (table III.5). India achieved a reduction of nearly 19 percentage points in the 1990s, although progress in addressing the underweight problem was slow in most other subregional countries. In South-East Asia, the rates of child undernourishment were generally lower, while the rates of reductions

The underweight children indicator reveals relatively slow progress

Table III.5. Trends in indicators for undernourishment during the 1990s

	Underweight children under 5 (Percentage of total)		Undernourished people (Percentage of total population)
	1990-1992	*1995-1999*	*1996-1998*
South and South-West Asia			
Bangladesh	66	56	38
Bhutan	..	19	..
India	64	45	21
Iran (Islamic Republic of)	16	11	6
Maldives	..	45	..
Nepal	49	47	28
Pakistan	40	38	20
Sri Lanka	..	33	25
Turkey	10	8	..
South-East Asia			
Cambodia	52	50	33
Indonesia	..	34	6
Lao People's Democratic Republic	..	..	29
Malaysia	25	20	..
Myanmar	32	28	7
Philippines	34	..	21
Thailand	20	10	21
Viet Nam	45	34	22
East and North-East Asia			
China	17	9	11
Democratic People's Republic of Korea	..	32	..
Mongolia	12	13	45
Pacific island economies			
Papua New Guinea	..	..	29
North and Central Asia			
Armenia	..	3	..
Azerbaijan	..	10	32
Georgia	..	3	23
Kazakhstan	..	8	5
Kyrgyzstan	..	11	17
Russian Federation	..	3	6
Tajikistan	..	..	32
Turkmenistan	..	..	10
Uzbekistan	..	19	11

Sources: UNDP, *Human Development Report 2001* (New York, Oxford University Press, 2001); World Bank, *World Development Indicators 2001* (CD-ROM); World Bank web site <http://www.developmentgoals.org/findout-data.html>, 6 February 2002; and national sources.

Notes: A child is considered to be underweight if his or her weight for age is less than minus two standard deviations from the median weight of the reference population, which is based on children from the United States. As to the second indicator, a person not getting the minimum required kilocalories (depending on his or her weight, height, age, sex and activity level) from the consumption of food is categorized as undernourished. It is very difficult not only to estimate the exact energy requirement of each person in a country but also to estimate the kilocalories of food consumed by them. Therefore, data on both indicators should be interpreted with particular caution.

were also slow, except Thailand. Exceptionally, China appears to have already achieved the goal, the rate of child malnutrition having fallen from 17.4 per cent in 1990 to 9 per cent in 1999.

Dietary energy requirements, measured in kilocalories per person per day, depend on the weight, height, age, sex and activity level of the person concerned. Anyone not receiving the minimum required kilocalories, as a result of either the small quantity of consumption intake or the low quality of food, or both, is categorized as undernourished. Generally, however, it is very difficult to estimate not only the exact energy requirements of each person in the country but also the kilocalories of food consumed by that person. Caution is thus needed in interpreting this particular indicator of hunger and malnutrition.

Country-level time-series data are not readily available, and only single observations are reported in table III.5. However, aggregate data on the undernourished population by subregion are available for the 1990s (table III.6). From these estimates, it is clear that South Asia had the highest percentage of the undernourished in the population (27 per cent) and East Asia the lowest (16 per cent) during the early 1990s. Progress in tackling this issue has been somewhat slow and uneven in all the subregions. For Asia and the Pacific as a whole, the percentage of the undernourished fell from 21 per cent in the early 1990s to 17 per cent in the second half of the 1990s. However, the incidence of undernourishment has apparently worsened among the Pacific island economies.

The second indicator shows the prevalence of hunger and under-nourishment

Table III.6. Percentage of undernourished people in the population in selected subregions of Asia and the Pacific during the 1990s

	1990-1992	*1996-1998*
South Asia	27	23
South-East Asia	18	13
East Asia	16	12
Pacific island economies	26	29
Asia and the Pacific	21	17

Source: FAO, *The State of Food and Agriculture 2001* (Rome, 2001).

Note: The data refer to developing economies only. Asia and the Pacific does not include Central Asia.

Without the availability of more comprehensive data, it is not possible at this stage to make any definitive statement on the possibilities of achieving the target as regards hunger and malnutrition. It is also very difficult to predict the feasibility of attaining the target concerning malnutrition among children under 5 years of age using the underweight children indicator. However, the achievement of the target at the regional level may be possible on the indicative basis of the proportion of undernourished people in the total population as a whole.

Inadequate data make it difficult to predict the achievement of the set target concerning hunger

Policy issues and strategies

Diverse challenges for different countries in poverty reduction

Progress in poverty reduction has been highly uneven among the developing economies of the ESCAP region. The major challenge for those countries that have made great strides in this regard is to sustain their success in the future, despite any temporary setback or constraint that may emerge from current or future economic downturns. However, there is a need for greater efforts to reach the set target among other economies in the region. As can be expected, the root causes of persistent poverty and the related problems of hunger and malnutrition are equally diverse from country to country. Any single policy package would not be suitable for all countries or over time. Nevertheless, certain common elements of a poverty alleviation strategy can be identified and are highlighted below.

A broad strategy in poverty alleviation includes a pro-poor growth approach

- Economic growth is necessary for sustained poverty alleviation. Therefore, growth-promoting policies should be pursued while maintaining sound macroeconomic balance and financial discipline. Closer monitoring of all macroeconomic indicators and proper interpretation of the signals they provide are important to prevent the recurrence of a crisis such as that of 1997, and the consequent erosion of hard-earned progress in poverty reduction.

- Rising income inequality can reduce the gains in poverty alleviation even in a growing economy. Therefore, establishing a pattern of economic growth which would benefit the poor equally, or even more than others, is a laudable objective.

Income growth alone is not likely to produce the desired result of eliminating hunger

- Income growth alone is not likely to produce the desired result without more and better direct interventions with regard to food intake and nutrition matters (box III.2). Among other options, information should be widely disseminated and people educated about improved processing and preservation of food products as well as their nutritional values and status.

- Hunger and undernourishment relate not just to availability but also to access. Improved distribution of food at various geographical levels and from various sources is pertinent in this context. The incomes of the poor could also be raised in kind to enhance their access to the available food supplies.

Human resources development is key to broad-based growth

- Broad-based growth should create productive employment opportunities for all groups, including young people and women. Meanwhile, the job prospects of young people could be brightened through increased investment in education and vocational training, and in facilities for ongoing learning.

Box III.2. Thailand's impressive success in reducing child undernourishment

Thailand was able to reduce undernourishment rates among pre-school children from over 50 per cent in 1982 to under 20 per cent in 1991, and further to 10 per cent in 1996.[a] This success was mediated through a holistic approach whereby intervention measures were integrated not only with the existing primary health-care activities but also with community development initiatives at the local level. Moreover, self-reliance was emphasized at the community level by developing local need-based programmes. Planning, integration, social mobilization and local action-oriented surveillance were the four major elements of the strategy.

Planning at both the macro and micro levels included the adoption in 1986 of the basic minimum needs approach using simple indicators for village-level social planning. Among such indicators were those relating to child malnutrition, low birth-weight, the prevalence of micronutrient deficiency, immunization coverage, antenatal care services, the availability of safe drinking water, and sanitary services. These indicators of basic minimum needs helped in setting locally valid programme objectives, targeting appropriate resources to the areas of greatest need, promoting better integration of multisectoral services and providing a framework for evaluation.

Microlevel planning involved the participation of representatives of the community and non-governmental organizations, nutrition and health professionals and government officials, especially those at the local level. Following this community-based planning process, actions relevant to nutrition were initiated and macrolevel planning supported those processes by promoting closer collaboration with relevant sectors such as health, agriculture, education and rural development. A good example of macrolevel planning was the inclusion of specific goals for the reduction of child malnutrition in the five-year national economic and social development plans of the country.

Improved nutrition was seen as encompassing components from several sectors, such as health, education and agriculture. The health component focused on ensuring the better health of mothers, monitoring child growth and development and promoting breastfeeding and appropriate complementary feeding. Immunization, oral dehydration therapy, deworming, the treatment of local epidemic diseases, the provision of safe drinking water and improved sanitation services were also integral components of the programme activities. Agricultural activities and education were used to achieve long-term nutritional improvements by enhancing food security, raising income-generation opportunities and inducing changes in nutrition behaviour.

For social mobilization, service providers, particularly in the area of health, worked closely with community leaders and gradually emerged as facilitators for community activities. Well-respected individuals, preferably women, who usually provided guidance or assistance to people in emergency situations, were selected by the communities themselves as community health and nutrition volunteers or mobilizers. The mobilizers were given appropriate training and served to link service delivery with the communities concerned and to foster local community-based nutrition initiatives. The mobilizers did not receive cash incentives or salary, but they benefited from free medical services for themselves and their families and from organized visits to other communities. To recognize their meritorious service, they were also honoured with volunteer badges, uniforms, certificates and awards.

Local action-oriented comprehensive nutritional surveillance was instituted through growth monitoring and promotion. All pre-school children were weighed and their health checked every three months at community weighing posts. These periodic monitoring opportunities were also used to educate mothers and mobilizers in child nutrition and remedial action was suggested for children with slow physical growth. As a result, mothers took greater responsibility for the nutritional improvement of their children. This approach placed greater emphasis on community education and involvement.

In sum, strong political will, translated into prioritized, effective and explicit nutrition-relevant action on the part of the Government, has contributed to Thailand's success in improving child nutrition. The driving forces were programme planning at both the macro and micro levels, sustained integrated action in the form of enabling sectoral policies and programmes, and systematic monitoring, all fuelled by a process of social mobilization and community ownership.

---

[a]   This box is largely based on an article by K. Tontisirin and S. Gillespie, "Linking community-based programs and service delivery for improving maternal and child nutrition", *Asian Development Review,* vol. 17, Nos. 1 and 2 (1999).

- Human resources development is the key to a pro-poor growth approach. This requires more sustained investment in education, health and other elements of social capital to better complement investment in physical infrastructure for growth promotion purposes.

The promotion of agriculture and agro-processing and rural small and medium-sized enterprises will have a major impact on poverty

- Since most of the poor and malnourished live in rural areas, rural development, particularly through agriculture and agro-processing activities, is essential for equitable growth. In particular, agricultural productivity and food production can be raised and food prices lowered through the dissemination of both modern inputs and low-cost simple technologies for the benefit of small farmers.

- Lower food prices can affect the incomes of the rural poor adversely and this trade-off could be counterbalanced with higher opportunities for off-farm employment. A pertinent policy option in this context is the promotion of rural industrialization, food processing in particular, and of industrial development activities with strong and extensive linkages to the rural sector.

- Small and medium-sized enterprises should be promoted for their employment-generating potential, among other advantages. The informal sector also provides job opportunities to the poor with few skills and financial resources. The provision of credit, training and infrastructure would help to enlarge and diversify such enterprises or informal undertakings and improve their productivity.

- A well-functioning and diverse financial sector should be developed to mobilize and allocate savings to those capable of investing efficiently, including women and small farmers in the rural sector.

Comprehensive population policies and target-oriented programmes

- Comprehensive population policies and programmes are needed, as many countries with low per capita income and a high incidence of poverty and malnutrition tend to be facing high population pressure.

- The hard-core poor are those who have not been able to benefit from economic growth or who have remained in the poverty trap. The provision of social safety nets, including food-for-work arrangements, can lessen their hardships, especially in times of economic crisis, as can the existence of long-term social protection schemes for all social and economic groups, such as women, the young, older persons, the infirm and the disabled. At the same time, the outreach and impact of existing social safety-net and social security programmes can be much enhanced through improved targeting and delivery, greater administrative transparency and better governance.

- Corrupt practices have implications for poverty alleviation efforts in developing countries; not only do they deprive the poor of huge financial resources that could have been used for raising their own welfare, but low-level corruption and inadequate or unaffordable access to justice and legal protection affect their lives directly. The essential ingredients of good governance are the rule of law, effective State institutions, transparency and accountability in the management of public affairs, respect for human rights and the participation of all citizens in the decisions that affect their lives. Therefore, improving governance will entail, directly and indirectly, enhanced poverty reduction, including through reduced corruption and non-transparent practices.

Improving governance with a focus on combating corruption should be a priority

- The timely and cost-effective realization of the millennium development goals implies closer cooperation and interaction among public sector authorities, business, external stakeholders, and civil society and other community-based organizations. The poor should also be given a voice in decision-making and implementation, so that policies and programmes address their needs and priorities.

Closer collaboration between all stakeholders is another prerequisite

- Developed countries need to remove their trade barriers and accelerate the opening of their markets to developing country exports, particularly agricultural products, clothing and textiles. More generally, globalization has to be better managed so as to moderate its dislocating effects while distributing its positive effects more equitably, especially among the large number of countries that have been marginalized in the process.

- International peace and stability are essential for the achievement of the millennium development goals. A reversal of the declining trend in ODA, along with further debt relief for heavily indebted poor countries in the region, would go a long way towards stimulating development and reducing extreme poverty. Some of these issues are discussed at greater length in the next chapter of this *Survey*.

Goal 2. Achieving universal primary education

Education is the key to both human development and human resources development. It serves to enhance the productivity levels of all beneficiaries, including the poor, and thus narrows the earning differentials among people, an important step in the alleviation of both absolute and relative poverty. Indeed, the available empirical evidence from developing countries in the ESCAP region shows that the incidence of poverty falls as the level of education of the household heads rises.

The target for this goal is universal primary schooling for all children, boys and girls alike, by 2015. Its two primary indicators are the net enrolment ratio in primary education and the proportion of pupils starting grade 1 who reach grade 5. A secondary indicator for this target is the literacy rate of persons in the 15-24 age group, or the youth literacy rate.

High net enrolment ratios in primary schooling in a large part of the region

The net enrolment ratio in primary education represents the number of children of primary-school age (as defined by the education system concerned) actually enrolled in primary school over the total population in the corresponding age bracket. The available data on this net enrolment ratio, contained in table III.7, reveal a high and rising percentage in South-East Asia, mostly 90 per cent or over. The ratio was comparatively lower in the Lao People's Democratic Republic, but it had expanded rapidly from 61 to 72 per cent between 1991 and 1996. The net enrolment rates were also high generally, 90 per cent or more, in East and North-East Asia, the Pacific island economies, and North and Central Asia. The ratios need to be improved in a number of countries in South Asia.

The net enrolment ratios are not available for some countries. As a proxy indicator, the gross enrolment ratio can be used. It is defined as the number of students enrolled in a level of education, regardless of age, as a percentage of the population of official school age for that level. It may exceed 100 per cent in cases where some pupils are below or above the official school age for a particular level of education. In South Asia, gross enrolment rates were around 100 per cent in most countries, except Bhutan (73 per cent) and Pakistan (75 per cent). In the other subregions, the gross enrolment ratios were around 100 per cent in most countries.

High ratios of persistence through grade 5

While enrolment rates capture the quantitative aspect of education, another equally important dimension is the quality of education, which comes from better teachers, improved school facilities and a curriculum that attracts students and keeps them in school. The persistence indicator on children reaching grade 5 measures the percentage of children starting primary school who eventually reach grade 5. Children who completed grade 4 (and are enrolling in grade 5) have basic literacy and numeracy skills. Survival to grade 5 implies the completion of a basic education. The proportion of pupils starting grade 1 and reaching grade 5 is over 80 per cent in most countries for which data are available (table III.7).

The secondary indicator of youth literacy is defined as the percentage of people aged 15-24 who can read and write a short, simple statement on their everyday life. However, the adult literacy rate, applicable to people aged 15 and above, is more commonly used. The emphasis on youth literacy aims at prioritizing the provision of education to the younger generation, who are capable of learning more easily.

Table III.7. Trends in indicators for universal primary education during the 1990s

| | Primary school enrolment ratio | | | | Persistence to grade 5 (Percentage of cohort) | | Youth literacy rate (Percentage of people aged 15-24) | |
| | Net | | Gross | | | | | |
	1990-1991	*1995-1997*	*1990*	*1995-1997*	*1990-1991*	*1995-1997*	*1990*	*1999*
South and South-West Asia								
Bangladesh	64	75	72	92	..	..	44	50
Bhutan	..	..	..	73	82	..	..	..
India	..	77	97	100	59	..	64	72
Iran (Islamic Republic of)	99	90	112	98	90	..	87	94
Maldives	..	97	..	128	..	..	98	99
Nepal	..	78	108	113	52	..	46	59
Pakistan	..	67	69	75	..	..	49	63
Sri Lanka	..	100	106	109	94	83	95	97
Turkey	89	99	99	107	98	..	93	96
South-East Asia								
Brunei Darussalam	91	91	115	106	95	92	98	99
Cambodia	..	98	121	113	..	49	46	58
Indonesia	97	95	115	113	84	88	95	98
Lao People's Democratic Republic	61	72	105	112	53	55	55	69
Malaysia	..	100	94	101	98	..	95	97
Myanmar	..	..	106	121	..	..	88	91
Philippines	97	100	111	117	..	..	97	99
Singapore	..	93	104	94	..	..	99	100
Thailand	..	..	99	89	..	..	98	99
Viet Nam	86	91	103	114	..	..	95	97
East and North-East Asia								
China	97	100	125	123	86	94	95	98
Hong Kong, China	..	90	102	94	100	100	100	100
Macao, China	81	..	99	..	97	..	..	..
Mongolia	..	81	97	88	..	90	70	79
Republic of Korea	100	93	105	94	99	98	100	100
Pacific island economies								
Fiji	100	..	125	116	..	..	98	99
French Polynesia	..	100	130	..	..	..	..	..
Kiribati	..	..	..	..	98	95	..	..
New Caledonia	97	..	129	..	..	..	..	..
Papua New Guinea	..	..	72	80	59	..	69	75
Samoa	..	96	122	100	..	86	83	87
Solomon Islands	..	..	84	97	85	..	..	..
Tonga	..	..	..	..	84	..	..	..
Vanuatu	..	..	96	..	90	..	..	..
North and Central Asia								
Armenia	..	..	..	87	..	100	100	100
Azerbaijan	..	..	114	106	..	93	..	..
Georgia	..	90	97	88	..	98	..	..
Kazakhstan	..	95	87	98	..	92	..	..
Kyrgyzstan	..	95	111	104	..	97	..	..
Russian Federation	..	93	109	107	..	..	100	100
Tajikistan	..	..	91	95	..	..	100	100
Uzbekistan	..	..	81	78	..	..	94	96

Sources: UNESCO web site <http://www.unesco.org/education/information/wer/htmlENG/tablesmenu.htm>, 6 November 2001; World Bank, *World Development Indicators 2001* (CD-ROM); Mahbub ul Haq Human Development Centre, *Human Development in South Asia 2000* (New York, Oxford University Press, 2000); and national sources.

Youth literacy nearly universal in a large number of countries in the region

Youth literacy is nearly universal in South-East Asia, East and North-East Asia, and North and Central Asia. Cambodia, the Lao People's Democratic Republic, Myanmar and Mongolia need to intensify their efforts to further improve their rates in this regard. However, youth literacy in several parts of South Asia is far from satisfactory, despite some progress made during the 1990s (table III.7). Youth illiteracy rates were high in Bangladesh (50 per cent), India (28 per cent), Nepal (41 per cent) and Pakistan (37 per cent) in 1999. They were also sizeable in Papua New Guinea (25 per cent) and Samoa (13 per cent) among the Pacific island economies. A sustained effort is thus needed in all these countries to raise enrolment rates in primary education and, more important, to induce students to complete their primary education.

The goal of universal primary education can be achieved

By and large, the millennium development goal of universal primary education can be achieved in the developing countries of the ESCAP region by 2015. Primary school enrolment rates in most regional countries have already reached or are approaching the 100 per cent level. Satisfactory progress in this direction in South Asia, a relatively populous subregion, will ensure the attainment of the goal. The falling fertility rates in almost all countries of the region constitute another positive factor in reaching the target.

Policy issues and strategies

Lack of education and poverty are closely linked

Children from poor families are normally unable to attend school because their parents cannot afford the cost of education and, equally important, they themselves are a source of free labour in earning a livelihood for their families. Thus, these children tend to remain poor in adulthood and the vicious cycle of poverty continues. Some policy issues and strategies specific to universal primary education are outlined further below.

Compulsory and free primary education with private sector involvement, as appropriate

- Primary education should be made compulsory and free in each country. In addition, textbooks, uniforms and school lunches should be provided free, particularly to children from poor families.

- The main responsibility for providing, expanding and upgrading primary education should rest with the public sector. The private sector should also be encouraged to participate in providing primary education, but under tight regulation so as to ensure proper educational standards. The natural concentration of private schools in urban areas would facilitate the allocation of a larger share of public sector resources to localities where the urban poor are predominant, or to rural and remote areas. At the same time, tax incentives can be given to induce more private schools to locate in those disadvantaged areas.

- Better-quality education is a major determinant of the degree of persistence and interest among students. More resources should be invested in training teachers and improving facilities as well as in addressing inadequate school facilities and overcrowded conditions, especially in remote areas and rural locations. Decentralization of education and the efficient utilization of scarce financial resources, including through better governance and enhanced transparency, are other appropriate policy efforts and options.

Improving the quality of education should be a priority

Goal 3. Promoting gender equality and empowering women

The empowerment of women and, more generally, equality between women and men, are needed not only for fairness but also for accelerating the process of economic, social and sustainable development. Investment in women's education has been one of the most important determinants of socio-economic advancement and mobility, with positive implications and spillover effects on various economic sectors and social strata. Differing parental and family needs and cultural diversity are partly the cause of the revealed variations in the school enrolments of boys and girls in countries of the region.[9]

Without the full involvement of women in all activities, a country cannot realize its full development potential

The millennium development goal is to eliminate gender disparity in primary and secondary education, preferably by 2005, and at all levels of education no later than 2015. The primary indicator of progress towards these targets is the ratio of girls to boys in primary, secondary and tertiary education. Suggested secondary indicators comprise the ratio of literate females to males in the 15-24-year age group; the share of women in wage employment in the non-agricultural sector; and the proportion of seats held by women in national parliaments.

The ratio of girls to boys at a particular level of education is gauged as the gross enrolment ratio for girls as a percentage of the same ratio for boys at that educational level.[10] A ratio equal to 100 per cent signifies gender equality, while the disparity borne by girl students is embodied in a lower value.[11] As to primary education, the situation is

The situation is generally satisfactory at the primary education level but marginally less so at the secondary level

---

[9] In some countries, boys have to help their parents in earning a livelihood and thus girls may have more opportunities to go to school. In others, boys are encouraged to attend school owing to cultural preferences, and girls have to take care of most household chores.

[10] The size of the population of girls and boys is not relevant here. For example, if the population of girls is smaller than that of boys and both genders are fully enrolled in schools, the indicator will show a value of 100 per cent.

[11] A ratio above 100 per cent indicates a greater participation of girls than boys at that level of education. This may be due to cultural differences or to the accelerated participation of males in formal or informal labour. It could also reflect the presence of older girls at that level of education (for example, if education has been delayed).

generally satisfactory, with the girls-to-boys enrolment ratio approaching 100 per cent in most countries in South-East Asia, North-East Asia, North and Central Asia, and the Pacific island economies (table III.8). South Asia has recorded considerable progress in levelling the gender disparity, although further steps need to be taken in some of the countries in this regard as well as in universal primary education. The enrolment disparity ratio is less favourable at the secondary level for a larger group of countries, mostly in South Asia and the Pacific island subregion, and among the least developed countries.

The elimination by 2005 of the gender disparity in primary and secondary education combined may not be achieved in the region as a whole

As a whole, it appears that the elimination by 2005 of the gender disparity at both the primary and secondary education levels may not be achievable in South Asia and in some countries in other subregions. The ratio of female-to-male students at the tertiary level was higher than 100 per cent in 10 out of 21 economies for which data were available. Most of these cases were in North and Central Asia. The ratios were generally lower in South Asia. However, the short interval between the reported data, 1990 and 1996, makes it difficult to try to discern progress over time.

A secondary indicator is the female youth literacy rate expressed as a percentage of male youth literacy rate. As discussed earlier, overall youth literacy (female and male combined) has been nearly universal in South-East Asia, East and North-East Asia, and North and Central Asia. The rates of female youth literacy as compared with those of males are lower in many countries in South Asia. Improvements in gender enrolment rates at both the primary and secondary levels of education should help to bridge the gap in literacy between males and females in South Asia in the coming years.

Data are not readily available on the share of women in wage employment in the non-agricultural sector, another secondary indicator of this goal. The proportion of seats held by women in national parliaments, another secondary indicator, is quite low in most countries, ranging from 2 per cent in Papua New Guinea and Solomon Islands to 26 per cent in Turkmenistan and Viet Nam in 2000. Ideally, the proportion should be close to 50 per cent.

Policy issues and strategies

Investment in female education translates directly and quickly into poverty alleviation through enhanced income generation, better nutrition for the whole family, better health care, better education of future generations, declining fertility and better environment through improved sanitation. Some specific measures to promote the education of girls and the empowerment of women are highlighted below.

Table III.8. Trends in indicators for gender equality and the empowerment of women during the 1990s

| | Ratio of girls to boys at different levels of education | | | | | | Ratio of literate females to males 15-24 years old | | Seats in parliament held by women (Percentage of total) |
| | Primary | | Secondary | | Tertiary | | | | |
	1990-1991	1996-1998	1990-1991	1996-1998	1990	1996	1990	1999	2000
South and South-West Asia									
Bangladesh	86	..	52	..	19	..	59	65	9
India	76	82	60	67	55	63	74	81	9
Iran (Islamic Republic of)	90	93	72	90	45	60	89	95	..
Maldives	..	97	..	106	..	..	100	101	6
Nepal	61	74	43	66	30	..	41	54	6
Pakistan	48	..	50	..	61	..	51	64	..
Sri Lanka	98	98	108	108	66	..	98	99	5
Turkey	94	93	65	71	52	57	91	95	4
South-East Asia									
Brunei Darussalam	94	96	108	114	..	151	101	101	..
Cambodia	..	84	42	54	..	26	40	55	9
Indonesia	97	96	83	87	..	55	97	99	8
Lao People's Democratic Republic	78	82	61	67	..	44	52	69	21
Malaysia	100	100	105	116	88	..	99	100	12
Myanmar	97	..	100	103	..	160	96	99	..
Philippines	96	98	99	101	137	130	100	100	13
Singapore	97	97	94	..	69	..	100	100	4
Thailand	98	..	97	..	..	..	99	99	..
Viet Nam	..	96	94	96	..	..	99	100	26
East and North-East Asia									
China	92	100	76	90	51	53	94	97	22
Hong Kong, China	101	102	105	107	72	..	101	101	..
Macao, China	95	..	110	..	48	100	..	..	..
Mongolia	102	109	114	137	189	229	78	87	8
Republic of Korea	100	100	97	100	49	64	100	100	4
Pacific island economies									
Fiji	100	..	96	..	..	..	99	100	11
French Polynesia	96	..	116	..	..	..	..	..	..
New Caledonia	97	..	110	112	..	..	..	..	..
Papua New Guinea	85	85	67	65	..	50	83	88	2
Samoa	109	99	122	110	..	..	100	101	8
Solomon Islands	86	86	65	67	..	..	..	..	2
Vanuatu	96	..	76	..	..	..	..	..	..
North and Central Asia									
Armenia	..	..	..	79	..	133	100	100	3
Azerbaijan	99	97	100	111	69	104	..	..	12
Georgia	100	99	98	98	118	112	..	..	7
Kazakhstan	..	101	102	111	..	128	..	..	11
Kyrgyzstan	100	98	102	111	..	111	..	..	..
Russian Federation	100	99	105	..	127	130	100	100	6
Tajikistan	98	97	..	89	62	49	100	100	..
Turkmenistan	..	..	..	..	..	..	..	..	26
Uzbekistan	99	96	91	88	..	..	95	97	7

Sources: UNESCO web site <http://www.unesco.org/education/information/wer/WEBtables/Ind8web.xls>, 6 November 2001; World Bank, *World Development Indicators 2001* (CD-ROM); and UNDP, *Human Development Report 2000* (New York, Oxford University Press, 2001).

Publicity campaigns, the provision of incentives and the creation of improved job opportunities are important for raising female enrolment and literacy rates

- Families with low incomes and those in rural areas are the two groups with traditionally low female enrolment rates. They need to have a better understanding of the importance of female education and, in this connection, more resources should be devoted to publicity campaigns to persuade parents to send their daughters to school. Local communities should be closely involved in this effort.

- Scholarships, school meals and take-home rations can be given as incentives to poor households to send girls to, and keep them in, school until they complete their education (box III.3). Supplementary and complementary measures include improved job opportunities for females coupled with the elimination of job discrimination against women.

- Girls, particularly those in rural areas, help their parents in household chores and other activities. Some flexibility in school hours may thus encourage parents to let their daughters attend school. More generally, however, the school system should be adapted to the needs of local communities.

Greater participation of women in government and other decision-making bodies

- The inclusion of a larger number of women, as well as greater female representation, in government and other decision-making bodies, at a high level should be encouraged and supported. Indeed, some countries have reserved a certain proportion of seats for women in legislative assemblies (in addition to openly contested seats) in an effort to redress gender disparities in political life.

Goal 4. Reducing infant and child mortality

The survival of infants and children is not just a measure of the availability, accessibility and affordability of health services: it is also a broader reflection of the social, economic and environmental influences and forces impinging on children's lives. Infant and child mortality rates provide a good approximation of a community's current health status and, by implication, of the welfare of a population and the quality of life itself. The millennium development goal is to reduce the under 5 mortality rate by two thirds between 1990 and 2015; the primary indicator for monitoring this target is the mortality rate of children under 5 years of age, that is, the number of children who die before reaching 5 years of age, expressed per 1,000 live births.

Box III.3. Some successful approaches to enhancing girls' enrolment in schools

Both demand- and supply-side interventions have helped to increase girls' enrolment in schools in a number of countries. In Bangladesh, for example, a school stipend programme was established in 1982 to subsidize various expenses for girls enrolling in secondary school.[a] The enrolment ratio increased significantly in the pilot project area, from 27 to 44 per cent, over a five-year period in the 1980s, or more than twice the national average. In 1992, the tuition fee for girls was eliminated and the stipend programme extended to all rural areas in the country. As a result, the school enrolment ratio of girls rose more rapidly than that of boys in the succeeding years. This also pushed up the women's enrolment ratio at intermediate colleges. In this regard, it is worth noting a similar programme implemented in Mexico, as part of a comprehensive multisectoral programme of poverty reduction in 1997. Specifically, poor families are given a grant for each child under 18 who is enrolled between the third grade of primary school and the third grade of secondary school. The grants are slightly higher for girls than for boys and increase with the higher levels of the school grade involved. For the final year, the grant is roughly equivalent to half of the average earnings of an agricultural worker. Any child missing more than 15 per cent of school days becomes ineligible for a grant in that particular month. The programme increased enrolments ratios at all levels, particularly at the transition level from primary to secondary education, when traditionally many children tend to drop out.

The level of female literacy is quite low in Pakistan. As part of the national effort to ensure universal primary education by 2006, several pilot projects were initiated targeting girls' enrolment in Balochistan, the largest but most sparsely populated province of Pakistan.[b] To overcome budgetary constraints, these projects were designed to rely on partnerships with local neighbourhoods or communities to leverage public support in cash or in kind. One pilot project provided a subsidy to private sector/non-governmental organizations to open primary schools in urban slum areas of Quetta, Balochistan's capital. While both boys and girls could attend the school, the government subsidy was linked to enrolled girl students. The local community was involved in selecting a school operator; approving the school's fee structure, site and management policies; and helping to ensure sufficient school enrolment. As a result of this initiative, the school enrolment of both girls and boys increased sharply in urban slum areas. A similar project was started in the rural areas of Balochistan. To take into account cultural sensitivities, only girls are allowed to attend these schools. The Government pays for locally recruited female teachers, training and supplies, while the village provides school premises and monitors teacher and student attendance. The establishment of such schools has increased the enrolment rates of both girls and boys.

Under both projects, boys' enrolment responded positively to the establishment of girls' schools. This shows the underlying complementarities between the schooling of girls and boys in the view of the parents. Therefore, a policy that encourages girls' schooling may have spillover benefits for boys. The success of these projects shows that the enrolment rate of girls can be increased by improving physical access through the establishment of schools in the neighbourhood, providing subsidies involving the local community and paying attention to cultural sensitivities.

---

[a] World Bank, *World Development Report 2000/2001: Attacking Poverty* (New York, Oxford University Press, 2000).

[b] J. Kim, H. Alderman and P.F. Orazem, *Evaluation of the Balochistan Rural Girls' Fellowship Program: Will Rural Families Pay to Send Girls to School?,* World Bank Departmental Working Paper 22983 (Washington, 1999).

Unhealthy conditions around the time of birth are a major cause of infant mortality. Diseases such as pneumonia, diarrhoea, malaria and measles frequently kill very young children, while malnutrition, unsafe water and the spread of HIV/AIDS are other contributing factors. To reflect these circumstances better, two secondary indicators are suggested: one is the infant mortality rate, thus focusing on children under the age of 1, and the other is the proportion of 1-year-old infants immunized against measles.

High rates of child and infant mortality in many countries

211

The data in table III.9 show that under-5 mortality rates were very high, 100 or more (per 1,000 live births) in 2000, in a number of countries, namely, Afghanistan, Azerbaijan, Bhutan, Cambodia, the Lao People's Democratic Republic, Myanmar, Nepal, Pakistan and Papua New Guinea. However, the rates were very low (10 or less) in Brunei Darussalam; Hong Kong, China; Malaysia; the Republic of Korea; and Singapore. Infant mortality rates (that is, the number of children who die before reaching 1 year of age) are lower than under-5 mortality rates, since the first is a subset of the second. The conclusions drawn for the under-5 mortality rates are more or less applicable to those of infants as well.

Progress in reducing child mortality rates has been uneven across countries and, if present trends continue, the achievement of the above goal appears doubtful for the ESCAP region as a whole

The millennium development goal is to reduce the child mortality rate by two thirds (or about 66 per cent) between 1990 and 2015. Countries achieving roughly a 30 per cent reduction during the 1990s are thus well on the way to meeting the target. A large number of countries with very high under-5 mortality rates in 1990 were able to reduce those rates in line with, or even faster than, the required target. However, the performance of some countries, including Afghanistan, Myanmar, Mongolia and Papua New Guinea, was less than desired. Some countries, such as China and Thailand, with initial relatively low mortality rates showed slower progress. Data for Central Asian countries are not available for 1990. However, high mortality rates in a number

Table III.9. Trends in indicators for child mortality during the 1990s

	Mortality rate (per 1,000 live births)				Immunization against measles (Percentage of children under 12 months)	
	Under 5		Infants			
	1990	2000	1990	2000	1989-1990	2000
South and South-West Asia						
Afghanistan	292	257	167	165	20	40
Bangladesh	180	82	114	54	54	71
Bhutan	189	100	123	77	89	76
India	142	96	94	69	87	50
Iran (Islamic Republic of)	59	44	46	36	83	99
Maldives	..	80	..	59	..	86
Nepal	189	100	123	72	67	73
Pakistan	158	110	104	85	97	54
Sri Lanka	35	19	26	17	83	95
Turkey	80	45	69	38	67	80

(Continued on next page)

Table III.9 *(continued)*

	Mortality rate (per 1,000 live births)				Immunization against measles (Percentage of children under 12 months)	
	Under 5		Infants			
	1990	2000	1990	2000	1989-1990	2000
South-East Asia						
Brunei Darussalam	..	7	9	6	..	94
Cambodia	193	135	123	95	34	55
Indonesia	97	48	71	35	86	71
Lao People's Democratic Republic	152	105	104	90	13	71
Malaysia	29	9	22	8	90	88
Myanmar	88	110	65	78	44	85
Philippines	69	40	43	30	85	79
Singapore	9	4	8	4	87	93
Thailand	34	29	26	25	80	96
Viet Nam	65	39	49	30	87	93
East and North-East Asia						
China	42	40	30	32	98	90
Democratic People's Republic of Korea	35	30	26	23	99	34
Hong Kong, China	7	5	6	3	41	..
Macao, China	..	..	10	6	57	..
Mongolia	84	78	64	62	86	93
Republic of Korea	30	5	23	5	95	85
Pacific island economies						
Fiji	31	22	25	18	72	75
Kiribati	..	70	65	56	75	62
Marshall Islands	..	68	..	55	52	93
Micronesia (Federated States of)	..	24	39	20	81	79
New Caledonia	..	12	13	7	..	..
Palau	..	29	..	24	..	96
Papua New Guinea	80	112	56	79	66	57
Samoa	..	26	27	21	89	91
Solomon Islands	36	25	29	21	70	96
Tonga	27	21	25	17	86	97
Vanuatu	70	44	56	35	66	94
North and Central Asia						
Armenia	..	30	..	25	..	91
Azerbaijan	..	105	..	74	..	99
Georgia	..	29	..	24	..	80
Kazakhstan	..	75	..	60	..	91
Kyrgyzstan	..	63	..	53	..	97
Russian Federation	31	22	23	18	85	97
Tajikistan	..	73	..	54	..	79
Turkmenistan	..	70	..	52	..	97
Uzbekistan	..	67	..	51	..	96

Sources: UNICEF, *The State of the World's Children 1992* (New York, Oxford University Press, 1992), UNICEF, *Official Summary: The State of the World's Children 2002* (United Nations publication, Sales No. E.02.XX.1); and World Bank, *World Development Indicators 2001* (CD-ROM).

of those countries in 2000 could be the result of a possible upward movement of the rates during the 1990s in line with the rising incidence of poverty.

Immunization rates of infants against measles were high in most countries

Immunization rates were also high (over 80 per cent) in most countries. Interestingly, many with low rates in 1990 or 2000 had recorded higher rates in some of the intervening years (for which data are not shown in table III.9). The immunization rate in Bangladesh, for example, was only 71 per cent in 2000, as against 97 per cent in 1997. Similarly, in Indonesia, the rate was 93 per cent in 1997 as compared with 71 per cent in 2000. There thus appears to be a need for a more stable and consistent performance regarding the immunization of children. Afghanistan, Cambodia and the Lao People's Democratic Republic achieved more consistent rates, although they remained below 80 per cent throughout the 1990s.

Policy issues and strategies

Child mortality rate can be considered an indicator of the health status of a country

Most of the policy issues and strategies highlighted below relate to health-care services, although good health is the net result of many other factors, such as nutrition, education and sanitation.

- Public provision of or support for health services is crucial to the poor who, in many cases, cannot afford the fees and costs charged by private providers. Those who can afford to do so should be required to pay user charges for public health facilities and services, and the resources generated in this way should be used to enlarge access and availability for the poor.

- Child immunization and vaccination programmes have been very successful in most countries; these programmes should be continued and, as appropriate, further strengthened and upgraded.

- The quality of public health services, particularly in rural and remote areas, should be improved to enhance their effectiveness and coverage.

- Information and knowledge on better childcare at the family level should be widely disseminated, among other preventive measures.

- Better basic hygiene and nutrition practices are crucial to child survival, growth and development.

Goal 5. Improving maternal health

While virtually non-existent in developed countries, maternal deaths are generally high in developing countries. Most of these deaths are due to lack of quality maternal health-care services, among other factors. It needs to be pointed out that skilled health personnel not only attend births but also provide mothers with basic information about prenatal and post-natal care for themselves and their children. The millennium development goal in this context is to reduce the maternal mortality ratio by three quarters between 1990 and 2015.

The primary indicator for this goal is the maternal mortality rate, that is, the number of women who die as a result of pregnancy and childbirth complications per 100,000 live births. However, maternal deaths are not easy to measure because of conceptual and practical problems, including difficulties in determining the exact cause of death and the lack of proper records of such deaths, particularly in poor countries. Time-series data on this ratio are also rare. However, some comparisons can be made between countries, albeit with great difficulty.[12] The maternal mortality rates varied from a high of 830 in Nepal to only 9 in Singapore (table III.10). A matter of concern is that the rates were quite high (over 200) in many countries, including several in South Asia as well as Indonesia, the Lao People's Democratic Republic, Papua New Guinea and the Philippines.

The available estimates of maternal mortality ratios by subregion reveal a considerable decline in maternal mortality ratios between 1990 and 1995 (table III.11). For Asia and the Pacific as a whole, the estimated ratios fell from 390 to 280 over the same period, with Pacific island economies recording a reduction of nearly two thirds. Estimates of maternal mortality for South and Central Asia were generally higher than those for South-East Asia and East Asia.[13]

A secondary indicator for this millennium development goal is the proportion of births attended by skilled health personnel such as physicians, nurses, midwives and primary health-care workers trained in midwifery skills. Trained health workers with midwifery skills greatly

Maternal mortality is to be reduced by three quarters

Owing to the lack of reliable time-series data, it is difficult to reach any conclusions on the feasibility of the target for maternal mortality for individual countries

---

[12] Different methods have been employed to derive maternal mortality ratios for different countries, rendering cross-country comparisons fraught with difficulties. For details, see WHO, "Maternal mortality in 1995: estimates developed by WHO, UNICEF, UNFPA" (WHO/RHRO1.9), 2001.

[13] It should be pointed out that, because of the very large margins of uncertainty associated with estimated maternal mortality ratios, their use for monitoring short-term trends is not recommended. For details, see the WHO source given in the previous note.

Table III.10. Trends in indicators for maternal health during the 1990s

	Maternal mortality ratio (Per 100,000 live births)	Births attended by health staff (Percentage of total)	
	1990-1996	1990-1991	1995-2000
South and South-West Asia			
Bangladesh	600	7	13
Bhutan	500	16	15
India	440	44	..
Iran (Islamic Republic of)	130	78	86
Maldives	390	55	90
Nepal	830	8	9
Pakistan	200	40	..
Sri Lanka	60	85	94
Turkey	55	77	81
South-East Asia			
Brunei Darussalam	22	..	98
Cambodia	590	47	34
Indonesia	390	47	56
Lao People's Democratic Republic	660	..	14
Malaysia	39	..	96
Myanmar	170	94	56
Philippines	208	..	56
Singapore	9	..	100
Thailand	44	71	71
Viet Nam	95	95	77
East and North-East Asia			
China	60	..	67
Democratic People's Republic of Korea	35	..	100
Hong Kong, China	..	100	..
Mongolia	65	100	93
Republic of Korea	20	95	98
Pacific island economies			
Fiji	20	..	..
French Polynesia	..	98	..
Marshall Islands	..	..	97
Papua New Guinea	390	..	53
Samoa	..	52	76
Solomon Islands	60	85	85
Vanuatu	..	..	79
North and Central Asia			
Armenia	29	..	97
Azerbaijan	37	..	100
Georgia	22	..	..
Kazakhstan	80	..	98
Kyrgyzstan	80	..	98
Russian Federation	74	..	99
Tajikistan	120	..	79
Turkmenistan	65	..	96
Uzbekistan	60	..	98

Sources: WHO, "Maternal mortality in 1995: estimates developed by WHO, UNICEF, UNFPA" (WHO/RHRO1.9), 2001. UNICEF, *The State of the World's Children 2001* (United Nations publication, Sales No. E.01.XX.1); World Bank, *World Development Indicators 2001* (CD-ROM); and World Bank web site <http://genderstats.worldbank.org/query/default.htm>, 31 October 2001.

increase the safety of childbirth, and their services are affordable to women with limited financial resources. Nevertheless, the percentage of births attended by skilled health personnel was below 50 per cent in some countries of the region (table III.10). Not surprisingly, the rate was particularly low in countries with high maternal mortality ratios, for example, several of those in South Asia. In the absence of reliable time-series data on maternal mortality, raising the prevalence or avail-ability of skilled care at birth to 90 per cent by 2015 should be a target for countries with lower rates. There are a large number of countries in the region that have a long way to go in achieving this target.

The proportion of births attended by skilled health personnel is a proxy indicator for tracking progress in reducing maternal mortality

Table III.11. Maternal mortality estimates by subregions of Asia and the Pacific, 1990 and 1995

	Maternal mortality ratio (Maternal deaths per 100,000 live births)	
	1990	*1995*
East Asia	95	55
South-East Asia	440	300
South and Central Asia	560	410
Pacific island economies	680	260
Asia and the Pacific	390	280

Source: WHO, "Maternal mortality in 1995: estimates developed by WHO, UNICEF, UNFPA" (WHO/RHRO1.9), 2001. ESCAP secretariat staff have derived estimates for Asia and the Pacific as a weighted average of subregional estimates.

Policy issues and strategies

Some major policy issues and strategies of direct relevance to maternal health are outlined below.

Increased investment in health-care services, including family planning services and skilled health personnel for births

- More investment is needed in health-care systems to improve the quality and coverage of delivery services, including skilled health personnel for births, and to provide prenatal and post-natal care for the poor.

- As appropriate, women should be empowered so that they are able to make decisions for themselves, particularly regarding family size. This can be complemented by the provision of affordable family planning services. A smaller family size tends to have a positive impact on both maternal and child health.

Annex table III.1. Incidence of poverty in rural and urban areas in selected countries based on national poverty lines during the 1990s

	Period	Rural poverty		Urban poverty	
		First year	Final year	First year	Final year
Bangladesh	(1992, 1996)	46.0	39.8	23.3	14.3
Cambodia	(1994, 1997)	43.1	40.1	24.8	21.1
India	(1988, 1999)	39.1	27.1	38.2	23.6
Indonesia	(1990, 1999)	14.3	20.2	16.8	15.1
Kazakhstan	(1996, 2000)	39.0	34.2	30.0	30.0
Kyrgyzstan	(1993, 1997)	48.1	64.5	28.7	28.5
Malaysia	(1989, 1999)	21.8	13.2	7.5	3.8
Mongolia	(1995, 1998)	33.1	32.6	38.5	39.4
Pakistan	(1991, 1999)	23.6	34.8	18.6	25.9
Philippines	(1991, 2000)	55.1	54.0	35.6	24.3
Republic of Korea	(1988, 1996)	7.2	9.4	8.9	6.1
Viet Nam	(1993, 1998)	66.0	45.0	25.0	9.0

Source: ESCAP, *Growth with Equity: Policy Lessons from Selected Asian Countries* (United Nations publication, Sales No. E.00.II.F.14); ADB, country papers prepared for the Inception Workshop on Building a Poverty Database, held at Manila in July-August 2001; World Bank, *World Development Report 2000/2001: Attacking Poverty* (New York, Oxford University Press, 2001); and national sources.

Annex table III.2. Income or consumption share of the bottom 20 per cent of the population in selected countries during the 1990s

	Period	First year	Final year
Bangladesh	(1992, 1996)	9.4	8.7
China	(1990, 1998)	7.3	5.9
India	(1990, 1997)	8.9	8.1
Indonesia	(1990, 1999)	9.2	9.0
Kazakhstan	(1993, 1996)	7.5	6.6
Pakistan	(1990, 1997)	8.1	9.4
Philippines	(1991, 1997)	5.8	5.3
Republic of Korea	(1988, 1996)	7.4	7.7
Sri Lanka	(1990, 1995)	8.9	8.0
Thailand	(1990, 1999)	4.9	3.9
Viet Nam	(1992, 1999)	7.8	5.6

Source: ESCAP, *Survey 1998*, pp. 144-147; World Bank web page, "Global poverty monitoring", at <http.//www.worldbank.org/research/povmonitor/index.htm>, 30 October 2001; and national sources.

REGIONAL DEVELOPMENT COOPERATION IN ASIA AND THE PACIFIC

INTRODUCTION

O DA has been an important resource in the process of economic growth and social advancement of developing countries, including those in the Asian and Pacific region.[1] It will remain so for the foreseeable future. Indeed, external aid is seen as one of the principal means to enable developing countries to achieve the poverty reduction and human development goals set by the United Nations Millennium Summit in its Declaration adopted by the General Assembly in September 2000. It is thus a major catalyst to socio-economic development, particularly in those countries which have the right policy environment but lack the infrastructure and capabilities necessary to mobilize sufficient domestic resources and to attract private capital flows.

External aid is a principal means for developing countries to reduce poverty

The Secretary-General of the United Nations, in his report entitled "Road map towards the implementation of the United Nations Millennium Declaration",[2] urged industrial and other donor countries to provide ODA equal to 0.7 per cent of their GNP; to distinguish between the portion of aid spent on development and that spent on humanitarian assistance so as to prevent erosion of the former; and to allocate ODA to

---

[1] ODA as defined by the Development Assistance Committee of OECD comprises those flows to developing countries and multilateral institutions provided by official national agencies mainly for the promotion of economic development and welfare. It includes technical cooperation. ODA is concessional in nature and has a grant element of at least 25 per cent. Flows meeting this test but directed to countries and territories in transition, including more advanced developing countries, are considered to be official aid (OA). Thus, ODA grants made by Governments or official agencies are transfers, in money or in kind, for which no repayment is required (unrequited official transfers). ODA/OA loans are those with maturities of over one year and meeting the criteria of ODA. However, repayment of both principal and interest in convertible currencies or in kind is required. Other official flows are official transactions whose main objective is not primarily development or whose grant element is below the 25 per cent threshold. Private sector transactions consist of direct investment, bank lending, investment in bonds and equities and export credits. Total net resource flow is defined as the sum of net ODA, net other official flows and net private sector flows.

2 A/56/326.

countries that need it most as well as to those whose policies are effectively directed towards reducing poverty. The Third United Nations Conference on the Least Developed Countries reconfirmed that 0.15-0.20 per cent of the GNP of developed countries should be directed to the least developed countries as ODA. The special role of development assistance in facilitating the realization of the millennium development goals is to be considered at the International Conference on Financing for Development, scheduled to be held at Monterrey, Mexico, in March 2002. The Secretary-General of the United Nations has urged the Conference to adopt an additional $50 billion in ODA, a doubling of current levels, as an interim, short-term target, achievable within two or three years.[3]

These targets are challenging in themselves, given the number of issues pertinent to development cooperation arising in the Asian and Pacific region:

ODA to the ESCAP region declined, notwithstanding reforms

- Several developing countries, including many in Asia and the Pacific, undertook major economic and political reforms in the 1990s, a decade which also witnessed a considerable improvement in the fiscal situation of most donor countries. However, the overall level of ODA to developing countries in the region declined, instead of increasing, throughout most of the decade.

- Development assistance has tended to flow towards recipient countries able to create and sustain an environment in which ODA could have a rapid and measurable impact on socio-economic development and poverty alleviation.

A dilemma between aid and need may have emerged

- This suggests that a dilemma between aid and need may have emerged. Countries that remained the least able to implement ancillary economic reform and restructuring measures effectively were often among the poorest and least developed. However, those countries did not necessarily receive the level

---

[3] The report of the High-level Panel on Financing for Development (known as the "Zedillo report") estimated the additional cost of achieving the millennium development goals at approximately $50 billion per year (see "Recommendations of the High-level Panel on Financing for Development" transmitted to the General Assembly as part of the above report, in document A/55/1000). More recently, the World Bank has estimated that attaining these goals will require between $40 and $60 billion annually in additional ODA, provided that the recipient countries improve their policy and institutional environment to make them more conducive to aid and assuming that FDI flows and the world trading system remain essentially unchanged (see World Bank, "The costs of attaining the millennium development goals", available at <http://www.worldbank.org/html/extdr/mdgassessment.pdf>).

of assistance, or, for that matter, FDI, needed to enable them to take full advantage of the wide range of concessions and preferences accorded them, especially in their global integration efforts, including trading relationships with the donor community itself.[4]

- A more judicious convergence of donor interests and preferences, and recipient capabilities in aid absorption, is needed to maximize the total impact of financial and non-financial ODA. Better coordination of aid programmes and projects, including those of a bilateral nature, is also necessary. Moreover, the active participation of recipient countries in the design and implementation stages could enhance ODA effectiveness. At the same time, ways and means should be found to lessen administrative burdens, particularly in smaller recipient economies.[5]

Donors' preferences and recipient capabilities need to converge more judiciously

- Development cooperation is no longer confined exclusively to financial and technical flows from developed to developing countries, especially in Asia and the Pacific. In fact, certain components of the ODA programmes of several developing countries in the region are comparable in size and scope to those offered by traditional, developed country donors. Indeed, in several cases, the duality of their roles (as both aid recipients and donors) could help considerably in the development of unique yet effective partnerships between those countries and a wide range of ODA recipients.

South-South cooperation is increasing in importance

- Effective coordination of programmes and projects from developing country donors, as well as between those donors and developed countries, combined with local ownership of projects and programmes, could generate considerable synergies. A good case in point is embodied in such triangular modalities as third-country training programmes conducted by local experts and consultants from developing countries but funded or sponsored by developed countries.

Triangular modalities can generate considerable synergies

---

[4] The role of ODA in meeting the financing gap of the least developed countries, and associated trade policy issues, was discussed in *Review of Implementation of the Programme of Action for the Least Developed Countries for the 1990s: Asia and the Pacific* (ST/ESCAP/2121) and *Review of Implementation of the Programme of Action for the Least Developed Countries for the 1990s: Subregional Studies* (ST/ESCAP/2084).

[5] For an analysis of issues concerning aid administration and effectiveness from the recipients' points of view, see ESCAP, *Enhancing Effectiveness of Aid* (United Nations publication, Sales No. E.99.II.F.63), in which case studies from Bangladesh, the Lao People's Democratic Republic, Nepal and Vanuatu are presented.

- The continuing support for those programmes by the donor community, including international and regional funding agencies, is encouraging. Nevertheless, the untying of bilateral aid from traditional donors is often a prerequisite to technical and other assistance of a triangular nature.

PATTERNS OF DEVELOPMENT COOPERATION IN ASIA AND THE PACIFIC

Global aid flows into the region

Aid flows recovered in 2000

The net flow of ODA from all donors to developing economies of the ESCAP region fell from a peak of over $19 billion in 1992 to around $14 billion in 1997, but recovered to over $16 billion in 2000 (figure IV.1). The proportion of global ODA going to those economies fluctuated between a low of 27.6 per cent in 1990 and a high of 34.4 per cent in 1999. In 2000, the share was 32.9 per cent. On a subregional basis (figure IV.2), economies in South and South-West and South-East Asia were

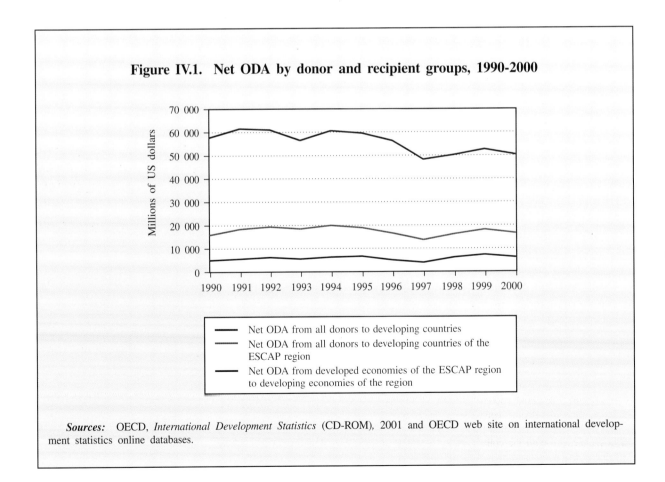

Figure IV.1. Net ODA by donor and recipient groups, 1990-2000

Millions of US dollars

—— Net ODA from all donors to developing countries

—— Net ODA from all donors to developing countries of the ESCAP region

—— Net ODA from developed economies of the ESCAP region to developing economies of the region

Sources: OECD, *International Development Statistics* (CD-ROM), 2001 and OECD web site on international development statistics online databases.

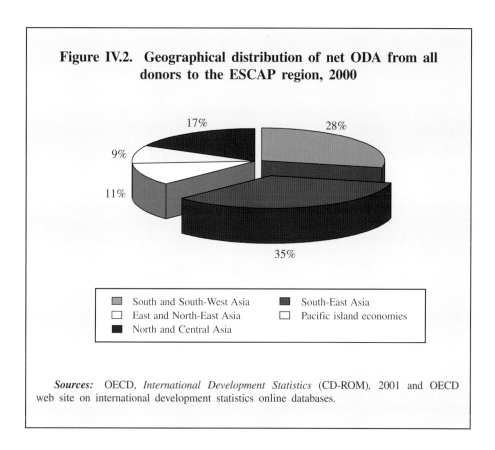

Figure IV.2. Geographical distribution of net ODA from all donors to the ESCAP region, 2000

17%

28%

9%

11%

35%

- ▨ South and South-West Asia
- ☐ East and North-East Asia
- ■ North and Central Asia
- ■ South-East Asia
- ☐ Pacific island economies

Sources: OECD, *International Development Statistics* (CD-ROM), 2001 and OECD web site on international development statistics online databases.

the destination for over $10 billion in ODA in 2000; China and Indonesia each received more than $2 billion a year, while Bangladesh, India, Thailand and Viet Nam were allocated at least $1 billion each. In the Pacific island economies, French Polynesia, Micronesia (Federated States of), New Caledonia and Papua New Guinea were the largest recipients in 2000. Net ODA flows to the economies in transition in North and Central Asia rose significantly, from $2 billion in 1992 to nearly $3 billion in 2000. Most of these flows were directed to the Russian Federation. Over the same period, the economies in Central Asia and the Caucusus, where aid flows had been relatively small in the early 1990s, saw a 20-fold increase in ODA. Bilateral donors provided nearly three quarters of ODA to Asia and the Pacific in 2000 (figure IV.3), in part reflecting sharply increased assistance in the aftermath of the 1997 crisis.[6] Multilateral flows reached a peak in 1994, decreasing more or less continually thereafter.

---

[6] Notably, developing countries in the Middle East provided an estimated total of $6 billion to other developing countries in 1990 and net flows to the ESCAP developing region peaked at more than $1 billion in 1991, Afghanistan, Bangladesh and Turkey being among the major recipients. With the collapse of oil prices in the last decade, net ODA from countries in the Middle East amounted to just over $12 million in 1999.

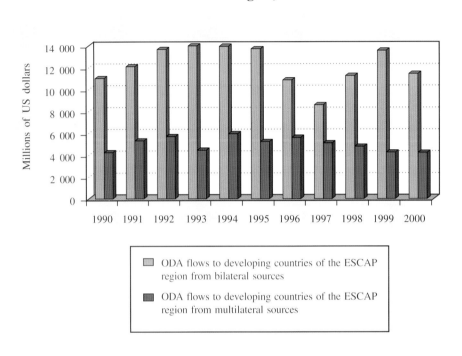

Figure IV.3. Bilateral and multilateral net ODA flows to developing countries of the ESCAP region, 1990-2000

Sources: OECD, *International Development Statistics* (CD-ROM), 2001 and OECD web site on international development statistics online databases.

Japan's share of ODA to Asia was 45 per cent

In Asia, the top three donors in 1999 were Japan, the International Development Association and the United States (table IV.1). Japan accounted for a very substantial share of ODA, 45 per cent, to Asia, which received 62 per cent of all Japanese aid. In the Pacific, France accounted for over 50 per cent of ODA flows (mainly to its territories in the region), followed by Australia and the United States. Among the recipients in Asia, China, Indonesia and the Russian Federation received the most ODA flows, while in the Pacific, French Polynesia, New Caledonia and Papua New Guinea headed the list (table IV.2).

ODA in per capita terms takes on a different nuance

ODA takes on a different nuance in per capita terms (table IV.3). Reflecting the fall-off in global ODA in absolute terms, external aid per head of population in the ESCAP region declined from $4.1 in 1995 to $3.2 in 2000. Economies in the Pacific continued to receive the most ODA on a per capita basis, although the amount declined considerably

Table IV.1. ODA donors to regional ESCAP members

	Top 10 donors in Asia, 1999				Top 10 donors in the Pacific, 1999		
Donor	*Millions of US dollars*	*Percentage of all ODA[a]*	*Percentage of donor ODA[b]*	*Donor*	*Millions of US dollars*	*Percentage of all ODA[a]*	*Percentage of donor ODA[b]*
Japan	6 609	45	62	France	724	51	17
International Development Association	1 895	13	46	Australia	229	16	31
United States	1 053	7	15	United States	183	13	2
Asian Development Fund	914	6	88	Japan	138	10	1
Germany	886	6	26	New Zealand	66	5	65
European Union	582	4	11	Asian Development Fund	22	2	2
United Kingdom	463	3	20	United Kingdom	20	1	1
Australia	267	2	37	United Nations Transitional Administration in East Timor	9	1	2
France	240	2	11	European Union	8	1	<1
Netherlands	238	2	6	International Development Association	5	<1	<1
Others	1 700	11	14	Others	20	1	<1
Total	14 847	100	28	Total	1 424	100	2

Sources: OECD, *International Development Statistics* (CD-ROM), 2001 and OECD web site on international development statistics online databases.

[a] Aid from each donor to ESCAP economies in Asia and the Pacific as a percentage of aid from all donors to ESCAP economies in Asia and the Pacific.

[b] Aid from each donor to ESCAP economies in Asia and the Pacific as a percentage of aid from each donor to all aid recipients.

between 1995 and 2000.[7] South-East Asia and North and Central Asia both received over $9 in ODA per capita in 2000, while East and North-East Asia and South and South-West Asia received less than $2 per capita in the same year. South and South-West Asia consist of economies with

---

[7] This result is likely to be a statistical artifact owing to the transfer of French Polynesia and New Caledonia from the list of ODA-eligible territories to OA countries in 2000.

Table IV.2. ODA recipients among regional ESCAP members

Top 10 aid recipients in Asia, 1999			*Top 10 aid recipients in the Pacific, 1999*		
Recipients	*Millions of US dollars*	*Percentage of all Asian economies*	*Recipients*	*Millions of US dollars*	*Percentage of all Pacific economies*
China	2 385	14	French Polynesia	352	25
Indonesia	2 216	13	New Caledonia	315	22
Russian Federation	1 946	12	Papua New Guinea	216	15
India	1 491	9	Micronesia (Federated States of)	108	8
Viet Nam	1 429	9	Marshall Islands	63	4
Bangladesh	1 215	7	Wallis and Futuna	50	4
Thailand	1 010	6	Solomon Islands	40	3
Pakistan	733	4	Vanuatu	37	3
Philippines	696	4	Fiji	34	2
Nepal	351	2	Palau	29	2
Others	3 260	19	Others	181	13
Total	16 732	100	Total	1 424	100

Sources: OECD, *International Development Statistics* (CD-ROM), 2001 and OECD web site on international development statistics online databases.

the lowest GNP per capita as well as the largest concentration of poverty in the Asian and Pacific region. On this basis, aid does not appear to have flowed to the countries most in need of it.

Table IV.3. ODA and GNP per capita in ESCAP subregions

(US dollars)

	1990		1995		2000	
	ODA per capita	*GNP per capita*	*ODA per capita*	*GNP per capita*	*ODA per capita*	*GNP per capita*
ESCAP region	3.8	632.0	4.1	977.9	3.2	1 051.6
South and South-West Asia	3.2	505.6	2.4	509.4	1.7	615.3
South-East Asia	9.5	689.8	8.8	1 320.3	9.2	1 082.2
East and North-East Asia	1.3	738.2	2.1	1 187.7	1.1	1 469.4
North and Central Asia	..	..	8.6	1 903.0	9.6	1 308.1
Pacific	204.4	961.5	246.7	1 195.9	80.5	1 844.1

Source: DAC.

Note: Figures are in current prices.

Regional aid inflows from all DAC member countries

The net amount of ODA to developing countries from member countries of DAC (figure IV.4) also declined, from about $43 to $36 billion, between 1991 and 2000.[8]   However, DAC-based aid to developing countries of the ESCAP region had expanded by nearly a third of the total flow to all developing countries to reach over $13 billion in 1999, partially as a response to the severity of the 1997 economic crisis in East and South-East Asia, before falling back to $11 billion in 2000.

Regional aid flows from DAC members were also down

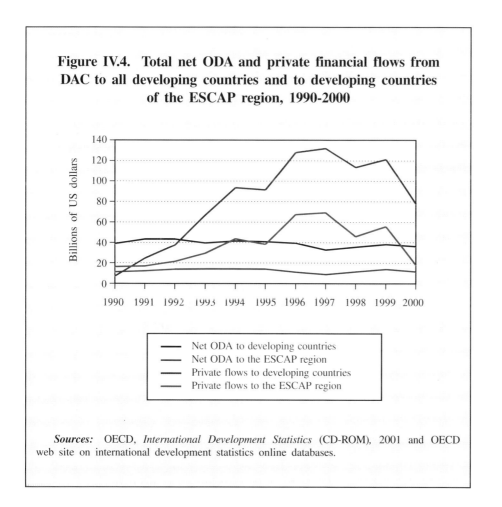

Figure IV.4. Total net ODA and private financial flows from DAC to all developing countries and to developing countries of the ESCAP region, 1990-2000

— Net ODA to developing countries
— Net ODA to the ESCAP region
— Private flows to developing countries
— Private flows to the ESCAP region

Sources: OECD, *International Development Statistics* (CD-ROM), 2001 and OECD web site on international development statistics online databases.

---

[8] DAC members are Australia, Austria, Belgium, Canada, Denmark, Finland, France, Germany, Greece, Ireland, Italy, Japan, Luxembourg, the Netherlands, New Zealand, Norway, Portugal, Spain, Sweden, Switzerland, the United Kingdom of Great Britain and Northern Ireland, the United States of America and the Commission of the European Communities.

Grants to developing economies in the region from DAC members, at $8.3 billion, continued to exceed loans, totalling $7.6 billion, in 2000. Nearly 49 per cent of the loans were directed to countries in South-East Asia, the region most seriously affected by the 1997 economic crisis (figure IV.5a). In contrast, a third of ODA grants, were directed to that subregion in 2000 (figure IV.5b). It is notable that the grant component exceeded the amount of loans extended to Pacific island economies by a factor of seven, a clear indication of the special needs and greater economic vulnerability of this subregion.

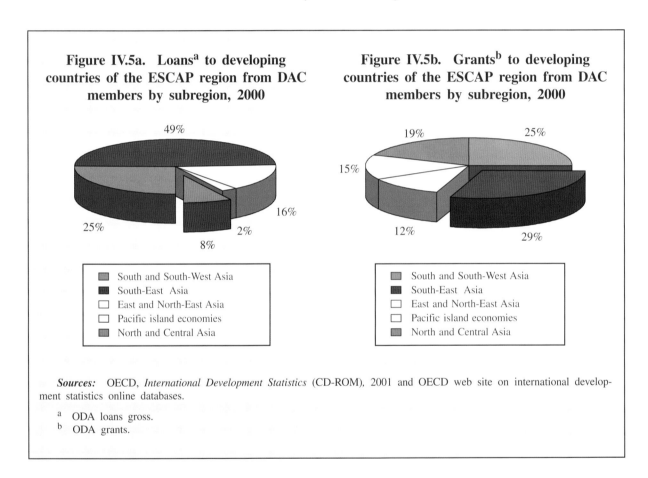

Figure IV.5a. Loans[a] to developing countries of the ESCAP region from DAC members by subregion, 2000

49%
16%
25%
2%
8%

☐ South and South-West Asia
■ South-East Asia
☐ East and North-East Asia
☐ Pacific island economies
▨ North and Central Asia

Figure IV.5b. Grants[b] to developing countries of the ESCAP region from DAC members by subregion, 2000

19%   25%
15%
12%   29%

☐ South and South-West Asia
■ South-East Asia
☐ East and North-East Asia
☐ Pacific island economies
▨ North and Central Asia

Sources: OECD, *International Development Statistics* (CD-ROM), 2001 and OECD web site on international development statistics online databases.

[a] ODA loans gross.
[b] ODA grants.

Allocations to the social sector were increased

Bilateral, DAC-based ODA commitments to economic infrastructure and services, and to the production sectors of the developing countries of the ESCAP region, have shown a gradual decline. However, ODA channelled to social infrastructure and services, programme assistance and emergency assistance recorded a significant increase. The allocations for economic and social infrastructure and services were 30 and 27 per cent respectively of the total net bilateral ODA commitments in 1999 (figure IV.6). Again, this pattern of aid allocation partially reflects donor response to the growing impact of the Asian economic crisis.

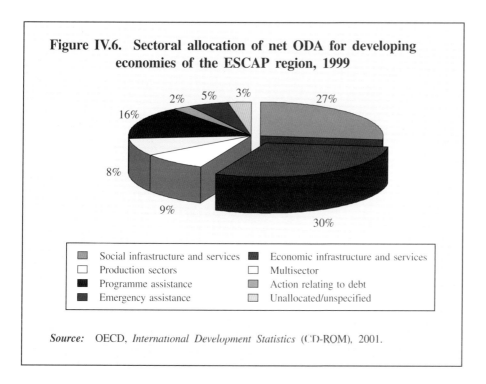

Figure IV.6. Sectoral allocation of net ODA for developing economies of the ESCAP region, 1999

Legend:
- Social infrastructure and services
- Production sectors
- Programme assistance
- Emergency assistance
- Economic infrastructure and services
- Multisector
- Action relating to debt
- Unallocated/unspecified

Source: OECD, *International Development Statistics* (CD-ROM), 2001.

The most striking trend in the 1990s, however, was the phenomenal rise in DAC-based private financial flows to developing countries prior to the 1997 crisis (figure IV.4) and the almost equally dramatic subsequent fall. The instability of these flows to developing countries of the ESCAP region was notable, from $16 billion in 1990 to $68.8 billion in 1997, falling to $55.5 billion in 1999 and just under $18 billion in 2000. Private financial flows had overtaken ODA from DAC countries as the major type of development finance for the region as a whole. However, their great volatility presents a challenge to policy management for stable and sustainable growth. In addition, the flows are concentrated heavily in a small number of East and South-East Asian economies. Clearly therefore, for most of the relatively poorer economies in Asia and the Pacific, private financial resources are not yet a substitute for ODA.

Private financial flows increased greatly, but were volatile

Regional aid inflows from regional member countries of DAC

Amount and distribution

ODA from ESCAP regional members in DAC, Australia, Japan and New Zealand, went up from less than a third to nearly half of total ODA to the ESCAP developing region during the period 1991-1999. South-East Asia received the lion's share of intraregional aid, accounting for nearly 54 per cent in 2000 (figure IV.7). Japan, which devoted 0.35 per cent of GNP

Regional DAC members increased their share of ODA to the ESCAP region to half

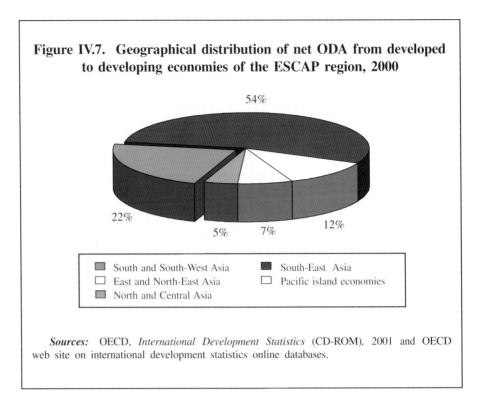

Figure IV.7. Geographical distribution of net ODA from developed to developing economies of the ESCAP region, 2000

Legend:
- South and South-West Asia
- East and North-East Asia
- North and Central Asia
- South-East Asia
- Pacific island economies

Sources: OECD, *International Development Statistics* (CD-ROM), 2001 and OECD web site on international development statistics online databases.

to aid in 1999 and is the world's largest donor, has been the region's biggest source of aid by far for over a decade, providing $5.5 billion in 2000, or 89 per cent of such intraregional ODA, compared with $4.5 billion in 1990 (figure IV.8). Indeed, nearly two thirds of Japan's global ODA has been directed towards developing countries in Asia and the Pacific (table IV.1). The 10 largest recipients of this assistance were all in Asia; among them, China, India, Indonesia and Thailand together were allocated more than $5 billion in 1999, China and Indonesia alone receiving over $1.5 billion each.

Low- and lower-middle-income countries in the region received three quarters of Japanese aid

Generally, some three quarters of Japan's gross bilateral ODA in 1998-1999 was channelled to low- and lower-middle-income countries, and a tenth to all least developed countries. A third of Japan's overseas assistance was used for the development of economic infrastructure; this was followed in importance by aid for the production sectors, programme assistance, and education, health and population.

An issue of much concern is the possible decline in intraregional aid from the three developed member countries in the ESCAP region, particularly Japan, whose ODA was cut by 10 per cent under the fiscal reform package announced in 1997. The prospects for higher assistance have become uncertain, in spite of the offsetting provision of new aid resources and the freezing of further cuts.

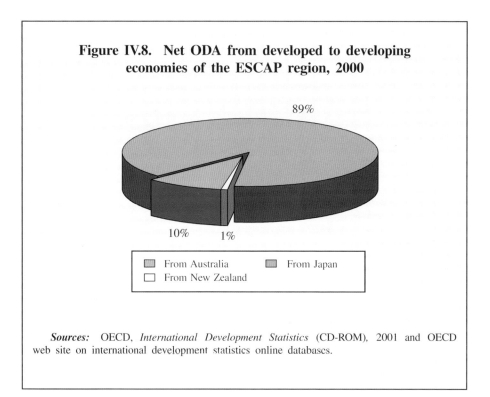

Figure IV.8. Net ODA from developed to developing economies of the ESCAP region, 2000

89%

10%   1%

☒ From Australia   ☒ From Japan
☐ From New Zealand

Sources: OECD, *International Development Statistics* (CD-ROM), 2001 and OECD web site on international development statistics online databases.

Net ODA from Australia declined gradually after 1995, when it peaked at nearly $705 million, before recovering to reach $620 million in 2000, while that from New Zealand fell from its peak of almost $73 million in 1997 to about $54 million in 2000. The Australian Agency for International Development estimates that the ODA-to-GNP ratio declined to 0.26 per cent in 1999, compared with the highest ratio of 0.65 per cent reached in 1975. However, Australia supports the United Nations target for ODA of 0.7 per cent of GNP and will try to maintain aid at the highest level, consistent with the needs of partner economies and its own economic circumstances and capacity to assist. In contrast, New Zealand has maintained the share of GNP devoted to ODA at 0.27 per cent; it ranked thirteenth in terms of this ratio among DAC member countries in 1999 and fifteenth in 1998.

Aid from Australia and New Zealand declined in the 1990s

With regard to geographical distribution, Papua New Guinea and East Timor received nearly a quarter of gross bilateral ODA from Australia on average in 1998 and 1999; Indonesia, the Philippines and Viet Nam were also in the top five recipients. However, the 10 largest recipients of New Zealand aid were from the Pacific island subregion, with the exception of Indonesia. New Zealand also directed nearly a quarter of its aid to least developed countries in the ESCAP region. More than half of Australian and New Zealand aid was allocated to the sectors of education, health, population and other social infrastructure.

Countries in the immediate geographical vicinity were major aid recipients

Recent changes in orientation and management

There have recently been fundamental changes in both the policy direction and the organization of the development cooperation programmes of Australia, Japan and New Zealand. Generally, more resources are channelled directly to programmes targeted at the poor and the basic sources of poverty, with poverty alleviation and eradication in recipient countries being the ultimate goal of development. In particular, against the visible negative impact of the Asian economic crisis, Japan has increasingly endorsed the idea that economic growth is only a means to achieve human-centred development and enhance people's welfare.

More importance will be attached to quality in Japanese aid programmes

The future direction of Japanese ODA, as outlined in the report prepared by Japan's Council on ODA Reforms for the 21st Century in January 1998, involved reprioritization of the areas for ODA assistance. The report provided guidelines on refocusing aid programmes from quantity to quality considerations and stressed the need for heightened public understanding of the ODA process (box IV.1). The Japanese philosophy on ODA is largely based on the country's own experience after the Second World War, when it obtained World Bank loans to develop its core infrastructure and industry. However, in many developing countries, the capacity to use external aid effectively, a highly literate population, a burgeoning private sector and a solid national planning system with an effective revenue collection capacity are still missing, and the parallel to the Japanese experience often does not exist. In May 2001, the Second Consultative Committee on ODA Reform was established, and tasked with proposing, among other things, measures for a more focused, effective and efficient ODA programme, and clarifying the philosophy and target of assistance as well as its role in foreign policy, given Japan's domestic economic difficulties and fiscal constraints and the rapid changes in the international environment.

Development cooperation is a strand of Australia's external policy

An Australian White Paper on foreign and trade policy, entitled "In the national interest", issued in 1993, integrated development cooperation as a strand of external policy, along with foreign trade, defence and immigration policies. Thus, overseas aid is seen to advance the national interest in helping developing countries to reduce poverty and achieve sustainable development. It is to be governed by six key principles for policy formulation and programme implementation: it must promote partnerships, be responsive to urgent needs and development trends, practical, targeted and outward-looking, and incorporate an Australian identity. Health, education, agriculture and rural development, infrastructure and governance are the five sectors accorded priority attention, along with two critical cross-cutting issues: gender equality and the environment. The approach of the Australian Agency for International

---

Box IV.1. Recommendations of the Council on ODA Reforms for the 21st Century for improving Japanese ODA

Effectiveness	• Emphasis on efforts in poverty alleviation and social development with a focus on human-centred development
	• Accent on basic education and primary health care
	• New directions in infrastructure development, using ODA only for projects that cannot be funded privately; more bundling with technical assistance; and teaming-up with multilateral institutions
	• Emphasis on environmental issues
	• Support for women in development
	• Stronger emphasis on human resources development
	• Formation of global partnerships
	• Increase in cross-border regional cooperation
	• Assistance in conflict prevention and post-war conflict development
	• Technical cooperation in legal and financial systems
	• Enhancement of the role of the private sector
Modalities	• Increased public participation, particularly by non-governmental organizations and recipient country stakeholders
	• Disclosure of information; enhanced development
	• Fostering of international aid experts for placement in multilateral institutions
Implementation	• Increased collaboration of agencies
	• Increased delegation of authority to the field
	• Improved evaluation by the inclusion of other donors, examination of the environmental and social impacts, and disclosure of more information
	• Enhanced collaboration with the private sector and multilateral institutions
	• Increased policy dialogue with recipient countries

Source: DAC.

Development to poverty reduction therefore emphasizes investment in human and social capital and the protection of the most vulnerable groups in society.

Through ODA, the contribution of New Zealand to the promotion of economic and social advancement, maintaining security and protecting the environment is well known, especially in the Pacific island subregion. As the principal beneficiaries and partners of New Zealand's aid are small island economies, the focus and management of bilateral country programmes, which also tend to be administratively intensive,

New Zealand's focus on the small island economies of the Pacific is well known

---

Box IV.2. Trust funds

Trust funds and revenue equalization reserve funds have been introduced in Kiribati, the Marshall Islands, Tonga and Tuvalu to smooth out the periodic variations in government receipts as a result of high reliance on external aid, royalties from natural resources and other volatile forms of revenue. The Tuvalu Trust Fund, for example, was established in 1987 as a publicly-owned investment fund, the earnings of which are used to help to bridge the gap between government revenue and expenditure. In addition to the Tuvalu Government itself, other major contributors to the Fund are Australia, New Zealand and the United Kingdom. Together with smaller grants from Japan and the Republic of Korea, the Fund totalled $27 million at its inception and, through reinvested earnings and additional donor inputs, its estimated value was $66.6 million in September 2000.

Source: Department of Foreign Affairs and Trade, Australia.

constitute a challenge. The pursuit of poverty reduction, including by addressing the multisectoral characteristics of the issue, adds another dimension to budget allocations in support of activities in health, environment and good governance, which are comparatively modest. Australia and New Zealand have both contributed to revenue equalization and trust funds in the Pacific island subregion (box IV.2). The importance of these funds is difficult to overestimate.

Debt relief and the untying of aid

Japan has made grants for debt relief

The high levels of external indebtedness of many developing countries and the associated financial difficulties, including in debt servicing, have both domestic and international implications. Elements of moral hazard are involved in debt-forgiveness considerations, and Japan's approaches are mediated mainly through making grants for debt relief. For example, the related assistance provided to a total of 14 developing countries to cover interest and principal due to Japan was worth $233 million in fiscal year 1997. The cumulated effects of some measures were equivalent to debt cancellation of over 80 per cent.

Australia has contributed to the Heavily Indebted Poor Countries Initiative

Although Australia now has only a grant aid programme, the country is owed about $2.2 billion in sovereign debts as of March 1999; mixed credits were previously extended as part of the discontinued Development Import Finance Facility. While debt relief is not a substitute for development assistance, the World Bank and IMF Heavily Indebted Poor Countries Initiative is viewed as the most credible way to provide debt relief.[9] Through supplementary allocations to the aid budget, Australia contributed $19 million in June 1998, followed by a commitment of another $19 million in September 1999.

---

[9] The Lao People's Democratic Republic, Myanmar and Viet Nam are the only three countries in the region to qualify for the Initiative. A decision point has not as yet been reached for the first two; the debt level in Viet Nam has been judged to be potentially sustainable.

Aid tends to be tied to the offsetting purchase of goods and services from the donor country for various reasons. Tied ODA can lead to greater support for aid programmes and increase their visibility. However, it can also function as a subsidy to enterprises and service providers in donor countries. It is estimated that tied aid could raise the cost of procured goods and services by 15 to 30 per cent and increase the administrative burden on both recipients and donors. Moreover, it could also favour projects requiring capital-intensive imports or donor-based techniques, which do not always conform to the priorities or absorptive capacity of the recipient countries.[10] The gradual untying of aid could thus increase the impact of development assistance through ongoing capacity-building leading to greater and better aid absorption in recipient countries.

The tying of aid can lead to inefficiency and greater costs

Japan has been one of the most prominent and vocal advocates of untied aid and virtually all (over 90 per cent) of its ODA is now untied. However, procurement under grant projects and technical cooperation activities is normally limited to Japanese goods and service providers. The procurement procedures and contract information for ODA loans are already fairly open and, to increase transparency, information is provided on bidders and contracts for both grant aid and loans. DAC has encouraged Japan to promote further untying of its ODA, particularly to least developed countries.

Virtually all Japanese aid is untied

Australia and New Zealand are reviewing the way in which their aid programmes could integrate the provision of goods and services from developing countries. In particular, although a third of Australia's bilateral ODA is tied, four fifths consist of goods and services supplied from Australia. Furthermore, only firms registered with the Australian Securities and Investments Commission, or with a head office in Australia or New Zealand, can be engaged to manage projects. As a result, the principle of promoting the Australian identity needs to be reconciled with considerations of partnership (through the building up of local ownership and capacity), cost-efficiency and impact maximization. However, the field operations of the Australian Agency for International Development encourage local partners to take greater leadership roles whenever this can be done effectively and accountably. The use of local talent, currently limited mainly to project review and implementation, could be broadened, as appropriate, to include accounting and financial management services.

Australia and New Zealand are seeking to increase the provision of goods and services from developing countries

---

[10] OECD, "Untying aid to the least developed countries", Policy Brief (*OECD Observer*, July 2001).

DEVELOPMENT COOPERATION AMONG DEVELOPING COUNTRIES

ODA has traditionally been viewed as the flow of resources from developed countries (commonly referred to as the North) to developing countries (the South). Such resource transfers, whether in cash or in kind, aim at supporting programmes and activities that build and upgrade capacity, help the poor, protect the environment and stimulate socio-economic growth as well as opportunities for domestic and foreign investment in the South. In this context, the world's commitment to the developing countries embodies not only a moral imperative but also a desire to address problems of common concern or promote matters of mutual interest.

South-South cooperation

Major gains in development efforts can be realized through cooperation between developing countries

There is heightened awareness, however, that major gains in development efforts can be realized through the promotion of South-South cooperation. Such cooperation enables developing countries themselves to bring their experience to bear on similar development problems in other developing countries. It also provides a cost-effective way to utilize the financial resources and technical expertise available from multilateral assistance programmes and activities. In this respect, the process can be greatly facilitated and extended through "triangular" or "trilateral" cooperative arrangements whereby developed countries provide the necessary inputs in support of South-South cooperation initiated and implemented by the developing countries themselves.

During the 1970s, South-South cooperation formally emerged as a strategy to support mutual development among developing countries and to promote their collective self-reliance. It was needed to ensure their more effective participation in global affairs and as a complement to the extensive economic relationships between the developed and developing countries.[11] The role of the United Nations in promoting this type of cooperation is described in box IV.3.

---

[11] Denis Benn, "South-South cooperation: a strategic dimension of international development cooperation" (web site <http://www.undp.org/tcdc/benn4.htm>). The principles behind South-South cooperation were reflected in the Action Programme for Economic Cooperation among Non-Aligned and Other Developing Countries, adopted by the Conference of Foreign Ministers of Non-Aligned Countries held at Georgetown in 1972; the Buenos Aires Plan of Action on Promoting and Implementing Technical Cooperation among Developing Countries, adopted at the United Nations Conference on Technical Cooperation among Developing Countries held at Buenos Aires in 1978; and the Caracas Programme of Action on Economic Cooperation among Developing Countries, adopted by the Group of 77 in 1981. From the framework of these broad principles came various initiatives designed to strengthen South-South cooperation through formal arrangements for subregional and regional integration, as well as through more informal modalities with a focus on strengthening subregional and regional trade and financial interaction, and technical capabilities.

Box IV.3. The role of the United Nations in the promotion of South-South cooperation

The United Nations has played an important role in the promotion of South-South cooperation since the 1970s. In particular, the Economic and Social Council and the General Assembly have endorsed programmes of action on TCDC and ECDC and have called upon the organizations and agencies of the United Nations system and the international community to support such programmes.

UNCTAD and UNDP have special responsibility for the promotion of ECDC and TCDC. The Special Standing Committee on ECDC provides broad policy guidance on programmes implemented by the UNCTAD secretariat. Within UNDP, the Special Unit for TCDC serves as the secretariat for the High-Level Committee on the Review of Technical Cooperation among Developing Countries. This is a subsidiary body of the United Nations General Assembly and meets biennially to review progress on TCDC within the United Nations system as a whole. Its report and recommendations are submitted to the General Assembly through the Economic and Social Council.

In its consideration of the agenda item New directions for TCDC, as a response to the imperatives of, and impulses from, economic globalization and liberalization, in June 1995 the High-Level Committee called for the promotion of high-priority TCDC activities in such areas as trade and investment, debt, macroeconomic coordination and aid management, poverty alleviation and the environment. In addition, it emphasized the need for closer operational integration between TCDC and ECDC, the identification of pivotal countries in each region to serve as catalysts for TCDC and the introduction of new modalities, especially the concept of "triangular cooperation" whereby developed countries would be encouraged to become involved in providing direct financial and technical support for the promotion of TCDC activities.

At the regional level, ESCAP has facilitated the implementation of TCDC and ECDC among developing countries. This is mediated through the strengthening of TCDC national focal points, particularly in least developed, landlocked and island developing countries, and economies in transition, and through facilitating the participation of developing countries in the region in the operational TCDC activities implemented by the ESCAP secretariat. In collaboration with the Government of China, the secretariat thus organized the Workshop on TCDC National Focal Points, held at Hangzhou, China, in November 2000. Its objective was to ensure better awareness, including through information dissemination, of the opportunities available in the TCDC programmes of China, Malaysia, the Philippines, Singapore and Thailand.

In 2000, the ESCAP secretariat funded the participation of 55 officials from least developed, landlocked and island developing countries, and economies in transition, in TCDC activities implemented through third-country training programmes. These included training courses on national economic management, poverty eradication and IT management in the public sector within the cooperation framework between ESCAP and the Government of Malaysia. Training courses implemented in collaboration with the Government of Singapore were focused on tourism management and development.

Sources: ESCAP, "Technical cooperation activities of ESCAP and announcement of intended contributions" (E/ESCAP/1221); and Denis Benn, "South-South cooperation: a strategic dimension of international development cooperation" (web site <http://www.undp.org/tcdc/benn4.htm>).

South-South cooperation embraces both TCDC and ECDC, but they are often pursued as separate initiatives. The High-level Committee on the Review of Technical Cooperation among Developing Countries, meeting in New York in 1995, recognized the need for closer operational integration between TCDC and ECDC, with TCDC being seen as an instrument for achieving the broader objectives of economic cooperation.

South-South cooperation is both technical and economic

Under the Buenos Aires Plan of Action for Promoting and Implementing Technical Cooperation among Developing Countries, the UNDP/TCDC modality to promote a partnership for development at the global, regional and bilateral levels was based on cost-sharing between participants, with the recipient country being responsible for international travel costs and the host country absorbing all local costs.

National and collective self-reliance is fostered through TCDC modalities

The TCDC modalities foster goals of national and collective self-reliance while broadening the scope and quality of international cooperation. Under TCDC, institutions of developing countries share experiences, pool and exchange information, transfer technical skills and strengthen organizational capacity to manage development activities, using their own human and financial resources as well as assistance from external sources. Such modalities often require the establishment of broad partnerships between Governments, international agencies, non-governmental organizations, community-based organizations and the private sector. In general, the modalities for TCDC are: (a) the identification and replication of effective or best practices; (b) the compilation and dissemination of information on capacities of developing countries; (c) subject-specific meetings and workshops; (d) study tours; (e) capacities and needs matching; (f) facilitating the establishment of networks; (g) the "pivotal country" approach; and (h) third-country cooperation arrangements.

South-South cooperation in the ESCAP region[12]

Growth in incomes and increased development are fostering South-South cooperation in the ESCAP region

In the Asian and Pacific region in particular, development cooperation is no longer confined exclusively to financial and technical flows from developed countries to their developing counterparts. There has been an ongoing upward movement in the income and development of many regional developing countries over the past three decades. Both Hong Kong, China, and Singapore have standards of living and per capita incomes comparable to those of many industrialized countries, while the Republic of Korea and Turkey are now OECD member countries. In fact, the ODA programmes of several developing countries in the region are comparable in size and scope to those offered by traditional donors, expanding as they have from the TCDC modality to include ODA loans and country-based programmes. In some cases, development cooperation programmes have shed the political identity of South-South cooperation.

---

[12] The secretariat circulated surveys on current development cooperation activities to developing member countries of the region in order to prepare this section. Responses were received from the Republic of Korea; Singapore; Sri Lanka; Thailand; and Turkey. Responses were also received from Hong Kong, China; and Macao, China.

Development cooperation among developing countries in Asia and the Pacific is possible as a result of differences in geographical location, income, human and financial resources and technological capability among countries in the region. Owing to these differences, the development experiences of countries in the region vary greatly and all have an opportunity to learn from the successful and unsuccessful experiences of their neighbours. Developing countries thus emphasize that their development cooperation programmes reflect their own first-hand development experience and differ to some extent from those offered by developed countries. Box IV.4 illustrates China's development cooperation programmes with least developed countries in the Asian and Pacific region. Another illustration of South-South cooperation is provided in box IV.5, in which Bangladesh's development cooperation activities are discussed.

Development cooperation between developing countries rests on first-hand experience

---

Box IV.4. China's development cooperation programmes with the least developed countries of the region

China, one of the strongest advocates of South-South cooperation, has long underlined its commitment by providing assistance to a diverse group of countries, including its neighbouring least developed countries. Scholarships have been made available to exchange students from Afghanistan, Bangladesh, Kiribati, the Lao People's Democratic Republic, Nepal, Samoa and Vanuatu and, starting in 2001, Bhutan. Fifteen exchange visits in various fields, ranging from the arts to sports, broadcasting and photography, are made every year with Nepal. Since 1990, medical teams have been sent to Kiribati, Samoa and Vanuatu.

China has also provided technical assistance in strengthening the industrial capacity and infrastructure of least developed countries in South Asia. Areas covered in bilateral exchange visits and cooperation projects with Bangladesh include flood control and regulation of rivers, water conservation, dike arrangement, watercourses and silt movements relating to sections of the Brahmaputra River. Under the first agreement on economic and technological cooperation between China and Maldives, signed in August 1981, assistance was provided in the installation of small power generators and in apartment-building in connection with the Male housing project. Subsequently, six similar agreements were concluded, the most recent being in February 2000, involving the provision of grant aid worth Y10 million to Maldives. Nepal was granted some $645 million in aid during the period 1956-1999, while around 25 contract projects in a wide range of production activities have been implemented since 1981. Materials and equipment ranging from grain and table salt to trucks and trolleys were also made available to Nepal.

With regard to least developed countries in South-East Asia, China has development cooperation agreements with Cambodia, the Lao People's Democratic Republic and Myanmar. The many economic and technical assistance activities include a joint economic and trade commission with Cambodia; the establishment of television satellite ground stations and hydropower and electricity grid stations in the Lao People's Democratic Republic; and some 22 construction projects, including the Yangon-Thanlyin bridge, in Myanmar, where bilateral economic and technological cooperation with China started in 1961.

Source: Ministry of Foreign Affairs, China.

Box IV.5. Bangladesh and its development cooperation activities

Although Bangladesh is still a least developed country, it has offered capacity-building in areas where it has specific expertise, such as microcredit, population policies and rural development. The Bangladesh Academy for Rural Development, the Rural Development Academy and the Bangladesh Public Administration Training Centre have considerable expertise in microcredit, rural banking and income-generation activities, and can cater for the training needs of developing countries. Grameen Bank has also organized microcredit training programmes for participants from Indonesia, Malaysia, Nepal and countries in Africa, and played an active role in organizing a summit on microcredit, which was held in Washington in February 1996. Bangladesh has a strong track record in establishing population policies, programmes and services that have helped to improve the general conditions of maternal and child health, lower birth rates and slow population growth. In recognition of this, the Partners in Population and Development secretariat was established in Dhaka to provide technical cooperation in the field of family planning to Colombia, Egypt, Indonesia, Kenya, Mexico, Morocco, Thailand, Tunisia and Zimbabwe.

Source: Ministry of Finance, Bangladesh.

Size of programmes

Given the administrative costs of managing development cooperation programmes, developing countries without the regional presence to administer their programmes independently have traditionally participated in development cooperation through grants and capital subscriptions to multilateral organizations.[13] Countries with extensive bilateral programmes thus tend to be upper-middle-income developing countries, such as the Republic of Korea, Singapore and Turkey, or large developing countries, such as China and India with significant domestic institutional capacity.

Developing countries of the ESCAP region received nearly 66 per cent of the Republic of Korea's aid in 2000

In 1999, the Republic of Korea provided $317.5 million of ODA, equivalent to 0.08 per cent of its GNP, of which two fifths were bilateral aid and the rest multilateral. Although this falls far below the 0.24 per cent average of DAC member countries, the volume of ODA in 1999 was five times larger than in 1991. Around 30 per cent of bilateral assistance was grant aid and technical cooperation, while the rest consisted of concessional development loans. Developing countries in the ESCAP region received approximately 82.5 per cent of ODA from the Republic of Korea in 1998-1999, but this share declined to 65.6 per cent in 2000. Aid from Turkey, which, together with the Republic of Korea, is a member of OECD but not of DAC, to all developing countries amounted to $44.8 million in 1998 but has fallen steadily since then, to $25.8 million in 2000. Developing countries of the ESCAP region, mainly in North and

---

[13]   Both Hong Kong, China, and Macao, China, contributed to the Asian and Pacific Development Centre. Hong Kong, China, also contributed to UNDP and the Asian Development Fund established by ADB.

Central Asia, received 72.4 per cent of the total in 1998, but this share had also fallen to 49.3 per cent in 2000. Likewise, as the Asian economic crisis affected middle-income developing countries such as Thailand, their development cooperation programmes measured in dollar terms declined in some cases to as low as a quarter of previous levels. Despite these difficulties, however, Thailand still contributes $2.3 million to programmes focused on the promotion of closer economic ties with countries in Indochina.

Distribution and focus

Although most development cooperation programmes of developing countries are extended primarily to their immediate neighbours, some member countries maintain programmes with a global coverage. India's bilateral assistance programme, the Indian Technical and Economic Cooperation Programme, launched on 15 September 1964, and the Special Commonwealth African Assistance Plan have provided technical assistance to 130 developing countries in Asia, Africa, Latin America and Eastern Europe. The Republic of Korea's aid programme has placed primary emphasis on countries in Asia and provided its strongest support to China, Indonesia, Kazakhstan, Mongolia, the Philippines, Sri Lanka, Uzbekistan and Viet Nam in 2001. The Russian Federation maintained one of the largest programmes until the 1990s, giving extensive financial and technical assistance to Cambodia, the Lao People's Democratic Republic, Mongolia and Viet Nam as well as to countries which had formed part of the former Soviet Union. A significant proportion of Turkey's grant and technical cooperation was directed to Azerbaijan and Turkmenistan. Assistance programmes have been extended to cover member countries of the Black Sea Economic Cooperation region, the Organization of the Islamic Conference and CIS.

Immediate neighbours are usually the major beneficiaries

Development cooperation among developing countries focuses on strengthening the capacity of those countries through human resources development and supporting their efforts to combat poverty through the sharing of experience (box IV.6). In addition to these overall themes, developing countries have cited as objectives of their development cooperation efforts the need to promote a market economy and free trade, build capacity for policy development and administration and address global issues such as environmental degradation, population and women in development. The Republic of Korea, for example, points out that humanitarian considerations, enlightened self-interest and solidarity among all people to address common problems and pursue common aspirations drive its development cooperation programmes. Since poverty reduction is its ultimate objective, the programme is furthermore seen as a political and diplomatic instrument to contribute to peace and prosperity, advance vital and mutually beneficial economic interests and reflect the humanitarian

Human resources development is the principal focus

Box IV.6. Human resources development

Training courses and study visits

India

Since 1964, the Indian Technical and Economic Cooperation Programme has provided civil training to improve human resources in diplomacy, foreign trade, management, audit and accounts, banking and IT to Cambodia, the Central Asian republics, Indonesia, Mongolia, the Philippines and Viet Nam. Under the study visit programme, in which India bears all expenses, senior decision makers are invited to India for an exchange of views and guided exposure to Indian capacity in small-scale industry, agriculture, health and education and trade. Between 1995 and 1998, delegations from Azerbaijan, Kyrgyzstan, Mongolia and the Russian Federation visited agricultural universities, export processing zones and research laboratories.

Philippines

The Philippine Technical Cooperation Program offers non-degree and other training courses in areas in which the Philippines has developed expertise and which are relevant to the development efforts of beneficiary countries, such as aquaculture management, entrepreneurship and management programmes for women, and energy management. When it is more feasible, Filipino experts and trainers may be sent to countries requesting such assistance.

Republic of Korea

To assist the development of technical and managerial skills, the Republic of Korea invited nearly 10,000 government officials, technicians and researchers for training between 1991 and 2000. The Invitation of Trainees Program is the core programme to assist developing countries in human resources development. The kinds of training provided cover regular training courses at the request of developing countries; region-specific training courses for a country; joint training courses with the cooperation of international organizations and donor agencies of other countries; on-the-job training at industrial locations to give first-hand experience; and long-term diploma courses for policy makers.

Singapore

Under the administration of the Technical Cooperation Directorate of the Singapore Ministry of Foreign Affairs, bilateral technical assistance programmes of the Singapore Cooperation Programme provide training courses and study visits on communications and transport, economic development, trade promotion, management and productivity for developing countries. The Singapore Technical Assistance Programme for Sustainable Development, for example, assists developing countries in achieving economic progress without damaging the environment by training officials in urban planning, transport management, water treatment and environmental health. Other components of the Programme include Singapore Cooperation Programme Training Awards, the Small Island Developing States Technical Cooperation Programme and the Viet Nam-Singapore Technical Training Centre, which offer courses designed to foster technical manpower development by training high-school graduates in technical skills.

Thailand

For Cambodia, the Lao People's Democratic Republic, Myanmar and Viet Nam, the bilateral programme under the Thai International Cooperation Program provides group training courses in education, health and agriculture designed according to the specific needs of each group. The courses are supplemented by the provision of experts and equipment and the implementation of technical projects. For other developing countries, the Department of Technical and Economic Cooperation organizes a series of international training courses, implemented by Thailand's academic and technical institutions, to address a variety of development concerns. It provides fellowships to support participation by developing countries.

Advisers

India

Indian experts are on a long-term mission to the Lao People's Democratic Republic to advise the Government on technical subjects.

Republic of Korea

The Republic of Korea has dispatched 22 medical doctors to 19 countries in Africa, Asia and the Pacific. Experts in agriculture, forestry, fisheries and electronics were sent to provide guidance, research and training in 42 countries. Korea Overseas Volunteers has provided training to technicians in auto maintenance, computer education and civil engineering, and has helped to increase rural incomes by teaching advanced techniques in agriculture, livestock-raising and fisheries in 24 countries. Other volunteers have worked as nurses, public health managers and nutritionists to improve health in the communities in which they serve, while others have specialized in the community development and social welfare.

Feasibility studies

Republic of Korea

As a type of technical grant aid, Development Study covers feasibility studies for socio-economic development projects through the sharing of specialized technical know-how to improve planning. It provides Governments with policy-making data prior to project implementation and, based on a field study, reviews the economic and technical implications of the proposed project. After completion of the study, a final report is forwarded to the recipient Government for use in policy-making or as a basis for securing project loans from international development banks or aid agencies, including possible loans from the Economic Development Cooperation Fund.

Source: DAC; Ministry of External Affairs, India; Korea International Cooperation Agency; Ministry of Foreign Affairs, Singapore; and Department of Technical and Economic Cooperation, Thailand.

---

concern of its people.[14] In the case of Thailand, the emphasis on strengthening social infrastructure to support human resources development and rural poverty alleviation is clearly visible in the sectoral distribution of aid; three quarters of its budget was spent on education, health and social development. Spending on agriculture also received a significant share.

As the focus of development cooperation programmes organized by developing countries is mainly on human resources development, most of the activities involved are mediated through the modalities of group training and the provision of study visits and technical advisers. However, countries such as China, India and the Republic of Korea have greatly widened the scope of their activities and implemented country projects as well as providing equipment to recipient countries.

Modalities include group training, study visits and technical advisers

Technical cooperation can be a link to furthering economic ties between countries. Malaysia is currently the largest foreign investor in Cambodia, and its exports to, and imports from, Cambodia amounted to $71.8 million and $17.2 million respectively in 2000. Cambodia and Malaysia have also signed agreements and cooperation frameworks such as the Bilateral Trade Agreement, the Investment Guarantee Agreement and the Economic, Scientific and Technical Cooperation Agreement to improve economic relations and facilitate trade and investment flows between the

Technical cooperation and economic ties often go hand-in-hand

---

[14] Korea International Cooperation Agency (<http://www.koica.or.kr>).

two countries. As part of its initiative to assist Cambodia, Malaysia has extended assistance and cooperation to Cambodia in the area of human resources development. Through the Malaysia Technical Cooperation Programme, Malaysia has provided training in human resources development, project planning, fisheries, veterinary sciences, property valuation and cooperative management, and trade and investment, to 195 Cambodian officials at various training institutions in Malaysia. A 16-member technical team led by the Economic Planning Unit visited Cambodia in September 2000 to assist in the preparation of a blueprint for the economic development of Cambodia.

India and Bhutan have a special relationship

There is a special relationship between India and the landlocked country of Bhutan. India extended financial assistance to Bhutan from the launch of the First Five-year Development Plan in 1961 and continues to be the principal donor to Bhutan. Of Bhutan's eight five-year plans, the first two were completely financed by India, whose contribution comprised around 28 per cent of the total resources for all plans. A significant portion of India's assistance has focused on infrastructure development in Bhutan, with hydropower generation and the construction of roads, bridges and hospitals among the priority sectors. Other major projects carried out with Indian assistance were the Paro airport, Bhutan Broadcasting Service, the electricity distribution systems for Thimphu and Paro and the Indo-Bhutan microwave link. The Penden cement plant, a gift from India, began commercial production in 1982 and exports surplus cement to neighbouring Indian States. India will also provide financing for the Dungsum cement plant, plans for which were initiated during the Seventh Five-year Development Plan.

Institutional and managerial arrangements

Coordination of aid programmes is usually done by existing institutions

Separate institutions to administer aid are maintained by only a few donor developing countries in the ESCAP region, since many of their aid programmes are relatively small but often cover a wide range of substantive areas. In general, the role of coordinating the development programme is delegated to an existing agency, while various academic and government institutions are responsible for its actual implementation. The Singapore Cooperation Programme, established in 1992, brings various technical assistance programmes within one framework. In Thailand, the Department of Technical and Economic Cooperation, under the Office of the Prime Minister, is responsible for the administration of technical cooperation between the Government of Thailand and foreign Governments and international organizations, and handles cooperation in which Thailand is a donor as well as recipient. The Department coordinates closely with the Ministry of Foreign Affairs in policy formulation and with the Ministry of Finance and the Bureau of the Budget in programme financing. At the implementation level, the Department coordinates with line agencies to provide training as well as training partners (box IV.7). In the Philippines, the Technical Cooperation Council, which has the

---

Box IV.7. Bank of Thailand and regional development cooperation

Although a single agency is usually responsible for coordinating development cooperation programmes, different agencies of the Government may be responsible for the actual implementation of activities. The Bank of Thailand, for example, participates in two regional forums aimed at strengthening institutional capacity. The Conference of Governors of South East Asian Central Banks (SEACEN), provides a forum for its member countries to exchange information and ideas on matters affecting their economies and financial systems; the SEACEN Research and Training Centre, opened in 1977 in premises provided by Bank Negara Malaysia, provides training courses led by resource persons from member countries and international organizations in various areas of central banking, including financial programming, monetary policy and financial accounts. SEACEN recently established an expert group on capital flows to draft proposals on capital flow management. The Bank of Thailand also participates in the Conference of Governors of Central Banks in South-East Asia, New Zealand and Australia which aims to strengthen central bank human resources through central bank training courses organized every two years on a rotation basis. In line with the Thai Government policy to pursue closer cultural, economic and trade links with countries in Indochina, the Bank of Thailand and Thammasat University organized an MBA course and offered scholarships in economics, banking and finance in the Lao People's Democratic Republic. The Bank of Thailand has also provided grants and training programmes in connection with the establishment of the National Bank of Cambodia.

Source: Bank of Thailand.

---

responsibility for formulating and executing the technical cooperation programme, is co-chaired by the Department of Foreign Affairs and the National Economic and Development Authority and includes members drawn from other relevant departments and technical centres.

Countries higher up the income scale have created special coordinating institutions

As development cooperation becomes an increasingly important component of national policy and trade, however, aid programmes tend to be administered by separate agencies. Among countries that maintain separate institutions are the Republic of Korea and Turkey. The Korea International Cooperation Agency, under the Ministry of Foreign Affairs and Trade, administers aid and technical cooperation programmes, while the Export-Import Bank of Korea administers the Economic Development Cooperation Fund of the Ministry of Finance and Economy and the Ministry of Foreign Affairs and Trade. In Turkey, the Turkish International Cooperation Agency, founded in 1992, executes development cooperation programmes along with other government agencies. The State Planning Organization coordinates technical cooperation activities, while the State Institute of Statistics keeps the requisite statistics.

Multilateral and triangular cooperation programmes

A number of developing countries in the ESCAP region offer multilateral cooperation programmes, either through third-country training programmes or on a cost-sharing basis, in which the Government co-sponsors the provision of group training, subregional cooperation programmes, partnership programmes and TCDC activities with other

Many countries offer multilateral and triangular cooperation programmes

countries or international organizations. Singapore's participation in these programmes is illustrated in box IV.8. Thailand, for example, organized research studies, training programmes and study tours in Thailand for participants from other developing countries who were sponsored by international organizations or donor countries. The Department of Technical and Economic Cooperation executes these programmes and covers administrative costs, while sponsoring agencies absorb the programme costs. Thailand has placed particular emphasis on co-funding for technical development projects in human resources development, agriculture, forestry, fisheries, industry, science and technology, and communication and transport management for neighbouring developing countries.

Box IV.8. Singapore and third-country training programmes

In joint training, otherwise known as third-country training programmes, assistance is provided to recipient countries in collaboration with another developed or developing country, or an international organization. Singapore has third-country training programmes with 11 countries, including Australia, Japan, the Republic of Korea and Thailand, as well as international organizations such as ADB, the Colombo Plan Secretariat, the Commonwealth Secretariat and ESCAP. In these programmes, the experience, expertise and resources of two partners are combined to provide training programmes for the benefit of developing countries in Asia as well as in other regions. Singapore and IMF signed an agreement in September 1997 to establish the IMF-Singapore Regional Training Institute in Singapore. The Institute, which is the first IMF regional training institute in Asia, offers joint training courses for developing countries in the region in the area of macroeconomics, statistics and national income accounting. Similarly, the World Bank Institute and the Ministry of Foreign Affairs offer joint training courses in banking, environmental management and public finance under the Singapore-World Bank Third Country Training Programme. Singapore also works jointly with UNDP to extend technical assistance under the TCDC programme. The Japan-Singapore Partnership Programme, established in 1994, offers joint training courses to participants from the Asian and Pacific region, while the Japan-Singapore Partnership Programme for the 21st Century, signed in May 1997, extends technical assistance from the Asian and Pacific region to Africa.

Source: Ministry of Foreign Affairs, Singapore.

The Philippines has also implemented triangular programmes such as the Japan/ASEAN/Cambodia Rural Development Programme, in which the Technical Cooperation Council of the Philippines facilitated the deployment of 10 agricultural experts to assist in the rehabilitation and reconstruction of Cambodia, and the UNIDO/Japan/Philippines/Kyrgyzstan Export-oriented Investment Promotion, under which experts from the Board of Investments conducted a two-week training course/workshop designed to develop Kyrgyzstan's capabilities in export-oriented investment policy formulation, the development of SMEs and export market penetration. For these programmes to be successful, however, the untying of aid is essential, so that donor countries which fund the multilateral cooperation programmes are able to fund programmes that best fit the needs of the recipient countries.

Since the 1957 issue, the *Economic and Social Survey of Asia and the Pacific* has, in addition to a review of the current situation of the region, contained a study or studies of some major aspect or problem of the economies of the Asian and Pacific region, as specified below:

1957:   Postwar problems of economic development

1958:   Review of postwar industrialization

1959:   Foreign trade of ECAFE primary exporting countries

1960:   Public finance in the postwar period

1961:   Economic growth of ECAFE countries

1962:   Asia's trade with western Europe

1963:   Imports substitution and export diversification

1964:   Economic development and the role of the agricultural sector

1965:   Economic development and human resources

1966:   Aspects of the finance of development

1967:   Policies and planning for export

1968:   Economic problems of export-dependent countries. Implications of economic controls and liberalization

1969:   Strategies for agricultural development. Intraregional trade as a growth strategy

1970:   The role of foreign private investment in economic development and cooperation in the ECAFE region. Problems and prospects of the ECAFE region in the Second Development Decade

1971:   Economic growth and social justice. Economic growth and employment. Economic growth and income distribution

1972:   First biennial review of social and economic developments in ECAFE developing countries during the Second United Nations Development Decade

1973:   Education and employment

1974:   Mid-term review and appraisal of the International Development Strategy for the Second United Nations Development Decade in the ESCAP region, 1974

1975:   Rural development, the small farmer and institutional reform

1976:   Biennial review and appraisal of the International Development Strategy at the regional level for the Second United Nations Development Decade in the ESCAP region, 1976

1977:   The international economic crises and developing Asia and the Pacific

1978:   Biennial review and appraisal at the regional level of the International Development Strategy for the Second United Nations Development Decade

1979:   Regional development strategy for the 1980s

1980:   Short-term economic policy aspects of the energy situation in the ESCAP region

1981:   Recent economic developments in major subregions of the ESCAP region

1982:   Fiscal policy for development in the ESCAP region

1983:   Implementing the International Development Strategy: major issues facing the developing ESCAP region

1984:   Financing development

1985:   Trade, trade policies and development

1986:   Human resources development in Asia and the Pacific: problems, policies and perspectives

1987:   International trade in primary commodities

1988:   Recent economic and social developments

1989:   Patterns of economic growth and structural transformation in the least developed and Pacific island countries of the ESCAP region: implications for development policy and planning for the 1990s

1990:   Infrastructure development in the developing ESCAP region: needs, issues and policy options

1991:   Challenges of macroeconomic management in the developing ESCAP region

1992:   Expansion of investment and intraregional trade as a vehicle for enhancing regional economic cooperation and development in Asia and the Pacific

1993:   Fiscal reform. Economic transformation and social development. Population dynamics: implications for development

1995:   Reform and liberalization of the financial sector. Social security

1996:   Enhancing the role of the private sector in development. The role of public expenditure in the provision of social services

1997:   External financial and investment flows. Transport and communications

1998:   Managing the external sector. Growth and equity

1999:   Social impact of the economic crisis. Information technology, globalization, economic security and development

2000:   Social security and safety nets. Economic and financial monitoring and surveillance

2001:   Socio-economic implications of demographic dynamics. Financing for development

This publication may be obtained from bookstores and distributors throughout the world. Please consult your bookstore or write to any of the following:

Sales Section
Room DC2-0853
United Nations Secretariat
New York, N.Y. 10017
USA

Tel: (212) 963-8302
Fax: (212) 963-4116
E-mail: publications@un.org

Sales Section
United Nations Office at Geneva
Palais des Nations
CH-1211 Geneva 10
Switzerland

Tel: (41) (22) 917-1234
Fax: (41) (22) 917-0123
E-mail: unpubli@unog.ch

Chief
Conference and General Services Section
Division of Administrative Services
Economic and Social Commission for
    Asia and the Pacific (ESCAP)
United Nations Building
Rajadamnern Avenue
Bangkok 10200, Thailand

Tel: (662) 288-1234
Fax: (662) 288-1000
E-mail: likitnukul.unescap@un.org

For further information on publications in this series, please address your enquiries to:

Chief
Development Research and Policy Analysis Division
Economic and Social Commission for
    Asia and the Pacific (ESCAP)
Rajadamnern Avenue
Bangkok 10200, Thailand

Tel: (662) 288-1610
Fax: (662) 288-1000, 288-3007
Cable: ESCAP BANGKOK

READERSHIP SURVEY

The Development Research and Policy Analysis Division of ESCAP is undertaking an evaluation of this publication, *Economic and Social Survey of Asia and the Pacific 2002,* with a view to making future issues more useful for our readers. We would appreciate it if you could complete this questionnaire and return it, at your earliest convenience, to

> Chief
> Development Research and Policy Analysis Division
> ESCAP, United Nations Building
> Rajadamnern Avenue
> Bangkok 10200, THAILAND

QUESTIONNAIRE

	Excellent	Very good	Average	Poor
1. Please indicate your assessment of the *quality* of the publication on:				
• Presentation/format	4	3	2	1
• Readability	4	3	2	1
• Timeliness of information	4	3	2	1
• Coverage of subject matter	4	3	2	1
• Analytical rigour	4	3	2	1
• Overall quality	4	3	2	1
2. How *useful* is the publication for your work?				
• Provision of information	4	3	2	1
• Clarification of issues	4	3	2	1
• Its findings	4	3	2	1
• Policy suggestions	4	3	2	1
• Overall usefulness	4	3	2	1

3. Please give examples of how this publication has contributed to your work:

....

....

....

....

4. **Suggestions for improving the publication:**

    ....
    ....
    ....
    ....

5. **Your background information, please:**

    Name: ....

    Title/position: ....

    Institution: ....

    Office address: ....

    ....

Please use additional sheets of paper, if required, to answer the questions.
Thank you for your kind cooperation in completing this questionnaire.
